JAVA™ 1.2
by example
3RD EDITION

D0470719

JERRY R. JACKSON • ALAN L. McCLELLAN

Sun Microsystems Press
A Prentice Hall Title

The publisher offers discounts on this book when ordered in bulk quantities. For more information, contact Corporate Sales Department, Prentice Hall PTR , One Lake Street, Upper Saddle River, NJ 07458. Phone: 800-382-3419; FAX: 201- 236-7141. E-mail: corpsales@prenhall.com.

Editorial/production supervision: *Mary Sudul*
Cover design director: *Jerry Votta*
Cover designer: *Anthony Gemmellaro*
Cover illustration: *Karen Strelecki*
Manufacturing manager: *Alexis R. Heydt*
Acquisitions editor: *Gregory G. Doench*
SunSoft Press publisher: *Rachel Borden*

10 9 8 7 6 5 4 3

ISBN 0-13-079669-7

Sun Microsystems Press
A Prentice Hall Title

To Kelly, who makes it all worthwhile.

Jerry

To Julie, my wife and best friend.

Alan

Contents

Part 1 - Working With the Java Language

Chapter 4
Memory and Constructors, 51

Chapter 17

Java Database Connectivity, 383

Part 2 - Writing Java Applets

Part 3 - Appendixes

List of Tables

List of Examples

List of Figures

Preface

Why We Are Here

The Java language is maturing and growing by leaps and bounds. With that maturation and growth, we've found more than enough new material to sink our teeth into with this edition of *Java by Example*. Our approach has never been to explore every nook and cranny of the Java language. Rather, we've tried to concentrate on topics that we deem to have the greatest utility for programmers making the transition to Java and to provide fairly detailed examples of those topics. Our primary focus in this edition is to explore the Java inner classes mechanism, reflection, and the *collection* classes. We'll try to help burgeoning Java programmers comprehend the utility of these in practical use. Where appropriate, we also try to show powerful programming techniques enabled by Java.

We'll also revisit Java native methods. In light of the Java Native Interface (JNI) introduced in the JDK, there's now a much more formal and clean way to interface Java applications with existing programs than with the original native methods mechanism.

Two areas of focus that, to our dismay, caused some confusion in the previous edition, namely the Java Remote Method Invocation (RMI) mechanism and the Java Database Connectivity (JDBC), will receive a slight make-over in this new edition. The last time around, we worked with pre-release versions of RMI and JDBC. However, we were confounded by the fact that the implementations for those parts of the language changed between the pre-release and the official JDK release. With many apologies to users miffed by our attempt to bet on the stability of the pre-release, we'll revisit these two key features of the language.

Although we update our applets portion of *Java by Example*, we are consciously not taking on the scope of changes in the JDK 1.2 Abstract Windowing Toolkit (awt). There is simply too much there to try to cover in a book adequately. In reality, the best way to grasp the complexities of the AWT is to read *Graphic Java*, which comprehensively covers the awt.

The structure of the book is consistent with previous editions. Part 1 covers basics of the Java language, showing how to implement standard programming constructs such as reading and writing to a file, declaring arrays, allocating and initializing memory, using the Java RMI and JDBC, and so on. Part 2 covers basics of applet writing, specifically for programmers who are concentrating on programs that will run within a web browser. Part 3 covers a myriad of useful details that don't really fit with the focus of the first two parts.

Audience

This is not a book about authoring on the world-wide web, writing common-gateway interface (CGI) scripts, or maintaining web servers. This is a book for intermediate to experienced programmers interested in learning Java. Because of the sheer number of C and C++ programmers ready to make the transition to Java, we pay special attention to Java as it relates to C and C++.

For Mac Programmers

There seems to be some confusion in the Macintosh community, from which we've had requests for Mac editions of *Java by Example*. This is actually counter to one of the great advantages of Java—it's platform independence. Granted, there are some restrictions on the Macintosh, namely, the 31 character file name limit imposed by MacOS. To address this issue, we've provided the compiled programs in zip format for easy execution on the Mac

We hope these modifications ease use of this material by the Mac programming community.

Meanwhile, to keep an eye on Java updates for Mac OS, check out `http://www.apple.com/macos/java/`.

For C Programmers

For C programmers who are coming to an object-oriented (OO) language for the first time, we provide an appendix that discusses the essential constructs used in object-oriented programming. Note, however, that this discussion is simply an introduction to OO as it relates to Java. There are several books and courses dedicated to OO programming, and novice OO programmers may want to consult some of these for more information.

Internet Sources of Information

There are several online sources of information on Java. You can find online guides and tutorials on Sun's home page:

```
http://java.sun.com/
```

There are active net newsgroups dedicated to Java:

```
comp.lang.java.misc
```

```
comp.lang.java.programmer
```

There is also a mailing list where Java aficionados exchange ideas, questions, and solutions. To subscribe, send mail to `majordomo@xcf.berkeley.edu`. The subject must be blank, and the body of email must be the following:

```
subscribe advanced-java
end
```

From these newsgroups, mail aliases, and web sites, you'll be able to locate countless other resources, tutorials, Frequently-Asked-Questions (FAQs), and online magazines dedicated to Java.

For updates about this book and information about other books in the Sun Press Java Series, look on the web at:

```
http://www.sun.com/books/java_series.html
```

Conventions Used in This Book

Table P-1 shows the coding conventions used in this book.

Table P-1 Coding Conventions

Convention	Example
Class names have initial capital letters.	`public class LineOfText`
Method names have initial lowercase and the rest of the words have an initial capital letter.	`public int getLength()`
Variable names have initial lowercase and the rest of the words have an initial capital letter.	`private int length` `private int bufferLength`
Public methods and variables are presented first in code examples, because they represent the interface for the class.	N/A
Private methods and variables are presented last in code examples, because users of the class do not need to see these.	N/A

Braces are used in every control structure, even when there is only one statement. This is not required by Java, but rather a personal preference.	`if (num < 5) {`
	`    count++;`
	`}`

Table P-2 shows the typographic conventions used in this book.

Table P-2 Typographic Conventions

Typeface or Symbol	Description
`courier`	Indicates a command, file name, class name, method, argument, Java keyword, HTML tag, file content, or code excerpt.
`bold courier`	Indicates a sample command-line entry.
italics	Indicates definitions, emphasis, a book title, or a variable that you should replace with a valid value.

Applets, Applications, and Programming Aids

The CD that accompanies this book includes several Java programs that you can use, modify, or simply study to help you learn the language. These programs include:

- Applets that show simple to complex use of the Java graphics library, multiple threads, and multimedia.

- Applications that show basic input/output, interfaces, memory use, and more.

- Programs such as a public class parser that you can use to extract information about Java classes or your program's classes. We provide these as simple aids you can use to better learn and understand the Java language.

Many of these programs are discussed throughout the book, but some are presented simply for you to examine, play with, or mimic. Feel free to borrow or adapt these for your own purposes.

Java by Example CD Contents

The CD accompanying this book includes the applets and applications referred to within this book, as illustrated in Table P-3. These are stored in the `Code.zip` file.

Table P-3 CD Contents

Directory	Contents
applets	This directory contains several sample applets, including the supporting audio and image files in `.au` and `.gif` format, respectively. This directory also includes sample HTML files that can be used to view the applets with the Java `appletviewer`.
applications	This directory contains several illustrative Java applications, some of which are described in the book, some of which are just provided for your use.
classes.zip	The applet and application class files referred to in the book in `zip` format.

You do not have to copy the CD contents to run the applications and applets on it. To run the programs from the CD, extract the `Code.zip` file, set the CLASSPATH environment variable to point to the Java Development Kit `classes.zip` file and the *Java by Example* `classes.zip` file on the CD.

Acknowledgments

It's hard to believe that we're now publishing a third edition of *Java by Example*. In helping us achieve this goal, we owe a big thanks to Brian Smithey for his technical review of the new material and to Mary Lou Nohr, the most competent of editors. We must also highlight the contributions of John Gray. We could not have completed this work without his assistance in helping update all of the applets to work with the JDK 1.2 and to use the graphics features it provides.

As always, the support and encouragement of the folks at Prentice Hall and Sun Press is much appreciated. We owe thanks to Greg Doench, Rachel Borden, John Bortner, Mary Treacy, and Lisa Iarkowski.

There are countless others who contributed to the previous editions of *Java by Example*, helping us establish a foundation from which we could build subsequent editions. To all of those folks, we say thank you.

Since we currently hold down full-time jobs with a start-up company developing distributed, enterprise applications in Java, we end up stealing from family time in order to update our book. For allowing us those compromises, we are grateful for the patience and understanding of our families—Kelly, Amber, and Justin Jackson and Julie, Ian, Drew, and Li-Mae McClellan. Our dogs', too.

Lastly, we extend our thanks to our readers, who have found our style and approach to covering Java useful.

Part 1—Working With the Java Language

CHAPTER
1

- Java Overview

- Using the Java Compiler and Interpreter

- The Java CLASSPATH Environment Variable

- Using the appletviewer

- The Difference Between Java Applications and Applets

- Applets and Web Pages

About Java

What Is Java?

Java is a general purpose object-oriented programming language. It provides a number of extensions that support development of GUI applications, as well as development of client/server applications over local and wide area networks. Given all the attention and interest in the Java programming language, it's somewhat surprising that there is very little new in it. However, that may account for its sudden popularity. It is mostly a collection of familiar constructs and features from programming languages such as C, C++, Objective-C, SmallTalk, and Common Lisp. From C and C++, Java borrows its syntax and its variable scoping model. From Objective-C, Java uses the concept of interfaces. From SmallTalk, Java borrows its model of runtime extensibility, dynamic memory management, and multiple threads of execution (multithreading). To these, Java adds security, a simple programming paradigm, and more.

Another reason for Java's popularity among programmers is that it is architecturally neutral. It is an interpreted language, and you can run Java programs on any platform that has the Java interpreter and runtime environment. This enables programmers to write code (and write it once) that can execute on a variety of hardware platforms and operating systems, as illustrated in Table 1-1.

Table 1-1 Platforms/Operating Systems Supporting Java

Hardware Platform	Operating System
SPARC	Solaris, SunOS 4.x
Intel	WindowsNT, Windows95, Windows98, Windows 3.1, OS/2, OS2/Warp, Linux
Macintosh	MacOS

The list of hardware platforms and operating systems supporting Java continues to grow, ranging from IBM OS/390 mainframes, DEC Alpha, AIX, AmigaOS, SCI/IRIX, and more.

Java and the World-Wide Web

It's safe to say that the merits of the Java programming language have been highlighted by its suitability for use on the world-wide web. It is, in fact, the programming language of the web. Its popularity has grown with the web's growth and with the advent of web browsers (such as Netscape Navigator, Internet Explorer, and HotJava) that are capable of running Java programs to incorporate audio, video, and animation directly into a web page. The Java programming language gives commercial, educational, and recreational programmers a language they can use to change web pages that are static and flat into web pages that are dynamic, lively, and rich.

The Java Utilities You Need to Know About

There are a handful of Java utilities that are worth reviewing before diving into the language itself. You'll most likely be dealing with these utilities in everyday development and use of the language, so we'll dedicate a few page to cover them.

The Java Interpreter and Java Runtime Environment

Java is an interpreted language. In earlier versions of the Java Development Kit (JDK), the `java` interpreter was the only way to run a Java program from the command line. (Of course, running Java programs from a browser is a different story.) However, the JDK 1.1 introduced the Java Runtime Environment (`jre`), which you can also use to execute a program from the command line. The `java` and `jre` programs reside in the Java `bin` directory. For example, if the JDK were installed in a directory named `/local/jdk`, you'd find the `java` and `jre` programs in the `/local/jdk/bin` directory.

The `java` interpreter takes a class name as an argument.

If the class is part of a Java package — a collection of classes that can be imported by a program — the class name needs to be a fully qualified name. This is accomplished by including the package in the class name. For example,

```
java java.util.Date
```

Any arguments that follow the class name are treated as arguments to the `main` method in the class. We'll see examples of this later on. For example, we'll develop a `LongMult` program that multiplies long numbers. It takes arguments like this:

```
java LongMult 84148939284829 12934829848938484555
```

The Java interpreter executes the main method in the specified class and exits, unless the main method creates one or more threads. If the main method creates any threads, the interpreter exits after the last thread has been run.

As we'll discuss shortly, the Java interpreter expects the class on the command line to be a binary representation of the class.

The Java Runtime Environment is a scaled down version of the JDK. It's primary use is for client-side program execution, which does not require the full-blown Java development environment of the JDK. The Java Runtime Environment does not include the Java source code, debugger, and other developer related components included with the JDK. The `jre` program that comes with the Java Runtime Environment is similar to the Java interpreter in that it will execute a specified class from the command line. There's one caveat for Windows users. On Windows systems, the `jre` command ignores the soon-to-be-discussed `CLASSAPTH` variable. That means that on Windows systems, you need to use the `-cp` option with the `jre` command and specify the path to the class file you want to execute. For example, we would execute our long multiplier program something like this, assuming the `LongMult` class resided in the `C:\Test\Classes` directory:

```
jre -cp C:\Test\Classes LongMult 84148939284829 12934829848938484555
```

The Java Compiler

So your probably thinking, if Java's an interpreted language, what's the deal with the compiler. Yes, Java is an interpreted language, but it is unlike a Unix shell script or BASIC program, for example, in which the source file itself is interpreted. Instead, the Java interpreter interprets compiled bytecode.

The Java compiler (`javac`) converts the program source code into bytecodes that can be executed in the Java environment. The Java interpreter (`java`) executes the compiled bytecode on the local system.

The javac compiler automatically adds a .class file name extension to the class name on the compiler command line. So, the source file MyClass.java becomes the compiled file MyClass.class.

Like other Java utilities, the javac compiler resides in the bin directory of the Java Development Kit (JDK). For example, if the JDK were installed in a directory named /local/jdk, you'd find the javac compiler and java interpreter in the /local/jdk/bin directory.

The Appletviewer Program

An *applet* is simply a Java program that executes in the context of a web browser capable of executing that program. The JDK also includes an appletviewer program to enable you to view applets without having to start a web browser. Like the javac compiler and the java interpreter, the appletviewer program resides in the bin directory of the JDK. (*Writing, Compiling, and Viewing an Applet* on page 10 shows how to invoke the appletviewer program.)

The appletviewer command takes an HTML file as an argument and displays any applets in the HTML file in their own window. If the HTML file doesn't have any APPLET tag in it, the appletviewer doesn't do anything.

CLASSPATH

The use of the CLASSPATH environment variable seems to vex a number of Java users. Even experienced Java programmers pay close attention to the CLASSPATH to ensure programs run correctly.

The Java CLASSPATH is an environment variable that specifies the path to all necessary class files. These class files can be individual .class files or a group of class files that are compressed using zip or Java Archive (jar) compression.

The format for a CLASSPATH is:

```
set CLASSPATH=path1;path2 ...
```

On Windows systems, the path needs to be preceded by the drive name.

The two most common problems folks encounter with the CLASSPATH is that they don't include all the paths they need for their programs to run, or they include those paths in the wrong order. Specifically, the CLASSPATH needs to specify the following:

- The current directory. This is done by placing a . (dot) in the CLASSPATH. This should be the first path in a CLASSPATH specification, as in:

  ```
  set CLASSPATH C:.
  ```

- A directory above the directory with the actual class files:

```
set CLASSPATH C:\MyClasses
```

- A directory above a Java package:

```
set CLASSPATH C:\MyPackages
```

- The complete path to any class files in zip or jar format. For example:

```
set CLASSPATH C:\MyZippedClasses\classes.zip
```

You could put all of our sample paths together into one CLASSPATH by separating them with a semicolon, like this:

```
set CLASSPATH C:.;C:\MyClasses;C:\MyPackages; C:\MyZippedClasses\
classes.zip
```

The order in which you specify paths in the CLASSPATH variable specifies the order in which the Java interpreter will look for classes to execute. Say, for example, we issued the following command:

```
java MyZippedClass
```

Assume that MyZippedClass is a class file in the classes.zip file. In our example, when the Java interpreter is invoked, it will look for MyZippedClass in this order:

1. The current directory (.)

2. The classes in the MyClasses directory.

3. The Java package in the MyPackages directory.

4. The classes in the classes.zip file.

The Java interpreter will execute the first MyZippedClass that it finds.

The CLASSPATH can be set in one of two ways:

- By using a command line option when you invoke the compiler or interpreter
- By setting it in a system file such as the .cshrc or .ksh files on Unix system, or the autoexec.bat file on Windows systems

The former offers the advantage of always being up-to-date and accurate when invoked. The latter is easier, since you set it in one place and are done with it. The shell or window you're using will always have a reference to the location of all necessary Java class files. However, if the CLASSPATH ever changes, the CLASSPATH setting in the system file also needs to be updated. Note that if you set the CLASSPATH in a system file, you can override that CLASSPATH by using a command line specification.

Javadoc

The javadoc program takes a Java source file or package name as an argument and produces an HTML page that describes relevant class information, such as its interfaces, constructors, methods, and fields. javadoc generates one HTML file for each Java source file and each package name specified on the command line. It also produces a class hierarchy.

The javadoc program does this by parsing the source file for program documentation, looking for comments that are placed immediately before a class, interface, constructor definition or field declaration. You can also embed HTML tags within the comments, although using HTML head tags such as <H1>, <H2>, <H3>, and so on, confuses javadoc formatting. javadoc also parses class declarations and outputs their signatures.

These embedded comments are referred to as *doc comments*. They consists of the characters between the beginning /** and the ending */ comment markers.

Doc comments may include HTML tags, as in this example from Applet.java:

```
/**
 * An applet is a small program that is intended not to be run on
 * its own, but rather to be embedded inside another application.
 * <p>
 * The <code>Applet</code> class must be the superclass of any
 * applet that is to be embedded in a Web page or viewed by the Java
 * Applet Viewer. The <code>Applet</code> class provides a standard
 * interface between applets and their environment.
 *
 * @author      Arthur van Hoff
 * @author      Chris Warth
 * @version     1.42, 03/12/97
 * @since       JDK1.0
 */
```

The first sentence of each doc comment should be a summary sentence describing the item being declared. javadoc copies this first sentence to the member summary at the top of the corresponding HTML file. The summary ends at the first period that is followed by a blank, tab, or line terminator, or at the first tag (as defined below).

`javadoc` parses special tags that start with an "at" sign (@). Table 1-2 summarizes these tags.

Table 1-2 Javadoc @ Tags

Tag	Example	
@author	* @author	Jerry R. Jackson
@version	* @version	1.0, 10/1/98
@since	* @since	Java by Example, 3rd Edition
@see	* @see	java.lang.String
	* @see	java.applet.Applet#resize(Dimension)

These tags must start at the beginning of a line. The # character in a @see tag separates the name of a class from the name of one of its fields, methods, or constructors.

Applications and Applets

Java programs come in two flavors: standalone applications and web browser applets. Java applications and applets differ slightly in their structure. C programmers can find an equivalent to main() in a Java application, but it is missing altogether in applet code.

Writing, Compiling, and Running an Application

Example 1-1 shows a simple hello world application in Java.

Example 1-1 Hello World Application

```
public class HelloWorld {
  public static void main(String[] args) {
     System.out.println("Hello Brave New World!");
  }
}
```

Just as in a C or C++ program, main() is the first piece of code that is executed in a Java application.

To produce an executable program, you have to first compile the hello world program into bytecodes. Assume for the moment that the source file is named HelloWorld.java. (By convention, Java source files must be named *filename*.java.) Example 1-2 shows the command line to compile the program.

Example 1-2 Compiling Hello World

```
javac HelloWorld.java
```

The `javac` compiler produces a compiled bytecode file named *filename*.`class`. For instance, compiling the `HelloWorld.java` file produces a file named `HelloWorld.class`. To execute the program, you invoke the `java` interpreter, as in Example 1-3.

Example 1-3 Invoking the Java Interpreter

```
java HelloWorld
```

The compiled program is stored in a file named `HelloWorld.class`,. The `java` interpreter requires the class name (in this case, `HelloWorld`) as an argument.

Running the `java` interpreter on the `HelloWorld` program would produce the following output:

```
Hello Brave New World!
```

Writing, Compiling, and Viewing an Applet

A Java applet looks quite a bit different from a Java application. Example 1-4 shows a hello world applet.

Example 1-4 Hello World Applet

```
import java.applet.Applet;
import java.awt.Graphics;

public class HelloWorldApplet extends Applet {
  public void paint(Graphics g) {
     g.drawString("Hello Brave New World!", 50, 25);
  }
}
```

You'll notice that there's no `main()` statement. It is not required for applets. (An applet can also have a `main()` and execute as a standalone application. However, this means you have to manually add some support that is normally handled by the browser.) Java applets are invoked differently than Java applications. We'll get into the nitty-gritty of these differences later. For now, understand that applets rely on graphical support in the browser in which they will be displayed. Applications, if they are graphical in nature, require explicit programming to build the windows in which they will be displayed.

You use the `javac` compiler to compile all Java programs in the same way, whether they are applications or applets. (See Example 1-2.) However, an applet is normally going to execute within a web browser, so instead of invoking the `java` interpreter from the command line to execute an applet, you embed HTML tags that reference the applet within a web page. For developing rapid applet prototypes, it's helpful to use the `appletviewer`. To do so, create a minimal HTML file, as in Example 1-5 and include the name of the compiled applet (in this case, `HelloWorldApplet.class`).

Example 1-5 Minimal HTML File With an Applet Reference

```
<title>Hello World Applet</title>
<hr>
<applet code="HelloWorldApplet.class" width=250 height=80>
</applet>
<hr>
```

After you've created a minimal HTML file, you can use the `appletviewer` to view the applet. Simply run `appletviewer` from the command line and specify the HTML file as an argument. For instance, assuming an HTML file named `HelloWorldApplet.html`, you could use the command in Example 1-6 to view the applet with the `appletviewer`.

Example 1-6 Invoking the `appletviewer` Program

```
appletviewer HelloWorldApplet.html
```

Figure 1-1 shows sample output from this command on a Windows 95 system.

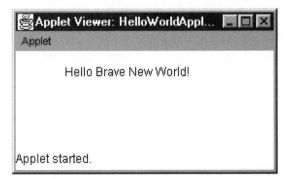

Figure 1-1 Displaying an Applet in the `appletviewer`

Of course, you can also include the HTML code in a web page and view the applet in a Java-enabled web browser. Then, when activated from the web page, the applet executes.

Incorporating Applets Into a Web Page

As previously mentioned, a Java program that runs within a web page is called an applet. However, not all web browsers are capable of executing Java applets. Netscape Navigator, Internet Explorer, and HotJava are the most prominent of the browsers currently capable of executing Java applets.

Although Java is a programming language, you don't have to be a programmer to incorporate a Java applet into your home page. A Java applet can be integrated easily into the HTML code that defines a web page. You just need to use the HTML `applet` tag, as in Example 1-7.

Example 1-7 The Basic HTML `applet` Tag Syntax

```
<applet code="applet_name.class" width=width height=height> </applet>
```

In this example, *applet_name* is name of the applet, including the `.class` extension of a compiled Java program. The *width* and *height* are numbers representing the width and height of the applet in pixels.

You can also include a set of parameters to specify exactly how you want the applet displayed. However, this only makes sense in the context of an applet with parameters, which we describe in *The HTML applet and param Tags* on page 544.

Summary

Java is a general purpose object-oriented programming language based on several already popular and familiar languages. Java programs can be written to be executed from a command line or from within a web browser. The former programs are Java applications, and the latter are referred to as Java applets. Applets can only execute in browsers that support Java. Those include Netscape Navigator and Microsoft Internet Explorer. The HTML `applet` tag is used to specify an applet within a web page.

Although Java is an interpreted language, Java programs must be compiled using the Java compiler (`javac`). The compiler converts the program source code into bytecodes that can be executed on the command line by the `java` interpreter or the `jre` program. The `jre` program is part of the Java Runtime Environment, a scaled down version of the JDK that is tailored for client-side execution of Java programs.

When Java programs are executed, the system references the CLASSPATH environment variable to see where it should look for classes to be run. You can set the CLASSPATH on the command line, but it is more convenient to set it in a system file such as the autoexec.bat file on Windows systems or the .cshrc or .ksh file on UNIX systems

Javadoc is a special Java utility for generating on-line documentation from program source code. The output of the javadoc program is a formatted HTML file describing a class in terms of its interfaces, constructors, signature, methods, and fields.

CHAPTER 2

Beginning With a Program

A Line Counter Program

To begin our discussion of Java, let's look at a simple program that counts the number of lines in a file. The program is used in the following way:

```
java CountLines file1 [file2 ... fileN]
```

The program will output the sum of lines in the files listed as arguments on the command line.

Much of the program will probably look familiar. You'll notice that Java looks a lot like C or C++. Java syntax was designed to be consistent with C usage where possible. First, we'll show the entire program in Example 2-1. Then, we'll take you through it, highlighting some key features.

Example 2-1 A Line Counter Program

```java
import java.io.*;


// The CountLines class will count and sum up the number of
// lines in the text files passed as arguments on the command line.

public class CountLines {

  public static void main(String[] args) {
    // Check usage. CountLines expects at least one file to count.

    if (args.length < 1) {
      System.err.println(
          "Usage: java CountLines <file1>...<fileN>");
        return;
    }

    // Initialize the line count.

    int lineCount = 0;

    // Loop through the file arguments and count the lines in each
    // file.

    for (int i = 0; i < args.length; i++) {

        // Wrap the processing of each file in a try/catch block in
        // case a read error occurs or the file can't be opened.
        // Save the current line count and revert to it if there
        // is an error processing the current file.

        int       savedLineCount = lineCount;
        Reader    in             = null;

        try {

            // Create a buffered reader connected to the current
            // file.

            in = new BufferedReader(
               new FileReader(args[i]));

            // The wasNewline flag is used to make sure we count a
            // final line that is terminated with EOF and has no
            // newline.
```

```
        boolean wasNewline = true;
        int     ch;

        // Loop through the characters and increment the
        // linecount when a newline is seen. The reader is
        // buffered so reading a character at a time is
        // efficient.

        while ((ch = in.read()) != EOF) {
            if (ch == '\n') {
                lineCount++;
                wasNewline = true;
            } else {
                wasNewline = false;
            }
        }

        // If we reached EOF and the previous character was not
        // a newline, increment the linecount.

        if (wasNewline == false) {
            lineCount++;
        }

    } catch (IOException e) {

        // If an exception occurred during the processing of
        // the current file, print a message and reset the
        // linecount.

        System.err.println(
            "Error while processing \"" + args[i] +
            "\": not counted.");
        lineCount = savedLineCount;
    }

    // Close the reader and any associated stream for this file.
    // The in variable might be null if an exception occurred
    // during stream creation

    if (in != null) {
        try {
            in.close();
        } catch (IOException e) {
        }

        in = null;
    }
```

```
    }
    // Display the final count.

    System.out.println(lineCount);
    }
    // A constant representing end of file.

    private static final int EOF = -1;
}
```

A Closer Look at the Line Counter

Now that you've had a chance to see a simple Java program, let's take a closer look at it. (Rather than define all the new terms and features right here, we'll point you to sections of this book where various topics are covered in more detail.)

Let's go through the program a piece at a time:

```
import java.io.*;
```

The first line is similar to an `include` statement in C or C++, except that an `import` doesn't actually insert anything into the current file. It just tells the compiler that the program will reference definitions in the named package. (Packages are described in more detail in *Packages and the import Statement* on page 47.) In this case, this class will reference definitions in the `java.io` package. The asterisk (*) is a wildcard character indicating that this class will have access to any class in the `java.io` package.

```
    // The CountLines class will count and sum up the number of
    // lines in the text files passed as arguments on the command line.
```

A series of comments follows the `import` statement. Java supports both C style (`/* */`) and C++ style (`//`) comments.

```
    public class CountLines {
```

A Java program consists of a set of class definitions. The first class defined in this program is called `CountLines`. The `public` keyword means that any other class may use this class. (Classes are discussed in our chapter on Chapter , *The Java Language Structure*, and scope modifiers such as `public` are discussed in *Method Modifiers and Their Scope* on page 36.) This is a standard opening statement for a class definition.

```
    public static void main(String[] args) {
```

A Java class that is used as the top level of an application must provide a `main()` method just as a C or C++ program provides a `main()` function. In Java, a `main()` method takes an array of `String` objects as its arguments and has no return value. (The `static` modifier is described in *Method Modifiers and Their Scope* on page 36.)

Unlike C or C++, the argument array for a `main()` method in Java does not contain the name of the program. The first element in the array is the first argument.

```
if (args.length < 1) {
    System.err.println(
        "Usage: java CountLines <file1>...<fileN>");
    return;
}
```

`System.err` is the standard error stream for a Java program. Java has predefined standard input, output, and error streams just like C and C++.

```
int lineCount = 0;
```

Variables may be declared anywhere in Java and not just at the top of a block as in C.

```
for (int i = 0; i < args.length; i++) {

    int       savedLineCount = lineCount;
    Reader    in             = null;
```

Arrays in Java have lengths associated with them. `args.length` returns the size of the argument array. Also note that the `in` variable is assigned `null`. This is an explicit `null` value that is distinct from all objects.

```
try {
```

This line is the start of the `try` block, used for *exception handling*. (Exceptions are described in detail *Exception Handling* on page 105.) Java deals with errors through an exception handling model. The Java exception handling model is almost identical to the one used in C++, but Java relies much more heavily on exceptions than does C++. Any error condition that arises within this `try` block will cause control to transfer to the `catch` block.

```
in = new BufferedReader(

        new FileReader(args[i]));
```

Java provides a building block approach to I/O. (See *Input/Output* on page 117 for details about the Java I/O.) This section of the `CountLines` program creates a `FileReader` to read from a file and obtains buffering by wrapping a `BufferedReader` around it.

```
boolean wasNewline = true;
int     ch;
```

Java has a primitive `boolean` type that is unrelated to the integer type. The `boolean` values are `true` and `false`.

```
while ((ch = in.read()) != EOF) {
    if (ch == '\n') {
        lineCount++;
        wasNewline = true;

    } else {
        wasNewline = false;
    }
}


if (wasNewline == false) {
    lineCount++;
}
```

The previous block of code looks almost exactly like C.

```
catch (IOException e) {

    System.err.println(
    "Error while processing \"" + args[i] +
        "\": not counted.");
    lineCount = savedLineCount;
}
```

This is the `catch` block that goes with the previous `try` block. If an error occurs in the `try` block, control will transfer to this `catch` block. In this case the errors are file I/O errors so we print a message and go on to the next file. Note that strings in Java may be concatenated using + .

```
if (in != null) {
    try {
        in.close();
    } catch (IOException e) {
    }

    in = null;
    }
}
```

In the previous block, the program closes each file before going to the next one. If an error occurs when closing the file, the `catch` block will trap the error.

```
    System.out.println(lineCount);
}
```

This is the end of the `main()` method. The `System.out.println()` method will display the sum of lines in all files listed as arguments to the program.

```
  private static final int EOF = -1;
}
```

This variable declaration defines the `EOF` constant used earlier in the program. The `Reader read()` method returns −1 on the end of file. The `final` modifier means the value of the variable will not change; it is treated as a constant.

Output From the Line Counter

The `CountLines` program outputs the number of lines in all files specified on the command line. For example, assuming a single file with 227 lines, the command line and output would look like this:

```
java CountLines file
227
```

Summary

This example shows that Java is closely related to C and C++. A programmer familiar with these languages can read simple Java programs fairly easily right away. Throughout the rest of this book, we will discuss the unique features of Java and the differences between it and the C family of languages.

In the next chapter, we'll delve into some necessary details about the Java language structure.

CHAPTER

3

- All About Classes and Methods

- Method Modifiers and Their Scope

- Variables, Methods, and Superclasses

- Packages and the import Statement

The Java Language Structure

Introduction

When working with a new programming language, there are basic language constructs and features that influence the way you develop your programs. We'll spend some time in the next few chapters describing these. We'll begin in this chapter by giving an overview of the basic structure of the Java language.

Classes and Methods

As we alluded to in the previous chapter, the fundamental structure in Java is a class. A class definition in Java corresponds to the definition of a structured type in C, and an *instance* of a class corresponds to a C structure. The fields or members of a structure in C also have an equivalent in Java. They are the *instance variables* of an instance of a Java class. For example, consider the following C structure:

```
struct point {
    int x;      /* a field/member */
    int y;
};
```

Now, here's a corresponding Java class definition:

```
class Point {
   int x;      // an instance variable
   int y;
}
```

An instance of a Java class can also have functions associated with it. These functions are called *methods,* and they act on the instance variables of the class, as illustrated in the following:

```
class Point {
   int x;
   int y;

   // A method that returns how far this Point is from (0,0).

   double distanceFromOrigin() {
     return Math.sqrt(x * x + y * y);
   }
}
```

Java has nothing that corresponds to C's global, free-standing functions (such as `printf`, `strcmp`, etc.). Each method is associated with a particular class and is referred to as a method of that class. Example 3-1 shows a sample class definition and the methods of that class. We'll present several new terms in this example and then explain them throughout the rest of this chapter

Example 3-1 Anatomy of a Class Definition

```
public class Card {

   // INSTANCE METHODS

   // Methods that return the suit and rank of a
   // particular card as Strings.

❶ public String getRank() {
     return ranks[rank];
   }

❷ public String getSuit() {
```

```
    return suits[suit];
  }

  // A method that returns whether the current card
  // is of higher rank than the argument card.

❸ public boolean higherRank(Card otherCard) {
    return rank > otherCard.rank;
  }

  // CLASS METHODS

  // Shuffle the deck.

❹ public static void shuffle() {
    for (int card = 0; card < cards.length; card++) {
      int otherCard    =
          (int)(Math.random() * 100) % DECKSIZE;
      Card temp        = cards[otherCard];
      cards[otherCard] = cards[card];
      cards[card]      = temp;
    }

    nextCard = 0;
  }

  // Deal a card.

❺ public static Card deal() {
    if (nextCard == DECKSIZE) {
      return null;
    } else {
      return cards[nextCard++];
    }
  }

  // INSTANCE VARIABLES

  // Variables representing the rank and suit of a particular
  // card.

❻ private int rank;
❼ private int suit;
```

```
  // CONSTRUCTORS

  // Construct a new card. Since there is a fixed set of 52 cards,
  // don't let anyone else call this.

❽ private Card(int newSuit, int newRank) {
    suit = newSuit;
    rank = newRank;
  }

  // CLASS VARIABLES

  // The deck.

  private static final int   DECKSIZE  = 52;
  private static final Card[] cards     = new Card[DECKSIZE];

  // Class variables representing different card suits and ranks.

❾ private static final int    NUMRANKS  = 13;
  private static final int    NUMSUITS  = 4;
  private static final String[] suits = {"C", "D", "H", "S"};
  private static final String[] ranks =
    {"A",  "2", "3", "4", "5", "6", "7", "8", "9",
     "10", "J", "Q", "K"};

  // Class variable holding the index of the next card to deal.

  private static int nextCard;

  // STATIC INITIALIZER

  // A static initializer that initializes the deck of cards.

❿ static {
    int cardNumber = 0;
    for (int cardSuit = 0; cardSuit < NUMSUITS; cardSuit++) {
      for (int cardRank = 0; cardRank < NUMRANKS; cardRank++) {
        cards[cardNumber++] = new Card(cardSuit, cardRank);
      }
    }
    shuffle();
  }
}
```

In Example 3-1:

❶, ❷, and ❸ on page 26 are instance methods of the `Card` class. Instance methods are associated with a particular instance of a class.

❹ and ❺ on page 27 are class methods of the `Card` class. Class methods deal with the class as a whole rather than with individual instances of the class.

❻ and ❼ on page 27 are instance variables for the `Card` class. Each card has its own copies of `rank` and `suit` just as a C structure would.

❽ on page 28 is the *constructor* for the `Card` class. A call to it creates a new instance of `Card`. (The next chapter, *Memory and Constructors*, describes constructors in more detail.)

❾ on page 28 begins a set of class variable definitions for the `Card` class. There is only one copy of each of these variables for the whole class.

❿ on page 28 is a *static initializer* for the `Card` class. It is used to initialize class data when a class is first created.

Now, having dissected the `Card` class, let's look at each feature in more detail.

Instance Methods

In Java, an *instance method* is a method associated with a particular instance of a class. When an instance method is called, it has access to the data contained in the instance it's associated with.

In the `Card` class example, the `getSuit()` method will return a `String` representing the suit of a particular card. Assume, for example, two cards— card1 and card2:

```
❶ card1.getSuit();
❷ card2.getSuit();
```

These are calls to instance methods. The call in line ❶ would return either C, D, H, or S, depending on the suit of card1. Likewise, the call in line ❷ would return either C, D, H, or S, depending on the suit of card2.

The Java syntax for invoking a method is:

<object>.*<method_name>*(*arg1*, *arg2*, ... *argN*)

In the case of an instance method, *<object>* must refer to an instance of a class that defines *<method_name>*.

Class Methods

Class methods are associated with a class as a whole, not with a particular instance. They are declared `static` in the class definition, in a manner similar to C++. The `shuffle()` and `deal()` methods in the `Card` class are class methods. They could be used as follows:

```
Card.shuffle();
Card nextCard = Card.deal();
```

Instead of calling the method on a particular instance of the `Card` class, you would call the method using the name of the class itself. The Java syntax for calling a class method is:

<class_name>.*<method_name>*(*arg1*, *arg2*, ... *argN*)

Class methods have a broader focus than instance methods. They can deal with information that is meaningful for the entire class. For instance, in the `Card` class example, the `shuffle()` and `deal()` methods manipulate an entire deck of cards, not just a single individual card.

Java allows class methods to be called in the same way as instance methods, but when this is done, the actual instance it is called on is irrelevant. For example:

```
❶ Card card1 = Card.deal();
❷ Card card2 = card1.deal();
```

In this example, line ❶ is a normal call to a class method. Line ❷ is a call to a class method, but using an instance-style reference to that method. Using `card1.deal()` is equivalent to finding the `deal()` method in `card1`'s class. This call is valid, but `card1` is only used to determine its class so the proper method can be called.

All class methods are implicitly *final* methods. As such, they cannot be overridden. (See *Final Methods* on page 36 for information.)

The main() Method

All Java applications include the equivalent of main(). It is a method declared in the top-level class in the program. (By top-level class here, we mean the class that is used as an argument to the java interpreter. The main() method in that top-level class controls the program's execution.)

You always define the main() method as in Example 3-2.

Example 3-2 The Java main() Method Declaration

```
  public class RunCalculator {
❶    public static void main (String[] args) {
     .
     .
     .
    }
  }
```

There are several things worth pointing out about the main() declaration. Note in line ❶ that the main() statement returns a void. Whereas in C and C++, main() returns a value (a status code), there is no return value associated with main() in Java. That is because main() status is handled by means of the Java exception handling model. (See *Exception Handling* on page 105 for details.)

You can actually have multiple main() methods within the classes used by a Java program. However, the only one that is recognized is the one in the class used as an argument to the java interpreter. For example, if the top-level main() method is in a class named RunCalculator, that main() method is executed by virtue of the command:

```
java RunCalculator
```

Overriding Methods

Java allows one class to be a subclass of another class. (See *Inheritance* on page 521 for more details about how this works.) All the attributes and methods of one class are applicable to the subclass as well. (This is not *strictly* true in Java, as we will see later in the discussion of method scope, but the reasons for its inaccuracy aren't relevant at the moment.) These attributes and methods are said to be *inherited* from the parent class, which is referred to as the *superclass*. If the new class you're defining behaves exactly like its superclass, except in areas that aren't defined for the superclass, then just inheriting everything from the superclass works fine. For instance, a RedWagon class is just like a Wagon class except in the area of color, which isn't defined for Wagon.

Consider, however, a class Window that represents windows on a computer screen. Let's say it has an instance method called draw() that displays windows on the screen. Now we want to create a window with a border. We could say that the WindowWithBorder class behaves just like Window, but we want to add a new drawBorder() method that covers the border area that isn't defined for Window. This approach seems reasonable, but what if we have a program that iterates through a list of windows and redraws them? Does it have to check each Window to see if it's a WindowWithBorder and, if so, call drawBorder() on it? What if there is also a WindowWithTitle?

To avoid building extensive knowledge about the structure of the Window class hierarchy into every program that wants to draw a Window, we need to take a different approach. We can say that drawing a WindowWithBorder means something different than just drawing a Window. We'd like draw() to do the normal Window drawing *and* draw the border for a WindowWithBorder. Java provides support for this approach by allowing you to override methods. You can create a WindowWithBorder class that inherits all the attributes and methods of the Window class, but you can redefine the draw() method. For instance, consider the code in Example 3-3.

Example 3-3 Overriding Methods

```
❶ public class WindowWithBorder extends Window {
      .
      .
      .
❷     public void draw() {
❸       super.draw();
❹       drawBorder();
      }

      private void drawBorder() {
        .
        .
        .
      }
   }
```

In line ❶ the use of the `extends` keyword guarantees that the
`WindowWithBorder` class will inherit everything in the `Window` class.

Now, when the program iterates through a list of windows and calls the `draw()`
method in line ❷ on a `WindowWithBorder`, it will draw the `Window` part and
then draw the border. The program can now just call `draw()` on any type of
`Window` and the right thing will happen.

To override a method, the new method (`WindowWithBorder.draw()` in our
example) must have the same name, argument types, and return type as the
corresponding method in its superclass. (The method name, argument types, and
return type are referred to as the *signature* of the method.) If you just want to
override the method in the superclass, that's all there is to it. If you want to extend
the method, as in Example 3-3, Java provides the `super` reserved word (as in line
❸) to invoke the superclass method from within the new method. A method
defined in the superclass may be invoked as follows:

```
super.<method_name>(arg1, arg2, ... argN)
```

In our example, we call `super.draw()` to draw the normal `Window` features
(that is, we call the `draw()` method of the superclass). Then we call
`drawBorder()` in line ❹ to complete the task.

Abstract Methods

Java provides the ability to specify the interface of a method without defining that method. Doing this can be very useful when you know that classes in your program will have to provide a particular operation, but the specifics of that operation may vary from subclass to subclass. For instance, in Example 3-4 we're writing a set of classes to support bank accounts.

Example 3-4 Abstract Methods

```
❶ public abstract class BankAccount {
     // Create a new BankAccount.
     public BankAccount(double balance, double interestRate) {
       accountBalance      = balance;
       accountInterestRate = interestRate;
       accountNumber       = nextAccountNumber++;
     }
     public double getbalance() {
       return accountBalance;
     }

     public double getInterestRate() {
       return accountInterestRate;
     }

     public int getAccountNumber() {
       return accountNumber;
     }

     // Compute interest. The method varies depending on the type of
     // account, so we declare it to be abstract.
❷    public abstract computeInterest();

     // The next account number is incremented each time an account
     // is created.
     private static int nextAccountNumber = 1;

     private double accountBalance;
     private double accountInterestRate;
     private int    accountNumber;
   }
```

We must declare BankAccount to be an abstract class as in line ❶ because it contains the abstract method, computeInterest(), which is not fully specified.

In line ❷, we declare computeInterest() to be an abstract method because there isn't any general body of code we could give it. However, we know that it needs to be defined in the subclasses of the BankAccount class. If we were to leave computeInterest() out of the BankAccount class definition and define it only in subclasses of BankAccount, we couldn't deal with BankAccount objects in a generic way. For example, if we wanted to write a method to calculate interest for all the BankAccount objects and print the results, we wouldn't be able to write the following loop because computeInterest() would not be defined for the BankAccount class:

```
for (int i = 0; i < numBankAccounts; i++) {
   BankAccount account = bankAccounts[i];
   System.out.println(account.getAccountNumber() + ": "
                 + account.computeInterest());
   }
```

By making computeInterest() an abstract method, we can specify that it's part of the BankAccount abstraction without being forced to put in some kind of dummy definition.

Native Methods

Not all code can be written in Java. Java is platform-independent, and it is sometimes necessary to write platform-specific code. Java programmers may also need to reuse code they've already written in other languages.

Java provides the capability to do this with a facility called *native methods*. Example 3-5 shows how to declare a native method in Java.

Example 3-5 Declaring a Native Method

```
// blink the dashboard lights
native void blinkLights(int numtimes);
```

Note that there is only a declaration; no method body is included.

The Java developers picked C as the default native method language, and they provided support for hooking C code into the Java interpreter. We'll describe the support for creating native methods in our chapter on *Linking With Native Code*.

Final Methods

Final methods are methods that cannot be overridden by methods in subclasses. (Recall that class methods are `final` methods.) When you declare a method `final`, you are saying that the implementation provided will never change. This allows the Java compiler to optimize by inlining final methods. (*Inlining* refers to replacing a call to a method with the body of the method after substituting for arguments—similar to macroexpansion.) This means that in many cases, the compiler can avoid looking up a method, which can lead to large speedups if the method-calling overhead is a significant part of the time required to execute the method.

Method Modifiers and Their Scope

Method modifiers in Java can be divided into two groups, based on whether or not they affect the scope of a method. *Scope* in a programming language refers to the region of a program in which a particular item such as a class, method, or variable may be accessed.

First, let's look at those modifiers that do not affect the scope of a method. Table 3-1 describes these modifiers.

Table 3-1 Method Modifiers That Do Not Affect Scope

Method Modifier Is...	Then...	Use for...
`final`	The method cannot be overridden by a method in a subclass.	Methods you do not want to change or methods you want the `javac` compiler to inline for performance reasons. (The `javac` compiler attempts to inline small `final` methods.)
`static`	The method is a class method.	Methods that do not rely on data internal to a particular instance of the class.

Table 3-1 Method Modifiers That Do Not Affect Scope (Continued)

Method Modifier Is...	Then...	Use for...
native	The method body will be written in C and linked into the interpreter.	Methods you want to be platform specific or methods you want to use to link in pre-existing code.
abstract	The method is not defined in the class. It must be defined in a subclass.	General-purpose methods that have no meaningful default operations. These methods are fully defined in subclasses.
synchronized	The method will acquire a lock on the instance (or on the class, if it is a class method) before running and will relinquish the lock when it completes. We describe synchronized methods in detail in *Multiple Threads of Execution* on page 171.	Methods that might interfere with each other in a threaded application.

Now let's look at those method modifiers that do affect a method's scope.

Methods in Java can have one of three primary scopes assigned to them: public, private, and *friendly*. Additionally, the protected modifier can be used to further define a method's scope. Table 3-2 summarizes how these modifiers affect the scope of a method.

Table 3-2 Method Modifiers That Affect Scope

Method Modifier Is...	Then...	Use to Define...
public	The method can be accessed by any class.	The external interfaces of your classes.
private	The method can be accessed only by methods within the same class.	Methods that are internal and only relevant to a particular class (and irrelevant to users of the class).
Not Explicitly Specified (a *friendly* Modifier)	The method can be accessed by methods in the class or methods in other classes in the same package as the class.	Methods you want other related classes to be able to access.
protected	The method can be accessed by methods in subclasses of the class.	Friendly methods that you want subclasses to also be able to access.

Method scope is important because the more narrowly the scope is defined on a part of a program, the simpler and more straightforward the program can be. This is evident by contrast. For example, in a traditional Basic program, there is only one scope. Everything in the program is accessible from everywhere. Unfortunately, this means that any part of the program might be dependent on any other part. Limiting the scope of each part of a program to the minimum necessary is one of the best ways of reducing program complexity, and the scope method modifiers in Java make this possible. With that in mind, let's look at these modifiers in a little more detail.

Scope of a public Method

A method defined to be `public` can be called by any part of the program. This is just like the Basic programming model. You would use the `public` modifier for the methods that define the external interfaces of your classes. The collection of publicly scoped methods defines the class as seen by users of the class.

Scope of a private Method

A method defined to be `private` can be called only by other methods in the same class. You would use the `private` modifier for methods that make up the implementation of the class. Users of the class have no reason to call these methods. For example, if you were writing a class that parsed input lines, you might have a `private` method named `getCharacter()` that extracted the next character from an internal buffer. This would be a useful abstraction in implementing a parsing class, but users of the class clearly have no reason to even know of its existence.

Scope of a friendly Method

By default, Java methods are *friendly*. A method that does not have an explicit scope modifier can be called by other methods in the class or by methods in any class in the same package.

Friendly method behavior in Java is similar to the `friend` access concept in C++. It is often the case when designing an object library that the abstraction presented to the users of the library consists of several interconnected classes. These interconnected classes commonly need access to parts of each other that aren't intended to be included in the external interfaces of the classes. In C++, a class can be made a friend of another class, giving it access to all the internals of the other class. In Java, friendship is supported by making the friendly classes part of the same package.

C++ programmers may be puzzled by the absence of the `friend` access concept in Java. However, C++ originally had no package concept. Without packages (or something like them) to provide *implicitly* friendly relationships between methods, the C++ developers implemented the `friend` method modifier, which provides *explicitly* friendly relationships between methods.

One significant difference between C++ friendship and Java friendly behavior is that friends in C++ actually have access to `private` members of their friends. In some cases, this gives friends greater access to class internals than the subclasses of the class enjoy.

Scope of a protected Method

A `protected` method is like a friendly method except that it can also be accessed by the subclasses of the class in which the method is defined.

Allowing subclasses access to a method that cannot be accessed by users of the class is often useful for extending a class. Allowing subclass access to class *data* is much less useful and is generally not recommended. (See Bjarne Stroustrup's *The Design and Evolution of* C++, page 301, for a discussion of the dangers of protected data.)

One additional constraint is placed on `protected` access. A method declared `protected` may only be accessed through a reference to the class attempting access or through one of its subclasses. For instance, consider the next example:

```
class A {
  protected void aMethod() {
  }
}
class B extends A {
  void anotherMethod() {
    aMethod();               // Correct. B is a subclass of A and
                             // the method is being called through
                             // a reference to B or one of its
                             // subclasses. (Through the "this"
                             // reference).

  }
  void aThirdMethod(A anA) {
    anA.aMethod();           // WRONG! The method is not being
                             // called through a reference to B or
                             // one of its subclasses. It's being
                             // called through a reference to A
                             // since anA is declared as being of
                             // type A.

  }
  void aFourthMethod(B aB) {
    aB.aMethod();            // Correct. The method is again being
                             // called through a reference to B or
                             // one of its subclasses.

  }
}
```

Variables

There are three kinds of variables in Java:

- Instance variables — Variables that hold data for an instance of a class
- Class variables — Variables that hold data that will be shared among all instances of a class
- Local variables — Variables that pertain only to a block of code

Before examining instance, class, and local variables in more detail, we first need to describe some basic features of all Java variables: supported types, modifiers, scopes and extents, and initial values. We introduce these here because they are important to understanding variables in Java.

Variable Type

A variable's type refers to the kinds of values that may be stored in it. Java variables can hold any of the Java primitive types—boolean, char, int, float, double—or an instance of a particular class. A variable of type Object can hold an instance of any class, since all classes are subclasses of Object.[1] Example 3-6 shows some sample variable type declarations.

Example 3-6 Sample Variable Type Declarations

```
   int a = 1;
   boolean flag = true;
❶ String s = "a string";
❷ Object o = s;
❸ s = o;                  // s = o Generates an error.
```

Note that in this example:

❶ Assigns an instance of the class String to s.

❷ Assigns s, a String, to o, an Object. This is okay, because the String class is a subclass of Object.

❸ Generates an error. Assigning the value of o to s fails because Object is not a subclass of String. (Not all objects are strings.) In this case, of course, we know that o is a String. We'll see how to make this assignment work later in our discussion of casting in *Runtime Typing and Class Loading* on page 133.

---

1. Unlike C++, but similar to Objective-C and SmallTalk, Java includes an Object class, which is the root of all other classes.

Variable Modifiers

You can use some of the same modifiers on variables that you can use on methods: `public`, `private`, `protected`, `final`, and `static`. Table 3-3 shows variable modifiers and describes their meaning.

Table 3-3 Variable Modifiers

Variable Modifier Is...	Then...
public	The variable can be accessed by any class.
private	The variable can be accessed only by methods within the same class.
protected	The variable can be accessed by subclasses of this class and classes in the same package.
static	The variable is a class variable.
final	The variable's value cannot be changed.
transient	The variable is not part of the persistent state of an object.
volatile	The variable can be changed asynchronously. The compiler will keep it in memory.

Variable Scope and Extent

Variables in a programming language are typically described in terms of two concepts: extent and scope. In Java, the scope of a variable is the same thing as the scope of a method. It is the region of the program from which the variable can be accessed.

Instance variables and class variables have the same scope modifiers as methods: they can be:

- `public`
- `private`
- friendly
- `protected`

(Local variables are completely different, so we'll talk about the scope of local variables separately.)

The *extent* of a variable refers to the duration for which the variable has meaning within the program. For example, the extent of an argument to a function is from the invocation of that function until it exits.

Table 3-4 summarizes variable scope and extent in Java.

Table 3-4 Variable Scope and Extent in Java

Variable Type	Scope Is...	Extent Is...
Instance Variable	Subject to these conditions: 1. `private` – only methods in this class can access the variable. 2. `public` – any class can access the variable. 3. *friendly* – this class or any class within the package can access the variable. 4. `protected` – any subclasses of this class or any class within the package can access the variable.	The time the instance is created until there are no more references to that instance.
Class Variables	Subject to the same scope as instance variables.	The time the class is loaded until there are no more references to that class.
Local Variables	Within the current block of code.	The time that the code block is active.

Instance Variables

Instance variables hold the data for an instance of a class. For example, recall the Card class:

Example 3-7 Sample Instance Variables

```
public class Card {
    .
    .
    .
    // INSTANCE VARIABLES

    // Variables representing the rank and suit of a particular
    // card.

❶   private int rank;
❷   private int suit;
```

In Example 3-7, `rank` and `suit` in lines ❶ and ❷ are instance variables. The extent of an instance variable is from the time the instance is created until all references to the instance are gone, at which point the instance may be *garbage collected*. (Java uses a garbage collection memory management model, which we'll describe in *Memory and Constructors* on page 51.)

You can explicitly specify the initial value of an instance variable, for example:

```
int a = 1;
```

However, if you do not specify the initial value of an instance variable, Java assigns a default value. Table 3-5 shows the default values assigned for each type of variable.

Table 3-5 Initialized Values of Primitive Types

If the Variable Is of Type...	Then the Java Compiler Initializes It to...
`float`	`0.0f`
`double`	`0.0d`
`int`	`0`
`byte`	`0`
`short`	`0`
`char`	`'\u0000'`
`long`	`0L`
`boolean`	`false`
all others	`null`

Note that `null` is a special value that can be assigned to any variable that holds an object. It is guaranteed to be distinct from any instance.

Class Variables

Class variables hold data that is shared among all the instances of a class. Conceptually, instead of there being a separate variable for each instance, there is just one variable for the whole class. If, for example, we wanted to keep a list of all the instances of a class, we could use a class variable like the one in Example 3-8.

Example 3-8 Class Variables

```java
import java.util.Vector;

public class ClassWithMemberList {

  // Construct a new member of the class and add it to the list.

  public ClassWithMemberList() {
    memberList.addElement(this);
  }

  // Return the list of members for this class.

  public static Vector getMembers() {
    return memberList;
  }

  // List of members of this class. It's static (and thereby, a
  // class variable) so that it is shared among all the members.
  private static Vector memberList = new Vector();
```

❶

The memberList variable in line ❶ is a class variable. All instances of ClassWithMemberList will share a memberList.

The extent of a class variable is from the time a class is loaded until the last reference to the class is lost. (Class loading is discussed in *Class Loading at Runtime* on page 137.) Class variables are initialized in exactly the same way as instance variables.

Local Variables

Java has local variables that are much like local variables in other languages. A local variable's scope is from its declaration until the end of the enclosing block. You may have already noticed in our examples that Java is like C++ in that you can declare local variables anywhere a statement is valid. This is useful because it allows a programmer to limit the scope of a variable to the smallest possible region of a program. The extent of a local variable is from the time it is initialized until its block is exited. Java requires that you initialize local variables before they are used. There are no default initial values for local variables.

Java also has a special declaration model for the variables in `for` loops. For example, look at this `for` loop:

```
for (int i=0; i<100; i++);
```

You can declare and assign the variable a value at the head of the `for` loop. This is similar to C++, which allows a declaration in the head of the loop. However, in C++, the variable is accessible until the end of the block that contains the loop. In Java, it is only valid until the loop ends.

Constants

Java does not really have constants as you may be accustomed to in other languages. To provide similar capability, Java includes the variable modifier `final`. When applied to a variable, `final` indicates that the value of the variable will not change.

It is fairly common to use `switch` statements with `case` values that are constants. In Java, you can accomplish this by declaring variables to be `final static`, as in Example 3-9.

Example 3-9 Using `final static` to Create a Constant

```
class CalcInput {

    private final static char SPACE   = ' ';
    private final static char TAB     = '\t';
    private final static char NEWLINE = '\n';
    private final static char DOT     = '.';
    private final static char MINUS   = '-';
        .
        .
        .
}
```

The variables TAB, NEWLINE, DOT, and MINUS can then be used as you would constants, since the `final` declaration means the variable's value cannot be changed.

Variables, Methods, and Superclasses

When you have variables and methods defined in the superclass of a class, you can access them by using the name of the superclass. For example, the following Foo class extends the Bar class, so you can directly access the variable x in the superclass.

```
public class Foo extends Bar {
    .
    .
    .
    public void setBar(int val) {
        Bar.x = val;
    }
}
```

Static Initializers

A static initializer is a block of code that is executed when the class containing it is loaded. Static initializers and variable initializers are executed in the order that they appear. For instance, consider the program in Example 3-10.

Example 3-10 Static Initializers

```
public class StaticInitExample {
    static string str  = "yes";
    static boolean flag;

    static {
        System.out.println(str);
        flag = true;
    }

    static boolean anotherFlag = flag;

    static {
        System.out.println(anotherFlag);
    }

    public static void main(String[] args) {
    }
}
```

This program would print the following output:

```
yes
true
```

A common use of static initializers is the loading of native libraries, as described in *Runtime Typing and Class Loading* on page 133.

Packages and the import Statement

Java allows related classes to be grouped together into a *package*. From within a package, all classes can access each other's friendly members. From outside a package, only `public` and `protected` classes, methods, and variables may be accessed.

To specify the package in which to place the classes in a file, you use the `package` statement. It is the first statement in a file. For example, the calculator program described in *Putting the Language Pieces Together* on page 319, begins with the following `package` statement:

```
package calc;
```

This line says that this class will be in the `calc` package and that this class will have access to all the classes in the `calc` package.

If there is no explicit package statement in a source file, the Java runtime system assigns the source file a default package with no name.

You can only use one package per Java source file, so if you want to access classes from other packages, you have to use the `import` statement. Table 3-6 shows acceptable syntax for an `import` statement.

Table 3-6 Forms of an `import` Statement

This `import` Syntax in a Source File...	Specifies...
`import <package_name>.<class_name>;`	The source file can access a single class in the package named *package_name*. For example, the following `import` statement enables the source file to access the `Stack` class in the `java.util` package: `import java.util.Stack;` Using this `import` syntax, you can then access the `Stack` class either as `java.util.Stack` or simply as `Stack`.
`import <package_name>.*;`	The source file can access any public class in the package named *package_name*. The wildcard (*) in the `import` statement matches all the `public` classes in the package. This `import` syntax is referred to as import-on-demand. For example, the following `import` statement enables the source file to import-on-demand all the public classes in the `java.io` package: `import java.io.*;`

An explicit single class `import` statement (as described in the first row of Table 3-6) or a local definition is intended to override a type name obtained through an import-on-demand statement. However, the Java compiler will signal an error if a conflict occurs.

Java assumes that the directory structure of your program files matches the package structure of your program. The `CLASSPATH` environment variable is available for you to set so that the Java runtime system knows where to find the classes in your program. (Refer to *CLASSPATH* on page 6.) The top-level directory containing the class definitions for Java is implicitly in your `CLASSPATH`. Say the top-level Java directory was named `classes`. Then the `java.util` package would be in the directory `util` under the directory `java` under the directory `classes`. Figure 3-1 shows this directory structure.

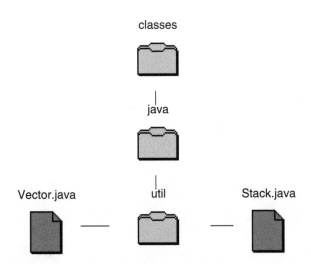

classes

java

Vector.java   util   Stack.java

Figure 3-1 Sample Package Hierarchy

Summary

In this chapter, we've covered a lot of basic material about the Java language. Remember that classes and methods are the fundamental building blocks of Java programs. Classes can *inherit* characteristics of other classes, and classes can access other, supporting classes by importing packages. Also, keep in mind the Java method and variable modifiers, which provide support for structuring applications and limiting access to the internal parts of a class.

CHAPTER 4

- Dynamic Memory Allocation and Garbage Collection

- Using Constructors and Creating Instances

- The Default Constructor

- Cleaning Up Resources (Finalization)

- Creating Linked Lists in Java

Memory and Constructors

Dynamic Allocation and Garbage Collection

Java implements a simple memory management scheme. You dynamically allocate memory within your program. Java frees it when that memory is no longer referenced.

Programming languages often implement a memory management scheme that optimizes for performance—at the expense of all other factors. Java, on the other hand, optimizes for reliability. Java programmers never explicitly free memory. It is always *garbage collected*, meaning that Java frees that memory and reuses it when there are no longer any references to it.

The current Java implementation is not guaranteed to garbage collect all unused memory. It uses a conservative garbage collector. Conservative garbage collectors are often used to add garbage collection to languages such as C and C++ [1], in which it is impossible to be sure if an address actually points to useful memory or not. The collectors are called conservative because in these cases, they will not collect memory that looks as if it might be in use.

---

1. For an overview of different garbage collection strategies, see Paul Wilson's paper, "Uniprocessor Garbage Collection Techniques," in the Proceedings of the International Workshop on Memory Management, St. Malo, France, September 1992. This has been published as Springer-Verlag Lecture Notes in Computer Science, no. 637.

The emphasis on reliability is at least one contributing factor in Java being garbage collected. Explicit memory deallocation is unsafe. If two parts of a program hold references to a piece of memory, and one of them frees it, the other part may perform an operation on corrupted data. Java keeps track of memory in use, and when that memory is no longer referenced within a program, Java automatically frees that memory (it *collects* the *garbage*) and reuses that memory.

Two sets of data types are available in Java, and allocating memory is handled differently for each. One set of data types is the Java primitive types—char, int, boolean, float, byte, short, long, double. These are allocated directly on the stack or in an instance. All other data types are subclasses of Object, and you must dynamically allocate them in your program.

Unlike C and C++, Java does not support global or stack allocation of structures and arrays. For example, Java does not have an equivalent to the C statement:

```
struct complex cnum;
```

In C, this might allocate space for a complex number on the stack. In Java, if you require a local structure, you need to dynamically allocate it—that is, you need to do something analogous to the C statement:

```
struct complex *cnum = malloc(sizeof(struct complex));
```

This line says to allocate space for a pointer to a complex number on the stack, and then allocate memory dynamically and place its address in cnum. To accomplish the same thing in Java, you would use the following declaration:

```
Complex cnum = new Complex();
```

The new Operator and Constructors

There are two components involved in allocating and initializing memory in Java:
1) the new operator and 2) a special method in each class called a *constructor*. Here
is how they work. You use the new operator to create a new instance of a class.
When the Java runtime system encounters a statement with the new operator in it,
the runtime system allocates memory for that instance. Then the constructor [2] is
called to initialize the newly allocated memory. For instance, in *Putting the
Language Pieces Together* on page 319, we show a calculator written in Java.
Example 4-1 shows use of the new operator to create an instance of a
Calculator class from that program.

Example 4-1 Creating an Instance With the new Operator

```
Calculator calc = new Calculator(System.in, System.out);
```

In Example 4-1, the new operator first *allocates* memory for an instance of the
Calculator class. Then, the constructor for the Calculator class is called to
initialize that memory. Example 4-2 shows a Calculator class constructor.

---

2.   Note that most object-oriented languages that support dynamic memory alloca-
     tion provide something similar to a Java constructor.

Example 4-2 Initializing Memory With a Constructor

```
public class Calculator {

❶ public Calculator(final Reader in, final Writer out) {

   BufferedReader dataIn;
   PrintWriter     printOut;

❷ if (!(in instanceof BufferedReader)) {
      dataIn = new BufferedReader(in);
   } else {
      dataIn = (BufferedReader)in;
   }

   if (!(out instanceof PrintWriter)) {
      printOut = new PrintWriter(out);
   } else {
      printOut = (PrintWriter)out;
   }

❸ input  = new CalcInput(dataIn);   // Object that handles all input.
   stack  = new CalcStack();         // Operand stack.
   output = printOut;                // Output writer.
   }

     .
     .
     .

}
```

In Example 4-2:

❶ Is the constructor declaration. The constructor *must* have the same name as the class and no return type.

❷ This is our first use of the `instanceof` operator, which performs type comparisons. Although not directly relevant to constructors, we mention it here for completeness.

❸ Is a series of items to be initialized when there is a new instance of the `Calculator` class. Specifically, after a new instance of the `Calculator` class is created (and memory is allocated for it), the `Calculator` constructor will create a reader instance to handle all input and an operand stack instance for the calculator. (Note that `input`, `stack`, and `output` are all `private` instance variables of the `Calculator` class.)

Using Multiple Constructors Within a Class

Although it's not illustrated in the previous example, you can include multiple constructors within a class. Doing so is useful if there is a common default initialization for a class. For example, if defining a complex number class, we might want a constructor that initializes the real and imaginary parts to 0.0 and another constructor that lets the user specify the initial values, as in Example 4-3.

Example 4-3 Using Multiple Constructors

```
public class Complex {
   public Complex() {
     realValue      = 0.0;
     imaginaryValue = 0.0;
   }

   public Complex(double real, double imaginary) {
     realValue      = real;
     imaginaryValue = imaginary;
   }
   .
   .
   .
   private double realValue;
   private double imaginaryValue;
}
```

In a program, we could use these constructors like this:

```
❶ Complex cnum1 = new Complex();
❷ Complex cnum2 = new Complex(0.0 1.0);
```

In this example, line ❶ allocates memory for a new instance of the Complex class and initializes that memory with a real value of 0.0 and an imaginary value of 0.0. Line ❷ allocates memory for a new instance of the Complex class and initializes that memory with programmer-defined values (0.0 and 1.0) for the real and imaginary parts.

The Default Constructor

If for some reason a class doesn't have a constructor defined in it, Java defines a default constructor. The default constructor does not have any arguments. What it does is call the constructor (with no arguments) for the immediate superclass. Once a class has at least one constructor, the default constructor is ignored.

It's important to note that instance variables in a new instance are initialized to the default values for their types (or to explicit initial values) before a constructor is called. If default initial values are all you require, an explicit constructor is not strictly necessary.

Using super and this in Constructors

There are two reserved words that have special meaning in constructors: super and this. You can use super to explicitly call a constructor from the superclass of the current class, and you can use this to call a constructor already defined within the same class. For instance, Example 4-4 shows use of super to call the constructor of the superclass.

Example 4-4 Using super to Call the Superclass Constructor

```
❶ class A {
     A(int x) {
       aValue = x;
     }

     int aValue;
   }

   class B extends A {
     B() {
❷      super(0);
     }
   }
```

In this example, super(0) in line ❷ calls A(0) in line ❶.

Without the call to `super()`, class B would fail to compile, since by default the first thing done in a constructor is to call the superclass constructor with no arguments, and class A has no constructor without arguments. (Note that since class A has a constructor defined, its default constructor is no longer available.) The empty constructor:

```
B() {}
```

is equivalent to:

```
B() {
    super();
}
```

You can use `this` to call other constructors in the same class. Example 4-5 shows how our previous complex number example could have been written using `this`.

Example 4-5 Using `this` to Call a Constructor in the Same Class

```
public class Complex {
  public Complex() {
❶    this(0.0, 0.0);
  }

❷  public Complex(double real, double imaginary) {
    realValue     = real;
    imaginaryValue = imaginary;
  }
    .
    .
    .
}
```

In this example, `this(0.0, 0.0)` in line ❶ calls `Complex(double, double)`, which is defined in line ❷.

The constructor to call is determined by matching the number and types of arguments. It is useful to use `this` when one constructor does a lot of setup work that all of the constructors need. This helps reduce redundant code.

When using `super` or `this` to call a constructor, you must make the call the first statement of the constructor.

Finalization

If an object has resources other than memory associated with it, such as open files or sockets, and the last reference to it is lost, Java provides a way for the programmer to release the resources. This is called *finalization*. In each class, you can define a method called `finalize()` with no arguments. Immediately before the object is garbage collected, the Java runtime system will call the `finalize()` method to clean up any outstanding resources. (The `finalize()` method is similar to a C++ destructor.) When defining a `finalize()` method, it is recommended that you *always* call `super.finalize()`.

A Sample Program Showing Linked Lists in Java

The following example demonstrates the use of linked lists in Java. It is a program for multiplying very long integers together. Each integer is represented as a linked list of digits. This example is particularly important for programmers wondering about the lack of *pointers* in Java. As the example will show, Java makes it very easy to build linked structures. In fact, each object reference in Java is actually a pointer, but its use is much more constrained than in C. The only operation defined on a Java pointer is to fetch a field from the object it points to.

The program is used in the following way:

```
java LongMult long_number1 long_number2 ... long_numberN
```

This long multiplication program uses the standard long multiplication algorithm taught in school. Multiply one number by each digit of the other and add the intermediate results. The addition of results uses the standard long addition algorithm. The program is optimized for clarity rather than speed; the only optimization applied is to always multiply the longer number by each digit of the shorter one to reduce the number of temporary results.

Figure 4-1 shows the simple structure of the long multiplier program, which consists of four classes. Table 4-1 shows a little more detail about the structure and function of these classes.

LongMult

The `LongMult` class multiplies long integers.

BigNum

The `BigNum` class represents long integers.

NumNode

The `NumNode` class represents a linked-list cell.

BigNumFormat Exception

The `BigNumFormatException` class handles errors.

Figure 4-1 Long Multiplier Class Structure
All the classes are defined in one source file, `LongMult.java`.

Table 4-1 Long Multiplier Program Class Summary

`LongMult` **Class**	
Package	`null`
Imports	`java.io.*` `java.util.Vector`
Subclass of	`Object`
Description	The `LongMult` class takes a list of long integers on the command line, multiples them together, and prints the result. This is the only `public` class in this program.

`Bignum` **Class**	
Package	`null`
Imports	None

Table 4-1 Long Multiplier Program Class Summary (Continued)

Subclass of	`Object`
Description	The `Bignum` class `represents` a long integer. It stores the digits of the integer in a linked list and provides `add()` and `mul()` methods.

`NumNode` **Class**	
Package	`null`
Imports	None
Subclass of	`Object`
Description	The `NumNode` class represents a single linked-list cell. It contains a numeric value and a reference to the next node in the list.

`BigNumFormatException` **Class**	
Package	`null`
Imports	None
Subclass of	`Object`
Description	The `BigNumFormatException` class represents all errors that occur during the construction of a `Bignum` object.

We will discuss each of these classes separately, but on the CD accompanying this book, all the classes are defined in one source file, `LongMult.java`. Now let's look at the long multiplier program in closer detail.

The LongMult Class and the main() Method

The `LongMult` class multiplies an arbitrary number of large integers (`Bignum`
objects) together. The digits of a `Bignum` are stored in a linked list, and the
multiplication is done using the standard long multiplication algorithm taught in
school:

```java
import java.io.*;
import java.util.Vector;

public class LongMult {
    public static void main(final String[] args) {

  // Check usage.  Any number of Bignum arguments may be specified.

  if (args.length < 1) {
     System.err.println("Usage: java LongMult <num1> ... <numN>");
     return;
  }

  try {

     // Initialize the total with the first argument translated into
     // a Bignum.

     Bignum total = new Bignum(args[0]);

     // Call Bignum.mul on the total and each new argument.

     for (int i = 1; i < args.length; i++) {
         total = total.mul(new Bignum(args[i]));
     }

     // Display the result.

     System.out.println(total);

  } catch (final Exception e) {
     e.printStackTrace();
     return;
  }
}
}
```

Java by Example

The BigNum Class

The Bignum class represents large integers. Each digit is stored independently in a linked list node. The number of digits is stored separately so that the smaller of two Bignum objects can be easily determined. Since this is a fairly lengthy class, we'll first show you the entire class definition and then highlight some specifics about it:

```java
private static class Bignum {

    Bignum(String stringNum) throws BignumFormatException {

        digits = stringNum.length();

        if (digits == 0) {
            System.err.println("Bignum has no value.");
            throw new BignumFormatException();
        }

        for (int index = 0; index < digits; index++) {

          int digitVal = Character.digit(stringNum.charAt(index), 10);

          if (digitVal == -1) {
            System.err.println(
            stringNum.charAt(index) + " is not a digit.");
            throw new BignumFormatException();
          }

          nodes = new NumNode(digitVal, nodes);
        }
    }

    Bignum(final NumNode nodeList) {
        nodes   = nodeList;
        digits = 0;

        for (NumNode node = nodes; node != null; node = node.next) {
            digits++;
        }
    }

    Bignum mul(final Bignum other) {
        Bignum arg1;
        Bignum arg2;

        if (digits > other.digits) {
            arg1 = other;
            arg2 = this;
        } else {
```

```
            arg1 = this;
            arg2 = other;
        }

        Bignum total = arg2.mul(arg1.nodes.val);

        int numZeros = 1;

        for (NumNode current = arg1.nodes.next; current != null;
            current = current.next) {

            // Multiply the longer Bignum by a digit of the shorter.

            Bignum partial = arg2.mul(current.val);

            // Scale the result to the correct tens position.

            partial.shift(numZeros);

            // Add the result to the running total.

            total = total.add(partial);

            // Add another zero.

            numZeros++;
        }
        return total;
    }

    Bignum add(final Bignum other) {

        // The list of nodes that will make up the resulting Bignum.

        NumNode total = null;

        // The current carry.  Always 1 or 0.

        int carry = 0;

        NumNode current;
        NumNode current2;

        for (current = nodes, current2 = other.nodes;
            current != null || current2 != null || carry != 0;
            current = next(current), current2 = next(current2)) {
```

```
        int tempVal = valof(current) + valof(current2) + carry;

        if (tempVal >= 10) {
            carry   = 1;
            tempVal = tempVal % 10;
        } else {
            carry = 0;
        }

    // Add the current result digit to the result list of digits.

    total = new NumNode(tempVal, total);
    }

    // Reverse the order of the digits to the normal Bignum
    // right to left order.

    return new Bignum(reverse(total));
}

public String toString() {
    final StringBuffer buf = new StringBuffer();

    fillBuffer(buf, nodes);

    return buf.toString();
}

private Bignum mul(int other) {

    NumNode total = null;
    int     carry = 0;

    for (NumNode current = nodes; current != null;
         current = current.next) {

        int tempVal = other * current.val + carry;

        if (tempVal >= 10) {
            carry   = tempVal / 10;
            tempVal = tempVal % 10;
        } else {
            carry = 0;
        }


        // Add the current result digit to the list of nodes.
        total = new NumNode(tempVal, total);
```

```
    }

    if (carry != 0) {
        total = new NumNode(carry, total);
    }

    return new Bignum(reverse(total));
}

private NumNode reverse(NumNode nodes) {

    NumNode after = nodes.next;
    nodes.next    = null;

    while (after != null) {
        NumNode temp = after.next;
        after.next    = nodes;
        nodes      = after;
        after      = temp;
    }

    return nodes;
}

// Add "n" zeros to the right end of a Bignum thus multiplying it
// by 10^n.

private void shift(int n) {
    while (n-- > 0) {
        nodes = new NumNode(0, nodes);
    }
}

private void fillBuffer(final StringBuffer buf, final NumNode
                        nodes) {
    if (nodes == null) {
        return;
    }

    // Add all the nodes after the current node first to
    // reverse the node order.

    fillBuffer(buf, nodes.next);

    // Now add the current node.

    buf.append(nodes.val);
}

private int valof(final NumNode node) {
```

```
        if (node == null) {
            return 0;
        } else {
            return node.val;
        }
    }

    private NumNode next(final NumNode node) {
        if (node == null) {
            return null;
        } else {
            return node.next;
        }
    }

    private NumNode nodes = null;
    private int     digits;
}
```

Now, let's go through this class to be sure you know how it's working. To begin with, notice how we create a new `Bignum` from a string of digits, and if any of the characters in the string are not digit characters, we throw a `BignumFormatException`:

```
Bignum(String stringNum) throws BignumFormatException {

    digits = stringNum.length();

    if (digits == 0) {
        System.err.println("Bignum has no value.");
        throw new BignumFormatException();
    }
```

We add each digit to the linked list nodes for the `Bignum`. The digits are stored in reverse order so we can process them later from right to left. We use the `Character.digit()` method to get the numeric value of a digit character. It returns -1 if the character does not represent a digit in the specified base.

```
    for (int index = 0; index < digits; index++) {

        int digitVal = Character.digit(stringNum.charAt(index), 10);

        if (digitVal == -1) {
            System.err.println(
            stringNum.charAt(index) + " is not a digit.");
            throw new BignumFormatException();
        }
        nodes = new NumNode(digitVal, nodes);
```

```
        }
    }
```

We create a `Bignum` from a list of nodes. This is used to create intermediate results for multiplication.

```
Bignum(final NumNode nodeList) {

    nodes  = nodeList;
    digits = 0;
    for (NumNode node = nodes; node != null; node = node.next) {
        digits++;
    }
}
```

We multiply two `Bignums`. The longer `Bignum` is multiplied by each digit of the shorter `Bignum` , and then the intermediate results are added. Note that we put the shorter number at the "bottom" of the long multiplication to reduce the number of intermediate results.

```
Bignum mul(final Bignum other) {
    Bignum arg1;
    Bignum arg2;

    if (digits > other.digits) {
        arg1 = other;
        arg2 = this;
    } else {
        arg1 = this;
        arg2 = other;
    }

    // Create the first intermediate result.

    Bignum total = arg2.mul(arg1.nodes.val);
```

We initialize the "zeros" counter, which is the number of zeros to tack on at the right of an intermediate result. Each intermediate result will be shifted left by one more position. In the for loop, we multiply each successive digit of the shorter number by the longer number, scale the result by the appropriate power of ten, and add it to the running total.

```
        int numZeros = 1;

        for (NumNode current = arg1.nodes.next; current != null;
```

```
              current = current.next) {

        // Multiply the longer Bignum by a digit of the shorter.

        Bignum partial = arg2.mul(current.val);

        // Scale the result to the correct tens position.

        partial.shift(numZeros);

        // Add the result to the running total.

        total = total.add(partial);

        // Add another zero.

        numZeros++;
    }
    return total;
}
```

The `add()` method adds the two `Bignum`s together. This method is used to add up intermediate results of a multiplication. Each corresponding digit of the two numbers is added with a carry. When the digits of one number run out, zeros are added until the other runs out. `NumNode` is the list of nodes that will make up the resulting `Bignum`.

`current` and `current2` are nodes from each `Bignum`. We traverse them right to left using the standard long addition algorithm.

In the for loop, we step through the nodes of each `Bignum`. The `next()` method keeps returning null once null is reached so we can keep stepping through whichever number is longer.

Notice that `valof()` returns the digit stored in a node or 0 if the node is null.

```
Bignum add(final Bignum other) {

    NumNode total = null;

    // The current carry.  Always 1 or 0.

    int carry = 0;

    NumNode current;
    NumNode current2;
```

```
for (current = nodes, current2 = other.nodes;
     current != null || current2 != null || carry != 0;
     current = next(current), current2 = next(current2)) {


    int tempVal = valof(current) + valof(current2) + carry;

    // If the temporary result is greater than ten, carry one.

    if (tempVal >= 10) {
        carry   = 1;
        tempVal = tempVal % 10;
    } else {
        carry = 0;
    }
}

    // Add the current result digit to the result list of digits.

    total = new NumNode(tempVal, total);
    }
```

We reverse the order of the digits to the normal `Bignum` right to left order, and then return a string representation of the `Bignum`.

```
    return new Bignum(reverse(total));
}

public String toString() {
    final StringBuffer buf = new StringBuffer();

    fillBuffer(buf, nodes);

    return buf.toString();
}
```

The `mul()` method multiplies a `Bignum` by a single decimal digit. This method is used by the general `Bignum * Bignum` multiplication method. `total` holds the list of digits resulting from multiplying the current `Bignum` by a single digit. Each digit of the `Bignum` is multiplied by the argument digit then the carry is added.

In the for loop, we multiply each digit in the `Bignum` by the argument digit, leaving the ones place in the current node and passing the tens place on as the carry.

```
private Bignum mul(int other) {

    NumNode total = null;
```

```
int     carry = 0;

for (NumNode current = nodes; current != null;
     current = current.next) {

    // Calculate the result for the current digit.  Multiply
    // the current digit by the argument and add the carry.

    int tempVal = other * current.val + carry;

    // If the current result is greater than ten, leave the
    // ones place and pass the tens place on as a carry.

    if (tempVal >= 10) {
        carry   = tempVal / 10;
        tempVal = tempVal % 10;
    } else {
        carry = 0;
    }

    // Add the current result digit to the list of nodes.

    total = new NumNode(tempVal, total);
}
```

If there is a carry left over after all the digits have been multiplied, it becomes the leftmost digit.

```
if (carry != 0) {
    total = new NumNode(carry, total);
}
```

Now, reverse the order of the digits to the normal `Bignum` right to left order.

```
    return new Bignum(reverse(total));
}
```

In the next block of code, the `reverse()` method destructively reverses the order of the nodes in a list. Notice that we save the next node before setting the next field of the first node to null.In the while loop, for each node in the list, we save the value in its next field, change the next field to point to the previous node, and continue with the saved value.

```
private NumNode reverse(NumNode nodes) {

    NumNode after = nodes.next;
    nodes.next    = null;
```

```
        while (after != null) {
                NumNode temp = after.next;
                after.next  = nodes;
                nodes       = after;
                after       = temp;
        }

        return nodes;
    }

    // Add "n" zeros to the right end of a Bignum thus multiplying it
    // by 10^n.

    private void shift(int n) {
        while (n-- > 0) {
                nodes = new NumNode(0, nodes);
        }
    }
}
```

The `fillBuffer()` method fills a `StringBuffer` with the nodes of a `Bignum`. Since the nodes are in reverse order, we call `fillBuffer()` recursively to generate the later nodes then add the current node.

```
    private void fillBuffer(final StringBuffer buf, final NumNode
                            nodes) {
        if (nodes == null) {
            return;
        }

        // Add all the nodes after the current node first to
        // reverse the node order.

        fillBuffer(buf, nodes.next);

        // Now add the current node.

        buf.append(nodes.val);
    }
```

We return the digit value of a node. If the node is null, return 0. This is used by `add()` to return a value when the nodes of one `Bignum` have run out.

```
    private int valof(final NumNode node) {
        if (node == null) {
            return 0;
        } else {
```

```
       return node.val;
       }
   }
```

We return the node after the current node. If the current node is null, return null. This is used by add() to continue stepping through the digits of one Bignum when the other has run out.

```
private NumNode next(final NumNode node) {
    if (node == null) {
   return null;
    } else {
   return node.next;
    }
}
```

```
// A Bignum consists of a list of digits and its length.
```

```
private NumNode nodes = null;
private int     digits;
   }
```

The NumNode and BigNumFormatException Classes

The NumNode class holds a single digit of a Bignum and contains a reference to the next NumNode in a list.

```
private static class NumNode {
  NumNode(final int intVal, final NumNode nextNode) {
    val  = intVal;
    next = nextNode;
  }

  int     val;
  NumNode next;

  }
```

Instances of the BignumFormatException class are returned whenever any error occurs trying to construct a Bignum.

```
private static class BignumFormatException extends Exception {}
}
```

Output From the Long Multiplier Program

After all the classes in the program have been compiled, you can call the `java` interpreter from the command line and multiply several long numbers:

```
java LongMult 594930002929 4332499002934 4545421112 123900922
14516202092787925733368898253842626126123232104
```

Summary

Java is a garbage-collected language. You never have to explicitly free memory, because the Java runtime system frees memory when there are no longer any references to it. To allocate memory in Java, you use the `new` operator to create a new instance of an object. The Java runtime system then creates a new object and allocates memory for it. To initialize that memory, the Java runtime system calls a special method, called a constructor, defined in the new object's class. The constructor defines how to initialize memory for the new object.

The long multiplier example shows how to build linked structures in Java. For programmers accustomed to using C-style pointers, this example illustrates how to accomplish the same result in Java.

CHAPTER
5

- Using Interfaces as Types
- Extending Interfaces
- A Tree Sort Program

Interfaces as Types

What Is an Interface?

Besides creating classes in your Java programs, you can also create special structures called *interfaces*. A Java interface is similar to a class, except there is no data associated with the interface. (We'll elaborate on that shortly.)

As we've seen, a class definition looks something like this:

```
public class MyClass {
    <class constructor, methods, and variables>
}
```

Similarly, you can define an interface:

```
public interface MyInterface {
    <methods—with no implementation details>
    <final variables>
}
```

The primary difference between a class and an interface is that the variables in an interface must be `final`, and the methods in the interface are only declarations. The way the method works is specified in any class that `implements` the interface. We'll show you exactly what this means in *Using Interfaces* on page 78, but first, let's consider the reason for interfaces.

Why Use an Interface?

We said earlier that the `public` methods of a class make up its external interface. In many ways, the external interface of a class is like a contract with users of the class. It defines the operations in the class that its instances can be counted on to perform. To draw a comparison to everyday life, we could say that people also enter into contracts that define the actions that are expected of them. It's not uncommon, however, for people to enter into multiple contracts with distinct sets of requirements: for example, a person might primarily be a family member, but also have responsibilities to the community, the church, the employer, and so on. In Java, a class may enter into multiple contracts by specifying multiple *interfaces* that it supports.

A class that *extends* another class is guaranteed to support the contracts entered into by its superclass. In Java, however, the extension mechanism alone does not provide the ability to enter into multiple contracts. (Java is a *single inheritance* language, and for C++ programmers, interfaces are used to approximate *multiple inheritance*.) Let's look at an example to illustrate this point:

```
❶ public class ColoredObject {
     public Color getColor() {
       return color;
     }

     public void setColor(Color newColor) {
       color = newColor;
     }

     private Color color = Color.white;
   }
❷ public class NamedObject {
     public String getName() {
       return name;
     }

     public void setName(String newName) {
       name = newName;
     }

     private String name = "";
   }
```

In this example, line ❶ is a class definition for `ColoredObject`, which includes methods for getting and setting color values. Line ❷ is a class definition for `NamedObject`, which includes methods for getting and setting name values.

Now assume we wanted to define a new class that extended both `NamedObject` and `ColoredObject`, as in the following:

```
   // The following is WRONG, because we can only extend one class.
❸ class NamedAndColoredObject extends NamedObject, ColoredObject {
   }
```

Line ❸ is an *invalid* class definition for `NamedAndColoredObject` because it extends both `NamedObject` and `ColoredObject`, which is illegal. We can't achieve what we want with `NamedAndColoredObject` because we can't extend more than one superclass. However, by using interfaces, we can achieve what we're trying to accomplish with `NamedAndColoredObject`.

Using Interfaces

Suppose we had an application that needed to determine if certain objects it manipulated were blue. We wouldn't expect each object to have a flag indicating whether or not it was blue, but we might want to fetch the object's color and compare it to blue. We know we can perform `getColor()` on instances of the `ColoredObject` class, and it seems right to have our `isBlue()` method operate on a `ColoredObject`. However, some of the classes we're working with already inherit from `NamedObject` and cannot be made subclasses of `ColoredObject`.

The question is, how can we make the `isBlue()` method work and still support contracts other than the one supported by `ColoredObject`? In Java, the answer is that we use an interface, as illustrated in Example 5-1.

Example 5-1 Defining Interfaces

```
❶ public interface ColoredObject {
      Color getColor();

      void setColor(Color newColor);
   }

❷ public interface NamedObject {
      String getName();

      void setName(String newName);
   }

   // Note the use of "implements" instead of "extends"
❸ public class NamedAndColoredObject implements
      ColoredObject, NamedObject {
      .
      .
      .
   }
```

In this example:

❶ and ❷ are now interface definitions instead of class definitions for `ColoredObject` and `NamedObject`.

❸ Is a *valid* class definition for `NamedAndColoredObject` because it implements the `ColoredObject` and `NamedObject` interfaces.

There are two things to note in this example:

- An interface provides no implementation for the methods it declares. The implementations must be provided by classes that implement the interface. `getColor()`, `setColor()`, `getName()`, and `setName()` only define method names, arguments, and return types.

- A class can extend only one other class, but it can implement any number of interfaces.

An interface is something like a shell or husk of a class—it has no inside. There is no local data associated with an interface. Table 5-1 shows the basic characteristics of variables and methods in an interface.

Table 5-1 Characteristics of an Interface

Variables are...	Methods are...
Treated like constants in an interface. They are always `final` and `static`, and they must be initialized.	Abstract. There's no implementation specified.

Any methods or variables declared in a public interface are implicitly `public`. All an interface actually does is specify a contract. That contract implicitly says that any class that implements the interface will provide a particular set of methods. [1]

The `ColoredObject` interface says that any class that implements it will provide `getColor()` and `setColor()` methods with specific arguments and return types. Given this, we can write `isBlue()` as in Example 5-2 on the next page.

---

1.   For those familiar with Objective-C, an interface in Java is similar to a protocol in Objective-C.

Example 5-2 Passing Classes That Implement an Interface

❶ ```
public interface ColoredObject {
   Color getColor();
   void setColor(Color newColor);
}
```

❷ ```
public class Car extends Vehicle implements ColoredObject {
   .
   .
   .
   public Color getColor() {
     return color;
   }

   public void setColor(Color newColor) {
     color = newColor;
   }

   private Color color = Color.white;
}
```

```
public class Example {
```
❸ ```
   public static boolean isBlue(ColoredObject o) {
     return o.getColor() == Color.blue;
   }
}
```

```
Car myAuto = new Car();
myAuto.setColor(Color.blue);
```
❹ ```
boolean colorIsBlue = Example.isBlue(myAuto); // returns true
```

In this example:

❶ Defines the `ColoredObject` interface. It declares `getColor()` and `setColor()` methods. It is up to any class that implements this interface to define what these methods do.

❷ Is a class definition for `Car`, which implements the `ColoredObject` interface. To uphold its end of the contract, `Car` defines what the `getColor()` and `setColor()` methods actually do.

❸ Defines the `isBlue()` method. The `isBlue()` method takes a variable of type `ColoredObject` as an argument. This means that `isBlue()` can be passed any object that is an instance of a class implementing the `ColoredObject` interface.

❹ Is a class method call to `isBlue()`. The key point here is that `Example.isBlue()` can accept `myAuto` as an argument because it is of type `Car`, which implements the `ColoredObject` interface.

As long as a class provides the `getColor()` and `setColor()` methods and specifies that it implements `ColoredObject`, instances of that class can be stored in variables of type `ColoredObject` and passed as arguments to methods expecting a `ColoredObject`.

Extending Interfaces

Interfaces may be extended just like classes. Unlike classes, however, interfaces may extend any number of other interfaces, as illustrated in Example 5-3.

Example 5-3 Extending an Interface

```
interface NamedAndColoredObject extends NamedObject, ColoredObject
{
    .
    .
    .
}
```

Some languages, such as C++ and CLOS, support multiple inheritance, which allows you to extend multiple classes. However, multiple inheritance introduces complexity and problems of its own. (For a good discussion of this issue, see Alan Snyder's paper, "Inheritance and the Development of Encapsulated Software Systems," in *Research Directions in Object-Oriented Programming*, edited by Bruce Shriver and Peter Wegner.)

A Sample Program Using Interfaces

The following program illustrates several features of Java we've discussed up to this point, and it demonstrates the use of interfaces. It also shows how interesting data structures can be constructed and provides an example of enumerations in Java.

The program sorts lines from a file using a binary tree. Each line is read in and inserted into the tree. The tree is then traversed and the lines are printed in sorted order. The traversal and printing are done using an enumeration of the tree. The program relies on a class that implements the `java.util.Enumeration` interface, which provides two methods: `hasMoreElements()` and `nextElement()`.

The `hasMoreElements()` method returns a `boolean` true value as long as there are elements that have not been enumerated. The `nextElement()` method returns an `Object`—the next element in the enumeration. Built-in enumeration classes are provided for Java classes such as `java.util.Vector`, `java.util.Hashtable`, and `java.util.Properties`. It is good practice to provide enumerations for new container classes so that Java code can be written in a consistent style.

This is the first program in which we use Java's package facility. We've grouped most of the classes into a package, which we call the `tree` package. The top-level file imports all the supporting classes in the `tree` package. The code for the tree sort program consists of five classes and one interface, as illustrated in Figure 5-1.

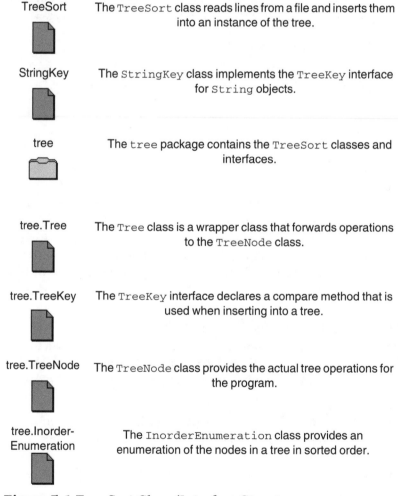

TreeSort   The `TreeSort` class reads lines from a file and inserts them into an instance of the tree.

StringKey   The `StringKey` class implements the `TreeKey` interface for `String` objects.

tree   The `tree` package contains the `TreeSort` classes and interfaces.

tree.Tree   The `Tree` class is a wrapper class that forwards operations to the `TreeNode` class.

tree.TreeKey   The `TreeKey` interface declares a compare method that is used when inserting into a tree.

tree.TreeNode   The `TreeNode` class provides the actual tree operations for the program.

tree.Inorder-Enumeration   The `InorderEnumeration` class provides an enumeration of the nodes in a tree in sorted order.

Figure 5-1 Tree Sort Class/Interface Structure

Table 5-2 shows a little more detail about the structure of these classes and interfaces.

Table 5-2 Tree Sort Program Class and Interface Summary

`TreeSort` **Class**	
Package	`null`

Imports	`java.io.*`
	`java.util.Enumeration`
	`tree.*`

Subclass of	`Object`
Interfaces	None
Description	The `TreeSort` class reads lines from a file and inserts them into an instance of the `tree.Tree` class. It then uses the `inorder()` enumeration of the tree to print sorted lines.

`StringKey` **Class**	
Package	`null`

Imports	`java.util.io*`
	`java.util.Enumeration`
	`tree.*`

Interfaces	`TreeKey`
Description	The `StringKey` class `implements` the `TreeKey` interface and constructs a new `StringKey` object for a given `String` object.

`Tree` **Class**	
Package	`tree`
Imports	`java.util.Enumeration` `java.util.Stack`
Interfaces	None
Description	The `Tree` class is a wrapper class that forwards operations to the `TreeNode` class. The `Tree` class exists so that empty trees can be manipulated. An empty tree has no `TreeNode` objects.

`TreeKey` **Interface**	
Package	`tree`
Imports	None
Description	The `TreeKey` interface declares a `compare()` method that is used when inserting into a tree. An instance of any class may be used as a key if its class `implements` the `TreeKey` interface.

Table 5-2 Tree Sort Program Class and Interface Summary (Continued)

`TreeNode` **Class**	
Package	`tree`
Imports	`java.util.Enumeration`
Subclass of	`Object`
Interfaces	None
Description	The `TreeNode` class provides the actual tree operations for the program. The `lookup()` method is not actually used in this program, but is included for completeness.

`InorderEnumeration` **Class**	
Package	`tree`
Imports	`java.util.Stack` `java.util.Enumeration`
Subclass of	`Object`
Interfaces	`Enumeration`
Description	The `InorderEnumeration` class provides an enumeration of the nodes in a tree in sorted order.

With these details in mind, we'll describe each class and interface and how they inter-relate to form a working, tree-sort program.

The TreeSort Class and the main() Method

The `TreeSort` class uses a binary tree to sort lines in a file and remove duplicated data. Each line is inserted into the tree and the tree is then enumerated to print each line. The keys for the tree must implement the `TreeKey` interface, which provides a comparison method for ordering the entries. We'll first show the entire class and then discuss some of it in detail.

```
import java.io.*;
import java.util.Enumeration;
import tree.*;

public class TreeSort {
    public static void main(final String[] args) {

      if (args.length < 1) {
        System.err.println("Usage: java TreeSort <file>");
        return;
      }
      try {
```

```
        final BufferedReader in =
          new BufferedReader(new FileReader(args[0]));

        final Tree tree = new Tree();
        String line;
        while ((line = in.readLine()) != null) {

            tree.insert(new StringKey(line), line);
        }

        final Enumeration entries = tree.inorder();

        while (entries.hasMoreElements()) {
            System.out.println(entries.nextElement());
        }

    } catch (final Exception e) {
        e.printStackTrace();
        return;
    }
}

private static class StringKey implements TreeKey {

    StringKey(final String val) {
        stringVal = val;
    }

    public int compare(final TreeKey other) {
        StringKey otherStringKey = (StringKey)other;
        final int compareResult =
                    stringVal.compareTo(otherStringKey.stringVal);

        if (compareResult < 0) {
            return TreeKey.LESS;
        } else if (compareResult == 0) {
                return TreeKey.EQUAL;
        } else {
                return TreeKey.GREATER;
        }
    }

    public String toString() {
        return stringVal;
    }

    private String stringVal;
}
```

```
}
```

Now that you've had a chance to review the entire class, let's looks at some details. First of all, notice that we create a `BufferedReader` so we can read a line at a time. We also create a new empty tree to which each line will be added. To read a line at a time, we create a `BufferedReader` object. (See *Input/Output* on page 117 for details about how this works.)

```
final BufferedReader in =
  new BufferedReader(new FileReader(args[0]));

final Tree tree = new Tree();
String line;
```

In the while loop, we insert the current line into the tree. The `StringTreeVal` class implements the `TreeVal` interface for Strings.

```
while ((line = in.readLine()) != null) {

    tree.insert(new StringKey(line), line);
}
```

In the next block of code, we create an enumeration for the tree that will print its entries in order. An "inorder" traversal of a tree prints the left subtree, the current node, and then the right subtree.

```
final Enumeration entries = tree.inorder();

while (entries.hasMoreElements()) {
    System.out.println(entries.nextElement());
}

} catch (final Exception e) {
    e.printStackTrace();
    return;
}
}
```

The `StringKey` class contains a `String` and implements the `TreeKey` interface. The `compare()` method compares the `String` in this `StringKey` to the `String` in "other" using the `compareTo()` method for Strings.

```
    private static class StringKey implements TreeKey {

      StringKey(final String val) {
        stringVal = val;
      }

      public int compare(final TreeKey other) {
        StringKey otherStringKey = (StringKey)other;
        final int compareResult =
                    stringVal.compareTo(otherStringKey.stringVal);

        if (compareResult < 0) {
          return TreeKey.LESS;
        } else if (compareResult == 0) {
            return TreeKey.EQUAL;
        } else {
            return TreeKey.GREATER;
        }
      }

      // Print a StringKey by printing its String.

      public String toString() {
        return stringVal;
      }

    private String stringVal;
    }
}
```

To read a line at a time, we create a `DataInputStream` object. (See *Input/Output* on page 117 for details about how this works.)

```
    try {

        DataInputStream in = new DataInputStream(
            new FileInputStream(args[0]));

        // Create a new empty tree. Each line will be added to it.

        Tree      tree   = new Tree();
        String    line;
```

The Tree Class

The `Tree` class stores objects in a binary tree based on the object's key. The objects in the tree may be looked up by the object's key or enumerated in sorted order. Most of the work is done by the `TreeNode` class. Operations are forwarded to the top level `TreeNode` of the tree.

```java
package tree;

import java.util.Enumeration;
import java.util.Stack;

public class Tree {

  // Construct a new tree with no entries.

  public Tree() {
    topNode = null;
  }

  // Insert an entry into the tree based on the compare method of
  // "key".

  public void insert(final TreeKey key, final Object val) {

    if (topNode == null) {
      topNode = new TreeNode(key, val);
    } else {
      topNode.insert(key, val);
    }
  }

  // Lookup an entry in the tree based on the compare method of "key"

  public Object lookup(final TreeKey key) {
    if (topNode == null) {
      return null;
    } else {
      return topNode.lookup(key);
    }
  }

  // Return an "inorder" enumeration of the tree.  This can be
  // used to sort the values in the tree.

  public Enumeration inorder() {
  return new InorderEnumeration();
```

The TreeNode Class

The TreeNode class defines the actual insert() and lookup() operations for trees. Each instance of TreeNode holds a key and a value and has left and right subtrees.

Notice the insert() method, which inserts a new entry. If the key compares less than the key in the current node, then it inserts the new value into the left subtree; if it compares greater, then it inserts the new value into the right subtree. Otherwise, it replaces the value in the current node.

Also, pay attention to the lookup() method, which looks up an entry in the tree based on the compare function of key. This method returns null if there is no matching entry.

```java
private TreeNode topNode;

private class TreeNode {

// Construct a new TreeNode with a specific key and value.

TreeNode(final TreeKey key, final Object val) {
    nodeKey   = key;
    nodeVal   = val;
    nodeLeft  = null;
    nodeRight = null;
}

// A special case for when the entry itself can serve as a key.

void insert (final TreeKey key) {
    insert(key, key);
}

void insert(final TreeKey key, final Object val) {

    // All TreeKeys implement the "compare" method.

    switch (key.compare(getKey())) {
    case TreeKey.EQUAL:
        nodeVal = val;
        break;
    case TreeKey.LESS:

        if (nodeLeft == null) {
            nodeLeft = new TreeNode(key, val);
        } else {
            nodeLeft.insert(key, val);
```

```
        }
        break;

     case TreeKey.GREATER:

   if (nodeRight == null) {
      nodeRight = new TreeNode(key, val);
   } else {
      nodeRight.insert(key, val);
   }
   break;
   }
}

Object lookup(final TreeKey key) {
    switch (key.compare(getKey())) {
    case TreeKey.EQUAL:
        return nodeVal;

    case TreeKey.LESS:
        if (nodeLeft == null) {
            return null;
        } else {

        return nodeLeft.lookup(key);
        }

    case TreeKey.GREATER:

        if (nodeRight == null) {
            return null;
        } else {

        return nodeRight.lookup(key);
        }
    }

    return null;
}

// These are Accessory methods for other classes in the package
// so that they do not need access to the instance variables of
// TreeNodes.

TreeNode getLeft() {
   return nodeLeft;
}
TreeNode getRight() {
```

```
            return nodeRight;
        }
        TreeKey getKey() {
            return nodeKey;
        }
        TreeKey getVal() {
            return nodeKey;
        }

        private TreeKey  nodeKey;
        private Object   nodeVal;
        private TreeNode nodeLeft;
        private TreeNode nodeRight;
    }
```

The InorderEnumeration Class

The `InorderEnumeration` class enumerates the entries in a tree one at a time in sorted order. The `hasMoreElements()` method returns false when all the entries have been enumerated. Each call to the `nextElement()` method returns the next entry in the tree. For each `TreeNode`, the left subtree, the node itself and then the right subtree are enumerated. The enumeration is performed using a stack. The stack's behavior mimics the behavior of the runtime stack in a recursive tree traversal, which might look like this:

```
void printTree(TreeNode node) {
  if (node != null) {
    printTree(node.getLeft());
    System.out.println(node.getVal());
    printTree(node.getRight());
  }
}
```

At each point where a value is printed, the state of the runtime stack will be duplicated in the enumeration. The first value to be printed will be the *leftmost* entry after the method has been called for each left subtree. At this point, all the leftmost entries will be on the runtime stack.

To initialize the enumeration, the `InorderEnumeration` class descends the leftmost branches of the tree, pushing each node on a stack. The top node on the stack is always the next to be enumerated. Following is the complete `InorderEnumeration` class:

```
private class InorderEnumeration implements Enumeration {

  public InorderEnumeration() {
```

```
      pushLeftNodes(topNode);
   }

         // When the stack is empty, there are no more entries.

   public boolean hasMoreElements() {
      return stack.empty() == false;
   }

   // After an entry is returned, we need to enumerate the right
   // subtree. so we set up the stack for the right subtree just as
   // we did at the top.

   public Object nextElement() {
      final TreeNode current = (TreeNode)stack.pop();
      pushLeftNodes(current.getRight());
      return current.getVal();
   }

   // Descend the leftmost branches of the tree pushing each node.

   private void pushLeftNodes(TreeNode node) {
      while (node != null) {
         stack.push(node);
         node = node.getLeft();
      }
   }

   private Stack stack = new Stack();
   }
}
```

The TreeKey Interface

The TreeKey interface defines a compare() method that can be used to order nodes in a tree. The compare() method should return either TreeKey.LESS, TreeKey.EQUAL, or TreeKey.GREATER depending on how the current TreeKey object compares to the argument TreeKey:

```
package tree;

public interface TreeKey {
    public static final int LESS    = -1;
    public static final int EQUAL   =  0;
    public static final int GREATER =  1;

    public int compare(final TreeKey other);
}
```

Output From the Tree Sort Program

After all the classes in the `tree` package and the `TreeSort` class have been compiled, you can call the `java` interpreter from the command line to start the tree sorter:

```
java TreeSort file
```

Assume that the source file had the following data:

```
Z Y X W
Z Y X W
z y x w
V U T S
v u t s
Q P O N
q p o n
M L K J
m l k j
I H G F
i h g f
E D C B
e d c b
A
a
```

The interpreter will display the following sorted output:

```
A
E D C B
I H G F
M L K J
Q P O N
V U T S
Z Y X W
a
e d c b
i h g f
m l k j
q p o n
v u t s
z y x w
```

Summary

Interfaces are the fundamental mechanism in Java for approximating multiple inheritance. You can design a class that may enter into multiple contracts by specifying multiple interfaces that it supports. An interface is similar to a class definition, except that the methods in an interface are essentially stubs. Each class that `implements` an interface must specify how the interface's methods are to operate. The `TreeSort` program shows the use of interfaces to provide a generic tree facility. An inorder enumeration enables the program to process each element of the tree when it is ready to. Without the enumeration, the program structure would have to mirror the tree structure.

CHAPTER
6

Arrays

Basics of Java Arrays

Arrays in Java are objects. As we discovered in our discussion of memory management, this means that arrays must be created with the new operator and cannot be allocated in place. For example, look at the following declaration:

```
int[] scores;
```

This declaration does not create an array. Instead, it creates a variable that can hold an array. To actually create an array of integers, it is necessary to use the new operator and create an instance, as in the following declaration:

```
scores = new int[10];
```

The size argument (in this case, 10) is required. Note that an array's size *cannot* be changed after it is created. (If you require a dynamically sized array, you can use the java.util.Vector class.) All the elements of the new array are initialized to the default value (0) for integers. All arrays in Java begin with element 0, so the first element is at index 0.

Array bounds are always checked in Java. If a subscript is less than 0 or greater than the array's length - 1, an `ArrayIndexOutOfBoundsException` is thrown. (We'll discuss throwing exceptions more in *Exception Handling* on page 105.)

Arrays of Objects

A common source of confusion arises when trying to create an array of objects. For example, consider the following statement:

```
String[] strings = new String[10];
```

This statement does *not* create an array of strings. Instead, it creates an array of ten `null` object references. In this respect, arrays of objects in Java are like arrays of pointers in C or C++. To populate the array with actual strings, it is necessary to store the `String` instances in the array explicitly, as in the following statement:

```
for (int i = 0; i < strings.length; i++) {
// All arrays have a public length instance variable.

❶    strings[i] = new String();
}
```

The statement in line ❶ stores a new instance of `String` in each element of the array.

The difference between declaring an array of a Java primitive type (`boolean`, `char`, `int`, `byte`, `short`, `long`, `float`, and `double`) and declaring an array of an object type is analogous to declaring a variable of a primitive type and a variable of an object type. For example, note the following two variable declarations:

```
❶ int foo;
❷ String bar;
```

In this example, line ❶ is a primitive variable declaration that creates a new integer variable, `foo`. Line ❷ is an object variable declaration (`String` is a subclass of `Object`) that creates a `null` reference to a `String`.

Multidimensional Arrays

Java does not support multidimensional arrays. You can, however, create arrays of arrays, just as you can in C and C++. This is natural since arrays in Java are objects, and it's possible to create arrays of any arbitrary object type. For example, the following declaration creates an array of null references to String arrays:

```
String[][] arrayOfStringArrays = new String[20][];
```

Note that the first dimension must be specified since the outermost array is actually being allocated. The elements of that array need to be allocated themselves, as illustrated in the following statement:

```
for (int i = 0; i < arrayOfStringArrays.length; i++) {
  // fill in each element of arrayOfStringArrays with an array of
  // strings.

  arrayOfStringArrays[i] = new String[10];
}
```

The following loop would actually fill the arrays with strings:

```
for (int i = 0; i < arrayOfStringArrays.length; i++) {
  for (int j = 0; j < arrayOfStringArrays[i].length; j++) {
    arrayOfStringArrays[i][j] = new String();
  }
}
```

A real program would probably combine the two loops like this:

```
for (int i = 0; i < arrayOfStringArrays.length; i++) {
   String[] newArray = new String[10];

   arrayOfStringArrays[i] = newArray;

   for (int j = 0; j < newArray.length; j++) {
     newArray[j] = new String();
   }
}
```

Again, the key points to remember are that Java arrays are objects that must be allocated, and arrays of Java objects are similar to arrays of pointers in C.

C++ Style Array Initialization

You can use the C++ style of enclosing an array's elements in opening and closing braces to initialize an array:

```
int[] scores = {1, 2, 3+4, 5};
```

Each element must be an expression that returns the array's component type. (Also, a comma after the last element is allowed.)

Array Expressions

You can also create a new array *on the fly*. You do this by using the type of an array followed by its elements in braces, as in the following example:

```
int result = sumArray(int[]{3,4,7*9});
```

Alternative Array Declaration Syntax

Java also allows arrays to be declared in a syntax similar to C arrays. For example, the declaration:

```
int[] scores;
```

can also be written as:

```
int scores[];
```

These two forms are completely equivalent, but the latter form makes it less clear that we're just declaring a variable that can hold an array rather than the array itself. For this reason we prefer to use the former syntax.

Arrays in the Object Hierarchy

Arrays are objects in Java, but their classes are unique. Each class defined in Java (either by the system or the user) along with the primitive types has a corresponding array class. The class `Object` has a corresponding `Object[]` class that has arrays of `Object`s as its instances. Array classes cannot be extended directly. They are extended when their corresponding classes are extended. If class `Y` is a subclass of class `X`, then class `Y[]` (the class of arrays of `Y`) is a subclass of class `X[]` (the class of arrays of `X`).

At first glance, this seems like a reasonable arrangement. However, there is a potential problem with this type of system. Let's examine the problem with arrays so as not to fall victim to it ourselves. Consider the following scenario:

```
class X {
   int a;
}

class Y extends X {
   int b;
}

class Z {
   static void broken(X[] arrayOfX, int index, X newValue) {
     arrayOfX[index] = newValue;
   }
}
```

Class Y is a subclass of class X. Thus, Y[] (array of Y) is a subclass of X[] (array of X). Here is the problem:

```
Y[] arrayOfY = new Y[10];
X valueOfTypeX = new X();

Z.broken(arrayOfY, 0, valueOfTypeX);
```

The problem is that Z.broken() will try to assign valueOfTypeX to element 0 of arrayOfY. Unfortunately, valueOfTypeX is not a Y! The Z.broken() method will try to assign something that isn't of type Y to an array of type Y. At runtime, this will lead to an ArrayStoreException being thrown.

In every other case where a runtime type check is necessary to determine if an operation can be applied, the Java compiler will point it out. An explicit cast is required. In this case, however, code that is not typesafe can slip by the compiler and cause problems later at runtime. [1]

Summary

The subtle difference between creating an array and creating a variable that can hold an array sometimes confuses programmers new to Java. A simple declaration such as this:

```
int[] scores;
```

only creates a variable that can hold an array. To actually create an array of objects, you must use the new operator:

```
scores = new int[10];
```

1. Some object-oriented languages, notably Eiffel, use this typing model (called covariance) deliberately because the Eiffel designers felt that it enhances the expressive power of the language. Other language designers consider it a bug.

This declaration initializes the 10 elements of the new array with 0, and the first element is at index 0.

Also, an array of object references is different from an array of primitive types. The elements of an array of object references must be explicitly created.

CHAPTER

7

- The Java Exception Handling Model

- Exceptions in Java

- The try and catch Blocks

Exception Handling

Exceptional Conditions

Java provides an exception handling model that allows you to check for errors *only* where it is relevant to do so. This is in contrast to C, in which you have to deal with errors in the normal path of a program. A large portion of a well-written program is concerned with what to do when things go wrong. When looking at a program written in a language like C, in which you are forced to handle errors via return codes, it can be hard to see the actual algorithm being used in a procedure because there is error checking code inserted every few lines.

Problems Using Return Codes for Error Processing

Returning an error code often forces the *real* return value of a procedure to be passed back in some other way. (Real return values are commonly returned via a reference argument. Note, however, that there are no reference arguments in Java. Returning multiple values in Java requires returning an instance of a class.) A more serious flaw with using return codes for error processing is that once an error code has been issued, it must be dealt with by every procedure in the chain of calls that led to the error. As the error code ascends the call chain, it becomes more and more out of context. As a result, programmers typically re-encode the error several times on its way up the chain of calls. Even if the program does not need to do anything with the error for several levels, the program must be written to process it at each one.

Let's look at an example in C. Suppose we're working with records in a set of files and we want to look up an entry in one of the files. Table names are associated with particular file names based on context. Errors are displayed to the user in the top level loop of the user interface:

```
/* Look up the entry for "Marianna" in the        */
/* "employee" table.                              */

/* On failure, "error" will be filled with a      */
/* structure containing details.                  */

ErrorStruct *error = NULL;
TableEntry  *entry = lookup("Marianna", "employee", &error);

if (entry == NULL) {
    return error;
}
```

In Java, we could rewrite this code to look something like this:

```
// Look up the entry for "Marianna" in the "employee"
// table.

// On failure, "error" will be filled in with details.

ErrorStruct error = new ErrorStruct();
TableEntry  entry = lookup("Marianna", "employee", error);

if (entry == NULL) {
    return error;
}
```

This version, unfortunately, requires that we allocate an ErrorStruct before the call—even if we don't end up using it. An alternative is to have lookup() return an instance of a class, as in the next example:

```
// Look up the entry for "Marianna" in the "employee" table.

// A variable of type "Result" contains a TableEntry and
// an ErrorStruct.

Result result = lookup("Marianna", "employee");

if (result.getEntry() == null) {
    return result.getError();
}
```

This version requires defining a Result class that is only used to return an extra value from the method. Following is another way to accomplish the same result:

```
// Look up the entry for "Marianna" in the "employee" table.

// The array returned will have a TableEntry and an ErrorStruct as
// elements 0 and 1.

Object[] result = lookup("Marianna", "employee");

if (result[0] == null) {
    return (ErrorStruct)result[1];
}
```

This version forces a type cast to be used, even though we know result[1] is an ErrorStruct.

As we can see, none of the previous three solutions are particularly satisfactory. The first version requires that we allocate an ErrorStruct when it isn't needed. The second version requires the definition of a Result class that is only used to return an extra value from the method. The third version forces an unnecessary type cast.

Catching and Throwing Exceptions

Rather than use the C-style error checking via return codes, Java recognizes that errors should *not* be dealt with in the normal path of a program. They are, in fact, *exceptional conditions.* Java implements a *catch and throw* model of exception handling similar to the one used in C++ . Using this model, you only have to pay attention to exceptional conditions where it makes sense to do so. Instead of returning errors from a method using the normal return value or parameter mechanism, Java provides an *exception handling* facility. Errors and other exceptional conditions are treated as distinct from the normal flow of control in the program, which, after all, they are. When an error occurs, an exception is *thrown.* Exceptions climb the chain of calls until they are *caught* or until the program exits.

The catch and throw method of exception handling offers two big advantages:

- An error condition can be dealt with only where it makes sense instead of dealing with it at every level between where it occurs and where it needs to be dealt with.

- Code can be written as if the operations in it will work.

Using Java's catch and throw method, we can simply rewrite the `lookup()` example as follows:

```
TableEntry entry = lookup("Marianna", "employee");
```

We can use `entry` without checking its value. This produces code that is much easier to read and modify.

try and catch

The fundamental language support for the catch and throw method of exception handling is the `try/catch` block. For example, at some higher level in our file database program, we could have the `try/catch` block in Example 7-1.

Example 7-1 `try` **Block in Java**

```
try {
    doFileProcessing();
    displayResults();

} catch (Exception e) {
    System.err.println("Error: " + e.getMessage());
}
```

Any error that occurred during the execution of `doFileProcessing()` or `displayResults()` would be *caught* by the `catch` and processed. If an error occurred during `doFileProcessing()`, `displayResults()` would never get called, and execution would proceed directly to the `catch` block. If, instead of having `(Exception e)`, we had a more specific error class, such as `(LookupException e)`, the actual error would have to be an instance of `LookupException` or one of its subclasses to be caught. Otherwise, the error would pass through this `try`/`catch` block and continue to climb the call chain until it reached a `catch` that matched it or the program exited. (Note that this code uses the `System` object, which provides standard input and output streams for reading character data and for printing output.)

You can also string multiple catches together to process different exception types differently. For example, look at Example 7-2.

Example 7-2 Multiple Catches in `try` Block

```
try {
    doFileProcessing();
    displayResults();

} catch (LookupException e) {
    handleLookupException(e);

} catch (Exception e) {
    System.err.println("Error: " + e.getMessage());
}
```

In this case, a `LookupException` would be caught and processed by the first `catch` and any other type of exception would be handled by the second `catch`.

The finally Statement

Exceptions can cause control to leave the current method without completing the method's execution. If there is cleanup code such as code to close files at the end of the method, it will never get called. To deal with this case, Java provides the `finally` statement [1].

---

1. The Java `finally` statement is equivalent to the Common Lisp `unwind-protect` special form.

The `finally` statement can be used in conjunction with a `try` block. Basically, it ensures that if an exception occurs, any cleanup work that is necessary is taken care of because the code in a `finally` statement is guaranteed to run even if an exception occurs. For example, look at Example 7-3.

Example 7-3 Using the `finally` Statement

```
try {
  doSomethingThatMightThrowAnException();
} finally {
  cleanup();
}
```

If `doSomethingThatMightThrowAnException()` throws an exception, the `cleanup()` method will still be called, and then the exception will continue to travel up the call chain. If an exception is not thrown, `cleanup()` will get called and execution will proceed after the `finally` statement.

The throw Statement

Up to this point, we've focussed on receiving and processing errors in the `try` and `catch` block. Conversely, we need to understand how an error originates. In Java, when an error condition arises in a program, we send an exception up the call chain by using the `throw` keyword. For example, let's go back to our file lookup example. Say we want to check that `entry` is assigned an appropriate value, and if it isn't, we want to send an exception up the call chain where it will be handled by the appropriate `try` and `catch` block. Example 7-4 shows how to throw the exception.

Example 7-4 Using `throw` in Exception Handling

```
TableEntry entry = fileLookup(name, filename);

if (entry == null) {
  throw new FileLookupFailureException(name, filename);
}
```

❶

In line ❶, the argument to `throw` can be any expression that returns an instance of a subclass of the `Throwable` class. (In general, this argument is almost always a subclass of `Exception`.)

The Java Exception class extends the Throwable class and represents exceptional conditions a user program may want to catch. The Throwable class provides some useful features for dealing with exceptions. Specifically, the Throwable class:

- Provides a slot for a message
- Contains a stack trace

It is often useful to create your own exception classes for special case exception handling within your program. This is normally done by creating a subclass of the Exception class.

The advantage of subclassing the Exception class is that the new exception type can be caught separately from other Throwable types, as in the LookupException example in Example 7-2 on page 109. We could simply define LookupException as in Example 7-5.

Example 7-5 Subclassing the Exception **Class**

```
public class LookupException extends Exception {
}
```

This would allow us to catch and specifically process a LookupException, without regard to other possible exceptions.

Errors

There is another high-level class in the Java runtime system that extends the Throwable class—the Error class. The runtime system uses the Error class for catastrophic failures that a program is not expected to be able to recover from.

A catch block such as the following is designed to catch all exceptions:

```
catch (Exception e) {
}
```

This catch block will not catch errors from the Error class, which is the desired behavior. If a program actually needs to trap *errors*, the following catch block will do:

```
catch (Error e) {
}
```

Declaring Exceptions

In Java, the exceptions a method can throw are considered part of its public interface. Users of a method need to know the exceptions it might throw so they can be prepared to handle them. Java requires that a method definition include a list of the exceptions the method throws. Example 7-6 shows the syntax for declaring these exceptions.

Example 7-6 Declaring Exceptions

```
public class Example {
❶   public static void exceptionExample() throws ExampleException,
    LookupException {
      .
      .
      .
    }
}
```

In line ❶, the exceptionExample() declaration includes the throws keyword, which is followed by a list of the exceptions this method might throw. In this case, that includes ExampleException and LookupException.

Defining the exceptions a method throws in the method declaration has one significant implication on the code you write. If you write a method that calls another method that can throw an exception, you must make sure the calling method does at least one of two things:

- Declares itself capable of throwing the same exception as the called method
- Includes a try/catch block to make sure the exception does not pass through to its caller

For example, the following code does both. It declares that `callExample` can throw an `ExampleException`, and it explicitly catches `LookupException`:

```
public class CallerExample {
   public static void callExample() throws ExampleException {
   try {
     Example.exceptionExample();
   } catch (LookupException e) {

     .

     .

     .

   }
}
```

Runtime Exceptions

There are a handful of common exceptions that can occur anywhere in a program. These include exceptions such as:

- `OutOfMemoryException`

- `NullPointerException`

- `ArrayIndexOutOfBoundsException`

These are referred to as *runtime exceptions*. Any exception that is a subclass of `RuntimeException` can be thrown from anywhere. Although you *can* declare them in a method declaration (and you should if you are explicitly throwing them) you do not have to explicitly declare the runtime exceptions. Doing so would introduce an unnecessary overhead in writing your programs.

It is legal to subclass `RuntimeException` and create your own exceptions that do not need to be declared. However, it's probably *not* a good idea since users of a method need to know the exceptions it might throw.

Remote Exceptions

The Java Remote Method Invocation (RMI) mechanism, described in *Exception Handling* on page 105, enables the development of distributed applications. As you might expect, there are a handful of exceptional conditions particular to the execution of remote objects in distributed applications. Remote methods throw `RemoteException`, which is the superclass of all remote method exceptions. Any method calling a remote method must be written to handle `RemoteException`.

Summary

The beauty of the Java exception handling model is that it allows you to treat errors and other exceptional conditions as distinct from the normal flow of control in a program. Unlike C, in which you are forced to return errors by using return values or passing parameters, Java provides a *catch and throw* model of exception handling similar to the one used in C++ . When an error occurs, an exception is *thrown*. Exceptions climb the chain of calls until they are *caught* or until the program exits.

The fundamental language support for the catch and throw model of exception handling is the `try/catch` block. If an exception causes a method to exit before the method's cleanup code has had a chance to execute, you can use the `finally` statement to release resources. You use the `throw` keyword to send an exception up the call chain.

To define your own exceptions, you can simply subclass the `Exception` class. A method must declare any exceptions it can throw.

CHAPTER
8

- Java I/O Classes

- Standard Streams for I/O

- Printing Text Output and Reading Text Input

- File I/O

- Data I/O

Input/Output

Introduction

Input and output in Java follow the C and C++ model in which I/O support is provided by a library, not by the language itself. In Java, of course, the I/O library is a class library—the `java.io` package—which we'll explore in this chapter.

Like C++, Java provides typesafe I/O. There is no equivalent to the C `printf()` function, which can crash if the wrong type is handed to it at runtime. In fact, there is no way to pass a wrong type to an output function in Java. This is consistent with Java's primary emphasis on code safety.

Java I/O Classes and Wrappers

The Java I/O classes are designed in a layered fashion. At the bottom level, there are basic `InputStream` and `OutputStream` classes. Added facilities such as buffering, connecting to files, printing data types other than bytes, and so on are provided by what we'll call *wrapper* classes. For example, say a program created an instance of an `InputStream` called istream, and we wanted to buffer the input. To do that, we could use a `BufferedInputStream` wrapper, as in Example 8-1.

Example 8-1 Using I/O Wrappers

```
BufferedInputStream bstream = new BufferedInputStream(istream);
```

This statement creates a new `BufferedInputStream` that forwards all the normal `InputStream` operations to `istream`. By wrapping the `InputStream` object in a `BufferedInputStream`, the program can now also buffer the input. Using different types of wrappers allows a program to access arbitrarily different and useful behavior from an `InputStream` or `OutputStream` object.

It's common for Java programs that perform I/O to check the types of the streams they are passed. In this way, programs can determine if they support the operations required and, if not, wrap them appropriately. For instance, Example 8-2 shows an excerpt from the calculator program described on page 327. This code checks to see if the input is of type `DataInputStream`.

Example 8-2 Checking Types of I/O Streams Passed

```
   public Calculator(InputStream in, OutputStream out) {

      DataInputStream dataIn;
      PrintStream      printOut;

❶    if (!(in instanceof DataInputStream)) {
        dataIn = new DataInputStream(in);

❷    } else {
        dataIn = (DataInputStream)in;
      }
        .
        .
        .
   }
```

In this example, the program checks to see if it already has a `DataInputStream` in line ❶. If it doesn't, the program wraps a `DataInputStream` around the `InputStream` in. If it does have a `DataInputStream`, the program casts the `InputStream` in as in line ❷.

Type casting and the `instanceof` operator are discussed in detail in *Runtime Typing and Class Loading*.

Standard Streams for a Java Program

When a Java program runs, there are three streams available by default:

- System.in

- System.out

- System.err

All three streams are stored in `static` variables of the `System` class. (The `System` class is in the `java.lang` package.

Table 8-1 summarizes the standard streams and their use.

Table 8-1 Standard Streams

Standard Stream	Stream Type	Use to...
System.in	InputStream	Read from user input.
System.out	PrintStream	Write user output.
System.err	PrintStream	Write user error output.

Printing Text Output in Java

The normal way of displaying output in Java is to use the `print()` and `println()` methods of the `PrintStream` class. `PrintStream.print()` sends its argument to the stream *without* a newline. `PrintStream.println()` sends its argument followed by a newline. For instance, look at the following example:

```
System.out.print("print and ");
System.out.println("println example");
```

The output from this example would look like this:

```
print and println example
```

A `PrintStream` object may not flush an output buffer until a newline is sent—unless the `PrintStream` is created with the `autoflush` option set to true. The `autoflush` option is an argument in one of the `PrintStream` constructors. In practical terms, this means that if a program needs to display a prompt, it may need to do an explicit call to `PrintStream.flush()` to make sure the prompt is displayed. For instance, look at Example 8-3.

Example 8-3 Displaying a Prompt

```
   // p is a PrintStream
   p.print("Please enter an integer: ");
❶ p.flush();
```

The prompt is not displayed until after the `p.flush()` in line ❶ is executed.

The standard `PrintStream` objects, `System.out` and `System.err`, are both created with `autoflush` set to true, so you do not need to explicitly call `flush()` when printing to them.

Java overloads the + operator for `String` objects, which makes printing much easier. Instead of being forced to construct long sequences of calls to `print()` and `println()`, a `String` argument may be constructed using +. In the following example, there are a series of `print()` and `println()` statements:

```
System.out.print("Ian is ");
System.out.print(10);
System.out.print(" and Drew is ");
System.out.print(8);
System.out.print(" and Li-Mae is ");
System.out.print(5);
System.out.println(" years old.");
```

Java provides the + operator to combine these statements into one statement, like this:

```
System.out.println("Ian is " + 10 + " and Drew is " + 8 + " and Li-
Mae is " + 5 + " years old. ");
```

Each argument to the + operator is converted to type `String` and then the string is converted. For primitive data types, this conversion occurs automatically. For instances of classes, the `toString()` method is called to do the conversion.

There's a default toString() method in the Object class that is called if there's no toString() method for that particular class. You can override the toString() method to define how you want your classes to be printed, as in the next example:

```
public class Person {
   public Person(String newName) {
     name = newName;
   }

   public String getName() {
     return name;
   }

❶  public String toString() {
     return "[" + getName() + "]";
   }

   private String name;
}

❷ Person kelly = new Person("Kelly");
  System.out.println(kelly);
```

In this example, line ❶ overrides the Object toString() method by defining how a Person is printed. Line ❷ prints [Kelly], using the new toString() method.

Reading Text Input in Java

There are three common ways of reading text input in Java:

- Reading some number of characters at a time

- Reading a line at a time

- Reading a token at a time

Let's look at each of these in more detail.

Reading Characters

Java supports reading some number of characters directly in the InputStream class. InputStream has read() methods for reading a single character and for reading an array of bytes. The following example shows how to read a single character:

```
// istream is an InputStream
int ch;

while ((ch = istream.read()) != -1) {
    <... do something with ch ... >
}
```

In this example, -1 in line ❶ indicates the end of the stream.

Reading an Array of Bytes

Example 8-4 shows how to read an array of bytes. The program is used in the following way:

```
java CopyFile file1 files2
```

Specifically, this program copies a file using InputStream.read(byte[]).

Example 8-4 Reading and Writing an Array of Bytes

```java
// CopyFile.java
import java.io.*;

public class CopyFile {
  public static void main(String[] args) {
    byte[] bytes = new byte[128];

    // Print usage line if no <src> or <dest> file are specified.
    if (args.length < 2) {
      System.err.println("Usage: java CopyFile <src> <dest>");
      return;
    }

    try {
      InputStream istream = new FileInputStream(args[0]);
      OutputStream ostream = new FileOutputStream(args[1]);
      int count;

      while ((count = istream.read(bytes)) != -1) {
          ostream.write(bytes, 0, count);
      }

      istream.close();
      ostream.close();
    } catch (final IOException e) {
      System.err.println(e);
      return;
    }
  }
}
```

❶
❷

❸
❹

❺

In this example:

❶ Opens the file named in args[0] and connects a FileInputStream object to it. (Remember that args[0] is the first argument and not the name of the program, as in argv[0] in a C main() declaration.)

❷ Opens the file named in args[1] and connects a FileOutputStream object to it.

❸ Reads the bytes in the input file.

❹ Writes the bytes to the output file. The 0 argument is the offset into the byte buffer, and count is the number of bytes to write.

❺ Closes both the input and output files.

Output of the CopyFile Program

The output of the CopyFile program is a duplicate file copied to the destination location. To use the CopyFile program, invoke the java interpreter from the command line and provide a source file and a destination file as arguments, as in the next example:

```
java CopyFile file newfile
```

Reading Text a Line at a Time

To read text a line at a time, you can use the readLine() method in the DataInputStream class. Example 8-5 shows an alternative to the previous program for copying a file; however, this program uses readLine(). The program is used in the same way as the previous program:

```
java CopyTextFile file1 files2
```

Example 8-5 Reading and Writing Text a Line at a Time

```java
// CopyTextFile.java
import java.io.*;

public class CopyTextFile {
   public static void main(final String[] args) {
     if (args.length < 2) {
        System.err.println("Usage: java CopyTextFile<src> <dest>");
        return;
     }

     try {
        final BufferedReader reader = new BufferedReader(
            new FileReader(args[0]));
        final PrintWriter writer   =
            new PrintWriter(new FileWriter(args[1]));

        String line;

        while ((line = reader.readLine()) != null) {
            writer.println(line);
        }

        reader.close();
        writer.close();

     } catch (final IOException e) {
        System.err.println(e);
        return;
     }
   }
}
```

In this example:

❶ Wraps a `BufferedReader` object around a `FileReader`. This will allow use of the `BufferedReader` `readline()` method, which reads a line of text and returns it as a string.

❷ Wraps a `PrintWriter` object around a `FileWriter`. This will allow use of the `PrintWriter.println()` method.

❸ Reads the input file a line at a time using the `readline()` method.

❹ Prints a line at a time to the output file using the `println()` method.

Output of the CopyTextFile Program

The output of the CopyTextFile program is a duplicate file copied to the destination location. To use the CopyTextFile program, invoke the java interpreter from the command line and provide a source file and a destination file as arguments, as in the next example:

```
java CopyTextFile textfile newtext
```

Reading a Token at a Time

To read text a token at a time, you can use the StreamTokenizer class. The syntax of tokens may be specified, and then the tokenizer can be used to read each token. For example, Example 8-6 shows how to read numbers and strings separated by the ; (semi-colon) character.

The program is used in the following way:

```
java TokenizerText file
```

The important distinction between this and the previous programs is that it wraps a StreamTokenizer object around a FileInputStream in order to deal with tokens.

Example 8-6 Reading and Writing a Token at a Time

```java
// TokenizerText.java
import java.io.*;

public class TokenizerText {
    public static void main(final String[] args) {
        if (args.length < 1) {
            System.err.println("Usage: java TokenizerTest <src>");
            return;
        }
        try {
            final StreamTokenizer stok = new StreamTokenizer(
                new FileReader(args[0]));
            stok.wordChars(0, ' ');

            // Declare ; to be the only separator char.
            stok.whitespaceChars(';', ';');
            int token;

            // token is filled with a code indicating what type of item
            // was just read.
            while ((token = stok.nextToken()) != stok.TT_EOF) {
                switch (token) {
                case stok.TT_NUMBER:

                    // If a number is read, the value is placed in the
                    // double variable nval.
                    System.out.println("Number: " + stok.nval);
                    break;
                case stok.TT_WORD:
                    // If a word is read, the value is placed in the
                    // String variable sval.
                    System.out.println("Word: " + stok.sval);
                    break;
                default:
                    break;
                }
            }
        } catch (final IOException e) {
            System.err.println(e);
            return;
        }
    }
}
```

❶

❷

In line ❶, the program creates a `StreamTokenizer` object that returns successive tokens on each call to `nextToken()` in line ❷. The `switch` following line ❷ is similar to a C `switch`.

Output of the TokenizerText Program

Assume we were to run the `TokenizerText` program on a file with the following data:

```
the truth; 96.8;is
out; there;
this is a; 42.5;test of
the;emergency broadcast
system
```

The output of the `TokenizerText` program is the source file, with all text separated by a semi-colon parsed according to whether it is a word or a number. Invoking the `TokenizerText` program on this file would produce the following output:

```
Word: the truth
Number: 96.8
Word: is
out
Word: there
Word: this is a
Number: 42.5
Word: test of
the
Word: emergency broadcast
system
```

File Input and Output in Java

The previous examples show simple stream-oriented file I/O in Java. Since the file classes `FileInputStream` and `FileOutputStream` are subclasses of `InputStream` and `OutputStream` respectively, they only support stream operations. However, there are often occasions when you need to be able to append to a file or treat a file as an array of bytes, which are not supported by the `InputStream` and `OutputStream` operations. The `RandomAccessFile` class provides this capability. (Note that a `RandomAccessFile` is not a stream. A `RandomAccessFile` has a file pointer associated with it that can be moved to any position within the file.)

You can open a `RandomAccessFile` in read (r) or read/write (rw) mode, and you can then change the file pointer position by using `seek()`.

Example 8-7 shows a program that appends its first file argument at the end of its second file argument.

Example 8-7 Appending Text to a File

```java
// AppendTextFile.java
import java.io.*;

public class AppendTextFile {
  public static void main(String[] args) {
    if (args.length < 2) {
      System.err.println(
          "Usage: java AppendTextFile <src> <dest>");
      return;
    }

    try {
      RandomAccessFile ifile = new RandomAccessFile(args[0],
          "r");
      RandomAccessFile ofile = new RandomAccessFile(args[1],
          "rw");

      ofile.seek(ofile.length());
      String line;

      while ((line = ifile.readLine()) != null) {
        ofile.writeBytes(line);
        ofile.writeByte('\n');
      }
      ifile.close();
      ofile.close();
    }
    catch (IOException e) {
      System.err.println(e);
      return;
    }
  }
}
```

❶
❷
❸
❹

In this example:

❶ Opens the first file argument in read (r) mode.

❷ Opens the second file argument in read/write (rw) mode.

❸ The file pointer starts at 0. Then, `ofile.seek(ofile.length())` repositions the pointer to the end of file so the program can append to it. The `RandomAccessFile` class supports the `length()` method to determine the end of the file.

❹ The `writeBytes()` method writes a string to the file, but it doesn't add a newline. (There is no `writelnBytes()`.)

Output of the AppendTextFile Program

The `AppendTextFile` program appends one file to the end of another file. Assume we were to use the `AppendTextFile` program to append a file with the following data:

```
plaid.
```

to another file with the following data:

```
Can't do
```

Running the `AppendTextFile` program on these two files would modify the second file so that it would read:

```
Can't do
plaid.
```

Data Input and Output in Java

Java also supports non-text data files. The `DataOutputStream` class has methods for writing primitive Java data types to a stream in a portable way. You can use the `DataInputStream` class to read them back in.

Java does not provide direct support for reading and printing user-defined objects. You must implement your own methods to do this.

Summary

Java stream I/O is based on the InputStream and OutputStream classes. Java also supports different types of I/O *wrappers*, which allow programs to apply a variety of useful operations to input and output streams.

Java provides three standard streams: System.in, System.out, System.err.

To display text output, Java provides the print() and println() methods of the PrintStream class. A user can specify how classes should be printed by defining toString() methods for them. Text input can be read using the read() methods of the InputStream class or the more specialized methods provided by the input wrapper classes.

To read and write binary data, Java provides the DataInputStream and DataOutputStream classes.

A file can be treated as an array of bytes using the RandomAccessFile class, which has a file pointer. Appending to a file is accomplished using the RandomAccessFile class by first seeking to the end of the file and then writing data to it.

CHAPTER
9

- Variable Assignments
- Casting One Type into Another
- Dynamic Class Loading

Runtime Typing and Class Loading

Introduction

Much of the power and flexibility of the Java language is the result of its dynamic runtime facilities. Java supports both runtime typing and runtime extensibility, which we'll discuss in this chapter.

Variable Types and Their Values

Most commonly used languages such as C assign types to variables. A value stored in a variable can be assumed to be of the variable's type. In Java, however, a variable may contain a value of a different type—provided that the type is a subtype of the variable's declared type. Specifically, an object stored in a variable of type T may actually be an instance of a subclass of type T. For instance, consider the variable assignments in the next example:

```
T data;

// Assume the SubclassOfT extends T.
SubclassOfT dataItem = new SubClassOfT();

// Object in the data variable is not directly of type T.
data = dataItem;
```

The `data` variable is not of type `T`, but the assignment is valid because `dataItem` contains a value that is an instance of a subclass of `T`.

Similarly, if a variable is declared to be an interface type, that variable can hold any object whose class implements that interface:

```
// I is an Interface type.
I data;

// The ImplementsI class implements the I interface.
ImplementsI dataItem = new ImplementsI();

// Object in data implements the I interface.
data = dataItem;
```

In this case, `data` can hold the object stored in `dataItem` because the `ImplementsI` class implements the `I` interface.

The instanceof Operator

The instanceof operator provides the means to perform type comparisons. Sometimes it is necessary to determine if a reference to an object declared to be of a particular class—say class A—actually refers to an object that is an instance of a specific subclass of class A. In our discussion of *Input/Output*, we looked at this example:

```
public Calculator(InputStream in, OutputStream out) {

    DataInputStream dataIn;
    PrintStream printOut;

    // Check if we already have a DataInputStream
    if (!(in instanceof DataInputStream)) {

        // If not, wrap one around the InputStream.
        dataIn = new DataInputStream(in);

    } else {

        // If so, cast the InputStream down.
        dataIn = (DataInputStream)in;
    }
    .
    .
    .
}
```

The type of the variable in is InputStream, but we need to know if its value is actually a DataInputStream. Java makes it easy to answer this kind of question because it keeps type information with each object. An object knows its type and the interfaces it implements. (C++ did not originally have this feature—called *manifest types*—but so many people ended up creating their own runtime-type information that the designers added it to the language.)

The instanceof operator syntax looks like this:

<object> instanceof *<type>*

In this syntax, *<type>* can be either a class name or an interface name.

Note that the `instanceof` operator does not tell you what the most specific type for an object is. In fact, the only way to determine the specific type of an object is to use `getClass()` to obtain the object's class and then use `getName()` to return the name of the class as a string. In practice, obtaining the specific type is not generally necessary, since what you usually want to know is if a particular operation will be valid on an object; asking if the object is an instance of a type that supports the operation is all that's required.

Type Casting

Now that we can find out that an object is an instance of a particular type, what can we do with that information? The `in` variable is still of type `InputStream`. (The variable that contains the instance is still of the superclass type—that is, `in` is of type `InputStream`, but it holds a value of type `DataInputStream`, which is a subclass of `InputStream`.) If we want to apply an operation from the subclass, we can't do it through the existing variable. For instance, look at the next example:

```
in.readLine();    // Error
```

We know the value held by `in` is of type `DataInputStream`. However, `in` itself is still of type `InputStream`. We can't use the `readLine()` method on `in` because `readLine()` is defined for variables of type `DataInputStream`, not `InputStream`.

Java deals with this problem by allowing one type to be *cast* into another type. This is just like type casting in C or C++, with one notable difference. In Java, you can only cast something into a type if it is an instance of that type or a subclass of that type. If the compiler cannot prove that the cast is valid, a runtime type check is inserted. If the type check fails at the time of the cast, a `ClassCastException` is thrown.

For example, consider this line from our calculator program:

```
dataIn = (DataInputStream)in;
```

If in did not actually contain a value of type DataInputStream, an exception would be thrown. However, since in does contain a DataInputStream value, the cast succeeds and we can call DataInputStream operations (such as the readLine() method) on dataIn:

```
dataIn.readLine(); // Correct
```

Alternatively, we could perform the cast directly in the call to readLine():

```
((DataInputStream)in).readLine(); // Also correct.
```

A cast from a class to a superclass is implicit and requires no runtime check. For example, we could call the Calculator() constructor (described in *Putting the Language Pieces Together* on page 319) with a DataInputStream without casting it to an InputStream:

```
Calculator c = new Calculator(new DataInputStream(System.in),
    System.out);
```

Class Loading at Runtime

The runtime type information provided by Java enables one of Java's most powerful features—*dynamic class loading*. At runtime, the Java system loads classes mentioned in a Java program. These classes are loaded from directories listed in a user's CLASSPATH environment variable. This class loading facility is also available to Java programmers.

It's never necessary to explicitly load a class that is mentioned directly in your program. All mentioned classes are loaded automatically. However, dynamic class loading is useful when a program defines an interface or abstract class that may have many different implementations.

The Applet class provides an excellent example. Every applet that is executed in a web browser extends the Applet class. The class browser mentions the Applet class by name, so it is automatically loaded. However, the class browser doesn't know about the subclasses of Applet until they are loaded. It doesn't really need to know, either, since the class browser only interacts with Applet subclasses through the methods defined by Applet. An applet browser could use the

following code to load a new applet. (Note that this code would only work if the applet was available through the user's CLASSPATH. If the applet was being loaded from an http server, a class loader would be required. See *Class Loaders* on page 138 for information on how class loaders work.)

```
Class  c    = Class.forName("Ticker");
Applet app  = (Applet)c.newInstance();
```

In this case, app could be manipulated using the public methods of the Applet class. (We use this technique in two of our examples: the Cellular applet described in *Putting the Language Pieces Together* on page 319, and the Lisp interpreter on the CD included with this book.)

Instances of the class Class contain information about particular classes that have been loaded into the Java runtime system. Each instance of Class contains information about one particular Java class. This information includes:

- The name of the class
- The name of its superclass
- The interfaces it implements
- Whether or not the class is itself an interface

All of this information is contained in the object representing the class.

static methods for a class cannot be called through the object that represents it. The only way of getting to the methods defined for a class is by creating an instance and casting the instance to the class. Each instance of Class defines a newInstance() method that calls the zero-argument constructor of the class it represents and returns the new instance. Class.newInstance() returns a value of type Object so it must be cast down to a particular class before the methods of the class can be accessed.

Class Loaders

To load classes from sources other than the paths specified in the CLASSPATH environment variable, you must define and use a class loader. A class loader has two jobs:

- Obtaining the bytes that represent a class from a source (for example, an http server)
- Installing the bytes as a class definition

Each new class loader extends the ClassLoader class. It defines the
loadClass() method, which reads in class data and calls the defineClass()
method to create an instance of the class Class. A loadClass() method for an
instance of ClassLoader generally goes through the following steps:

```
Look up the class in a local cache (usually an instance of
java.util.Hashtable).

IF not found
  Use findSystemClass to try to locate the class using the
  standard java classpath mechanism.

  IF not found
      Try to load the bytes for the class from the source
      associated with this class loader.
      IF successful
          Call defineClass to create an instance of Class
          Install the new class in the local cache.

      ELSE
          Throw a ClassNotFoundException.

IF the class needs to be resolved (i.e. if it mentions other
classes that are not yet known)

  Call resolveClass() to resolve it.

Return the class.
```

Class loaders commonly differ in how they retrieve the bytes for a class and what,
if any, security policies they enforce on classes they load.

Summary

This chapter highlights how Java variables can hold values of types other than the variable's type. Java provides extensive support for dynamic type operations and dynamic extension of the system. The type of an object may be determined at runtime and all casting between types is checked. An invalid cast will cause an exception to be thrown. New classes may be added to the system during operation and can include code written in C. Class loaders are used to install classes obtained from external sources.

CHAPTER 10

- The Java Native Interface

- Native Methods and Virtual Machine Dependencies

Linking With Native Code

Introduction

Java supports extending the system at runtime with code written in C. In the JDK 1.0, this was accomplished by using the native method interface. The JDK has since been extended with a more standard programming interface for writing native methods and embedding the Java virtual machine into native applications. This interface is called the Java Native Interface (JNI). We'll describe both in this chapter.[1] Be aware, however, that the old native method interface will not be supported on Java Hotspot, which is a high performance Java Virtual Machine. If you currently use the old native method interface, you should consider migrating to the JNI.

Why Link With Native Code

To link with native code, you can declare methods to be `native` and implement them in C. There are three reasons you might want to do this:

- To provide access to machine-specific code
- To use an existing library

---

1. For comprehensive coverage of the native method interface and the Java Native Interface, refer to Gordon, Rob (1998). *Essential Java, Java Native Interface*. Prentice Hall.

- To obtain higher performance

The first two reasons are obvious. Since Java is explicitly a cross-platform language, it's clear that you must leave Java in order to perform platform-specific operations. Also, if you have a large existing library in C, it's pointless to rewrite it in Java. The third reason deserves more discussion.

Clearly, code written in C is faster than the equivalent Java code. If someone absolutely needs performance today, writing critical code in C makes a lot of sense (with a few caveats, which we'll elaborate on shortly). In the future, however, there is no reason for Java code to be significantly slower than C. It's really a matter of compiler and runtime technology. People have been able to tame languages like CommonLisp, so we can expect that a fast Java will eventually be available.

Say you want the speed today. The typical place a C programmer would write inline assembler is in a tight inner loop. However, this is a bad idea when extending Java with C. The overhead of calling a native method is significant. In an inner loop you incur that overhead repeatedly. The only time it makes sense to write native code for speed is if you are going to write a sizeable routine completely in C (for example, an image processing routine). Many of the methods in Sun's JDK are native for speed, but these methods are built into the virtual machine and don't incur the same overhead as user-level native methods.

This overhead is a result of Java's cross-platform nature. Cross-platform doesn't just mean running the same on different hardware. It also means running the same on different Java virtual machines. Early attempts at native code interfaces (including the original JDK native method interface) were specific to each Java Virtual Machine. They exposed internal details of object representations and memory management. Even later releases of the same virtual machine were likely to break existing native code. The creators of Java (with help from Netscape) have since designed the new Java Native Interface, which hides the virtual machine from the programmer. This ensures compatibility and allows virtual machine implementors the flexibility required to produce high-performance virtual machines.

We'll look at an example that uses the JNI as well as examples that uses the older JDK native method interface for comparison. As we dig deeply into the internals of Java objects using the older interface, you'll see how its use locks one into a specific virtual machine and constrains the virtual machine implementation.

Note that the procedure to link Java programs with C code is fairly complex, so if you don't intend to link Java programs with C code, you may want to skip this chapter and go directly to *Multiple Threads of Execution* on page 171.

Using JNI

Java allows you to declare methods in classes to be `native` (see *Native Methods* on page 35). You can then implement the bodies of these methods in C. This can be useful when you require machine-specific code or you need extremely high performance.

Using methods written in C is a four-step process. You need to:

1. Declare native methods.

2. Generate a `.h` file that your C files can include. This `.h` file defines the interface between your native routines and the virtual machine.

3. Build a dynamic library containing C routines that match the names and signatures in the generated `.h` file.

4. Link the library into the Java runtime system.

Before showing some examples of native methods, let's go through each of these steps in detail for a Linux environment.

Declaring Native Methods

A native method is declared exactly like an abstract method, except the keyword `abstract` is replaced with the keyword `native`. Instead of defining the method body, you must terminate the declaration with a semi-colon. Following is the native declaration we'll use in our example:

```
public static native String getenv(String name);
```

That's all there is to declaring a native method.

Generating Include Files

In order to implement a native method, you must generate linkage information. To do this, you use the _javah_ program. Here is the `javah` command used for our first example:

```
javah -jni nat.Env
```

This generates the file `nat_Env.h`:

```
/* DO NOT EDIT THIS FILE - it is machine generated */
#include <jni.h>
/* Header for class nat_Env */

#ifndef _Included_nat_Env
#define _Included_nat_Env
```

```
#ifdef __cplusplus
extern "C" {
#endif
/*
 * Class:     nat_Env
 * Method:    getenv
 * Signature: (Ljava/lang/String;)Ljava/lang/String;
 */
JNIEXPORT jstring JNICALL Java_nat_Env_getenv
  (JNIEnv *, jclass, jstring);

/*
 * Class:     nat_Env
 * Method:    setenv
 * Signature: (Ljava/lang/String;Ljava/lang/String;)V
 */
JNIEXPORT void JNICALL Java_nat_Env_setenv
  (JNIEnv *, jclass, jstring, jstring);

#ifdef __cplusplus
}
#endif
#endif
```

The file contains method signatures for the native methods declared in the nat.Env class. Note that the method names are mangled. The mangled names are the names we'll use in our C definitions.

Building a Library

Let's assume that you've written the C functions for your native methods. (We'll see how this works in our examples). Now you need to create a dynamic library. On a Linux system, you would use the following compiler command:

```
gcc -I<path to jdk>/<jdkversion>/include -I<path to
jdk>/<jdkversion>/include/genunix -shared -o
env.so nat_env.c
```

This command line assumes that the include file nat_Env.h is in the current directory. The -shared flag says to create a dynamic library.

Now we have a library we can link into a Java system.

Linking a Library into Java

To link a dynamic library containing native methods into Java, you create a static initializer for a class. The static initializer uses either System.load(<*pathname*>) or System.loadLibrary(<*library name*>). If the

library is located within your dynamic library search path, you can use
`loadLibrary()`; otherwise you must specify a full path name. Here is the
`static` initializer we use in the example.

```
public class Env {
    static {
        System.load("<path to nat>/nat/env.so");
    }
    .
    .
    .
}
```

Let's start out with a simple example. We would like to access a program's
environment, but Java doesn't support this. We'll write native methods for
`getenv()` and `setenv()`. Here is the Java class:

Example 10-1 JNI Implementation for getenv() and setenv()

```
package nat;

// This class provides native implementations of getenv() and
// setenv() so that we can access a program's environment from Java.

public class Env {

  // The native methods that access the environment are contained in
  // the "env.so" library.

  static {
    System.load("/home/jrj/nat/env.so");
  }

  // Fetch a value from the environment.

  public static native String getenv(String name);

  // Set a value in the environment.

  public static native void setenv(String name, String value);
}
```

That was certainly simple enough. The C file, on the other hand, will need some
commentary:

```
#include <stdlib.h>
#include "nat_Env.h"

/* Fetch an environment variable */
```

```
jstring
Java_nat_Env_getenv(
    JNIEnv *env,   /* JNI environment */
    jclass klass, /* class reference for static method */
    jstring name  /* Java name string to pass to getenv() */
)
{
    /* Obtain a C string from the Java string. */

    const char *namestr = (*env)->GetStringUTFChars(env, name, 0);

    /* Retrieve the environment value as a C string. */

    const char *str = getenv(namestr);

    /* Create a Java string from the C string. */

    jstring result = (*env)->NewStringUTF(env, str);

    /* Tell the JNI we're finished with the Java string argument */

    (*env)->ReleaseStringUTFChars(env, name, namestr);

    /* Return the environment value. */

    return result;
}

/* Set an environment variable */
void
Java_nat_Env_setenv(
    JNIEnv *env,   /* JNI environment */
    jclass klass, /* class reference for static method */
    jstring name, /* Java name string */
    jstring value /* Java value string */
)
{
    /* Obtain C strings from the Java strings. */

    const char *namestr  = (*env)->GetStringUTFChars(env, name, 0);
    const char *valuestr = (*env)->GetStringUTFChars(env, value, 0);

    /* Set a value in the environment. "1" means overwrite. */

    setenv(namestr, valuestr, 1);

    /* Tell the JNI we're finished with the Java string arguments */
```

```
    (*env)->ReleaseStringUTFChars(env, name, namestr);
    (*env)->ReleaseStringUTFChars(env, value, valuestr);
}
```

The first argument to a native method is a JNIEnv *environment* reference.

```
    JNIEnv *env,   /* JNI environment */
```

All JNI functions are accessed via this argument through a double indirection. The environment reference is a pointer to a thread-local pointer to a function table:

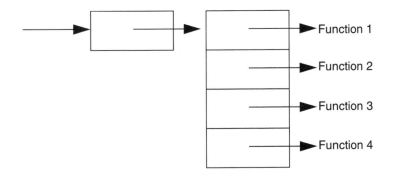

This structure allows the virtual machine great flexibility, but it requires a fairly ugly syntax for referencing functions:

```
(*env)->GetStringUTFChars(env, name, 0);
```

In this syntax:

env — Is a pointer to a pointer to a function table.

*env— Is a pointer to a function table.

(*env)->GetStringUTFChars — Refers to a particular slot in the table.

The second argument to a *non-static* native method is the object on which the method is being invoked. The second argument to a *static* method is the class containing the method. In our example, we're defining static methods, so the second arguments are class references like this:

```
    jclass klass, /* class reference for static method */
```

All the rest of the arguments are the actual Java method arguments.

The actual method implementations for getenv() and setenv() are pretty simple. The only noteworthy points are the calls to GetStringUTFChars() and ReleaseStringUTFChars(). GetStringUTFChars() extracts the bytes of a

Java string in UTF-8 format and returns a pointer to the `char` array.
`ReleaseStringUTFChars()` tells the virtual machine that we are finished with
the extracted string.

JNI, Native Methods, and the Java Virtual Machine

Let's delve into a more elaborate example that involves looking up the values of
variables in a Lisp interpreter. We'll look at four versions of the native method.
The first example will use the JNI and the other three use the original native
method interface. These last three examples will progressively expose the
internals of the Java Virtual Machine data structures. After looking at the
differences between these approaches, you'll see why portable code must use an
interface like the JNI.

The native method we'll implement is used to look up the value of a variable in a Lisp interpreter. Assume that the bottleneck in the interpreter is the speed of variable lookup, and we hope to improve performance by using a native method. The `environment` structure containing our variables consists of a set of linked `frames`, each containing a vector of names and a vector of values, like this:

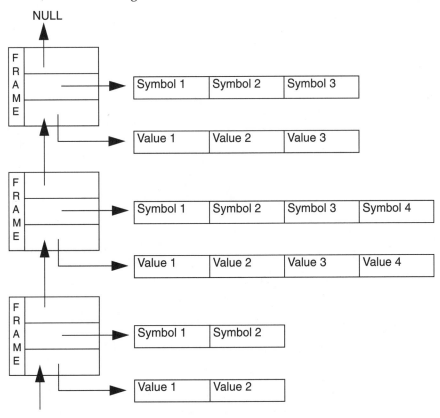

When a variable name is looked up, a search is done on the name vector of the current frame. If a match is found, the corresponding element of the value vector is returned. If no match is found, the search is repeated with the frame contained in the `parent` link of the current frame. If there is no match at the end of the frame, we check an immediate value slot in the symbol itself. If it is empty, we throw an `UnboundSymbol` exception. The method signature for our lookup method is:

```
public native Object fetch(LispSymbol sym) throws
    UnboundSymbolException;
```

Using the JNI for a Symbol Lookup

Our header file `lisp_LispEnv.h` generated from the `lisp.LispEnv` class looks like:

```
/* DO NOT EDIT THIS FILE - it is machine generated */
#include <jni.h>
/* Header for class lisp_LispEnv */

#ifndef _Included_lisp_LispEnv
#define _Included_lisp_LispEnv
#ifdef __cplusplus
extern "C" {
#endif
/*
 * Class:     lisp_LispEnv
 * Method:    fetch
 * Signature: (Llisp/LispSymbol;)Ljava/lang/Object;
 */
JNIEXPORT jobject JNICALL Java_lisp_LispEnv_fetch
  (JNIEnv *, jobject, jobject);
#ifdef __cplusplus
}
#endif
#endif
```

Here is the native lookup code:

Example 10-2 Symbol Lookup Code

```
#include "lisp_LispEnv.h"

/* This example shows how to manipulate Java fields, methods,
   exceptions, and arrays. This is _not_ a good example of when to
   use native methods. In fact, this native method is substantially
   slower than the corresponding Java method because of the overhead
   of fetching fields and methods through an opaque interface. Most of
   the method consists of field and method lookups with very little
   opportunity for optimization. However, the example will
   show where potentially big performance gains can be achieved via
   native methods when we look at how to manipulate primitive arrays.
*/

jobject
Java_lisp_LispEnv_fetch(
    JNIEnv *env,        /* JNI environment */
    jobject lisp_env,   /* Lisp environment object */
    jobject lisp_sym    /* Symbol to look up */
)
```

```
{
    int var_index;         /* Index into the local environment vector */
    jobject vec;           /* A Java Vector */
    jclass vec_class;      /* Class for java.util.Vector */
    jfieldID val_field;    /* Field in lisp.LispEnv containing symbol
                              values */
    jmethodID element_at;  /* Method id for java.util.Vector's
                              elementAt() */
    /* Get the lisp.LispEnv class. We'll need it. */

    jclass lenv_class = (*env)->GetObjectClass(env, lisp_env);

    /* If we were passed a null object, throw an exception. Note that
       calling ThrowNew() does not cause control to leave the
       function. The third argument to ThrowNew() is a message string
       for the exception. */

    if (lisp_env == 0 || lisp_sym == 0) {
        jclass npe = (*env)->FindClass(env,
                    "java/lang/NullPointerException");
        (*env)->ThrowNew(env, npe, "");
        return 0;
    }

    /* Call index_of to see if the symbol is located in the current
       frame */

    var_index = index_of(env, lisp_sym, lisp_env);

    /* If the symbol was not found, repeat the lookup in the parent
       frame; if there is no parent frame, check the symbol's local
       value. If there is no local value, throw an
       UnboundSymbolException. */

    if (var_index == -1) {
        /* In order to reference class fields we need to obtain
           "fieldIDs". The fieldIDs are used to access the actual
           object fields. */
        jfieldID parent= (*env)->GetFieldID(env, lenv_class,
                            "parent", "Llisp/LispEnv;");

    /* Fetch the parent environment frame */

    jobject parent_env = (*env)->GetObjectField(env, lisp_env,
                        parent);

        if (parent_env == 0) {
```

```
/* If there is no parent, we're at the top of the environment
   chain so we look in the symbol's local value slot */

/* Fetch the LispSymbol class so we can get the "localVal"
   fieldID */

jclass lsym_class  = (*env)->GetObjectClass(env, lisp_sym);

/* Fetch the localVal fieldID */

jfieldID local_val = (*env)->GetFieldID(env, lsym_class,
                     "localVal","Ljava/lang/Object;");

/* Fetch the localVal field */

jobject result = (*env)->GetObjectField(env, lisp_sym,
                 local_val);

/* If the field is null, raise an exception. */

if (result == 0) {

    /* An alternative approach to throwing an exception is to
       explicitly construct the exception and then use "Throw".
       This is needed when you must create an instance of an
       exception using a constructor with an extended argument
       list */

    jclass use = (*env)->FindClass(env,
        "lisp/UnboundSymbolException");
    jmethodID meth =
        (*env)->GetMethodID(env, use, "<init>", "()V");
    jobject ex = (*env)->NewObject(env, use, meth);
    (*env)->Throw(env, ex);

    return 0;

} else {
    /* We found a value, return it. */

    return result;
}
}
/* If we didn't find the symbol locally, climb the environment
   chain and look in the parent frame */

return Java_lisp_LispEnv_fetch(env, parent_env, lisp_sym);
```

```
    }

    /* We found the symbol in the current frame, extract the
       corresponding value and return it. */

    /* Fetch the fieldID for the "localVals" vector */

    val_field = (*env)->GetFieldID(env, lenv_class, "localVals",
        "Ljava/util/Vector;");

    /* Fetch the "localVals" vector */

    vec= (*env)->GetObjectField(env, lisp_env, val_field);

    /* Obtain the vector's class so we can get its methodIDs */

    vec_class = (*env)->GetObjectClass(env, vec);

    /* Fetch the "elementAt" method from the vector's class so we
       can extract one of the vector's elements. */

    element_at = (*env)->GetMethodID(env, vec_class, "elementAt",
        "(I)Ljava/lang/Object;");

    /* Extract the value at "var_index" within the vector. */

    return (*env)->CallObjectMethod(env, vec, element_at, var_index);
}

int
index_of(
    JNIEnv *env,      /* JNI environment */
    jobject sym,      /* Symbol to look up */
    jobject lisp_env  /* Lisp environment */
)
{
    int i; /* counter for search loop */
    int result = -1; /* index of element */

    /* Look up all the classes we'll need */

    jclass str_class = (*env)->FindClass(env, "java/lang/String");
    jclass vec_class = (*env)->FindClass(env, "java/util/Vector");
    jclass sym_class = (*env)->FindClass(env, "lisp/LispSymbol");
    jclass env_class = (*env)->FindClass(env, "lisp/LispEnv");

    /* Look up all the fields we'll need */
    /* The symbol vector for the environment frame. */
```

```
jfieldID vars_field =
    (*env)->GetFieldID(
      env,
      env_class,
      "localVars",
      "Ljava/util/Vector;");

/* The number of entries in a vector. */

jfieldID count_field =
    (*env)->GetFieldID(
      env,
      vec_class,
      "elementCount",
      "I");

/* The array of elements in a vector. */

jfieldID data_array_field =
    (*env)->GetFieldID(
      env,
      vec_class,
      "elementData",
      "[Ljava/lang/Object;");

/* The string name of a symbol. */

jfieldID sym_name_field =
    (*env)->GetFieldID(
      env,
      sym_class,
      "name",
      "Ljava/lang/String;");

/* The length of a string. */

jfieldID str_count_field =
    (*env)->GetFieldID(
      env,
      str_class,
      "count",
      "I");

/* The character array for a string. */

jfieldID str_value_field =
    (*env)->GetFieldID(
```

```
        env,
        str_class,
        "value",
        "[C");
```

```
/* Offset into the character array at which the string starts. */
```

```
jfieldID str_offset_field =
    (*env)->GetFieldID(
        env,
        str_class,
        "offset",
        "I");
```

```
/* Fetch the variable name vector out of the environment frame */
```

```
jobject vector = (*env)->GetObjectField(env, lisp_env,
                vars_field);
```

```
/* Fetch the elementData array out of the variable name vector */
```

```
jarray data_array = (*env)->GetObjectField(env, vector,
                data_array_field);
```

```
/* Fetch the number of elements in the variable name vector */
```

```
int count = (*env)->GetIntField(env, vector, count_field);
```

```
/* Fetch the Java string representing the name of the symbol */
```

```
jstring name = (*env)->GetObjectField(env, sym, sym_name_field);
```

```
/* Fetch the Java character array from the name string */
```

```
jarray val = (*env)->GetObjectField(env, name, str_value_field);
```

```
/* Extract a primitive array of java characters that can be
   accessed directly. The JNI allows a programmer to extract
   an actual primitive array that may be treated as a straight 'C'
   array. The primitive array may or may not be a copy depending
   on the JNI implementation. The third argument, if non-zero,
   should be the address of a jboolean. The jboolean pointed to
   by the argument will be set to JNI_TRUE if the primitive array
   is a copy and JNI_FALSE if it is not. We must release the
   primitive array later when we are finished with it. */
```

```
jchar* primarray = (*env)->GetCharArrayElements(env, val, 0);
```

158

```
/* Fetch the length of the name string */

jint strcount = (*env)->GetIntField(env, name, str_count_field);

/* Fetch the offset into the character array of the name string */

jint stroff = (*env)->GetIntField(env, name, str_offset_field);

for (i = 0; i < count; i++) {
    /* Fetch a symbol out of the variable name vector */

    jobject entry = (*env)->GetObjectArrayElement(env,
                    data_array, i);

    /* Fetch the name string out of the symbol */

    jstring ename = (*env)->GetObjectField(env, entry,
                    sym_name_field);

    /* Fetch the length of the local symbol name */

    jint estrcount = (*env)->GetIntField(env, ename,
                    str_count_field);

    jarray eval;  /* The character array for the local java name
                    string */

    jchar* localprim; /* The primitive array corresponding to the
                    java array */

    jint estroff; /* The offset of the local string */
    int j;        /* Counter for stepping through the main symbol's
                    name. */
    int k;        /* Counter for stepping through the local name */

    /* If the two strings are different lengths, they can't be
       equal. */

    if (estrcount != strcount) {
       continue;
    }

    /* Fetch the local java character array */

    eval = (*env)->GetObjectField(env, ename, str_value_field);

    /* Fetch the corresponding primitive character array. Here
       is where big gains can be made if a native method
```

manipulates large quantities of primitive data. An image
processing application could grab hold of a simple byte
array and process its elements directly without method
overhead or array bounds checking. This can lead to
significant performance wins. In this case, if
the average symbol name length were large, we might get a
speed improvement here but since they're not, we lose due
to the overhead of fetching the fields and methods. */

```
localprim = (*env)->GetCharArrayElements(env, eval, 0);

/* Fetch the offset for the local string */

estroff = (*env)->GetIntField(env, ename, str_offset_field);

/* Initialize counters. */

j = stroff;
k = estroff;

/* Step through each primitive array comparing characters. */

while (estrcount-- > 0) {
    if (primarray[j++] != localprim[k++]) {
        break;
    }
}

/* Free up the local primitive array. The fourth argument
defines what to do if the primitive array is a copy.
The options are:
0            - Copy the contents back into the original array and
               free the buffer.
JNI_COMMIT   - Copy back contents but don't free the buffer.
JNI_ABORT    - Free the buffer without copying back changes.
Since we've only been reading data and made no changes,
we'll use JNI_ABORT. */

(*env)->ReleaseCharArrayElements(env, eval, localprim,
                                 JNI_ABORT);

/* If all characters matched, we've found the right one. */

if (estrcount == -1) {
    result = i;
    break;
}
}
```

```
/* Free up the main primitive array */
(*env)->ReleaseCharArrayElements(env, val, primarray,
                        JNI_ABORT);

/* Return the found index or -1 if the symbol was not found. */

return result;
}
```

Using the Native Method Interface for Symbol Lookup

Now, in the next three examples use the native method interface specific to the Java Virtual Machine.

We'll go through the steps used to create a native method again for the last set of examples since they differ slightly from the process when you're using the JNI. Using the native method interface, you need to:

1. Declare native methods.

2. Generate .h files that your C files can include. These .h files describe the structure of the Java classes used by the native methods.

3. Generate the *stub* functions that the Java runtime will use to call your native methods.

4. Build a dynamic library with the generated stub functions and your C functions.

5. Link the library into the Java runtime system.

As you can see, the process is similar to using the JNI, except that there is an extra step required — the generation of *stub* functions. Let's go through these, as before.

Generating Include Files

In order to implement a native method, you must have C declarations for all the Java classes you use. You have to use the `javah` program to generate these C declarations. This `javah` program will generate the relevant information for a set of classes specified on the command line. For instance, following is the `javah` command used for our examples:

```
javah -o lisp/java_structs.h java.lang.String java.util.Vector
lisp.LispSymbol lisp.LispEnv
```

The native method in our examples uses two classes from the lisp package, along with the String and Vector classes. javah will create the structure declarations needed and place them in lisp/java_structs.h. Here is what the lisp/java_structs.h file looks like after being created by javah:

```
/* DO NOT EDIT THIS FILE - it is machine generated */
#include <native.h>
/* Header for class java_lang_String */

#ifndef _Included_java_lang_String
#define _Included_java_lang_String

typedef struct Classjava_lang_String {
  struct HArrayOfChar *value;
  long offset;
  long count;
/* Inaccessible static: InternSet */
} Classjava_lang_String;
HandleTo(java_lang_String);

#endif
/* Header for class java_util_Vector */

#ifndef _Included_java_util_Vector
#define _Included_java_util_Vector
struct Hjava_lang_Object;

typedef struct Classjava_util_Vector {
  struct HArrayOfObject *elementData;
  long elementCount;
  long capacityIncrement;
} Classjava_util_Vector;
HandleTo(java_util_Vector);

#endif
/* Header for class lisp_LispSymbol */

#ifndef _Included_lisp_LispSymbol
#define _Included_lisp_LispSymbol
struct Hjava_lang_String;

typedef struct Classlisp_LispSymbol {
  struct Hjava_lang_Object *localVal;
  struct Hjava_lang_String *name;
}Classlisp_LispSymbol;
HandleTo(lisp_LispSymbol);
```

```
#endif
/* Header for class lisp_LispEnv */

#ifndef _Included_lisp_LispEnv
#define _Included_lisp_LispEnv
struct Hlisp_LispEnv;
struct Hjava_util_Vector;

typedef struct Classlisp_LispEnv {
  struct Hlisp_LispEnv *parent;
  struct Hjava_util_Vector *localVars;
  struct Hjava_util_Vector *localVals;
} Classlisp_LispEnv;
HandleTo(lisp_LispEnv);

struct Hlisp_LispSymbol;
extern struct Hjava_lang_Object *lisp_LispEnv_fetch(struct
Hlisp_LispEnv *,struct Hlisp_LispSymbol *);
#endif
```

In the file, there are declarations for all the classes we asked for and a declaration for a function at the end of the file. This is the function that must be defined to implement the native method. Note that in the class and function declarations, each period (.) in a class name is replaced by an underscore (_).

It's important to understand the structure of a Java object in memory before writing native methods using a virtual machine specific native interface. We will be directly accessing the C slots of Java objects. This is completely non-portable but necessary when writing code that plugs in at this level. Each object referenced in a Java program consists of a structure with two fields:

- A pointer to its data slots

- A pointer to its methods

Collectively, these are called the *handle* on the object. Figure 10-1 shows how the LispEnv class we use in our example would look in memory.

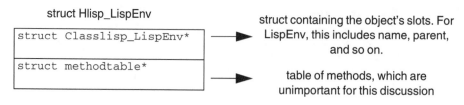

Figure 10-1 Structure of a Java Object in Memory

To make manipulating the slots of a Java instance more convenient, the C
unhand(x) macro will return the particular structure with slots, given a pointer
to a handle. So the following would be valid:

```
struct Hlisp_LispEnv* henv = ....;
Classlisp_LispEnv*    env  = unhand(henv);
```

Then, the following would be a correct reference:

```
env->localVars
```

We'll explore the manipulation of these objects shortly in our examples.

Generating Stub Functions

Java needs to embed the functions we write for our native methods into the
runtime system. It does this via stub functions that are also generated by the
javah program. To create stubs, it is necessary to use javah with the -stubs
option, as in the following:

```
javah -stubs -o lisp/stubs.c lisp.LispEnv
```

This command would create a file named lisp/stubs.c, which looks like this:

```
/* DO NOT EDIT THIS FILE - it is machine generated */
#include <StubPreamble.h>

/* Stubs for class lisp_LispEnv */
/* SYMBOL: "lisp_LispEnv/fetch(Llisp/LispSymbol;)Ljava/lang/Objec
t;", Java_lisp_LispEnv_fetch_stub */
stack_item *Java_lisp_LispEnv_fetch_stub(stack_item *_P_,struct
execenv *_EE_)
{
  extern void* lisp_LispEnv_fetch(void *,void *);
  _P_[0].p = lisp_LispEnv_fetch(_P_[0].p,((_P_[1].p)));
  return _P_ + 1;
}
```

Now, let's look at the examples. The only thing that will change in these three examples is the `index_of()` function, which looks up a `LispSymbol` in a frame.

Using the Native Method Interface, Example 1

In the first example, we will compare variable names by using the Java dynamic invocation interface to call the `String.equals()` method:

```
#include "java_structs.h"

/* look up a variable in a frame. If found, return the index;
   otherwise, return -1
*/

int
index_of(
    ClassArrayOfObject*    vec,    /* Vector of names */
    long                   len,    /* Length of the name vector */
    Classlisp_LispSymbol*  sym     /* Lisp symbol to look up */
)
{
  long i;

  /* Fetch the actual array of object pointers from the
     java.util.Vector */

  struct Hjava_lang_Object** oarray = vec->body;

  /* step through the array of objects and call String.equals to
     compare the entries with the argument symbol */

  for (i = 0; i < len; i++) {

    /* use "unhand" to get to the actual symbol object */

    Classlisp_LispSymbol* other_sym =
      unhand((Hlisp_LispSymbol*)oarray[i]);
    /* Call execute_java_dynamic_method to invoke String.equals.
       Arguments are:
       1) execution context (0 means current context).
       2) object to call method on.
       3) method name.
       4) method signature
          Translation:

              (                - beginning of arguments
              L                - argument is an instance of a class
              java/lang/Object - the name of the argument's class
```

```
        ;               - end of class description
        )               - end of arguments
        Z               - returns a boolean.

    5) method argument   */

  int result = execute_java_dynamic_method(
     0,
     (Hjava_lang_Object*)sym->name,
     "equals",
     "(Ljava/lang/Object;)Z",
     (Hjava_lang_Object*)other_sym->name);

  /* If the boolean result is true, return the index */

  if (result) {
    return i;
  }
}

/* The name was not found in the current frame */
return -1;
}

/* The function that implements the native "fetch" method */

struct Hjava_lang_Object*
lisp_LispEnv_fetch(
  struct Hlisp_LispEnv*    env,
  struct Hlisp_LispSymbol* sym
)
{
  int                  var_index;
  Classlisp_LispEnv*   lenv;
  Classlisp_LispSymbol*lsym;

  /* If we were passed a null object, throw an exception. Note that
     calling SignalError does not cause control to leave the
     function. The third argument to SignalError is a char* which
     can be passed a message string. */

  if (env == 0 || sym == 0) {
    SignalError(0, "java/lang/NullPointerException", 0);
    return 0;
  }

  /* Extract the symbol and environment from the handles */
```

```
lenv = unhand((struct Hlisp_LispEnv*)env);
lsym = unhand((struct Hlisp_LispSymbol*)sym);

/* Call index_of to see if the symbol is located in the current
   frame */

var_index = index_of(
  unhand(unhand(lenv->localVars)->elementData),
  unhand(lenv->localVars)->elementCount,
  lsym);

/* If the symbol was not found, repeat the lookup in the parent
   frame; if there is no parent frame, check the symbol's
   localValue. If there is no local value, throw an
   UnboundSymbolException */

if (var_index == -1) {
  if (lenv->parent == 0) {
    if (lsym->localVal == 0) {
      SignalError(0, "lisp/UnboundSymbolException", 0);
      return 0;
    } else {
      return lsym->localVal;
    }
  }

  return lisp_LispEnv_fetch(lenv->parent, sym);
}

/* return the value from the frame */

return unhand(unhand(lenv->localVals)->elementData)-
  >body[var_index];}
```

Using the Native Method Interface, Example 2

For the next two examples, we'll only show index_of() since everything else is
the same. In this version, we extract C strings from Java strings and compare them
using the strcmp() function. makeCString returns a pointer to garbage
collected memory containing a C version of a Java string. To obtain a pointer to a
C string allocated with malloc(), you would use allocCString():

```
int
index_of(
  ClassArrayOfObject*   vec,
  long                  len,
  Classlisp_LispSymbol* sym
)
```

```
{
  long                    i;

  /* Extract a C string from the argument symbol */

  char*                   s       = makeCString(sym->name);
  struct Hjava_lang_Object**  oarray = vec->body;

  for (i = 0; i < len; i++) {

    /* Extract a C string from the current frame entry */

    Classlisp_LispSymbol* other_sym =
      unhand((Hlisp_LispSymbol*)oarray[i]);

    /* Compare them the old fashioned way */

    if (strcmp(s, makeCString(other_sym->name)) == 0) {
      return i;
    }
  }

  /* not found */

  return -1;
}
```

Using the Native Method Interface, Example 3

The final version compares Java strings directly, avoiding the overhead of a method call as well as the overhead of copying strings:

```
int
index_of(
  ClassArrayOfObject*      vec,
  long                     len,
  Classlisp_LispSymbol*    sym
)
{
  long                       i;
  struct Hjava_lang_Object** oarray = vec->body;

  for (i = 0; i < len; i++) {
    struct Classlisp_LispSymbol* other_sym =
      unhand((struct Hlisp_LispSymbol*)oarray[i]);

    /* Get the actual string structures from the handles */

    Classjava_lang_String* symstring  =
```

```
     unhand(sym->name);
 Classjava_lang_String* otherstring =
     unhand(other_sym->name);

 /* A Java String contains a count of characters --
    If the counts differ, they don't match */

 if (symstring->count == otherstring->count) {
     long count = symstring->count;
     long j;

     /* Extract the unicode arrays from the strings. Since
        Java Strings are immutable, the implementation shares
        them and a particular String object may start at
        some offset into a unicode array */

     unicode* symchars   = unhand(symstring->value)->body +
         symstring->offset;
     unicode* otherchars = unhand(otherstring->value)->body +
         otherstring->offset;

     /* Compare the unicode arrays */

     for (j = 0; j < count; j++) {
         if (symchars[j] != otherchars[j]) {
             break;
         }
     }

     if (j == count) {
         return i;
     }
   }
 }

 return -1;
}
```

Summary

The Java development environment provides tools to assist in linking to platform-specific code. Because of the need to interface with native libraries and obtain platform specific performance gains, the interface to native code has been formalized in the form of the Java Native Interface (JNI). The JNI provides a general way to interface to native code, independent of the Java Virtual Machine.

You can also link to C code using the old-style native method interface, but it is dependent on a particular virtual machine. The old native method interface will not be supported on Java's high performance virtual machine, called Hotspot.

There are some obvious reasons you might want to link to native code — to provide access to machine-specific code, to use an existing library, or to obtain higher performance. Of these, be judicious when extending Java code with C for performance. The overhead of calling a native method is significant. The only time it makes sense to write native code for speed is if you are going to write a sizeable routine completely in C.

CHAPTER 11

- Creating Multiple Threads with the Thread Class

- Locking Resources and How They Work

Multiple Threads of Execution

Introduction

Until recently, the only programmers who had to worry about concurrent execution were those writing operating systems and embedded control software. Most application programmers wrote programs that just ran from start to finish. Some exceptions include multiuser applications that allocate a process to each user and process control programs like the UNIX shell, the sole purpose of which is to create multiple processes. Though these count as applications, they have a strong systems programming flavor.

This has changed with the advent of graphical user interfaces (GUIs). Prior to the use of GUIs, when a program interacted with a user, it was usually because it needed an input before it could continue. There wasn't much point to having multiple threads of control. Now a program's user interface often has its own state that the user can manipulate while the program underneath is doing something else. This is probably the most common use of *threads*. (For a complete discussion of the use of threads, see *Threads Primer: a Guide to Multithreaded Programming*, Bill Lewis and Daniel Berg, Sun Microsystems Press.)

Java has exceptionally good support for programming with multiple threads of execution. Unlike most languages in which support for threads is only available at the library level, Java builds thread support directly into the language. This includes built-in support for creating threads and for locking resources necessary for proper execution of multiple threads.

Creating Threads

There are two ways to create threads in Java:

- Define a class that *extends* the `Thread` class

- Define a class that `implements` the `Runnable` interface

Extending the Thread Class

The first way to create a thread is to define a new subclass of `Thread`. This is a simple matter of using the `extends` keyword, as in Example 11-1.

Example 11-1 Creating Multiple Threads With the Thread Class

```
❶ public class ExampleThread extends Thread {
❷    public void run() {
      < ... call synchronized methods and do whatever the thread needs to do ... >
      }
   }
```

In this example, line ❶ defines a class that `extends` the `Thread` class. Line ❷ defines a `run()` method. Every class that extends the `Thread` class needs to have a `run()` method that specifies whatever tasks are required when this thread is executed.

Now, to start a new thread, you use the `start()` method, which is defined in the `Thread` class. Example 11-2 shows how this works.

Example 11-2 Starting a Thread

```
ExampleThread ethread = new ExampleThread();
ethread.start();
```

When the new class is instantiated and its `start()` method is called, a new thread of control is created. The new thread then calls the `run()` method, which in this case is defined in the `ExampleThread` class.

Implementing the Runnable Interface

The second way to create a thread is to define a class that *implements* the `Runnable` interface. Any class can represent a thread if it implements the `Runnable` interface and defines a `run()` method, as in Example 11-3.

Example 11-3 Implementing Threads With the `Runnable` Interface

```
❶ public class ExampleRunnable implements Runnable {
❷    public void run() {
      <... perform tasks ... >
      }
```

```
    }
    ExampleRunnable er = new ExampleRunnable();
❸ new Thread(er).start();
```

In this example:

❶ Defines a new class that implements the `Runnable` interface.

❷ Defines a `run()` method that performs whatever tasks are required when this thread is executed.

❸ Creates a new `Thread` instance with a `Runnable` object (in this case, `er`) as an argument. The `start()` method of the new instance is then called. This starts a new thread of control.

This method of creating threads of control is very useful if the class we want to run in a thread already `extends` some other class. We can't extend `Thread` if we're already extending another class. By using the `Runnable` interface, we can still create multiple threads even when we're already extending another class.

We'll discuss the methods and attributes of the `Thread` class in more detail in *Part 2—Writing Java Applets*. Applets rely heavily on the use of threads, as we'll show in several examples.

Resource Locking

The most complicated area of programming with threads arises when multiple threads must access a shared resource. The problems that arise can be surprisingly subtle. Consider the following example:

```
public class BrokenThreadExample {
  public int nextCounter() {
    return counter++;
  }

  private int counter = 0;
}
```

This example looks innocent enough. You might think we could use it to supply an increasing counter to multiple threads. Unfortunately, it's broken in more than name. The problem can be hard to see because many programmers tend to think of the built-in operations in a language like Java as atomic units. The line:

```
return counter++;
```

is actually a compound operation. The current value of the counter is read, it is incremented by one, and the value is written back. What happens if another thread writes its value back between the read and the write? Here's a scenario that illustrates the problem:

Thread 1 reads `counter` and finds the value 0.
Thread 2 reads `counter` and finds the value 0.
Thread 1 adds one and writes 1 into `counter`.
Thread 2 adds one and writes 1 into `counter`.

Now, the `counter` value is set to 1, even though both threads incremented it.

Using the synchronized Modifier

To avoid this problem, we *lock* a resource (like the `counter` in our example) while a thread is accessing it. In Java, locking resources is extremely simple. Each object in Java has a lock associated with it. A method that uses the `synchronized` modifier automatically acquires the lock on its instance before proceeding. If the instance's lock is already held by another thread, the method will block until it can obtain the lock. So all that is needed to fix our example is to add `synchronized` to the `nextCounter()` method, as illustrated in Example 11-4.

Example 11-4 Locking Resources With the synchronized Modifier

```java
public class FixedThreadExample {
  public synchronized int nextCounter() {
    return counter++;
  }

  private int counter = 0;
}
```

Now, before Thread 1 reads the counter, it acquires the lock on the shared `FixedThreadExample` instance. It reads `counter`, increments it, and writes it back. Any other threads waiting to access the shared `FixedThreadExample` wait their turn.

Class methods may also need to be synchronized. If this is necessary, you can also use the `synchronized` modifier with these `static` methods. Each class has its own lock on resources just as instances do.

Using synchronized Blocks

It is possible for a method to acquire the lock on an object other than its own. This is done using a `synchronized` block, as in Example 11-5.

Example 11-5 Using a `synchronized` **Block**

```
public class SynchronizedBlockExample {
  public int getCounter() {
    return counter;
  }

  public void setCounter(int newValue) {
    counter = newValue;
  }

  private int counter = 0;
}

SynchronizedBlockExample myCounter =
  new SynchronizedBlockExample();

❶ synchronized (myCounter) {
    int currentCounter = myCounter.getCounter();
    myCounter.setCounter(currentCounter + 1);
  }
```

In line ❶, we lock a specific instance of a `SynchronizedBlockExample` rather than the current object. Within the `synchronized` block, we use the `getCounter()` method to read the counter and the `setCounter()` method to write a new value while holding the lock on `myCounter`. In this way, no other thread can access `myCounter`.

Summary

Unlike many other languages, Java builds thread support directly into the language. There is built-in support for creating threads and for locking resources necessary for proper execution of multiple threads.

You can create multiple threads of control by using the `Thread` class, in one of two ways: define a class that *extends* the `Thread` class or define a class that *implements* the `Runnable` interface. The latter method is particularly useful when a class already extends another class, but you still want it to run multithreaded.

Java also provides a simple way to lock resources necessary for the proper execution of multiple threads. By using the `synchronized` modifier, a method automatically acquires the lock on its class or instance before proceeding. If the object's lock is already held by another thread, the method will block until it can obtain the lock.

CHAPTER 12

Inner Classes

In this chapter we discuss facilities that assist in structuring Java applications. These facilities are collectively known as *inner classes*, though there are three distinct kinds:

- Member Classes
- Local Classes
- Anonymous Classes

These each serve their own purpose, so we'll discuss them separately. Together, however, they give a Java programmer fine-grained control over the organization of Java programs.

Member Classes

One of the foremost benefits of object-oriented programming is the ability to restrict information access to those parts of a program that need it. (See "Encapsulation" on page 522..) Member classes improve on Java's basic encapsulation facilities.

Consider the InorderEnumeration class from our tree sorting example or the NumNode class from our Bignum example in the Chapter , *Memory and Constructors* chapter. Both of these classes are declared as "friendly" classes. This designation specifies the most limited access available for top-level classes. They are each visible to all members of their respective packages. This is not ideal, however, because neither one makes sense outside the context in which it's used. Java provides a way to limit the scope of such a class even further. A class may be made a member of another class. `InorderEnumeration` may be a member of `Tree` and `NumNode` may be a member of `Bignum`. As members of other classes, they can be declared private and their uses limited to code within the surrounding classes.

For example, Example 12-1 shows how it would look to incorporate `InorderEnumeration` as a member class of the `Tree` class.

Example 12-1 Member Class

```
public class Tree {
  // ... other code ...

  // Return an "inorder" enumeration of the tree.
  // This can be used to sort the values in the tree.

  public Enumeration inorder() {
    return new InorderEnumeration();
    }

  private class InorderEnumeration implements Enumeration {

    // To initialize the enumeration, we descend the leftmost
    // branches of the tree pushing each node on a stack. The top
    // node on the stack is always the next to be enumerated.

    private InorderEnumeration() {
      pushLeftNodes(topNode);
    }

    // When the stack is empty, there are no more entries.

    public boolean hasMoreElements() {
      return stack.empty() == false;
    }

    // After an entry is returned, we need to enumerate the right
    // subtree, so we set up the stack for the right subtree just
    // as we did at the top.

    public Object nextElement() {
      TreeNode current = (TreeNode)stack.pop();
      pushLeftNodes(current.getRight());
      return current.getVal();
```

```
      }
      // Descend the leftmost branches of the tree pushing each node.

      private void pushLeftNodes(TreeNode node) {
        while (node != null) {
        stack.push(node);
        node = node.getLeft();
        }
    }
    Stack stack = new Stack();
    }
    private TreeNode topNode;
}
```

There are two things to note about this example. First, the
InorderEnumeration class is now *private*. It can only be used by its *enclosing
class*. This behavior is exactly what we want since it makes no sense to use the
class in any other way. An additional benefit is that there is no chance for a name
conflict with other classes in the package. Second, we no longer need to pass the
tree node as an argument to the constructor for InorderEnumeration. As a
member of the Tree class, InorderEnumeration has access to the other private
members of the class. In this case, the simplification is relatively small, but it can
be much greater.

Local Classes

Example 12-1 shows how member classes can take advantage of context and use
members from their enclosing classes directly. But what about more specific
contexts? That's where *local classes* come in. They are defined within individual
blocks, not just within classes. To understand how this works, imagine we're
writing a text editor like Emacs. The action performed by each keystroke can be
configured but starts out by simply inserting the character. So, we have an inner
class called CharacterAction that has access to all the editor's members:

```
package editor;

public class TextEditor {

    // ... public methods ...

    abstract class CharacterAction {
      abstract void performAction();
    }

    // ... data structures (buffers, etc.) ...

}
```

Let's assume that for the default behavior for each ASCII keystroke, we want to insert the corresponding character. To accomplish this, we'll refer to an array of `CharacterAction` objects indexed by character. Using member classes, we can hide the definitions of our `CharacterAction` class and its subclasses within `TextEditor`, as in Example 12-2.

Example 12-2 Text Editor Using Member Classes

```java
public class TextEditor {
    // public methods

    public void insert(int character) {
        // ...
    }

    // ... public methods ...

    // Class representing an action taken when a key is pressed.

    abstract private class CharacterAction {
        abstract public void performAction();
    }

    private void initializeActions() {
        // Set the default action for each character.
        for (int i = 0; i < MAX_CHARS; i++) {
            charActions[i] = new DefaultCharacterAction(i);
        }
    }

    final private class DefaultCharacterAction extends
            CharacterAction {
        public DefaultCharacterAction(int character) {
            this.character = character
        }

        public void performAction() {
            // Call the insert() method from TextEditor.
            insert(character);
        }

        private int character;
    }

    private CharacterAction[] charActions = new
            CharacterAction[MAX_CHARS];
```

```
    private static final int MAX_CHARS = 127; // ASCII

    //     ... data structures (buffers, etc.) ...
}
```

Note that we have a complete definition of `DefaultCharacterAction` when all we really care about is its `performAction()` method. With *local* classes, we can rewrite it, as in Example 12-3.

Example 12-3 Text Editor Using Local Classes

```
public class TextEditor2 {
    // public methods

    public void insert(int character) {
        // ...
    }

    // ... public methods ...

    // Class representing an action taken when a key is pressed.

    abstract private class CharacterAction {
        abstract public void performAction();
    }

    private void initializeActions() {
        // Set the default action for each character.

        for (int i = 0; i < MAX_CHARS; i++) {
            final int character = i;

            class DefaultCharacterAction extends CharacterAction {
                public void performAction() {
                    // Call the insert() method from TextEditor.

                    insert(character);
                }
            }

            charActions[i] = new DefaultCharacterAction();
        }
    }

    private CharacterAction[] charActions = new
        CharacterAction[MAX_CHARS];
    private static final int MAX_CHARS = 127; // ASCII
    // ... data structures (buffers, etc.) ...
}
```

Now we have eliminated the need for a constructor for
DefaultCharacterAction. The DefaultCharacterAction class is now
local to the *block* defined by the loop.

There are two points to highlight in this example:

First, the performAction() method references a variable from *outside the class*.
You might think that the value of character would be unavailable once the loop
was finished, but the Java compiler arranges for it to be stored in the heap so that
it will persist. A local variable used in this way must be declared final.

Second, we're actually creating 127 different classes! Each time through the loop,
we create a new class in a different context. This isn't as inefficient as it sounds
because the Java compiler translates this code into basically the same thing as
Example 12-1, which does not use local classes. Conceptually, however, there is a
class for each character.

Now, the DefaultCharacterAction class really consists of nothing more than
a performAction() method.

Anonymous Classes

In our local class example, the DefaultCharacterAction class consists of only
a performAction() method. You might question whether or not we really need
a named class definition for this. As it turns out, we don't. A local class that is
instantiated in only one place can be made *anonymous*. We'll see later that
anonymous classes support a powerful style of programming commonly used in
languages like CommonLisp and Smalltalk. In the meantime, Example 12-4
shows how the TextEditor example looks when we use anonymous classes.

Example 12-4 Anonymous Classes

```
public class TextEditor3 {
  // ... public methods ...

  public void insert(int character) {

  // ...
  }

  // ... public methods ...

  // Class representing an action taken when a key is pressed.
  abstract private class CharacterAction {
    abstract private void performAction();
  }
```

```
  private void initializeActions() {
    // Set the default action for each character.

    for (int i = 0; i < MAX_CHARS; i++) {
      final int character = i;

      charActions[i] = new CharacterAction() {
          private void performAction() {
              // Call the insert() method from TextEditor.

              insert(character);
          }
      }
    }
  }

  private CharacterAction[] charActions = new
    CharacterAction[MAX_CHARS];
  private static final int MAX_CHARS = 127; // ASCII

  //    ... data structures (buffers, etc.) ...
}
```

Now we've completely eliminated the DefaultCharacterAction class. The code simply says, "Create an instance of the subclass of CharacterAction() with the defined performAction() method." The same notation could be used to say, "Create an instance of the class that implements an interface with the defined performAction() method."

Anonymous classes may not have constructors. This makes sense if you think about it. Constructors match the name of a class and anonymous classes don't have names, so there would be nothing to call a constructor for an anonymous class. Any arguments passed in a new expression are forwarded to the constructor for the superclass of the anonymous class.

Scoping and Inner Classes

There are several issues involving scope and member and local classes. Let's look at those now.

Scoping and Member Classes

A member class is considered part of the implementations of its containing classes. This means that the containing classes (and other members of the containing classes) may access the private parts of the member class. In fact, it's possible to make everything in a member class private. Consider the following example:

```java
public class QuestionableScoping {
    private static class X {
        private void foo() {
            System.out.println("foo!");
        }
    }

    private static class Y extends X {
        private Y() {
        }

    private void bar() {
        foo();
    }

    private void foo() {
        System.out.println("not foo!");
    }
  }

  public static void main(String[] args) {
    new Y().bar();
  }
}
```

Running `main()` prints the following:

```
not foo!
```

Notice that we are able to override `foo()` even though it is `private`. We are able to invoke `bar()` even though it is `private`. Finally, we are able to create an instance of `Y()`, even though it's constructor is `private`.

This works, but it doesn't really express a programmer's intent. Some methods and fields are external and some are internal. If they're all declared `private`, there is no distinction. Here is an improved version of the previous example that behaves identically:

```java
public class VirtuousScoping {
    private static class X {
```

```
❶      protected void foo() {
           System.out.println("foo!");
       }
   }

   private static class Y extends X {
❷      public Y() {
       }

❸  public void bar() {
       foo();
   }

   protected void foo() {
       System.out.println("not foo!");
   }
   }

   public static void main(String[] args) {
     new Y().bar();
   }
}
```

In this rewrite, we do the following:

❶ We indicate that `foo()` is intended to be overridden in subclasses by making it `protected`.

❷ We indicate that Y() is intended to be instantiated by making its constructor `public`.

❸ We indicate that `bar()` is intended to be invoked from outside `Y()` by making it `public`.

With these changes, this example is completely equivalent to the previous one! Why is this?

Since classes `VirtuousScoping.X` and `VirtuousScoping.Y` are `private`, no external class can hold a reference to either one. The `public` and `protected` methods are externally unavailable since there is no way to obtain an instance on which to invoke them. The only way external code can ever refer to an instance of a `private` class is under the following conditions:

- The `private` class extends a `public` class or implements a `public` interface *and* ...

- One of the `private` class's surrounding classes contains a method that returns instances of the private class.

For example, consider this class definition:

```java
import java.util.*;

public class PublicAccessToPrivate {
  private static class X extends Hashtable {
    public int size() {
      return super.size() * 2;
    }
  }

  public static X getXHash() {
    return new X();
  }
}
```

Now, assume the following class to exercise `PublicAccessToPrivate`:

```java
import java.util.*;

public class PublicAccessToPrivateUser {
  public static void main(String[] args) {
    Hashtable xhash = PublicAccessToPrivate.getXHash();

    xhash.put("Ian", Boolean.TRUE);
    xhash.put("Drew", Boolean.TRUE);
    xhash.put("Li-Mae", Boolean.TRUE);
    xhash.put("Amber", Boolean.TRUE);
    xhash.put("Justin", Boolean.TRUE);

    System.out.println("xhash.size() = " + xhash.size());
  }
}
```

Here, running the `main()` method will print:

```
xhash.size() = 10
```

Even though `X` is a `private` class, `PublicAccessToPrivateUser` can invoke the `getXHash()` method and manipulate an instance of `X` because it only does so through the `public Hashtable` interface.

So, a sensible convention to adopt for member classes is to give their members the same scopes as you would if they were top-level classes and control access through the scopes of the member classes themselves.

Static Member Classes

Something we haven't yet touched upon is the distinction between static and non-static member classes. Instances of static member classes, like static methods, are not associated with particular instances of surrounding classes. Let's look at

Example 12-5 Scoping With Static/Non-Static Member Classes

```
import java.util.Hashtable;

// This class represents arbitrary objects with fields that can be
// defined at runtime. A call to setField() will associate a field
// name with a value and a call to getField() will retrieve the value.
// This differs from a Hashtable in the following ways:
//
// 1) An attempt to fetch a field that has never been set will throw
//    an UnknownFieldException rather than returning null.
// 2) A field may contain null.

public class GenericObject {
  // Return a specified field if it exists.

  public Object getField(String fieldName) throws
      UnknownFieldException {
    return whash.get(fieldName);
  }

  // Associate a field name with a value.

  public void setField(String fieldName, Object value) {
                whash.put(fieldName, value);
  }

  // The exception generated when a field is fetched before it is
  // set.

  public static class UnknownFieldException extends Exception {
    public UnknownFieldException(GenericObject obj, Object key) {
      super("Unknown field: " + obj + "." + key);
    }
  }

  // A Hashtable that allows nulls by wrapping them in Wrapper
  // objects.

  private class WrappedHash {
    // Return the value associated with a key if one exists;
    // otherwise throw an UnknownFieldException.
```

```
    public Object get(Object key) throws UnknownFieldException {
      Wrapper w = (Wrapper)hash.get(key);

      if (w == null) {
          throw new UnknownFieldException(GenericObject.this, key);
      }

      // Return the value contained in the wrapper.

      return w.value();
    }

    // Associate a key with a wrapped value.

    public void put(Object key, Object value) {
      hash.put(key, new Wrapper(value));
    }

    private Hashtable hash = new Hashtable();
  }

  // A container to store in a Hashtable so that null values can be
  // distinguished from missing values.

  private static class Wrapper {
    public Wrapper(Object toBeWrapped) {
      this.wrapped = toBeWrapped;
    }

    public Object value() {
      return wrapped;
    }

    private Object wrapped;
  }
  private WrappedHash whash = new WrappedHash();
}
```

The GenericObject class might be used like this:

```
public class GenericObjectUser {
  public static void main(String[] args) {
    try {
      GenericObject go = new GenericObject();

      go.setField("name", "Jess");
      go.setField("type", "cat");
```

```
        System.out.println("Name: " + go.getField("name") + "\nType:
                        " + go.getField("type"));

        go.getField("age");

    } catch (GenericObject.UnknownFieldException ufe) {
        System.err.println(ufe.getMessage());
    }
  }
}
```

In this example, the GenericObject.UnknownFieldException class is intended to be visible to external code so that it may be explicitly caught. It is *static* because an instance of the class is not associated with any particular instance of GenericObject.

The Wrapper class is static as well, for the same reason. The WrappedHash class is private because it is strictly part of the implementation of GenericObject. It is non-static because each instance of WrappedHash is part of a specific instance of GenericObject.

Note the unusual construct of GenericObject.this in the WrappedHash class. Instances of non-static member classes are contained in other instances. We can refer to the containing instances by using the this keyword. This is useful when we want to return a reference to a surrounding instance, as in our example. It is also useful if a surrounding class defines a method or field with the same name as one in the member class:

```
public class NonStatic {
  private class X {
    public void a() {
      System.out.println("a");
    }

    private class Y {
      public void b() {
❶       X.this.a();
      }

      public void a() {
        System.out.println("not a");
      }
    }
  }
```

```
public static void main(String[] args) {
  new NonStatic().new X().new Y().b();
}
}
```

Note the call to X.this.a() in line ❶. This will invoke the a() method from X rather than Y.Also, in line ❷, notice the incredibly convoluted object construction:

```
new NonStatic().new X().new Y().b();
```

Read this line as:

Invoke the b() method of a new instance of NonStatic.X.Y contained in a new instance of NonStatic.X contained in a new instance of NonStatic.

Whew!

Since each instance of a non-static member class is part of an instance of a surrounding class, the surrounding class instance must be specified when creating an instance of the member class. Within an *instance* context of a surrounding class, the associated surrounding instance is implicit. This is why we could simply use the construct "new WrappedHash()" in the GenericObject example. In our NonStatic example, however, we're creating instances from within a static method. There are no implicit surrounding instances, so we must explicitly name the surrounding instances using an extended form of the new syntax:

```
<instance>.new <member class>(<args>)
```

Scoping of Local Classes

Local classes can be treated in the exactly the same way as member classes with the simplifying constraints that they are always private to the block containing them and they are effectively always static.

Anonymous Classes and Higher-Order Programming

A style of programming known as *higher-order* programming has been developed in the functional language community. This style involves treating functions as values that can be passed as arguments and returned as values. Something similar is done in C when function pointers are used. Since Java doesn't have functions, the equivalent style must be based on classes and methods. Anonymous classes can be used to simulate functions as values. Let's look at Example 12-6, which involves iterating through a Vector and checking for a match. If a match is found, we return the matched object.

Example 12-6 Anonymous Class to Simulate Functions as Values

```
package higherorder;

import java.util.*;

// Search for an object within a Vector that satisfies the
// SearchMethod argument.

public class VectorSearcher {
  public Object search(SearchMethod searchMeth, Vector vector) {

    for (int i = 0; i < vector.size(); i++) {
      Object obj = vector.elementAt(i);

      if (searchMeth.match(obj)) {
          return obj;
      }
    }

    return null;
  }
}
```

This class abstracts the mechanics of searching a `Vector`. To search for an object with a particular property, we only need to define the appropriate `SearchMethod()` method. Here is the definition of `SearchMethod()`:

```
package higherorder;

// Represents a predicate used for searching. match() should
// return true if its argument satisfies the predicate.

public interface SearchMethod {
  public boolean match(Object o);
}
```

And here is an example of the use of these classes:

```
VectorSearcher searcher = new VectorSearcher();

boolean result = searcher.search(
    new SearchMethod() {
        public boolean match(Object o) {
            return ((NamedObject)o).getName().equals("BAR");
        }
    }
    vec);
```

This code would search a vector for an element named `"BAR"` and return the element if found. Although this may not seem much simpler than the equivalent loop, it would be much simpler than the equivalent code for searching a tree or some other more complicated data structure. The structure traversal code need only be written once and can be used repeatedly by changing the search method.

An Extended Example: Anonymous Classes, Closures, and Continuation Passing Style

Use of anonymous classes enables powerful new programming techniques. A particularly useful one is known as continuation passing style. Although this topic goes a beyond the narrow scope of exploring the Java language, we want to bring it to your attention to highlight the full utility of anonymous classes. If your focus is on basic understanding of the language, you may want to skip this section and return to it after you're more comfortable writing Java code. Otherwise, follow along as we examine a more involved example that demonstrates the power of anonymous classes.

In the example, we'll implement a pattern-matching program for trees. Such a program could be used in any context where structured data needs to be manipulated according to a predefined set of patterns. Some common uses would be in code generation for a compiler, macro expansion, or, as we'll use it later, for source-to-source transformation of programs (actually, parse-tree to parse-tree transformation).

Though pattern matching may seem esoteric, it will directly demonstrate some of the most powerful uses of anonymous classes. We'll see how anonymous classes allow us to take advantage of context to clarify code, and we'll explore a program-structuring technique known as continuation passing style.

First, though, we need to discuss the concept of a *closure*.

A closure consists of a function or some other operation and the environment in effect when the function or operation is defined. For example, in the programming language Scheme, we could define a function that adds 2 to its argument in the following way:

```
(define (addtwo n)
   (+ n 2))
then: (addtwo 5) => 7
```

Using closures, however, we could define a generic solution to constructing *adders*:

```
(define (addn n)
```

```
(lambda (x)    ; "lambda" in Scheme means "make function"
  (+ x n)))
```

and use it in this way:

```
(define addtwo (addn 2))
```

The value returned from addn is called a closure because it consists of a function (constructed by the lambda expression) and the environment in which it was defined (in the case of the definition of addtwo, an environment where n = 2). Other calls to addn() would return functions defined in different environments, where n might have different values.

Now, on to our example.

The trees we'll be matching come from the Lisp interpreter provided with our book (discussed in the Chapter, *Reflection* chapter). A tree consists of pairs that make up the structure of the tree and data, which can be arbitrary objects. Each pair has two slots, like this:

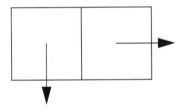

These slots are generally referred to as the *car* and the *cdr* [1].

Such pairs can be composed to create arbitrary tree structures; for example, a list of three items, "a," "b," and "c" (usually written as (a b c)):

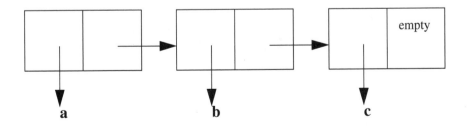

---

1. These names are derived from the machine instructions, Contents of Address Register and Contents of Decrement Register, provided by the first machines used to implement Lisp.

Consider this tree:

It would usually be expressed as (a (b c d) e). We could represent it graphically, as in the following illustration:

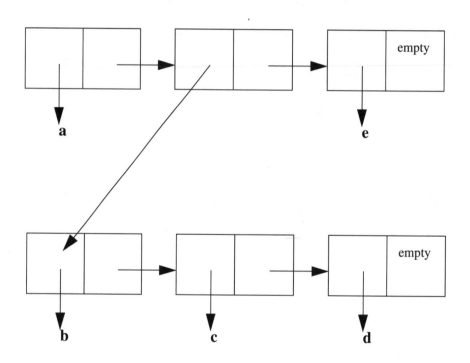

We use the following conventions to describe patterns:

?x — a particular item

$x — a particular sequence

So, our sample tree, `(a (b c d) e)`, would be matched by any of the following patterns:

```
($x)              ; after matching: $x = (a (b c d) e)
(?x ($y) ?z)      ; after matching: ?x = a, $y = (b c d), ?z = e
($x (?y c $z) ?q) ; after matching: ?x = a, ?y = b, $z = (d), ?q = e
(?x $y)           ; after matching: ?x = a, $y = ((b c d) e)
(?x (?y $z) ?q)   ; after matching: ?x = a, ?y = b, $z = (c d), ?q = e
```

We'll also want to be able to put conditions on a match like this:

```
(?x:isNumber $y)
```

This statement says that we want to match a list consisting of a number followed by anything. The thing that makes pattern matching particularly interesting is the potential need for backtracking. For example, if we want to match the tree:

```
(a b (c b a) b)
```

and our pattern looks like:

```
($q ?x $r ($s ?x $t) ?x)
```

we might start out matching by assigning:

```
$q = ()
?x = a
$r = (b)
$s = (c b)
$t = ()
```

and not actually fail until we reach the final `?x` and find that it doesn't match our assignment. We would have to backtrack to our original assignment for `$q` and start over, eventually ending up with:

```
$q = (a)
?x = b
$r = ()
$s = (c)
$t = (a)
```

If we didn't have to worry about backtracking, the natural way to approach a tree traversal would be to write one or more recursive methods to navigate the tree structure. The pattern of recursive calls would mimic the structure of the tree, and the built-in system stack would take care of our bookkeeping. The typical reaction at this point would be to sigh heavily and then begin to sort out the requirements for implementing our own explicit stack to maintain state, giving up on the simple recursive solution. This response is unfortunate because a program built around an explicit stack is much more complicated a recursive solution. In our particular example, the explicit stack model also bad since we may want to add new pattern types later and we don't necessarily know what kind of state we'll need to save. The stack model may need to be updated in arbitrary ways.

Let's return to our recursive traversal and see where it fails. We would presumably have code that looks like this:

```java
public boolean match(Object tree, BindingMap bindings) {
    if (tree instanceof LispCons) {
    // The LispCons class implements pairs
    LispCons treecons = (LispCons)tree;

    if (carPattern().match(treecons.getCar(),bindings) != null) {
       return cdrPattern().match(treecons.getCdr(), bindings);
    }
  }
}
```

The process of matching would establish bindings for the pattern variables (like ?x or $y) in the BindingMap that is passed in.

So, what goes wrong? If the second call to match fails, there is no way to resume the first call in order to find a different set of bindings. The fundamental problem is that the first call to match *returns* and loses any information about where it was in the matching process. Clearly, then, the solution is simple: don't return! This may sound silly at first blush, but this is, in fact, exactly how we'll fix the problem. Actually, we will return from a matching operation, but only on a failure. Successful matches won't return and will thus save their state.

We will construct our matcher by using a programming technique known as continuation passing style (cps). Think of a continuation as the entire future of a computation wrapped up into a function or method. So, given the program:

```java
public class Simple {
    public static void main(String[] args) {
        System.out.println(3*4+5);
    }
}
```

after multiplying 3*4, the continuation could be thought of as the method:

```java
    private static void cont(int x) {
        System.out.println(x+5);
    }
```

That is, the future of the value returned from the multiplication is to have 5 added to it and then be printed. Writing a program in continuation passing style makes such continuations explicit. If our simple class were completely translated into cps, it would look like this:

```
import higherorder.*;
// This class is a simple example of continuation passing style
// without using anonymous classes.

public class Simple {
  public static void main(String[] args) {
    mult(3, 4, new MultCont());
  }

  // Multiply two integers and pass the result to the continuation.

  private static void mult(int x, int y, IntContinuation cont) {
    cont.eval(x*y);
  }

  // Add two integers and pass the result to the continuation.

  private static void add(int x, int y, IntContinuation cont) {
    cont.eval(x+y);
    }

  // The continuation for the call to mult().

  static class MultCont implements IntContinuation {
    public void eval(int x) {
      add(x, 5, new AddCont());
    }
  }

  // The continuation for the call to add().

  static class AddCont implements IntContinuation {
    public void eval(int x) {
      System.out.println(x);
    }
  }
}
```

The `IntContinuation` interface is defined as:

```
package higherorder;

  public interface IntContinuation {
```

```
    void eval(int x);
}
```

Each call includes a new argument, the *continuation*, that will be invoked on the result. Note that none of the methods return until the computation is finished. Also note that this is very awkward, not so much because of the continuation passing but because the `AddCont` and `MultCont` classes are out of context. They are each used only in one place and make no sense as stand-alone classes. A better way to create continuations would be to use anonymous classes, like this:

```java
package higherorder;
// This class is a simple example of continuation passing style
// using anonymous classes.

public class Simple2 {
  public static void main(String[] args) {
    mult(3, 4,
      new IntContinuation() {
        public void eval(int x) {
          add(x, 5,
            new IntContinuation() {
              public void eval(int x) {
                System.out.println(x);
              }
            });

        }
      });
  }

// Multiply two integers and pass the result to the continuation.

  private static void mult(int x, int y, IntContinuation cont) {
    cont.eval(x*y);
  }

// Add two integers and pass the result to the continuation.

  private static void add(int x, int y, IntContinuation cont) {
    cont.eval(x+y);
  }
}
```

This example, though still somewhat syntactically awkward, places the continuations in context. The single-use, stand-alone classes are gone. In our matcher, we won't translate everything to cps; there's no need. We will only translate recursive matching calls into cps so we can maintain state. Each successful match will invoke its continuation and each failed match will return. If we make it through the complete matching process successfully, we will throw a special success exception all the way out to the original match invocation, dropping our saved state in the process.

Table 12-1 shows the classes we'll discuss.

Table 12-1 Packages and Classes for Inner Class Example

highorder Package	
Closure	The interface that our continuations will implement
Predicate	The interface that represents predicates items must satisfy in order to match
match Package	
Match	The top-level interface to the matcher
MatchExp	The root class for all pattern classes
AnyExp	A pattern that matches anything
PairExp	A pattern that matches a pair (i.e., a LispCons)
VarExp	A pattern that matches anything and binds a name (e.g., ?x)
SeqVarExp	A pattern that matches a sequence and binds a name (e.g., $x)
ListExp	A pattern that matches a list of items
SeqClosure	A support interface
BindingMap	A table of bindings returned from a match
Cell	A support class for BindingMap
NoSuchBindingException	The exception thrown if a BindingMap is asked for an unknown entry
lisp Package	
LispCons	The class used to build tree structures
LetSpecialForm	A sample use of the matcher

Each Exp class represents a particular type of pattern and defines a match() method. A complete pattern is constructed by composing instances of the various pattern classes. The external interface into the matcher consists of the Match class, the MatchExp class, and the BindingMap class. Users create an instance of MatchExp to use as a pattern via pattern construction calls defined in Match. They then invoke the matcher itself via other calls defined in Match. Optionally, a BindingMap is returned from the match process so that the variable assignments from the match may be queried.

Now, let's examine these classes.

Closure Interface

The Closure interface, listed in Example 12-7, represents an arbitrary operation that can be invoked.

Example 12-7 higherorder.Closure Class

```
package higherorder;

public interface Closure {
    void eval() throws Exception;
}
```

Note that the eval() method of Closure does not take any arguments. We'll get any required information into our closures from the environment that is active when they are created.

Predicate Interface

The Predicate interface, listed in Example 12-8, represents an arbitrary predicate that can be invoked and that will return true or false.

Example 12-8 higherorder.Predicate Class

```
package higherorder;

public interface Predicate {
    boolean eval(Object x);
}
```

Match Class

The Match class (Example 12-9) is the top-level interface to the pattern matcher. It defines the match operations and also provides shortcuts for creating patterns. A pattern to match the tree

```
(a (b a) a)
```

could be constructed via:

```
Match.list(
  Match.var("x"),
  Match.list(
    Match.any(),
    Match.var("x")),
  Match.var("x"))
```

Each of the calls would return an instance of a subclass of `MatchExp`. The two main methods, `Match.match()` and `Match.matches()`, both pass a special success continuation into the match process that will throw a success exception when the match is complete.

Example 12-9 match.Match Class

```java
package match;

import java.util.*;
import higherorder.*;

public class Match {

    // Check if a pattern matches a tree without returning bindings.
    // Used as a simple test.

    public static boolean matches(MatchExp exp, Object item) {

        // Even though we don't return bindings, we need to track them
        // so we can compare multiple instances of the same variable.

        BindingMap bindings = new BindingMap();

        try {
            // Invoke the match method of the pattern expression with
            // a continuation that will throw to here on success.

            exp.match(item, bindings, SUCCEED);
        } catch (SuccessException se) {
            // If we received a success exception, the match was
            // successful.
            return true;
        } catch (Exception e) {
            e.printStackTrace();
            System.exit(1);
        }

        // If we returned normally from the match call, the match failed.
        return false;
    }

    public static BindingMap match(MatchExp exp, Object item) {
        // Check if a pattern matches a tree and return bindings on
        // success. Return null on failure.

        BindingMap bindings = new BindingMap();
```

```
  try {
     // Invoke the match method of the pattern expression with
     // a continuation that will throw back out to here on success.

     exp.match(item, bindings, SUCCEED);
  } catch (SuccessException se) {
     // If we received a success exception, the match was
     // successful.

     return bindings;
  } catch (Exception e) {
     e.printStackTrace();
     System.exit(1);
  }
  // If we returned normally from the match call, the match failed.
  return null;
}

// Shortcuts for creating patterns.

// Create a pattern object that will match anything.

public static MatchExp any() {
  return new AnyExp();
}

// Create a pattern object that will match a LispCons.

public static MatchExp pair(MatchExp car, MatchExp cdr) {
  return new PairExp(car, cdr);
}

// Create a pattern object that will match anything and bind a
// name.

public static MatchExp var(String name) {
  return new VarExp(name);
}

// Create a pattern object that will match any item that satisfies
// a predicate and bind a name.

public static MatchExp var(String name, Predicate p) {
  return new VarExp(name, p);
}

// Create a pattern object that will match any sequence and bind
```

```
// a name.

public static MatchExp svar(String name) {
  return new SeqVarExp(name);
}

// Create a pattern object that will match any sequence that
// satisfies a predicate and bind a name.

public static MatchExp svar(String name, Predicate p) {
  return new SeqVarExp(name, p);
}

// Create a pattern object that will match any list (i.e., a tree
// that ends in the empty list like (a b c))

public static MatchExp list(MatchExp[] exps) {
  return new ListExp(exps);
}

// The next six methods are just shorthand for various length lists
// since Java doesn't support methods with arbitrary numbers of
// arguments.

public static MatchExp list() {
  return list(new MatchExp[] {});
}

public static MatchExp list(MatchExp exp) {
  return list(new MatchExp[] {exp});
}

public static MatchExp list(MatchExp exp1, MatchExp exp2) {
  return list(new MatchExp[] {exp1, exp2});
}

public static MatchExp list(MatchExp exp1, MatchExp exp2, MatchExp
  exp3) {
  return list(new MatchExp[] {exp1, exp2, exp3});
}

public static MatchExp list(
  MatchExp exp1,
  MatchExp exp2,
  MatchExp exp3,
  MatchExp exp4
)
{
```

```
    return list(new MatchExp[] {exp1, exp2, exp3, exp4});
  }

  public static MatchExp list(
    MatchExp exp1,
    MatchExp exp2,
    MatchExp exp3,
    MatchExp exp4,
    MatchExp exp5
  )
  {
    return list(new MatchExp[] {exp1, exp2, exp3, exp4, exp5});
  }

  // A special exception class that will signal a successful match.
  public final static class SuccessException extends Exception {}

  // An instance of SuccessException to throw after a successful
  // match.

  private final static SuccessException SUCCESS = new
    SuccessException();

  // A special continuation that will throw a success exception.

  private final static Closure SUCCEED = new Closure() {
    public void eval() throws SuccessException {
      throw SUCCESS;
    }
  };
}
```

MatchExp Class

The `MatchExp` class (Example 12-10) is the root class for all patterns in the matcher. Each pattern defines a `match()` method to implement its special match semantics. A default implementation of `seqMatch()` is provided for all patterns that do not explicitly deal with sequences.

Example 12-10 match.MatchExp Class

```
package match;

import java.util.*;
import higherorder.*;
import lisp.LispCons;

public abstract class MatchExp {
```

```
// Match a tree against this pattern. Add any resulting bindings
// to the binding map that is passed in. On a successful match,
// invoke the continuation; return on failure.

public abstract void match(
  Object item,
  BindingMap bindings,
  Closure continuation
) throws Exception;

// The default behavior of a pattern in a sequence match is to
// match the pattern against the "car" of the sequence and invoke
// the sequence continuation on the "cdr." This allows a pattern
// that explicitly matches a sequence to invoke the match
// operations of subpatterns and then continue matching the rest
// of the sequence.

public void seqMatch(
  final LispCons seq,
  final BindingMap bindings,
  final SeqClosure continuation
) throws Exception {
    // If the cdr of this tree cell is not itself a cell,
    // then we're not looking at a true sequence and the
    // match should fail (i.e., return).

    if (seq.getCdr() instanceof LispCons) {
        final LispCons seqCdr = (LispCons)seq.getCdr();

        // Invoke the match routine for this pattern and
        // continue matching the sequence via the continuation
        // on success.

        match(
            seq.getCar(),
            bindings,
            new Closure() {
                public void eval() throws Exception {
                    continuation.eval(seqCdr);
                }
            });
    }
  }
}
```

AnyExp Class

The AnyExp class (Example 12-11) represents a wildcard pattern that matches anything. It always succeeds and simply invokes its continuation.

Example 12-11 match.AnyExp Class

```
package match;

import java.util.*;
import higherorder.*;

public class AnyExp extends MatchExp {
  // Always succeed in matching.
  public void match(
    Object item,
    BindingMap bindings,
    Closure continuation
  ) throws Exception
  {
    continuation.eval();
  }
}
```

PairExp Class

The PairExp class (Example 12-12) represents a pattern that matches a pair (LispCons). It is constructed from two other patterns that match the car and cdr. The match call for the car takes a continuation that will invoke the match on the cdr.

Example 12-12 match.PairExp Class

```
package match;

import java.util.*;
import higherorder.*;
import lisp.*;

public class PairExp extends MatchExp {
  // Create a new PairExp pattern from two subpatterns.

  public PairExp(MatchExp car, MatchExp cdr) {
    this.car = car;
    this.cdr = cdr;
  }

  // Match a LispCons against the car and cdr patterns of a PairExp.
```

```
public void match(
  final Object item,
  final BindingMap bindings,
  final Closure continuation
) throws Exception
{
  // If the item is not a LispCons the match should fail and return.
  if (item != LispCons.emptyList && item instanceof LispCons) {
    // Note that the following two variables _must_ be declared
    // final so that they may be referenced by the anonymous
    // class we create as a continuation. This is a Java
    // restriction on anonymous classes -- they may only reference
    // local variables that are final.

    final LispCons consItem = (LispCons)item;
    final MatchExp cdrExp   = cdr;

    // Invoke the match operation defined by the "car pattern."
    // On success, the continuation will invoke the match defined
    // by the cdr pattern. If the cdr match is successful, the
    // continuation passed into the pair match is invoked.

    car.match(
        consItem.getCar(),
        bindings,
        new Closure() {
            public void eval() throws Exception {
                cdrExp.match(consItem.getCdr(), bindings,
                    continuation);
            }
        });
  }
}
private MatchExp car;
private MatchExp cdr;
}
```

Notice that PairExp illustrates a very important inner class feature: inner classes can reference the local environment in effect when they are created. In the segment below, observe how the anonymous class we are passing into the car.match() calls references consItem and cdrExp. These are *local* variables in the current method, yet they can be accessed at a later time from within the anonymous class. This is a very powerful mechanism for taking advantage of context, and we will use it repeatedly in the pattern matcher.

```
final LispCons consItem = (LispCons)item;
final MatchExp cdrExp   = cdr;
```

```
// Invoke the match operation defined by the "car pattern."
// On success, the continuation will invoke the match defined
// by the cdr pattern. If the cdr match is successful, the
// continuation passed into the pair match is invoked.

car.match(
    consItem.getCar(),
    bindings,
    new Closure() {
        public void eval() throws Exception {
        cdrExp.match(consItem.getCdr(), bindings,
            continuation);
        }
    });
```

VarExp Class

The VarExp class (Example 12-13) represents a pattern that matches anything and establishes a binding for a name. If a VarExp with a particular name, say, a, has already matched something, any other VarExp with the same name must match the same thing (or at least something *equal* to it).

Example 12-13 match.VarExp Class

```
package match;

import java.util.*;
import higherorder.*;

public class VarExp extends MatchExp {
  // Create a new VarExp pattern.
  public VarExp(String name) {
    this.name = name;
  }

  // Create a new VarExp pattern with a predicate that must be
  // satisfied for a match to be successful.

  public VarExp(String name, Predicate p) {
    this.name = name;
    this.pred = p;
  }

  // Match an item. If this VarExp's name has already been bound,
  // check that the binding is equal to the object being matched. If
  // this VarExp contains a predicate, make sure it is satisfied.
  // If a later match fails, undo any binding that was established
```

```java
      // during the match.

      public void match(
        Object item,
        BindingMap bindings,
        Closure continuation
      ) throws Exception
      {

        // Check to see if this variable already matched something.

        Cell binding = bindings.get(name);

        // If no binding, we create one.

        if (binding == null) {
          // If there's a predicate and it doesn't match, fail.

          if (pred != null && !pred.eval(item)) {
            return;
          }

          // Create a new binding

          bindings.put(name, new Cell(item));

          // Invoke the continuation.

          continuation.eval();

          // If we got here, a later match failed, so we remove the
          // binding we added.

          bindings.remove(name);

        } else if (binding.value().equals(item)) {
          // If there's a predicate and it doesn't match, fail.

          if (pred == null || pred.eval(item)) {
            // Since the binding for this variable is already
            // established, we can just invoke the continuation.

            continuation.eval();
          }
        }
      }
      private String name;
      private Predicate pred;
    }
```

SeqVarExp Class

The SeqVarExp class (Example 12-14) represents a pattern that can match against a subsequence of a list (for example, $y in (?x $y ?z)) and bind a name. If a SeqVarExp with a particular name has already matched something, another SeqVarExp with the same name must match an equal item.

Example 12-14 match.SeqVarExp Class

```
package match;

import java.util.*;
import higherorder.*;
import lisp.*;

public class SeqVarExp extends MatchExp {
   // Create a new SeqVarExp pattern.

   public SeqVarExp(String name) {
     this.name = name;
   }

   // Create a new SeqVarExp pattern with a predicate that must be
   // satisfied for a match to be successful.

   public SeqVarExp(String name, Predicate p) {
     this.name = name;
     this.pred = p;
   }

   // Match a complete sequence. If a binding already exists for this
   // name, compare the binding to the sequence being matched. This
   // method is used when a sequence variable is being matched
   // against an entire list rather than a subsequence of a list.

   public void match(
     Object item,
     BindingMap bindings,
     Closure continuation
   ) throws Exception
   {
     // Check to see if this variable already matched something.

     Cell binding = bindings.get(name);

     // If a binding exists, compare against it.

     if (binding != null) {
```

```java
            if (binding.value().equals(item)) {
                // If there's a predicate and it doesn't match, fail.

                if (pred == null || pred.eval(item)) {
                    continuation.eval();
                }
            }

        } else if (item instanceof LispCons) {
            // If there's a predicate and it doesn't match, fail.
            if (pred == null || pred.eval(item)) {

                // Create a new binding

                bindings.put(name, new Cell(item));

                // Invoke the continuation.

                continuation.eval();

                // If we got here, a later match failed, so we remove the
                // binding we added.

                bindings.remove(name);
            }
        }
    }


    // Match a subsequence of a list. This method is called when
    // a match is attempted within a ListExp pattern. The current
    // subsequence is compared against any existing binding for this
    // SeqVarExp. This is done without actually extracting a copy of
    // the current subsequence or the bound subsequence for
    // efficiency.

    public void seqMatch(
        final LispCons seq,
        final BindingMap bindings,
        final SeqClosure continuation
    ) throws Exception {

        // Check to see if this variable already matched something.

        Cell binding = bindings.get(name);

        // If a binding exists, compare against it.

        if (binding != null) {
```

```
    seqBindingMatch(
        (SeqBinding)binding.value(),
        seq,
        bindings,
        continuation);
  } else {
    // Otherwise, create a binding and invoke the continuation.
    seqMatchAux(seq, seq, bindings, continuation);
  }
}


// This class represents a sequence binding. It is used to
// maintain a binding without actually extracting the subsequence
// from a list. It stores a reference to the beginning of the
// subsequence and a reference to the end of the subsequence.
// Later, when the actual value is required, a value is copied out
// of the original sequence.

public static class SeqBinding {
  // Create a new sequence binding.

  SeqBinding(LispCons seq, LispCons tail) {
    this.seq  = seq;
    this.tail = tail;
  }

  // Extract a value subsequence. Cache the result the first time
  // it is created and retrieve the cached copy on subsequent
  // calls.

  public Object value() {
    // If we haven't retrieved the value yet, compute it.
    if (val == null) {
      // If the subsequence continues to the end of the
      // outer list, don't copy it out, just return a
      // reference to it.

      if (tail == null) {
        val = seq;
      } else {
        // Create a copy of the subsequence.
        val = listDifference(seq, tail);
      }
    }

    return val;
  }
```

```
  // Accessors for the beginning and end of the subsequence.

  public LispCons getSeq() {
     return seq;
  }

  public LispCons getTail() {
     return tail;
  }

  // Display the subsequence.

  public String toString() {
     return value().toString();
  }

  // Extract a copy of the subsequence from the outer list.

  private static LispCons listDifference(LispCons seq, LispCons
     tail) {
     // If the beginning equals the end, it's an empty list.

     if (seq == tail) {
        return LispCons.emptyList;
     }

     // Create a new pair consisting of the first element of
     // the subsequence followed by a copy of the tail.

     return new LispCons(
        seq.getCar(),
        listDifference((LispCons)seq.getCdr(), tail));
  }

  private LispCons seq;
  private LispCons tail;
  private LispCons val;
}

// Compare a subsequence with an existing binding and, if
// successful, invoke the continuation.

private void seqBindingMatch(
  SeqBinding binding,
  LispCons item,
  BindingMap bindings,
  SeqClosure continuation
) throws Exception
```

```
{
  // Compare against the existing binding.

  Cell result = seqBindingCompare(binding, item);

  if (result != null) {
    // If there's no predicate or predicate is successful, invoke
    // the continuation.

    if (pred == null || pred.eval(binding.value())) {
      continuation.eval((LispCons)result.value());
    }
  }
}

// Compare a subsequence against an existing binding. Return null
// on failure; a new binding cell on success.

private Cell seqBindingCompare(SeqBinding binding, LispCons
  item) {
  // Extract the start and end of the subsequence from the
  // binding and compare.

  return compareAux(binding.getSeq(), binding.getTail(), item);
}
// Recursively compare a list against a list defined in terms
// of its start and end. Return null on failure; a new binding
// cell on success.

private Cell compareAux(LispCons seq, LispCons tail, LispCons
  item) {
  // If we've reached the end of our binding, it's a success.

  if (seq == tail) {
    return new Cell(item);
  } else if (seq.getCar().equals(item.getCar())) {
    // If the first elements match, recursively compare the tails.

    return compareAux(
        (LispCons)seq.getCdr(),
        tail,
        (LispCons)item.getCdr());
  } else {
    // If the first elements don't match, fail.

    return null;
  }
```

```
}

// Attempt to bind this SeqVarExp to a subsequence and invoke the
// continuation to match the remainder of the sequence. Repeatedly
// extend the subsequence and try again on match failure. (i.e.,
// if matching (a b c), first match (a); then, if that fails, match
// (a b), then (a b c)).

private void seqMatchAux(
  LispCons seq,
  LispCons tail,
  BindingMap bindings,
  SeqClosure continuation
) throws Exception
{
  // Create a sequence binding given a start and end. On the
  // initial call to seqMatchAux, the start and end will be the
  // same and the matched subsequence will be empty.

  SeqBinding sb = new SeqBinding(seq, tail);
  // If there's no predicate or the predicate succeeds, create
  // a binding and invoke the continuation.

  if (pred == null || pred.eval(sb.value())) {
    bindings.put(name, new Cell(sb));
    continuation.eval(tail);
  }
  // If we've reached the end and we can no longer extend the
  // sequence, fail (i.e., return). Remove any bindings.

  if (tail == LispCons.emptyList) {
    bindings.remove(name);
    return;
  }

  // If we're not yet at the end, extend the matched sequence and
  // retry matching the remainder of the outer list.

  Object newTail = tail.getCdr();

  // If the tail is not a LispCons, this is not a proper
  // sequence, so fail; otherwise, recursively match after
  // extending the sequence.

  if (newTail instanceof LispCons) {
    seqMatchAux(seq, (LispCons)newTail, bindings, continuation);
  } else {
    bindings.remove(name);
```

```
    }
  }
  private String name;
  private Predicate pred;
}
```

ListExp Class

The `ListExp` class (Example 12-15) represents a pattern that matches complete sequences. Within the context of a `ListExp` pattern, `SeqVarExp` patterns can match subsequences. Matches of subpatterns are invoked via the `MatchExp.seqMatch()` method, which maintains the sequence context. After a subpattern matches, its continuation proceeds with matching the rest of the sequence.

Example 12-15 match.ListExp Class

```
package match;

import java.util.*;
import higherorder.*;
import lisp.*;

public class ListExp extends MatchExp {
  // Create a new ListExp pattern.
  public ListExp(MatchExp[] exps) {
    this.exps = exps;
  }

  // Match against a proper sequence (a set of LispCons instances
  // chained together and ending with the empty list such as:
  // (a b c)).

  public void match(
    final Object item,
    final BindingMap bindings,
    final Closure continuation
  ) throws Exception
  {
    // If the object being matched is not a LispCons, it cannot
    // represent a proper sequence.

    if (item instanceof LispCons) {
      // Create a final variable containing the subpatterns so
      // that it can be accessed from within the continuation.

      final MatchExp[] expArray = exps;
```

```
        // Invoke the matchAux routine, which keeps track of the
        // index into the vector of subpatterns.
        // A sequence match call uses a different closure type,
        // SeqClosure, whose eval method takes the remainder of the
        // sequence to match as an argument.

        matchAux(
            0,
            (LispCons)item,
            bindings,
            new SeqClosure() {
                public void eval(LispCons seq) throws Exception {
                    continuation.eval();
                }
            });
    }
}

// A helper method that keeps track of the index within the set of
// subpatterns for this pattern.

private void matchAux(
    final int       index,
    final LispCons item,
    final BindingMap bindings,
    final SeqClosure continuation
) throws Exception
{
    // If we've reached the end of the subpatterns and the current
    // item being matched is the empty list, the match succeeded so
    // invoke the continuation.

    if (index == exps.length) {
        if (item == LispCons.emptyList) {
            continuation.eval(item);
        }

    } else {
        // Match the next subpattern through its seqMatch() call.
        // Pass a continuation that will match the remainder of
        // the subpatterns.

        exps[index].seqMatch(
            item,
            bindings,
            new SeqClosure() {
                public void eval(LispCons seq) throws Exception {
                    matchAux(
```

```
                         index + 1,
                         seq,
                         bindings,
                         continuation);
                }
            });
    }
 }
 private MatchExp[] exps;
}
```

SeqClosure Interface

The SeqClosure interface (Example 12-16) represents a continuation used in matching sequences. The argument to eval is the remainder of the sequence to match.

Example 12-16 match.SeqClosure Interface

```
package match;

import lisp.LispCons;

public interface SeqClosure {
   void eval(LispCons exp) throws Exception;
}
```

BindingMap Class

The BindingMap class (Example 12-17) represents a minor extension of Hashtable. There are two main differences:

1.   Null values may be stored because all entries are wrapped in Cell objects.
2.   The valueOf() method automatically extracts a sequence from a Seq-VarBinding during a fetch and unwraps any entries from their Cell wrappers.

Example 12-17 match.BindingMap Class

```
package match;

import java.util.Hashtable;

public class BindingMap {
   // Retrieve a binding and return the contents of the Cell object.
   // If the contents represent a sequence binding, extract the
   // actual sequence before returning.

   public Object valueOf(String name) throws NoSuchBindingException {
```

```
   // Retrieve the binding.

   Cell c = get(name);

   if (c == null) {
      throw new NoSuchBindingException(name);
   }

   // Extract the contents of the cell.

   Object result = c.value();

   // If it's a sequence binding, extract the sequence.

   if (result instanceof SeqVarExp.SeqBinding) {
      return ((SeqVarExp.SeqBinding)result).value();
   }

   return result;
 }

 // Store a new cell.

 public void put(String name, Cell value) {
   ht.put(name, value);
 }

 // Retrieve a binding.

 public Cell get(String name) {
   return (Cell)ht.get(name);
 }

 // Remove a binding.

 public void remove(String name) {
   ht.remove(name);
 }
 public String toString() {
   return ht.toString();
 }

 private Hashtable ht = new Hashtable();
}
```

Cell Class

The Cell class (Example 12-18) is a simple wrapper, so null references can be stored in a Hashtable.

Example 12-18 match.Cell Class

```
package match;

public class Cell {
  // Create a Cell.
  public Cell(Object o) {
    this.obj = o;
  }

  // Extract the Cell's value.
  public Object value() {
    return obj;
  }
  public String toString() {
    return "{" + obj.toString() + "}";
  }

  private Object obj;
}
```

NoSuchBindingException Class

The NoSuchBindingException class (Example 12-19) is the exception thrown when a BindingMap is asked for a nonexistent entry.

Example 12-19 match.NoSuchBindingException Class

```
package match;

public class NoSuchBindingException extends Exception {
  public NoSuchBindingException(String name) {
    super("No binding found for: " + name);
  }
}
```

LispCons Class

The LispCons class (Example 12-20) represents a node in a Lisp tree structure. The class provides methods for accessing the car and cdr fields, printing a list, and comparing for equality.

Example 12-20 lisp.LispCons Class

```
package lisp;

public class LispCons {
  // Create a single special instance to stand for the empty list.

  public static final LispCons emptyList = new LispCons(null, null);
    // Initialize the empty list.

    static {
      emptyList.car = emptyList;
      emptyList.cdr = emptyList;
    }

    // Create an empty LispCons.

    public LispCons() {
      car = emptyList;
      cdr = emptyList;
    }

    // Create a LispCons with a specified car and cdr.

    public LispCons(Object newCar, Object newCdr) {
      car = newCar;
      cdr = newCdr;
    }

    // Extract the car field.

    public Object getCar() {
      return car;
    }

    // Extract the cdr field.

    public Object getCdr() {
      return cdr;
    }

    // Store a new value into the car field.

    public void setCar(Object newCar) {
      car = newCar;
    }

    // Store a new value into the cdr field.
```

```java
public void setCdr(Object newCdr) {
   cdr = newCdr;
}

// Compare two lists for equality. Compare the cars, then
// compare the cdrs.

public boolean equals(Object other) {

   // If the two conses are the same object, then they are equal.

   if (this == other) {
      return true;
   }

   // A cons can't be equal to a noncons.

   if (!(other instanceof LispCons)) {
      return false;
   }

   // Recursively compare the cars and cdrs.

   LispCons otherCons = (LispCons)other;
      return car.equals(otherCons.car) &&
         cdr.equals(otherCons.cdr);
}

// Construct a string representation of a list.

public String toString() {
   StringBuffer buf = new StringBuffer();
   write(buf, true);
   return buf.toString();
}

// Recursively output a list.

private void write(StringBuffer buf, boolean first_element) {

   // Handle the empty list special case.
   if (this == emptyList) {
      buf.append("()");
      return;
   }

   // If we're writing the first element of a list, write out
```

```
    // the opening parenthesis; otherwise, write a space.

    if (!first_element) {
        buf.append(' ');
    } else {
        buf.append('(');
    }

    // If the car is itself a cons, recursively use write() to
    // output it.

    if (getCar() instanceof LispCons) {
        ((LispCons)getCar()).write(buf, true);
    } else {
        // otherwise, print it according to conventions defined
        // by LispPrinter.

        buf.append(LispPrinter.toLispString(getCar()));
    }

    // If we're at the end of the list, print the closing
    // parenthesis.

    if (getCdr() == emptyList) {
        buf.append(')');
    } else if (getCdr() instanceof LispCons) {
        // If the cdr points to another cons, recursively use
        // write() to output it.

        ((LispCons)getCdr()).write(buf, false);
    } else {
        // If the cdr is not a cons, output a vertical bar to
        // signal this, output the final entry, and print the
        // closing parenthesis.

        buf.append(" | ");
        buf.append(LispPrinter.toLispString(getCdr()));
        buf.append(')');
    }
  }

  private Object car;
  private Object cdr;
}
```

LetSpecialForm Class

The LetSpecialForm class (Example 12-21) translates Lisp expressions of the form:

```
(let ((x 4)
      (y 5))
  (+ x y))
```

into the equivalent:

```
((lambda (x y)
    (+ x y))
  4 5)
```

This translation is done by use of the pattern matcher defined in the match package. By using the pattern matcher, we avoid the ugly and complicated code required to check the shape of the "let" expression and extract the relevant pieces.

Example 12-21 lisp.LetSpecialForm Class

```java
package lisp;

import higherorder.*;
import match.*;

public class LetSpecialForm extends LispSpecialForm {
  // Evaluate a 'let' expression.
  public Object eval(LispCons exp, LispEnv env, LispInterpreter
    interp)
    throws Throwable {

    // Create a predicate that will match a LispSymbol. Each
    // binding like (x 4) in the class description consists of
    // a symbol and an arbitrary tree.

    final Predicate isSymbol =
      new Predicate() {
        public boolean eval(Object x) {
          return x instanceof LispSymbol;
        }
      };

    // Create a predicate that will determine if a list is a
    // proper binding list like ((x 4) (y 5)).

    final Predicate allBindings = new Predicate() {
      public boolean eval(Object x) {
```

```
            LispCons c = (LispCons)x;

            // We don't need to check that each element is
            // a LispCons since the sequence var would not
            // have matched unless they were.

            while (c != EMPTY_LIST) {
                // Match a binding. It should consist
                // of a list containing a symbol and any
                // other arbitrary expression.

                if (!Match.matches(
                    Match.list(
                        Match.var("sym", isSymbol),
                        Match.any()),
                    car(c))) {
                    return false;
                }

                c = (LispCons)cdr(c);
            }
            return true;
        }
    };
    // The complete pattern for a let expression. We can use
    // "any" for the actual 'let' symbol since we would not be
    // in the LetSpecialForm eval method unless the first element
    // was 'let'. Basically, we want to match:
    // (? ($bindings:allBindings) $expressions)

    MatchExp letPattern =
        Match.pair(
            Match.any(),
            Match.pair(
                Match.list(Match.svar("bindings", allBindings)),
                Match.list(Match.svar("expressions")))));
    try {
        BindingMap results = Match.match(letPattern, exp);

        if (results == null) {
            throw new LispException("Invalid let syntax: " + exp);
        }

        // If the match succeeded, extract the bindings from
        // the binding map.
```

```
    LispCons letBindings = (LispCons)results.valueOf("bindings");
    LispCons[] separated = separateBindings(letBindings);

    // Create the lambda expression.

    exp =
        cons(
            cons(
                interp.getReader().intern("lambda"),
                cons(
                    separated[0],
                    results.valueOf("expressions"))),
            separated[1]);
  } catch (NoSuchBindingException nsbe) {
    throw new LispException("Invalid let syntax: " + exp);
  }

  // Evaluate the translated expression.

  return interp.getEvaluator().eval(exp, env, interp);
}

// Extract the names and values from the bindings into separate
// lists. Once again, we needn't check types of the objects
// along the way since the match would have failed if they
// were incorrect.

private LispCons[] separateBindings(LispCons letBindings) {
  LispCons varResult = EMPTY_LIST;
  LispCons valResult = EMPTY_LIST;

  while (letBindings != EMPTY_LIST) {
    varResult= cons(caar(letBindings), varResult);
    valResult= cons(cadar(letBindings), valResult);
    letBindings= (LispCons)cdr(letBindings);
  }

  return new LispCons[] {varResult, valResult};
}
}
```

Summary

Inner classes provide low-level control over how you structure your Java programs. Inner classes can be grouped into three types:

- **Member Classes** — Classes that are made members of other classes.

- **Local Classes** — Classes that are defined within individual blocks of code and not just within classes.

- **Anonymous Classes** — Local classes that are instantiated in only one place can be made *anonymous*. They do not have constructors. Any arguments passed in a new expression are forwarded to the constructor for the superclass of the anonymous class. They allow you to write single-use classes in meaningful contexts and reference the dynamic environment. They are Java's version of stand-alone methods and closures

Out pattern matching example demonstrates static inner classes, anonymous classes, and continuation passing style. Several things should be taken from this example. Named inner classes support good program structure by allowing you to encapsulate code that does not need to be exposed. Anonymous classes allow you to write single-use classes in meaningful contexts and reference the dynamic environment. They are Java's version of stand-alone methods and closures. Recursive routines written in continuation passing style are a convenient alternative to explicit stack manipulation.

CHAPTER 13

Collection Classes

One of the most notable and useful changes in the JDK 1.2 is the addition of a set of data structures that provide standard implementations of linked lists, balanced trees, sets, and more. These data structures come in the form of the Java collection classes. This chapter describes background for use of the collection classes and goes into some detail on their everyday use.

Standard Data Structures

Processing complicated data structures in a language without garbage collection always involves a significant amount of memory management, making it difficult to provide simple abstract facilities for users. Consider a hash table. When a user has finished with it, what should happen to its components? Should the entries be deleted? Let's look at a few cases that highlight some of the implicit issues.

- **Case 1 — A hash table used to store named objects** — Each key is a string and its value is an arbitrary object. After inserting a new entry, the user will not typically hold on to the property name independently of the hash table. The values, on the other hand, are likely to be used outside of the hash table, possibly connected through references to other objects. So, when the hash table is deleted, the keys should be deleted, but the values should not.

- **Case 2 — A hash table used to store named numeric properties** — Each key is a string and its value is a number. Neither a key nor a value is likely to have a unique identity. When the hash table is deleted, both the keys and the values should be deleted.

- **Case 3 — A hash table used to store dynamic object attributes** — Each key is an object of arbitrary type, and each value is a list of attributes. The key has a unique identity, and so do parts of the values. When the hash table is deleted, neither the key nor the interior attribute values should be deleted, but the attribute list itself should be.

These are only a few scenarios illustrating the complexity of managing key/value pairs in a hash table. The important point here is that the lifetimes of keys and values are not really parts of the *hash table* abstraction. In fact, forcing users to deal with these issues breaks the intended abstraction.

Garbage-collected languages, on the other hand, stand out in their ability to handle data structures. In a garbage-collected language like Java, components are freed when they are no longer used, period. Partly for this reason, garbage-collected languages have traditionally provided significantly better built-in support for data structures than languages with explicit memory management.

However, until the release of JDK 1.2, Java lagged behind the other dynamic languages. It provided very few collections (`Hashtable`, `Vector`, `BitSet`, and so on.) and no unifying framework. These deficiencies have resulted in a significant overuse of the `Vector` class, even in situations where it is inefficient.

Overuse of the `Vector` class, despite its inefficiencies, is likely because of the common notion that anything built into the language must be efficient. People are often confused by this notion when they first venture into languages that provide higher-level abstractions. In a language like C, anything built into the language *is* efficient—but only because C provides no high-level features. Other factors also come into play. A programmer is likely to prefer a built-in solution in general because it is standard and presumably fully debugged.

While these are valid reasons for use of built-in language solutions, what is really required is a complete set of built-in, standard, debugged data structures so that a programmer can choose the appropriate structure for the task—without compromising efficiency. The JDK 1.2 supplies just such a set of data structures: the Java collection classes. The Java collection classes provide standard implementations of linked lists, balanced trees, sets, and more. They also provide a framework that supports the easy creation of new collections that can be used in a consistent way.

Besides letting the programmer choose the appropriate data structure for the task and providing a framework for creating new collections, these data structures provide another advantage. That is, they encourage code reuse, because different programs tend to share representations. For example, Lisp functions always exhibit a high degree of reuse because of the common use of the list data structure.

Java Collection Classes Hierarchy

Java provides a set of classes that implement the vast majority of commonly used data structures. The classes are arranged into simple hierarchies based on class characteristics. Methods are provided to search, sort, and combine different structures. We'll look at the collection class hierarchies in detail, even though this goes somewhat against our basic approach of describing the Java language rather than its class libraries. However, almost every significant program in Java will make use of one or more of these classes, so we would argue that the collection classes warrant this special attention.

The major collection classes fall into two groups:

- Simple collections of elements such as lists and sets
- Mappings between pairs of elements such as hash tables

From these two groups, we'll explore four main hierarchies:

1. The `Collection` interface hierarchy
2. The `Map` interface hierarchy
3. The `Collection` class hierarchy
4. The `Map` class hierarchy

There are also support classes, such as `Iterator` and `Comparator`, that we will discuss in context.

The Collection Interface Hierarchy

Figure 13-1 shows the interface hierarchy of the Collection class.

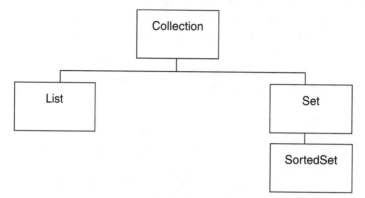

Figure 13-1 Collection Interface Hierarchy

The Map Interface Hierarchy

Figure 13-2 shows the Map interface hierarchy.

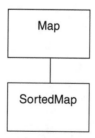

Figure 13-2 Map Interface Hierarchy

The Collection Class Hierarchy

Figure 13-3 shows the Collection class hierarchy. Note the following relationships:

- All the subclasses of AbstractCollection implement Collection.
- All the subclasses of AbstractList implement List.
- All the subclasses of AbstractSet implement Set.
- TreeSet implements SortedSet.

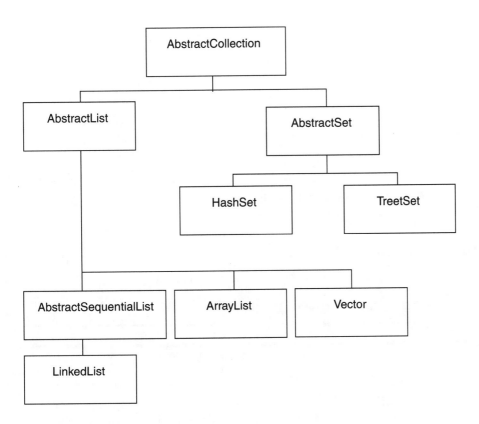

Figure 13-3 Collection Class Hierarchy

The Map Class Hierarchy

Figure 13-4 shows the `Map` class hierarchy. Note that all the subclasses of `AbstractMap` implement `Map`, and `TreeMap` implements `SortedMap`.

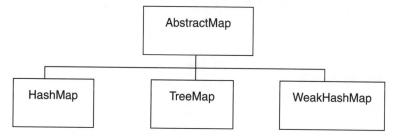

Figure 13-4 Map Class Hierarchy

Operations on Collections

The `Collection` interface provides the operations in Table 13-1.

Table 13-1 Collection Operations

Method	Description
`boolean add(Object)`	Adds an object to the collection if it is not present or if the collection allows duplicates. Returns true if the object was actually added.
`boolean addAll(Collection)`	Adds all the elements of a specified collection to the collection if the elements are not already present or if the collection allows duplicates. Returns true if *any* of the objects were actually added.
`void clear()`	Removes all the elements from the collection.
`boolean contains(Object)`	Returns true if a particular object is contained in the collection.
`boolean containsAll(Collection)`	Returns true if all the elements of a specified collection are contained in the collection.
`boolean isEmpty()`	Returns true if there are no elements in the collection.
`Iterator iterator()`	Returns an iterator (similar to an Enumeration) over the collection.

Table 13-1 Collection Operations (Continued)

Method	Description
`boolean remove(Object)`	Removes one copy of an object from the collection if it is present. Returns true if the object was removed.
`boolean removeAll(Collection)`	Removes all the elements of a specified collection from the collection. Returns true if *any* of the objects were removed.
`boolean retainAll(Collection)`	Removes all but the elements of a specified collection from the collection. Returns true if *any* objects were removed.
`int size()`	Returns the number of elements in the collection.
`Object[] toArray()`	Returns an array containing the elements from the collection. If the particular collection provides an ordering on elements, the ordering will be preserved in the newly created array.
`Object[] toArray(Object[])`	Returns an array containing the elements from the collection. If the particular collection provides an ordering on elements, the ordering will be preserved in the newly created array. If the argument array is large enough to hold all the elements of the collection, they are copied into it; otherwise, a new array (the same type as the argument array) is allocated and filled with the elements of the collection. If the array is larger than the collection, any remaining array elements are set to `null`. Note that this method, unlike the zero-argument `toArray()` method, allows an array to be returned whose type is more specific than `Object`. Given a collection c of instances of `Foo`, the call: `c.toArray(new Foo[0])` will return an array of `Foo` rather than an array of `Object`.

Operations on Maps

The Map interface provides the operations in Table 13-2

Table 13-2 Map Operations

Method	Description
`void clear()`	Removes all keys and values from the map.
`boolean containsKey(Object)`	Returns true if the object is a key in the map.
`boolean containsValue(Object)`	Returns true if the object is a value in the map.
`Set entrySet()`	Returns a set of `Map.Entry` objects representing the key/value pairs in the map.
`Object get(Object)`	Returns the value in the map that corresponds to the specified key if one exists; otherwise returns `null`. A return value of null does not imply that the key is not present since a key may explicitly be mapped to null.
`boolean isEmpty()`	Returns true if the map contains no entries.
`Set keySet()`	Returns a set consisting of all the keys in the map.
`Object put(Object, Object)`	Associates a key with a value in the map. If the key already exists in the map, any previous value is discarded.
`Object putAll(Map)`	Adds all the entries from a specified map to the map.
`Object remove(Object)`	Removes the map entry with the specified key.

All of the operations provided by `Collection` and `Map` that modify the object are optional. It is acceptable for instances of `Collection` or `Map` to throw an exception when optional operations are invoked. This allows for the creation of immutable instances.

Subinterfaces of Collection and Map

Each of the interfaces that extend `Collection` or `Map` represents a `Collection` or `Map`, respectively, with specific properties. Let's look at those properties.

List

A List is an ordered Collection. Elements can be inserted or accessed by position, starting at 0. Table 13-3 shows the operations that are specific to lists.

Table 13-3 List Operations

Method	Description
void add(int, Object)	Inserts a new element at a particular position.
Object get(int)	Returns the element at a particular position.
int indexOf(Object)	Returns the index of the first occurrence of an object or –1 if the object is not in the list.
int lastIndexOf(Object)	Returns the index of the last occurrence of an object or –1 if the object is not in the list.
ListIterator listIterator()	Returns a ListIterator over the elements of the list. A ListIterator differs from a simple iterator in that it allows a list to be traversed in forward and backward directions and supports replacing and adding elements instead of just removing them.
ListIterator listIterator(int)	Returns a ListIterator over the elements of the list beginning at a particular index.
Object remove(int)	Removes the element at a particular position.
Object set(int, Object)	Replaces the element at a position with a new element. The old element is returned.
List subList(int, int)	Returns a list consisting of the elements of the list between a start index and an end index. The returned list is backed by the original list, so changes made to the sublist are reflected in the original list.

Set

A Set is a Collection with no duplicate elements. Set does not add any new operations to Collection.

SortedSet

A `SortedSet` is a `Set` whose elements are ordered according to a comparison method. If the elements implement the `Comparable` interface, the natural ordering of elements may be used; otherwise, an instance of `Comparator` that can order any two elements must be provided at `Set` creation time. Table 13-4 shows the operations specific to `SortedSet`.

Table 13-4 SortedSet Operations

Method	Description
`Comparator comparator()`	Returns the instance of `Comparator` associated with the set, or `null` if the set uses the natural ordering of its elements.
`Object first()`	Returns the element of the set that comes first in the set's ordering.
`SortedSet headSet(Object)`	Returns a set of all the elements of the set that come before a specific object in the ordering. The returned set is backed by the original set, so changes to the returned set are reflected in the original set.
`Object last()`	Returns the element of the set that comes last in the set's ordering.
`SortedSet subSet(Object, Object)`	Returns a set of all the elements in the set that fall between two objects in the set's ordering. The returned set is backed by the original set, so changes to the returned set are reflected in the original set.
`SortedSet tailSet(Object)`	Returns a set of all the elements of the set that come after a specific object in the ordering. The returned set is backed by the original set, so changes to the returned set are reflected in the original set.

SortedMap

A `SortedMap` is a map whose elements are ordered according to a comparison method. If the elements implement the `Comparable` interface, the natural ordering of elements may be used; otherwise, an instance of `Comparator` that can order any two elements must be provided at `Map` creation time. The operations specific to `SortedMap` are shown in Table 13-5.

Table 13-5 Sorted Map Operations

Method	Description
`Comparator comparator()`	Returns the instance of `Comparator` associated with the set, or `null` if the set uses the natural ordering of its elements.
`Object firstKey()`	Returns the key of the map that comes first in the map's ordering.
`SortedMap headMap(Object)`	Returns a map of all the entries of the map whose keys come before a specific key in the ordering. The returned map is backed by the original map, so changes to the returned map are reflected in the original map.
`Object lastKey()`	Returns the key of the map that comes last in the map's ordering.
`SortedMap subMap(Object, Object)`	Returns a map of all the entries in the map whose keys fall between two keys in the map's ordering. The returned map is backed by the original map, so changes to the returned map are reflected in the original map.
`SortedMap tailMap(Object)`	Returns a map of all the entries of the map whose keys come after a specific key in the ordering. The returned map is backed by the original map, so changes to the returned map are reflected in the original map.

Tips

Once you understand the `Collection`, `List`, `Set`, `Map`, `SortedSet`, and `SortedMap` interfaces, you know basically how to use the Java collection classes. The remaining questions revolve around the selection of specific concrete classes that implement the interfaces. For the most part, they differ only in the relative efficiencies of various operations. Here are some guidelines to keep in mind.

- For lists, `ArrayList` supports constant time access to elements and high-speed searching via `Collections.binarySearch()` but performs badly if many elements need to be added or deleted anywhere except at the end.

- `LinkedList` supports efficient addition or deletion but requires time, proportional to the length of the list, for element access.

- For sets and maps, `HashSet` and `HashMap` are clear winners, as long as there is no requirement that the elements be ordered; otherwise, `TreeSet` and `TreeMap` are appropriate.

- The `Hashtable` and `Vector` classes are largely obsoleted by the new `HashMap` and `ArrayList` classes. They differ in being implicitly synchronized (we'll see how to synchronize arbitrary `Collections` and `Maps` later) and in not allowing null elements. While implicit synchronization is sometimes convenient, it's arguably a bug that nulls are not supported.

The WeakHashMap Class

One subclass of `Map` deserves its own section: the `WeakHashMap` class. It's only useful in very special circumstances; yet, when appropriate, it is extremely useful. A `WeakHashMap` is a `Map` whose values are stored via a `WeakReference`. This means that any value in the map that is not referred to by an object outside the map will be garbage collected. Why would you want this behavior? A common example is a cache for an object database system. Queries return object instances with identity. If multiple queries return the same row from the database, they should return the same instance. This constraint is usually dealt with via a hash table that maps database keys to objects. However, a simple hash table has the unfortunate property that it will hold on to its entries even if nobody holds references to them. This property can lead to an enormous waste of space if an application performs a query, manipulates the returned objects, and finishes with them. They never leave the hash table. If a `WeakHashMap` is used instead, any entries for an object will be removed when the object has no more references.

Using Collections — Large Strings

To demonstrate many of the uses of the Java collection classes, we'll create string classes that perform well in the areas in which the Java `String` class performs poorly—modifications and equality testing for large strings. In particular, our classes will support concatenating strings containing millions of characters in a reasonable time, and one of the classes will implement equality testing as a pointer comparison. The string classes will implement the `java.util.List` interface so that they can be treated as a *list* of characters. We'll also show how to

create a new `List` class by extending the `java.util.AbstractList` class. As
you go through the example, notice that we make use of numerous classes and
features mentioned previously in this chapter, including the
`java.util.LinkedList`, `java.util.ListIterator`, and the
`java.util.WeakHashMap` classes.

First, here are some usage examples:

```
CharList cl  = new CharList("All work");
CharList cl2 = new CharList(" and no play");
CharList cl3 = new CharList(" makes Jack a dull boz.");
cl.addAll(cl2);
cl.addAll(cl3);
// Whoops, not a "boz"...
cl.set(cl.size() - 2, 'y');
// Make 1024 copies, (easier than typing them...)
for (int i = 0; i < 10; i++) {
    cl.addAll(cl);
}
```

Figure 13-5 shows the high-level structure of instances of our string classes—the `collections.CharList` class and the `collections.UniqueCharList` class.

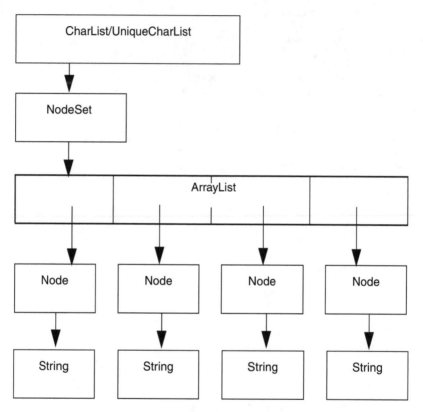

Figure 13-5 Collection Example

Each node contains a string with start and end offsets. Below a threshold string size value, adds, sets, and removes are done by replacing the individual string values referred to by nodes. Above the threshold, nodes are split into pieces. Figure 13-6 shows node relationships when a string is inserted in the middle of a node that is larger than the threshold value.

1

A node is made up of a string, start offset, and end offset.

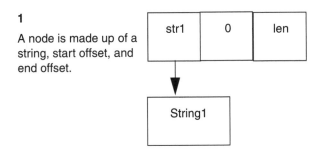

2

When a string is inserted, the nodes maintain this relationship.

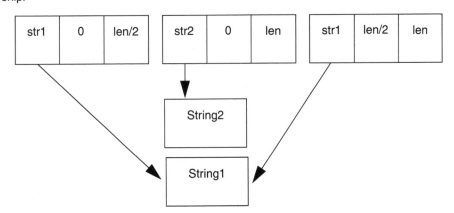

Figure 13-6 Inserting a String

Figure 13-7 shows the node relationships when a string of length n is removed from the middle of a node that is larger than the threshold value.

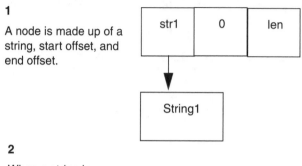

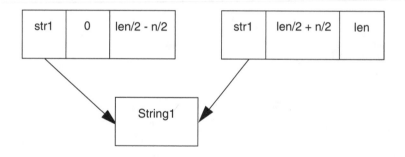

Figure 13-7 Removing a String

Collections Package Classes

There are six classes in our string example:

- `collections.CharList` — The main class representing a list of characters. The `CharList` class extends the `java.util.AbstractList` class and provides all the necessary `List` operations as well as an extended set of bulk operations. As we'll observe, one of the useful things about the Java collection classes is how much of an implementation can be inherited from the existing classes. Since this class represents a list of characters, all the normal `List` operations provided work on individual characters. These operations have been augmented with operations that work on strings, so that an entire string or CharList may be added, set, removed, etc.

- collections.UniqueCharList — The class representing strings that have been *canonicalized*. That is, each unique string value is represented only once by the UniqueCharList class. All UniqueCharList instances that represent the same string share the same NodeSet (see Figure 13-6). When a UniqueCharList is modified, a new NodeSet is created for it. The NodeSet is looked up in a WeakHashMap, and, if an existing NodeSet contains the same characters, the existing set is used in its place. A WeakHashMap is used so that canonical NodeSets are not needlessly kept around when no one is referring to them. Using UniqueCharLists reduces the space required to store CharLists and allows equality testing via a pointer comparison on NodeSets at the cost of slowing down modifications.

- collections.Canonicalizer — The class that is a wrapper around a WeakHashMap. The wrapper is necessary because a standard WeakHashMap is ineffective when the contained values hold references to their keys. Values in a WeakHashMap are held by strong references, so, if they refer to their keys, the keys (and values) will never be garbage collected. Our Canonicalizer class stores its values in explicit WeakReference objects so that both the keys and values may be reclaimed if they are not referenced from outside the Canonicalizer.

- collections.CharList.NodeSet — The class that contains the bulk of the implementation for a CharList. A NodeSet maintains a List of Node objects and character offsets for the starts of each node.

- collections.CharList.Node — A simple class that maintains a reference to a string along with start and end positions. Methods are provided for fetching characters and creating new nodes with portions added, removed, or modified.

- collections.CharList.CharIterator — A class that allows the characters in a CharList to be generated in order.

The CharList Class

The CharList class (Example 13-1) represents strings that are optimized for modifications. The strings are built out of chunks that are strung together. When the chunks are above a threshold size, changes to the string consist of adding chunks and splitting chunks. Many operations are inherited from the java.util.AbstractList class, including all iteration support and indexing operations.

Example 13-1 collections.CharList Class

```java
package collections;

import java.util.List;
import java.util.ArrayList;
import java.util.LinkedList;
import java.util.AbstractList;
import java.util.ListIterator;
import java.util.Iterator;
import java.util.Collection;
import java.util.NoSuchElementException;

public class CharList extends AbstractList {
  // Create a CharList with a string as initial contents.

  public CharList(String s) {
    this();
    add(0, s);
  }

  // Create a CharList with another CharList as initial contents.
  public CharList(CharList c) {
    this();
    addAll(c);
  }

  // Create an empty CharList.
  public CharList() {
    nodeset = new NodeSet(new ArrayList());
  }

  // Return the number of characters in the CharList. Part of the
  // List interface.
  public int size() {
    return nodeset.size();
  }

  // Is the number of characters zero? Part of the
  // List interface.
  public boolean isEmpty() {
    return size() == 0;
  }

  // Fetch the Character at a particular index. This is done using
  // a binary search based on the initial character offsets of the
  // nodes in the CharList. Part of the List interface.
  public Object get(int index) {
```

```
    return nodeset.get(index);
}

// Fetch the char value at a particular index. This is done using
// a binary search based on the initial character offsets of the
// nodes in the CharList.
public char getChar(int index) {
  return nodeset.getChar(index);
}

// Store a char value at a particular index.
public char set(int index, char value) {
  return ((Character)set(index,
         new Character(value))).charValue();
}

// Store a Character, a String, or a CharList at a particular
// index. This method is an extended part of the List interface.
// The normal List interface would only support storing individual
// items (i.e. Characters), but we have extended it to support bulk
// set operations.

public Object set(int index, Object element) {

  // Allow any object to be stored as a string.

  String s      = element.toString();
  Object result = get(index);

  // By default, we assume the new entry will be in a Node by
  // itself.

  Node newNode = new Node(s);
  nodeset      = getNodeSetToEdit(nodeset).set(index, newNode);
  return result;
}

// Insert a Character, a String, or a CharList at a particular
// index.
// This method is an extended part of the List Interface.

public void add(int index, Object element) {

  // If we're inserting another CharList, use an optimized routine
  // that works at the Node level rather than the Character or
  // String level.

  if (element instanceof CharList) {
```

```
    addAll(index, (CharList)element);
  }

  // Allow any object to be added as a string.

  String s      = element.toString();
  Node newNode = new Node(s);
  nodeset       = getNodeSetToEdit(nodeset).add(index, newNode);
}

// Remove a single Character from a CharList. Part of the List
// interface.

public Object remove(int index) {
  Object result = get(index);
  nodeset        = getNodeSetToEdit(nodeset).remove(index);
  return result;
}

// Add all the items from another Collection to the CharList.
// This could be inherited from AbstractList, but we want to allow
// concatenation of a CharList with itself. The default
// AbstractList.addAll() operation does not support adding a
// Collection to itself. Part of the List interface.

public boolean addAll(Collection c) {
  return addAll(size(), c);
}

// Insert all the items from another Collection into the CharList.
// If the other Collection is itself a CharList, it is handled as
// a special case. Returns true if the CharList was modified. In
// the case of a List Collection (as opposed to a Set), this will
// always be true unless the added Collection is empty. Part of
// the List interface.

public boolean addAll(int index, Collection c) {

  // If we're not adding a CharList, use the method derived from
  // AbstractList. If the index is out of range, let the
  // AbstractList method generate the error.

  if (!(c instanceof CharList) || index < 0 || index > size()) {
    return super.addAll(index, c);
  }

  // If the added Collection is empty, do nothing and return false.
```

```
  if (c.size() == 0) {
     return false;
  }

  // If a CharList is being added, add its nodes directly without
  // extracting the characters first.

  CharList cl          = (CharList)c;
  NodeSet currentNodes = nodeset;
  NodeSet clNodes      = cl.nodeset;

  nodeset = currentNodes.insertNodes(index, clNodes);
  return true;
}

// Two CharLists are equal if their NodeSets are equal.
public boolean equals(Object o) {
  if (o == null || !(o instanceof CharList)) {
     return false;
  }

  return nodeset.equals(((CharList)o).nodeset);
}

// When we build a contiguous string, we replace the existing
// nodes with a single node containing the entire string.
public String toString() {
  nodeset = nodeset.flatten();
  return nodeset.getNodeString(0);
}

// The following set of methods declared "protected" are to be
// used in the implementation of CharList subclasses.
// Return the current nodeset.
protected NodeSet getNodeSet() {
  return nodeset;
}

// Replace the current nodeset.
protected void setNodeSet(NodeSet set) {
  nodeset = set;
}

// Return the set of nodes to manipulate on a modification. This
// method can be overridden in a subclass to copy the nodes,
// allowing nodesets to be shared.
protected NodeSet getNodeSetToEdit(NodeSet n) {
  return n;
```

```
    }

    // The NodeSet class encapsulates all node-level manipulations.
    // It contains an ArrayList of Node objects and an integer array
    // of offsets. Each offset is the character position of the
    // beginning of a node. A get() operation finds a character by
    // performing a binary search on the offset array. All NodeSet
    // node operations begin with a call to
    // CharList.getNodeSetToEdit(), which returns the set of nodes to
    // operate on. In the base CharList class, this returns the
    // NodeSet argument. In the derived class UniqueCharList, it
    // returns a copy of the NodeSet.

    protected static class NodeSet implements Cloneable {
      // The equality test for a NodeSet iterates through its
      // characters and the characters of the other NodeSet
      // comparing each for equality.
      public boolean equals(Object o) {
        if (o == null || !(o instanceof NodeSet)) {
          return false;
        }

        NodeSet other = (NodeSet)o;
        int mySize  = size();
        int otherSize = other.size();

        // If the NodeSets do not contain the same number of
        // characters, they're not equal.

        if (mySize != otherSize) {
          return false;
        }

        // Use CharIterators to generate successive characters to
        // compare.
        CharIterator i1 = new CharIterator(this);
        CharIterator i2 = new CharIterator(other);
          while (i1.hasNext()) {
            if (i1.next() != i2.next()) {
              return false;
            }
          }
          return true;
      }

        // Generate a hash code for the NodeSet. Since CharLists are
        // intended to potentially grow to great length, we don't
        // incorporate every character into the hash. We use
```

```
// characters from the front, characters from the end, and a
// character from the middle. We use the same hash generation
// mechanism that java.lang.String does.

public int hashCode() {
    int count = 0;
    int code = 0;
    int numNodes = nodes.size();
    int numChars = size();

    // Iterate over HALF_HASH_MAX characters from the front of
    // the string updating the code. Loop for each node and
    // each character within a node.

    for (int i = 0; i < numNodes; i++) {
        String nodeString = getNode(i).toString();
        int nodeLength  = nodeString.length();

        for (int j = 0; j < nodeLength; j++) {
            code = 31 * code + nodeString.charAt(j);

            if (count++ > HALF_HASH_MAX) {
                break;
            }
        }
    }
    count = 0;

    // Iterate over HALF_HASH_MAX characters from the end of
    // the string updating the code. Loop for each node and
    // each character within a node.

    for (int i = numNodes - 1; i >= 0; i--) {
        String nodeString = getNode(i).toString();
        int nodeLength  = nodeString.length();
        for (int j = nodeLength - 1; j >= 0; j--) {
            code = 31 * code + nodeString.charAt(j);

            if (count++ > HALF_HASH_MAX) {
                break;
            }
        }
    }

    // Grab a character from the middle of the string and
    // update the code.

    if (numChars > HASH_MAX) {
```

```
            code = 31 * code + getChar(numChars / 2);
        }

        return code;
    }

    // Create a copy of a NodeSet.

    protected Object clone() {
        return new NodeSet(
            (List)((ArrayList)nodes).clone(),
            (int[])offsets.clone(),
            offsetLength);
    }

    // Create a new NodeSet containing a specified set of nodes.
    protected NodeSet(List nodes) {
        this.nodes = nodes;

        // Calculate the character offsets for each node.

        computeOffsets();

        // If the average node size is too small for the size of
        // the CharList, merge small nodes together.

        coalesce();
    }

    // Flatten a NodeSet into a single node. This method is used
    // to generate a java.lang.String from a NodeSet.

    protected NodeSet flatten() {
        int numNodes = nodeCount();

        // If we're already a single node, just return a copy.

        if (numNodes == 1) {
            return (NodeSet)clone();
        }

        // Build a single String by appending each node into a
        // StringBuffer.

        StringBuffer buf = new StringBuffer();

            for (int i = 0; i < numNodes; i++) {
                buf.append(getNodeString(i));
```

```
            }

        // Get a new interned string from the StringBuffer.

        String s = buf.toString().intern();

        // Create a new NodeSet containing a single Node.

        ArrayList nodes = new ArrayList();
        nodes.add(new Node(s));
        return new NodeSet(nodes);
    }

    // Return the string contained in a particular node.

    protected String getNodeString(int index) {
        return getNode(index).toString();
    }

    // Create a new NodeSet specifying all required values.

    private NodeSet(
        List nodes,
        int[] offsets,
        int offsetLength
    )
    {
        this.nodes          = nodes;
        this.offsets        = offsets;
        this.offsetLength   = offsetLength;

    // If the number of characters in the CharList is small
    // compared to the number of nodes in the CharList, merge
    // small nodes together.

        coalesce();
}

// Return a Character object containing the char value at a
// particular index.

private Object get(int index) {
    return new Character(getChar(index));
}

// Return the char value at a particular index.

private char getChar(int index) {
```

```
    // If we only have one node, don't bother binary searching to
    // find the node index.

    if (nodes.size() == 1) {
        return getNode(0).getChar(index);
    }

    // Binary search to find the node index.

    int nodeIndex = getNodeIndex(index);
    checkBounds(nodeIndex);

    // Fetch the character taking the offset of the current node
    // into account.

    return getNode(nodeIndex).getChar(index -
                        offsets[nodeIndex]);
    }

    // Return the number of characters in the NodeSet.

    private int size() {
        if (nodeCount() == 0) {
            return 0;
        }

    // The size is the last node offset plus the length of the
    // last node.

    int lastIndex = nodeCount() - 1;
    int result  = offsets[lastIndex] + getNode(lastIndex).size();
    return result;
    }

// Return the number of nodes.
private int nodeCount() {
    return nodes.size();
}

// Remove the character at a particular index. If the node
// containing the character is larger than the split
// threshold, split it in two at the position of the removed
// character; otherwise, create a new node without the removed
// character.

private NodeSet remove(int index) {
    // Find the node containing the character.
```

```
    int nodeIndex = getNodeIndex(index);
    checkBounds(nodeIndex);

    Node currentNode= getNode(nodeIndex);
    int currentNodeSize= currentNode.size();

    // Find the character offset within the node.

    int nodeCharIndex = index - offsets[nodeIndex];

    if (currentNodeSize == 1) {

    // If we're pointing at a node with only a single character,
    // just remove it.

    nodes.remove(nodeCharIndex);
    } else if (currentNodeSize > currentSplitThreshold()) {
        // If we're in the middle of a large node, split it at
        // the character position into two nodes minus the
        // character in the middle.

        List splitNodes = splitWithHole(currentNode,
                    nodeCharIndex, 1);

        // Use a "set" followed by an "add" so the ArrayList will
        // only have to adjust positions for other nodes once. If
        // we removed the existing node and added two more we would
        // require more adjustments.

        nodes.set(nodeIndex, splitNodes.get(0));
        nodes.add(nodeIndex + 1, splitNodes.get(1));

    } else {
        // The current node is too small to split. Replace it with
        // a new node.
        nodes.set(
            nodeIndex,
            currentNode.copyWithDelete(nodeCharIndex));
    }

    computeOffsets(nodeIndex);
    return this;
}

// Replace multiple characters in a CharList with a new string.
private NodeSet set(int index, Node n) {
    // Find the node containing the character.
```

```
int nodeIndex = getNodeIndex(index);
checkBounds(nodeIndex);

// Extract information about the original node.

Node original    = getNode(nodeIndex);
int newStrLen    = n.size();
int nodeCharIndex = index - offsets[nodeIndex];

// Find how much room is available in the current node. If
// the new string is larger than the current node, we'll have
// to alter other nodes as well.

int spaceRemaining = original.size() - nodeCharIndex;
String origString  = getNodeString(nodeIndex);

// If we're replacing characters in the last node in the
// CharList and the new string is too big, we can replace
// the node with a new node containing its original contents
// plus the new string.

if (nodeIndex == nodes.size() - 1) {
    StringBuffer buf = new StringBuffer();
    buf.append(origString.substring(0, nodeCharIndex));
    buf.append(n.str);

    if (newStrLen < spaceRemaining) {
        // If the new string fits in a single node,
        // just do the overwrite.
        buf.append(origString.substring(
            nodeCharIndex + newStrLen));
    }

    String s = buf.toString().intern();
    nodes.set(nodeIndex, new Node(s));
    computeOffsets(nodeIndex);
    return this;
}

// If the new string is too large to fit within the existing
// node, spread it across multiple nodes.

if (newStrLen > spaceRemaining) {
    String nodeString = n.toString();

    // First, replace the current node with a new node
    // containing the new string at the specified index.
```

```
nodes.set(nodeIndex,
    original.copyWithReplace(
        nodeCharIndex,
        nodeString.substring(0, spaceRemaining)));

// Chop off the portion of the new string that was
// placed in the first node.

newStrLen -= spaceRemaining;
nodeString = nodeString.substring(spaceRemaining);

// For each remaining node, while we still have
// characters to add, create a new node with the
// minimum of the length of the remaining new text and
// the size of the current node.

while (++nodeIndex < nodes.size()) {
    Node current = getNode(nodeIndex);

    // Calculate how much of the new string goes in
    // this node.

    int substringLen = Math.min(newStrLen,
                    current.size());

    // Replace the current node.

    nodes.set(nodeIndex,
        current.copyWithReplace(
            0,
            nodeString.substring(0, substringLen)));

    // Chop off the portion of the new string that was
    // placed in the current node.

    newStrLen -= current.size();
    nodeString = nodeString.substring(substringLen);

    // If we've run out of new string, quit.

    if (newStrLen < 0) {
        break;
    }
}

// If there's any leftover new string when we run out
// of nodes, add a new node containing the rest of the
// new string.
```

```
        if (newStrLen > 0) {
            nodes.add(new Node(nodeString));
        }

        computeOffsets(nodeIndex);
        return this;
    }

    // If the new string fits entirely within a node, either
    // split the node and insert a new node or replace the
    // existing node depending on whether or not the existing
    // node's size exceeds the split threshold.

    if (original.size() > currentSplitThreshold()) {
        // If the current node is big enough to split, split it
        // into two nodes, leaving out the portion being replaced.

        List splitNodes = splitWithHole(
            original,
            nodeCharIndex,
            newStrLen);

        // We minimize the number of node position adjustments for
        // the NodeSet by replacing the current node with the first
        // of three new nodes, then building up a small ArrayList
        // out of the other two nodes so we can do an addAll(),
        // which will insert both the nodes with only one
        // adjustment.

        nodes.set(nodeIndex, splitNodes.get(0));
        splitNodes.set(0, n);
        nodes.addAll(nodeIndex + 1, splitNodes);
        computeOffsets(nodeIndex);
        return this;
    }

    // If the new string fits in a node and the node is too small
    // to split, just replace the node.

    nodes.set(
        nodeIndex,
        getNode(nodeIndex).copyWithReplace(
            index - offsets[nodeIndex],
            n));

    computeOffsets(nodeIndex);
    return this;
```

```
}

// Insert a string into a NodeSet at a particular index. If
// the new string falls immediately before a node or at the
// end of the NodeSet, just add a new node. If the string
// falls in the middle of a node, either split it or replace
// it, depending on the size of the existing node.

private NodeSet add(int index, Node n) {
    // Find the node containing the character unless the new
    // string is being added at the end of the NodeSet.

    int nodeIndex = -1;

    if (index == size()) {
        nodeIndex = nodes.size();
    } else {
        nodeIndex = getNodeIndex(index);
    }

    checkBounds(nodeIndex);

    if (nodeIndex >= nodes.size()) {
        // If we're adding at the end.

        nodes.add(n);
        computeOffsets(nodeIndex);
        return this;
    }

    Node currentNode = getNode(nodeIndex);

    // Find the add position within an existing node.

    int nodeCharIndex = index - offsets[nodeIndex];

    if (currentNode.size() <= currentSplitThreshold()) {
        // The current node is too small to split.

        nodes.set(
            nodeIndex,
            currentNode.copyWithInsert(nodeCharIndex, n));
    } else if (index == offsets[nodeIndex]) {
        // If the new node immediately precedes another node,
        // just add it in without affecting the other nodes.

        nodes.add(nodeIndex, n);
```

```
    } else {
       // We're in the middle of a big node, so split it in two.

       List splitNodes = split(currentNode, nodeCharIndex);

       nodes.set(nodeIndex, splitNodes.get(0));
       splitNodes.set(0, n);
       nodes.addAll(nodeIndex + 1, splitNodes);
    }

    computeOffsets(nodeIndex);
    return this;
}

// Insert a CharList into a NodeSet at a particular index. If
// the new CharList falls immediately before a node or at the
// end of the NodeSet, just add the new nodes. If the CharList
// falls in the middle of a node, split it and add the new nodes
// in the middle.
private NodeSet insertNodes(int index, NodeSet other) {
    // If we're adding at the end, just add the new nodes.

    if (index == size()) {
       int lastNodeIndex = nodes.size() - 1;
       nodes.addAll(other.nodes);
       computeOffsets(lastNodeIndex);
       return this;
    }
    // Find the node into which we're inserting.

    int nodeIndex    = getNodeIndex(index);
    Node currentNode = getNode(nodeIndex);

    // If the new CharList falls immediately before a node,
    // just add the new nodes.

    if (index == offsets[nodeIndex]) {
       nodes.addAll(nodeIndex, other.nodes);
    } else {

       // Split the current node at the insertion position.
       int nodeCharIndex = index - offsets[nodeIndex];
       List splitNodes  = split(currentNode, nodeCharIndex);

       // Add the new nodes.

       nodes.set(nodeIndex, splitNodes.get(0));
       splitNodes.remove(0);
```

```
        splitNodes.addAll(0, other.nodes);
        nodes.addAll(nodeIndex + 1, splitNodes);
    }

    computeOffsets(nodeIndex);
    return this;
}
// Search for the node containing a character index by
// performing a binary search on the offset array.
private int getNodeIndex(int index) {
    int low   = 0;
    int high  = offsetLength - 1;

    while (low <= high) {
        // Start at the middle.

        int mid    = (low + high)/2;
        int offset = offsets[mid];

        // If the current offset is less than the index, the
        // character index might fall in the current node.
        // Check if the following offset is greater than the
        // character index.

        if (offset < index) {
            if (mid + 1 >= offsetLength ||
                offsets[mid + 1] > index) {
                return mid;
            }

            low = mid + 1;
        } else if (offset > index) {
            // If the current offset is greater than the index,
            // check if the previous offset is smaller than
            // the character index.

            if (mid - 1 <= 0 || offsets[mid - 1] < index) {
                return mid - 1;
            }

            high = mid - 1;
        } else {
            return mid;
        }
    }
    return high;
}
```

```
// Return the node at a particular index.
private Node getNode(int nodeIndex) {
   return (Node)nodes.get(nodeIndex);
}

// Split a node into two nodes, leaving out a piece in the middle.
// This is used to replace a segment of a node with a new node.

private List splitWithHole(Node n, int nodeCharIndex, int
                          holeSize) {
   String nodeString    = n.toString();
   List result          = new ArrayList();

   // Both the new nodes refer to the same original string.

   result.add(new Node(nodeString, 0, nodeCharIndex));
   result.add(
      new Node(
      nodeString,
      nodeCharIndex + holeSize,
      nodeString.length()));
   return result;
}

// Split a node in two with no gap in the middle. This is used
// to insert a new string within a node.
private List split(Node n, int nodeCharIndex) {
   return splitWithHole(n, nodeCharIndex, 0);
}

// If a CharList gets built out of an excessive number of very
// small nodes, merge some of the small nodes into larger ones
// to reduce the node count.

private void coalesce() {
   // Perform a quick check to see if it's worth the effort to
   // perform the manipulations.

   if (belowCoalesceThreshold()) {
      return;
   }

   // Create a LinkedList from the nodes so that our removals
   // won't require shifting the nodes around each time.

   List coalesceList = new LinkedList(nodes);
   int currentThreshold = currentSplitThreshold();
   ListIterator iter = coalesceList.listIterator();
```

```
int count = 0;
int firstAdjustIndex = -1;
int i;

// Iterate through the linked list, merging pairs of nodes
// that are small enough.

while ((i = iter.nextIndex()) < (coalesceList.size() - 1)) {
    // Stop one before the end.

    Node n1 = (Node)iter.next();
    Node n2 = (Node)iter.next();

    int sum = n1.size() + n2.size();

    if (sum <= currentThreshold) {
        // Track the first index at which we adjust so we
        // only recompute offsets for changed nodes.

        if (firstAdjustIndex == -1) {
            firstAdjustIndex = i;
        }

        // If the two current nodes together sum to less
        // than the current threshold, back up and remove
        // the second node, then back up again and replace
        // the first node with the new merged node.

        iter.previous();
        iter.remove();
        iter.previous();
        iter.set(n1.copyWithInsert(n1.size(), n2));

        // If we've done as much work as we're willing to
        // do in one operation, quit out.

        if (++count > MAX_COALESCE) {
            break;
        }
    }
}

// Turn the LinkedList back into an ArrayList and
// recompute node offsets.

nodes = new ArrayList(coalesceList);
computeOffsets(Math.max(firstAdjustIndex, 0));
}
```

```java
// See if the average node size is below a threshold based on
// the size of the CharList. If the CharList is large, we want
// to make sure we don't have an excessive number of nodes.
// Also, for small CharLists we want to avoid the situation
// where someone has added a lot of characters one at a time,
// producing one node per character.

private boolean belowCoalesceThreshold() {
   int charSize = size();
   int nodeSize = nodes.size();

   if (nodeSize < MIN_COALESCE_THRESHOLD) {
      return true;
   }

   return (nodeSize < charSize / NODE_ADJUSTMENT);
}

// Make sure the threshold for splitting a node is greater
// than twice the threshold for merging nodes so we don't
// oscillate.

private int currentSplitThreshold() {
   return (int)Math.max(
      MIN_SPLIT_THRESHOLD,
      (size() / NODE_ADJUSTMENT) * 2.5);
}

// Generate an exception for an index that is out of bounds. We
// always call this with a value returned by getNodeIndex().

private void checkBounds(int nodeIndex) {
   if (nodeIndex == -1) {
      throw new IndexOutOfBoundsException("Index: " + nodeIndex
         + ", Size: " + size());
   }
}

// Compute the character offsets for each node.

private void computeOffsets() {
   computeOffsets(0);
}

private void computeOffsets(int start) {
   offsetLength = nodes.size();
```

```
    if (offsets == null) {

        // If this is a fresh NodeSet, create a new offset array.

        offsets= new int[nodes.size()];
        start= 0;
    } else if (offsets.length < nodes.size()) {
        // If the number of nodes is greater than the size of
        // the offset array, create a new offset array at
        // least double the size of the existing array.

        int[] temp =
            new int[Math.max(offsets.length * 2, nodes.size())];
        System.arraycopy(
            offsets,
            0,
            temp,
            0,
            Math.min(offsets.length, start));
        offsets = temp;
    }

    // Loop through the nodes, incrementing the current offset
    // by the size of each node.

    int currentOffset =
        (start == 0
            ? 0
            : offsets[start - 1] + getNode(start - 1).size());

    for (int i = start; i < offsetLength; i++) {
        offsets[i]      = currentOffset;
        currentOffset += getNode(i).size();
    }
}

// Return the offset for a particular node.

private int getOffset(int nodeIndex) {
    return offsets[nodeIndex];
}

private List nodes = null;      // Set of nodes for the NodeSet
private int[] offsets = null;   // Set of offsets for the
                                // NodeSet.
private int offsetLength = 0;   // Number of slots in the offset
                                // array that are being used.
private static final int HASH_MAX        = 100;
```

```java
    private static final int HALF_HASH_MAX = HASH_MAX / 2;
}


// Return the node containing a particular character index.
private int getNodeIndex(int n) {
    return nodeset.getNodeIndex(n);
}


// The CharIterator class iterates through each node in the
// NodeSet and through each character in a node, returning them
// in succession. It includes a reset() method so that a higher
// level iterator can reset its state after a modification.

private static class CharIterator {
    // Create a new CharIterator starting at the beginning of the
    // NodeSet.

    private CharIterator(NodeSet n) {
        this.nodeset    = n;       // The NodeSet
        this.nodeIndex  = 0;       // Index of the current node
        this.charOffset = 0;       // Index of the current character
                                   // within the current node
        this.charIndex  = 0;       // Index of the current character
        this.end        = n.size(); // The maximum character index.

        if (charIndex < end) {
            this.currentNode = n.getNode(0);
        }
    }

    // Return true if we haven't reached the end.

    private boolean hasNext() {
        return charIndex < end;
    }

    // Return the next character in the NodeSet.

    private char next() {
        if (!hasNext()) {
            throw new NoSuchElementException();
        }

        // Get the character at the current character offset
        // within the current node.

        char c = currentNode.getChar(charOffset++);
```

```
        // Increment the current character count so we can easily
        // tell when we're done.

        charIndex++;

        // Move to the next node if necessary.

        if (hasNext() && charOffset >= currentNode.size()) {
            currentNode = nodeset.getNode(++nodeIndex);
            charOffset = 0;
        }

        return c;
    }

    // Provide a means of resetting all the internal variables
    // if a change to the NodeSet rearranges the nodes.

    private void reset(int newCharIndex) {
        this.charIndex = newCharIndex;
        this.nodeIndex = nodeset.getNodeIndex(newCharIndex);
        this.end       = nodeset.size();

        if (nodeIndex != -1) {
            this.charOffset = newCharIndex -
                        nodeset.getOffset(nodeIndex);
        }
    }
    privateNodeSet nodeset;       // The NodeSet
    private Node currentNode;  // The current node
    private int nodeIndex;     // Index of the current node
    private int charOffset;    // Index of the current character
                               // within the current node
    private int charIndex;     // Index of the current character
    private int end;           // The maximum character index.
}

// The Node class holds a String with start and end positions. It
// provides methods for copying nodes with insertions,
// replacements, and deletions.

private static class Node {
    // Return the string represented by a node.

    public String toString() {
        return str.substring(start, end);
    }
```

```java
// Fetch a Character object from a node.

private Character get(int index) {
    return new Character(getChar(index));
}

// Fetch a character from a node.

private char getChar(int index) {
    return str.charAt(start + index);
}

// Return the size of the string represented by a node.

private int size() {
    return end - start;
}

// Create a copy of a node with the string represented by
// another node inserted in the middle.

private Node copyWithInsert(int charIndex, Node n) {
    StringBuffer buf = new StringBuffer(str.substring(0,
                charIndex));
    buf.append(n.str);
    buf.append(str.substring(charIndex, str.length()));
    return new Node(buf.toString());
}
// Create a copy of a node with the string represented by
// another node replacing a substring.

private Node copyWithReplace(int charIndex, Node n) {
    return copyWithReplace(charIndex, n.toString());
}

// Create a copy of a node with a string replacing a substring.

private Node copyWithReplace(int charIndex, String s) {
    StringBuffer buf = new StringBuffer(str.substring(0,
                charIndex));
    buf.append(s);
    buf.append(str.substring(charIndex + s.length(),
                str.length()));
    return new Node(buf.toString());
}

// Create a copy of a node with a substring deleted.
```

```java
    private Node copyWithDelete(int charIndex) {
        StringBuffer buf = new StringBuffer(str.substring(0,
                        charIndex));
        buf.append(str.substring(charIndex + 1, str.length()));
        return new Node(buf.toString());
    }

    // Create a new node with start and end offsets.

    private Node(String str, int start, int end) {
        this.str   = str.intern();
        this.start = start;
        this.end   = end;
    }

    // Create a new node that represents a complete string.

    private Node(String str) {
        this.str   = str.intern();
        this.start = 0;
        this.end   = str.length();
    }

    String str;
    int start;
    int end;
}

private NodeSet nodeset = null;   // The NodeSet for a CharList

// The minimum length of a node to split
private static final int MIN_SPLIT_THRESHOLD = 100;

// The minimum number of nodes that must be present in a CharList
// to consider coalescing nodes
private static final int MIN_COALESCE_THRESHOLD = 100;

// The maximum number of coalesces to perform in a single pass
private static final int MAX_COALESCE = 50;

// The minimum ratio of characters to nodes that initiates
// coalescence.
private static final int NODE_ADJUSTMENT = 10;
}
```

UniqueCharList Class

The UniqueCharList class (Example 13-2) extends CharList with an additional property. Any two UniqueCharLists that represent the same string will share the same NodeSet object. This extension enables extremely fast equality checking even for large strings. It also minimizes the space required to store a set of CharLists. The operations on UniqueCharList operate by invoking the basic CharList operations and then running the NodeSet through a canonicalizing transformation.

Example 13-2 collections.UniqueCharList

```java
package collections;

import java.util.List;
import java.util.ArrayList;
import java.util.LinkedList;
import java.util.AbstractList;
import java.util.ListIterator;
import java.util.Collection;

public class UniqueCharList extends CharList {
  // Create a UniqueCharList with a string as initial contents.

  public UniqueCharList(String s) {
    this();
    add(0, s);
  }

  // Create a UniqueCharList with another CharList as initial
  // contents.

  public UniqueCharList(CharList c) {
    this();
    addAll(c);
  }

  // Create an empty UniqueCharList.

  public UniqueCharList() {
    setNodeSet(this.new NodeSet(new ArrayList()));
    canonicalize();
  }

  // Store a Character, a String, or a CharList at a particular
  // index. This method is an extended part of the List interface.
  // The normal List interface would only support storing individual
```

```
// items (i.e. Characters), but we have extended it to support bulk
// set operations. Invoke the method defined in CharList, then
// canonicalize the current NodeSet.

public Object set(int index, Object element) {
  Object result = super.set(index, element);
  canonicalize();
  return result;
}


// Insert a Character, a String, or a CharList at a particular
// index. This method is an extended part of the List Interface.
// Invoke the method defined in CharList, then canonicalize the
// current NodeSet.

public void add(int index, Object element) {
  super.add(index, element);
  canonicalize();
}


// Remove a single Character from a UniqueCharList. Part of the
// List interface. Invoke the method defined in CharList, then
// canonicalize the current NodeSet.

public Object remove(int index) {
  Object result = super.remove(index);
  canonicalize();
  return result;
}


// Add all the items from another Collection to the UniqueCharList.

public boolean addAll(int index, Collection c) {
  boolean result = super.addAll(index, c);

  if (result) {
    canonicalize();
  }

  return result;
}


// Since all equal UniqueCharLists share a common NodeSet, just
// compare the NodeSets for pointer equality.

public boolean equals(Object o) {
  if (o == null || !(o instanceof UniqueCharList)) {
    return false;
```

```
      }

    return getNodeSet() == ((UniqueCharList)o).getNodeSet();
  }

  // Create a String from the UniqueCharList by merging the
  // strings from all the nodes into a single node.

  public String toString() {
    return getNodeSet().flatten().getNodeString(0);
  }

  // Since NodeSets are shared for UniqueCharLists, copy the
  // existing ArrayList of nodes before modifying. The method in
  // CharList simply returns the current set of nodes.

  protected List createNewNodeArray() {
    return (List)((ArrayList)getNodes()).clone();
  }

  // Run the current NodeSet through a canonicalizer so that
  // we are referencing a shared NodeSet.

  private void canonicalize() {
    setNodeSet((NodeSet)canonicalizer.canonicalize(getNodeSet()));
  }
  private static Canonicalizer canonicalizer = new Canonicalizer();
}
```

Canonicalizer Class

The `Canonicaliser` class (Example 13-3) represents a *canonicalizing transformation* on objects. When `canonicalize()` is called on an object, a unique object equal to the argument is returned. The returned value may or may not be the same object that was passed in. As long as any other reachable object in the system maintains a strong reference to a canonicalized object, it will persist. Any two objects in the system that hold references to canonicalized versions of equal objects will refer to the same object.

Example 13-3 collections.Canonicalizer

```
package collections;

import java.lang.ref.WeakReference;
import java.util.WeakHashMap;

public class Canonicalizer {
  // Return a canonicalized reference. Ensure that any two objects
```

```
// that hold canonicalized references to equal objects refer to
// the same canonicalized object.

public synchronized Object canonicalize(Object o) {
  // See if there is already a canonicalized version of the object.

WeakReference wr  = (WeakReference)hash.get(o);
Object refVal     = null;

  // If the weak reference is not null, a canonicalized version
  // once existed but may have been garbage collected. Check
  // to see if the reference has been cleared.

  if (wr != null) {
     refVal = wr.get();
  }

  if (refVal == null) {
     // If there was no entry or the reference was cleared,
     // remove the old reference and add a new weak reference
     // to the argument object. It will become the canonicalized
     // version.

     hash.remove(o);
     hash.put(o, new WeakReference(o));
     return o;
  }else {
     return refVal;
  }
}

  private WeakHashMap hash = new WeakHashMap();
}
```

Summary

- Until the release of JDK 1.2, Java provided very few collection classes, resulting in a significant overuse of the `Vector` class, even in situations where it is inefficient.

- The JDK 1.2 provides a set of classes that implement the vast majority of commonly used data structures. These provide standard implementations of linked lists, balanced trees, sets, and more.

- These classes also provide a framework that supports the easy creation of new collections that can be used in a consistent way.

- The major collection classes fall into two groups:

  - Simple collections of elements such as lists and sets
  - Mappings between pairs of elements such as hash tables

- `WeakHashMap` implements `Map` and stores values via a `WeakReference`. This means that any value in the map that is not referred to by an object outside the map will be garbage collected.

CHAPTER
14

Reflection

In this chapter, we explore *reflection* in Java, including when its use is appropriate and, just as importantly, when it is not. As we shall see, many situations that might intuitively call for Java reflection can be addressed effectively with other Java features. When the need does arise, however, reflection support in Java is a powerful tool; we will work through an extended example of how to use it.

From Whence It Came

Java occupies a somewhat unique position among programming languages. It is half static and half dynamic. By static, we mean that it has strong compile-time type checking like C++. By dynamic, we mean that it has runtime types and garbage collection like Lisp or Smalltalk. These dynamic features have attracted many people from the dynamic language communities, who view Java as a language that is both reasonable—unlike C++—and viable.

This has been a positive trend. The C/C++ community has benefited from the influx of novel programming approaches, and the dynamic language communities have benefited from a wealth of new opportunities. As Java has evolved, more dynamic features have entered the language, no doubt influenced by dynamic language advocates. Reflection is one such feature.

Reflection in a programming language context refers to the ability to observe and/or manipulate the inner workings of the environment programmatically. The name is derived from the action of *reflecting* the environment into the space manipulated by a program.

Reflective capabilities in programming languages span a broad spectrum. On one end of the spectrum, you could view something as simple as determining the type of an object at runtime to be a form of reflection, because many language implementations maintain runtime type information for objects that they do not expose in the language. The "vtables" in a C++ implementation would be one such example.

On the opposite end of the spectrum, consider languages with "meta-object protocols" or MOPs. These languages actually allow programmers to assist in choosing the physical layouts of objects and the behavior of method invocation.

Java falls somewhere between these two extremes. It does not allow programmers to alter the behavior of the system itself, but it does allow them to directly observe and invoke the object creation, method invocation, and field access mechanisms. This access is enabled by *reflecting* classes, fields, methods, and constructors into the domain of objects that can be manipulated from Java. Objects that represent classes have always existed in the form of instances of `java.lang.Class`, although some new methods have been added to the JDK for this purpose. New classes representing fields, methods, and constructors have been added in the `java.lang.reflect` package.

Uses of Reflection

Reflection is called for when information about an object's type is not available at compile time. This situation is very uncommon. We're not talking about simply not knowing an object's specific type. Even when its specific type is unknown, a great deal can be known about an object's type. In most situations, what's important about an object's type is whether or not the object supports some set of operations. If one wants to print an object, all that's important is that it support a `toString()` method. The specific type of the object doesn't matter. This sort of dynamism is easily supported by Java's class inheritance and interface mechanisms. If you think about it, you almost always know in advance what sort of operations you want to perform on an object. After all, you generally write code to do particular things.

So, when do you really not know anything about the objects you'll be manipulating? When are you not told the operations you'll be performing until runtime? Generally, these cases occur when you are writing meta-applications. By meta-applications, we mean applications that deal with the features objects possess by virtue of being Java objects. For example, in an application dealing with vehicles, the description of a particular vehicle might include its fuel requirements, horsepower, number of wheels, and so on. In a meta-application, the description of a particular item includes its methods, fields, and supported interfaces. Note that even the objects in our vehicular example can be described at this level, but it's usually not interesting to do so.

Okay, so what are these meta-applications? The most common types are interpreters and debuggers—applications in which a user needs to invoke arbitrary operations on arbitrary objects at runtime. These applications need to be able to determine which operations are valid for an unknown object and to invoke those operations dynamically.

Even most interpreters and debuggers do not actually require the use of reflection. If someone writes an interpreter or debugger for some other language in Java, reflection is generally not needed. It's only when you want to interpret or debug Java itself that reflection comes into play. Without using reflection, you need to emulate the entire Java Virtual Machine in order to create a Java interpreter or debugger. Using reflection, you can easily take advantage of the built-in virtual machine.

When Not to Use Reflection

It's a common error for programmers new to reflection to try to use it like function pointer in C. Here's an example:

```
import java.lang.reflect.*;
import java.util.Vector;

// Search a vector for an item that satisfies a specified constraint.
// Use reflection to apply a user-specified boolean method to each
// element. Return the index of a matched item or -1 if no match.

public class RefSearcher {

  public static int search(
    Vector items,
    Method searchMethod
  ) throws Exception
  {
      Class returnType   = searchMethod.getReturnType();
      Class[] paramTypes = searchMethod.getParameterTypes();

      if (!returnType.equals(Boolean.TYPE) ||
```

```
                paramTypes.length != 1 ||
                !paramTypes[0].equals(Object.class)) {
                throw new Exception("RefSearcher -- Invalid method: " +
                    searchMethod);
            }

        int count = items.size();

        for (int i = 0; i < count; i++) {
        // Use reflection to invoke the search method.

        boolean result =
            ((Boolean)searchMethod.invoke(
                null, // A static method
                new Object[] { items.elementAt(i) })).booleanValue();
        if (result) {
            return i;
        }
    }

    return -1;
    }
}
```

This class could then be used like this:

```
import java.lang.reflect.*;
import java.util.Vector;

// Use the RefSearcher.search method to find a String within a
// Vector.

public class RefSearcherUser {
    // The search method to pass in.

    public static boolean isMyString(Object x) {
        return x.equals("soccer");
    }

    public static void main(String[] args) throws Exception {
        Vector v = new Vector();
        v.addElement("baseball");
        v.addElement("soccer");
        v.addElement("basketball");
```

```
    // Run the search.

    System.out.println(
        RefSearcher.search(
            v,
            RefSearcherUser.class.getDeclaredMethod(
                "isMyString",
                new Class[] { Object.class }))));
    }
}
```

Not only is this inefficient, but it also denies us compile-time type checking, forcing us to examine the method being passed in at run-time for compatibility. Since we know the desired type signature in advance, the preferable solution is to use interfaces:

```
public interface SearchMethod {
    public boolean invoke(Object item);
}
```

Here's an equivalent of the vector search program using interfaces.

```
import java.util.Vector;

// Search a vector for an item that satisfies a specified constraint.
// Use an interface to apply a user-specified boolean method to each
// element. Return the index of a matched item or -1 if no match.

public class InterfaceSearcher {
  public static int search(
    Vector items,
    SearchMethod searchMethod
  ) throws Exception
  {
    int count = items.size();

    for (int i = 0; i < count; i++) {
      boolean result = searchMethod.invoke(items.elementAt(i));
          if (result) {
              return i;
          }
    }

    return -1;
  }
}
```

The InterfaceSearcher could then be used like this:

```
import java.util.Vector;

// Use the InterfaceSearcher.search method to find a String within
// a Vector.

public class InterfaceSearcherUser {
  public static void main(String[] args) throws Exception {
    Vector v = new Vector();
    v.addElement("baseball");
    v.addElement("soccer");
    v.addElement("basketball");

    // Run the search.

    System.out.println(
      InterfaceSearcher.search(
        v,
        new SearchMethod() {
          public boolean invoke(Object item) {
            return item.equals("soccer");
          }
        }));
  }
}
```

Now the code is much clearer, it's type safe, and it's much more efficient to boot. Ain't interfaces grand?

The java.lang.Class Class and the java.lang.reflect Package

Most of Java's reflective capabilities are stored in the `java.lang.Class` class and the `java.lang.reflect` package. These provide a variety of reflective class operations. These can be divided into the following types of operations:

- Type introspection operations

- Public component access operations

- Locally declared component access operations

- Creation and invocation operations

"Reflective Class Operations in Java" on page 284 describes these operations in detail.

The `Class` class provides the reflection API support necessary to obtain information about a running Java application. Instances of the `Class` class represent the following in a running Java application:

- Classes and interfaces

- Arrays

- Primitive Java types (`boolean`, `byte`, `char`, `short`, `int`, `long`, `float`, and `double`)

- The `void` return type

The Java Virtual Machine automatically constructs `Class` objects when classes are loaded and when the class loader issues `defineClass()` method calls.

The `java.lang.reflect` package complements the `Class` class to enable reflection in Java. Among the classes in this package, `java.lang.reflect` provides:

- `Array`

- `Constructor`

- `Field`

- `Method`

- `Modifier`

These classes provide information about and access to the objects returned by `Class` methods.

Reflection and Primitive Types

Before getting into our detailed example, there's one issue we need to point out regarding Java reflection and primitive types. The reflection interfaces only accept arguments that are derived from `Object`, so primitive values like `int`s, `double`s, and `boolean`s cannot be passed directly to a reflective invocation. Java reflection deals with this by accepting instances of the classes `Integer`, `Double`, `Boolean`, and so on, instead of the primitive values. (New classes such as `Short` and `Byte` were added in JDK 1.1 to support reflection.) So, a method that expects an `int` and an instance of `Integer` would be invoked like this:

```
foo.invoke(<obj>, new Object[] {new Integer(5), new Integer(6)})
```

We would invoke it in this way, even though the first argument to the method is declared as an `int` and not as an `Integer`. We'll see shortly that this approach can introduce ambiguities if a user's intention is unknown.

Reflective Class Operations in Java

Before we delve into a detailed example, let's review the variety of Java's reflective class operations, as described in the following tables.

Table 14-1 Type Introspection Operations

Operation	Description
`Class.isInstance(Object obj)`	Returns true if `obj` is an instance of the class.
`Class.isAssignableFrom(Class other)`	Returns true if `other` is a subclass of the class.
`Class.isPrimitive()`	Returns true if the class represents a Java primitive type such as int, boolean, char, etc.
`Class.isArray()`	Returns true if the class represents an array type.
`Class.isInterface()`	Returns true if the class represents an interface.
`Class.getComponentType()`	If the class represents an array type, returns the type of objects held by the array; otherwise returns null.

Intuitively, the public component access operations apply to the entire public interface of a class, which naturally includes inherited components. They provide access to the view required by a user of the class.

Table 14-2 Public Component Access Operations

Operation	Description
`Class.getFields()`	Returns an array of field objects representing the public fields of the class, including inherited fields that are not hidden.
`Class.getMethods()`	Returns an array of method objects representing the public methods of the class including inherited methods that are not overridden.
`Class.getConstructors()`	Returns an array of constructor objects representing the public constructors of the class.

Table 14-2 Public Component Access Operations (Continued)

Operation	Description
`Class.getField(String name)`	Returns a field object representing the public field of the class with the given name which may be inherited. Throws a `NoSuchFieldException` if no public field exists with that name.
`Class.getMethod(String name, Class[] parameterTypes)`	Returns a method object representing the public method of the class with the given name and parameter types which may be inherited. Throws a `NoSuchMethodException` if no public method exists with that name and argument list.
`Class.getConstructor(Class[] parameterTypes)`	Returns a constructor object representing the public constructor of the class with the given parameter types. Throws a `NoSuchMethodException` if no public constructor exists with that argument list.

In contrast to the public component access operations, the locally declared component access operations apply to the all the components supplied by the class itself. They provide complete internal access to the class for use by its implementor.

Table 14-3 Locally Declared Component Access Operations

Operations	Description
`Class.getDeclaredFields()`	Returns an array of field objects representing the fields declared explicitly by the class — not inherited.
`Class.getMethods()`	Returns an array of method objects representing the methods declared explicitly by the class — not inherited.
`Class.getConstructors()`	Returns an array of constructor objects representing all the constructors of the class.

Table 14-3 Locally Declared Component Access Operations (Continued)

Operations	Description
`Class.getField(String name)`	Returns a field object representing the locally declared field of the class with the given name. Throws a `NoSuchFieldException` if no local field exists with that name.
`Class.getMethod(String name, Class[] parameterTypes)`	Returns a method object representing the locally declared method of the class with the given name and parameter types. Throws a `NoSuchMethodException` if no local method exists with that name and argument list.
`Class.getConstructor(Class[] parameterTypes)`	Returns a constructor object representing the constructor of the class with the given parameter types. Throws a `NoSuchMethodException` if no constructor exists with that argument list.

Table 14-4 Creation and Invocation Operations

Operations	Description
`Constructor.newInstance(Object[] initargs)`	Creates a new instance of the class containing the constructor.
`Array.newInstance(Class componentType, int length)`	Creates a new array with the specified `componentType` and length.
`Array.newInstance(Class componentType, int[] dimensions)`	Creates a new array with the specified `componentType` and `dimensions`.
`Array.get(Object array, int index)`	Returns the value at `index` in the array.
`Array.getBoolean(Object array, int index)`	Returns the boolean value at `index` in the array.
`Array.getByte(Object array, int index)`	Returns the byte value at `index` in the array.
`Array.getChar(Object array, int index)`	Returns the char value at `index` in the array.
`Array.getShort(Object array, int index)`	Returns the short value at `index` in the array.
`Array.getInt(Object array, int index)`	Returns the integer value at `index` in the array.

Table 14-4 Creation and Invocation Operations

Operations	Description
`Array.getLong(Object array, int index)`	Returns the long value at `index` in the array.
`Array.getFloat(Object array, int index)`	Returns the float value at `index` in the array.
`Array.getDouble(Object array, int index)`	Returns the double value at `index` in the array.
`Array.set(Object array, int index, Object value)`	Sets the value at `index` in the array.
`Array.setBoolean(Object array, int index, boolean value)`	Sets the boolean value at `index` in the array.
`Array.setByte(Object array, int index, byte value)`	Sets the byte value at `index` in the array.
`Array.setChar(Object array, int index, char value)`	Sets the char value at `index` in the array.
`Array.setShort(Object array, int index, short value)`	Sets the short value at `index` in the array.
`Array.setInt(Object array, int index, integer value)`	Sets the integer value at `index` in the array.
`Array.setLong(Object array, int index, long value)`	Sets the long value at `index` in the array.
`Array.setFloat(Object array, int index, float value)`	Sets the floatvalue at `index` in the array.
`Array.setDouble(Object array, int index, double value)`	Sets the double value at `index` in the array.
`Method.invoke(Object obj, Object[] args)`	Invokes the method on `obj`, which must be an instance of the class containing the method if the method is non-static. Otherwise, it is ignored.
`Field.get(Object obj)`	Returns the value for the field in object `obj`.
`Field.getBoolean(Object obj)`	Returns the boolean value for the field in object `obj`.
`Field.getByte(Object obj)`	Returns the byte value for the field in object `obj`.
`Field.getChar(Object obj)`	Returns the char value for the field in object `obj`.
`Field.getShort(Object obj)`	Returns the short value for the field in object `obj`.
`Field.getInt(Object obj)`	Returns the integer value for the field in object `obj`.
`Field.getLong(Object obj)`	Returns the long value for the field in object `obj`.

Table 14-4 Creation and Invocation Operations

Operations	Description
`Field.getFloat(Object obj)`	Returns the float value for the field in object `obj`.
`Field.getDouble(Object obj)`	Returns the double value for the field in object `obj`.
`Field.set(Object obj, Object value)`	Sets the value for the field in object `obj`.
`Field.setBoolean(Object obj, boolean value)`	Sets the boolean value for the field in object `obj`.
`Field.setByte(Object obj, byte value)`	Sets the byte value for the field in object `obj`.
`Field.setChar(Object obj, char value)`	Sets the char value for the field in object `obj`.
`Field.setShort(Object obj, short value)`	Sets the short value for the field in object `obj`.
`Field.setInt(Object obj, integer value)`	Sets the integer value for the field in object `obj`.
`Field.setLong(Object obj, long value)`	Sets the long value for the field in object `obj`.
`Field.setFloat(Object obj, float value)`	Sets the float value for the field in object `obj`.
`Field.setDouble(Object obj, double value)`	Sets the double value for the field in object `obj`.

An Interpreter Written in Java

Now, on to our example. In it, we'll look at an interpreter that allows users to perform arbitrary public operations on Java objects. There's a little irony here. Since an interpreter like this is one of the rare occasions when use of Java reflection is really warranted, we're actually obviating the need for most people to ever use reflection directly themselves.

One approach to writing such a Java interpreter is to mimic as closely as possible the syntax and semantics of Java in a dynamic fashion. This is probably what you would expect from a Java interpreter. However, this approach is not necessarily the most useful or convenient one. First, Java is not designed to be used interactively. All Java code is embedded in class definitions, but an interactive user often wants to write simple methods that can be independently invoked—similar to scripts. Second, the strong data typing of Java is somewhat painful for interactive use, forcing the user to do a lot of extra typing.

Rather than creating a pseudo-Java syntax with free-floating methods and dynamic typing, we've chosen to front-end our dynamic invocation mechanism with an interpreter for a Lisp-like language. This solution has the following advantages:

1. It simplifies the syntax—we don't need to write a complicated grammar and parser for a pseudo-Java syntax.

2. It provides natural support for dynamic typing—Lisp was originally designed to be dynamically typed.

3. It is expression oriented—languages based on expressions rather than statements are very convenient for interactive use.

The focus in the rest of this chapter is to show the parts of this interpreter that use Java's reflective facilities. Although in many cases, particular solutions shown are specific to the interpreter, the issues we are dealing with are common to most or all uses of reflection.

Refection at Work

Before we go into detail about individual uses of reflection in the interpreter, let's map out where reflection comes into play. Our interpreter uses reflection for the following purposes:

- Invoking methods

- Creating objects

- Fetching and setting fields

- Creating arrays

- Fetching and setting array slots

All except the last of these are implemented in a class named `lisp.Reflector`. Fetching and setting of array slots is implemented in two classes: `lisp.prim.LispAFetchFun` and `lisp.prim.LispAStoreFun`.

Now, let's look at these classes in detail and analyze how reflection is used.

The lisp. Reflector Class

The `Reflector` class provides support for invoking methods, accessing fields, and creating objects through reflection. Accessing fields is straightforward, but Java does not provide a simple way to invoke the "most specific method" with a given name and set of arguments. This is a significant issue when writing an interpreter for a dynamically typed language like Lisp. The only information available when evaluating an expression is the operation name and the arguments.

The most complicated part of the process involves differentiating between methods that take simple types like `boolean` and methods that take the corresponding objects like `java.lang.Boolean`. As we previously mentioned, reflection in Java requires invocation of a method that takes a `boolean` to use an instance of `java.lang.Boolean`. This requirement makes it difficult to determine from the arguments which type is actually intended. In our interpreter, we arbitrarily define a method that takes `boolean` to be more specific than one that takes `Boolean` and will select it first. This definition is largely pragmatic because methods in Java that operate on primitive types are much more common than methods that operate on the related objects.

Here's the logic the interpreter uses to select a most-specific method:

1. Find all methods with the specified name and number of arguments.

2. Select the method with the closest match to the actual arguments specified according to some distance measure. Our measure is different from the one used by standard Java because of the noted ambiguity between `int` and `Integer`, `boolean` and `Boolean`, and so on.

Selecting a method is complicated further when a method is defined to take arguments of primitive numeric types. If the defined argument types are shorter than the types passed at invocation, the call will fail. For example, if a method is defined to take a `short` and it is passed an `int`, no applicable method will be found because Java will not automatically perform type coercions that can lose information. In our interpreter, we handle this by supporting explicit casts between numeric types, like this:

```
(foo.bar (cast x java/lang/Short))
```

Now, consider Example 14-1. This is a fairly lengthy class file, so we'll highlight uses of reflection as we go along.

Example 14-1 lisp.Reflector Class

```
package lisp;

import java.util.*;
import java.lang.reflect.*;

public class Reflector {
  public static Object invokeField(Object item, String fieldName,
    Object[] args) throws Throwable
```

In line ❶ the Class.isArray() method returns true if a class represents an
array. The Array.getLength() method in line ❷ returns the length of an
arbitrary array.

```
   {
❶   if (item.getClass().isArray()) {
       if (fieldName.equals("length")) {
❷        return new Integer(Array.getLength(item));
       } else {
         throw new LispException(
             "The only field defined for arrays is: \"length\".");
       }
     }

     // Support extracting the actual class object from a
     // class reference so that it's convenient to invoke methods
     // defined on the class "Class". We want to allow something
     // similar to Java's "java.lang.String.class" construct.
     // In the interpreter it would be: "java/lang/String:class".

     if (fieldName.equals("class") && item instanceof ClassRef) {
       return ((ClassRef)item).getKlass();
     }

     // Allow for an explicit widening cast. A class that extends
     // another class may contain new fields with identical names.
     // In order to access the values of the fields defined in
     // the parent class, we must be able to specify that the
     // object being accessed should be treated as an instance
     // of the parent class when searching for a field.
     //
     // Given the following two classes:
     //
     // package snippets;
     //
```

```
// public class Wide {
//     public Wide(int x) {
//         this.x = x;
//     }
//
//     public void printIt() {
//         System.out.println("wide");
//     }
//
//     public int x;
// }
//
// package snippets;
//
// public class Narrow extends Wide {
//     public Narrow(int x) {
//         super(x+5);
//         this.x = x;
//     }
//
//     public void printIt() {
//         System.out.println("narrow");
//     }
//
//     public int x;
// }
//
// the only way to access the field named "x" defined in
// Wide for an instance of Narrow is to cast the instance
// to an instance of Wide:
//
// ==> (define n (snippets/Narrow.new 10))
// n
//
// ==> n:x
// 10
//
// ==> (cast n snippets/Wide):x
// 15

Class searchClass = null;

if (item instanceof Cast) {
  // An explicit widening cast.
  searchClass = ((Cast)item).getKlass();
  item        = ((Cast)item).getObject();
} else if (item instanceof ClassRef) {
  // A static field.
```

```
      searchClass = ((ClassRef)item).getKlass();
    } else {
      // A simple field.
      searchClass = item.getClass();
    }
```

The `Field.get()` method in line ❸ fetches the value from the corresponding slot of an object or class. The `Field.set()` method in line ❹ sets the value of the corresponding slot of an object or class.

```
    Field f = searchClass.getField(fieldName);

    // Note that the get() and set() calls work for static fields
    // since the instance arguments are ignored.

    switch (args.length) {
    case 0:
❸    return f.get(item);
    case 1:
      f.set(item, args[0]);
❹    return Boolean.TRUE;
    default:
      throw new LispException(
          "A field reference requires either 1 or 2 arguments, " +
          "got: " + args.length);
    }
  }

  // Invoke a most-specific instance method on an object.
  // Calls to "new" and "new[]" are handled separately.

  public static Object invokeMethod(
    final Object item,
    final String methodName,
    final Object[] args) throws Throwable
  {
    if (methodName.equals("new")) {
      return invokeConstructor(item, args);
    }
    if (methodName.equals("new[]")) {
      return invokeArrayConstructor(item, args);
    }

    // We don't need to allow for a widening cast here because
    // Java doesn't allow access to overridden methods from parent
    // classes. Given our previous two example classes "Wide" and
```

```
// "Narrow", there is no way to invoke the printIt() method
// defined in Wide on an instance of Narrow.

final Class searchClass =
    (item instanceof ClassRef
        ? ((ClassRef)item).getKlass()
        : item.getClass());

// Select the most-specific method.

final Method method = getMethod(searchClass, methodName, args);

if (method == null) {
    throw new LispException(
        "No applicable method found for: " + methodName +
        " on: " + searchClass.getName());
}
```

In the next block of code, Method.getParameterTypes() in line ❺ returns an array of classes representing the types of all the arguments to the method.

```
// Perform any necessary casts. These include casts explicitly
// specified by the user as well as widening casts between
// numeric types. In a Java program, an "int" will be
// implicitly coerced to a "long" when used as an argument to
// a method that expects a "long", but the reflection mechanism
// does not perform a coercion. We coerce such arguments
// ourselves before handing them to the reflection system.
```

❺
```
Class[] paramTypes = method.getParameterTypes();

for (int i = 0; i < args.length; i++) {
    Object arg = args[i];

    if (arg == null) {
        continue;
    }

    Class argType = arg.getClass();

    // Extract actual arguments from casts.

    if (arg instanceof Cast) {
        args[i] = ((Cast)arg).getObject();
    }
```

In line ❻, `Class.isAssignableFrom()` determines if a class is a subclass of another class or if it implements a particular interface. You'll notice this method used throughout this `Reflector` class definition.

```
        // If we're passing a numeric argument, perform any
        // required widening casts.

     if (isPrimAndObject(argType) &&
         Number.class.isAssignableFrom(argType) &&
         getPrimClass(argType) != paramTypes[i]) {

         if (paramTypes[i] != Object.class) {
             args[i] = convert((Number)args[i], paramTypes[i]);
         }
     }
  }
```

In the `try` block, `Method.invoke()` in line ❼ calls a method found via reflection. Recall that Java requires a method to declare any exceptions that can be thrown.
However, a reflected call could conceivably throw any instance of `Throwable`, so the reflection system wraps any exception thrown during invocation in an instance of the class `InvocationTargetException`. The `InvocationTargetException.getTargetException()` method in line ❽ retrieves an actual exception thrown during dynamic invocation.

```
  try {
     return method.invoke(item, args);
  } catch (InvocationTargetException ite) {
     throw ite.getTargetException();
  }
}

// Create an array. Unlike array creation in a static Java
// program, multidimensional arrays created through reflection
// are always completely fleshed out. In other words, there is
// no equivalent to:
//
// int[][] foo = new int[10][];
//

public static Object invokeArrayConstructor(
  Object item,
  Object[] args) throws LispException
{
```

```
    if (!(item instanceof ClassRef)) {
      throw new LispException(
          "\"new[]\" may only be invoked statically.");
    }

    int[] dimensions = new int[args.length];

    // Collect the specified dimensions, ensuring they are numbers.
    // Floating-point dimensions are truncated to integers.

    for (int i = 0; i < args.length; i++) {
      if (!(args[i] instanceof Number)) {
        throw new LispException(
          "Arguments to array constructors must be numbers.");
      }
      dimensions[i] = ((Number)args[i]).intValue();
    }
```

We use `Array.newInstance()` in line ❾ to actually construct the array given the class and dimensions. The method creates an instance of an arbitrary array type, given the `item` class and an array of `integer` dimensions.

```
❾    return Array.newInstance(((ClassRef)item).getKlass(),
        dimensions);
    }

    // Invoke a most-specific constructor on a class. This is
    // basically the same process as method invocation except that
    // the method name is implicit and the call is always static.

    public static Object invokeConstructor(
      final Object item,
      final Object[] args) throws Throwable
    {

      if (!(item instanceof ClassRef)) {
        throw new LispException("\"new\" may only be invoked
            statically.");
      }

      // Find the most-specific constructor.

      Class searchClass    = ((ClassRef)item).getKlass();
      Constructor    constructor = getConstructor(searchClass, args);

      if (constructor == null) {
```

```
       throw new LispException("No applicable constructor found
          for: " +
          searchClass.getName());
   }
```

In line ⑩, `Constructor.getParameterTypes()` returns an array of classes representing the types of all the arguments to the constructor.

```
       // Perform any necessary casts.

⑩     Class[] paramTypes = constructor.getParameterTypes();

       for (int i = 0; i < args.length; i++) {
          Object arg = args[i];

          if (arg == null) {
             continue;
          }

          Class argType = arg.getClass();

          // Extract actual arguments from casts.

          if (arg instanceof Cast) {
             args[i] = ((Cast)arg).getObject();
          }

          // If we're passing a numeric argument, perform any
          // required widening casts.

          if (isPrimAndObject(argType) &&
              Number.class.isAssignableFrom(argType) &&
              getPrimClass(argType) != paramTypes[i]) {
             if (paramTypes[i] != Object.class) {
                args[i] = convert((Number)args[i], paramTypes[i]);
             }
          }
       }
   }
```

In the next `try` block, `Constructor.newInstance()` in line ❶ creates a new class instance and initializes it, using the selected constructor. Notice use of the `InvocationTargetException.getTargetException()` once again to throw an exception thrown during dynamic invocation.

```
       try {
          // Invoke the constructor.
❶        return constructor.newInstance(args);
```

```
  } catch (InvocationTargetException ite) {
    throw ite.getTargetException();
  }
}

public static Number convert(
  Number n,
  Class convertTo) throws LispException
{

  // Find a converter that will convert from the class of
  // "n" to the specified class if such a converter exists.

  Converter conv = (Converter)converters.get(convertTo);
  if (conv == null) {
    System.err.println("No conversion defined from: " +
  n.getClass() + " to: " + convertTo);
    throw new LispException();
  }

  // Perform the conversion.

  return conv.convert(n);
}

// Define a constant which represents the "distance" between
// incompatible methods.

final private static int INFINITE_DISTANCE = Integer.MAX_VALUE;

// Find the appropriate constructor for a class.
private static Constructor getConstructor(
  final Class c,
  final Object[] args)
{
```

In line ❷, Class.getConstructor() finds the constructor for a class that
matches the argument types that are passed in. The
Class.getConstructors() method in line ❸ returns all constructors defined
for a given class.

```
  // If there are no arguments, there can only be one
  // matching constructor.

  if (args.length == 0) {
    try {
```

❷
```
        return c.getConstructor(new Class[0]);
    } catch (NoSuchMethodException nsme) {
        return null;
    }
}

// Collect the constructors from this class.
```
❸
```
final Constructor[] currentConstructors= c.getConstructors();

int minConstructorDistance    = INFINITE_DISTANCE;
Constructor currentConstructor = null;

// Loop through set of constructors with the same number of
// args and find the closest match.
```

Remember that `Constructor.getParameterTypes()` returns an array of classes representing the types of all the arguments to the constructor.

```
for (int i = 0; i < currentConstructors.length; i++) {
  if (currentConstructors[i].getParameterTypes().length !=
      args.length) {
      continue;
  }
  // Calculate the distance between the types in the
  // constructor invocation and the signature of a
  // particular constructor.

  final int currentDistance =
      calculateArgDistance(
          currentConstructors[i].getParameterTypes(),
          args);

  // If the current constructor is closer to the
  // invocation signature than the current saved constructor,
  // replace the saved constructor with the current one.

  if (currentDistance < minConstructorDistance) {
      minConstructorDistance = currentDistance;
      currentConstructor     = currentConstructors[i];
  }
}

return currentConstructor;
}

// Find the appropriate method for a class.
private static Method getMethod(
```

```
      final Class c,
      final String methodName,
      final Object[] args)
{
   // If the class is not public we must find any public methods
   // in one of the public interfaces implemented by the class.

   Vector interfaces = null;
   Vector methods    = null;

   if (Modifier.isPublic(c.getModifiers()) == false) {
      interfaces                     = new Vector();
      Class[] immediateInterfaces = c.getInterfaces();

      for (int i = 0; i < immediateInterfaces.length; i++) {
         if
(Modifier.isPublic(immediateInterfaces[i].getModifiers()) ==
               true) {
            interfaces.addElement(immediateInterfaces[i]);
          }
      }
   }

   if (args.length == 0) {
      if (interfaces == null) {
         // If there are no args and this is a public class,
         // there can only be one applicable method.

         try {
            return c.getMethod(methodName, new Class[0]);
         } catch (NoSuchMethodException nsme) {
            return null;
         }
      } else {
         for (int i = 0; i < interfaces.size(); i++) {
            // In this case, any method is as good as another
            // since the methods inherited from interfaces must
            // all be compatible.

            try {
               return
                  ((Class)interfaces.elementAt(i)).getMethod(
                     methodName, new Class[0]);
               } catch (NoSuchMethodException nsme) {
               }
         }

         return null;
```

```
        }
    }

    if (interfaces != null) {
        for (int i = 0; i < interfaces.size(); i++) {
            Method[] iMethods =
                ((Class)interfaces.elementAt(i)).getMethods();

            for (int m = 0; m < iMethods.length; m++) {
                methods.addElement(iMethods[m]);
            }
        }
    }

    // Collect the methods from this class.

    Method[] currentMethods = null;
    if (interfaces == null) {
        currentMethods = c.getMethods();
    } else {
        currentMethods = new Method[methods.size()];
        methods.copyInto(currentMethods);
    }

    int minMethodDistance    = INFINITE_DISTANCE;
    Method currentMethod     = null;

// Loop through set of methods with the same name and number of
    // args and find the closest match.

    for (int i = 0; i < currentMethods.length; i++) {
        if (!currentMethods[i].getName().equals(methodName) ||
            currentMethods[i].getParameterTypes().length !=
            args.length) {
            continue;
        }

        // Calculate the distance between the types in the
        // method invocation and the signature of a
        // particular method.

        final int currentDistance =
            calculateArgDistance(
                currentMethods[i].getParameterTypes(),
                args);

        // If the current method is closer to the
        // invocation signature than the current saved method,
```

```
              // replace the saved method with the current one.

              if (currentDistance < minMethodDistance) {
                  minMethodDistance = currentDistance;
                  currentMethod     = currentMethods[i];
              }
          }
          return currentMethod;
    }

    // Calculate a distance value for a method or constructor given its
    // parameter types and a set of arguments.

    private static int calculateArgDistance(
       final Class[] paramTypes,
       final Object[] args)
    {
       int methodDistance = 0;

       for (int pindex = 0; pindex < paramTypes.length; pindex++) {
           final Class paramType = paramTypes[pindex];

           // Null arguments are ignored since we don't know what
           // their types are. If a null argument is required to
           // disambiguate an invocation, it should be cast to the
           // appropriate type.

           if (args[pindex] == null) {
               continue;
           }

           Class argType  = args[pindex].getClass();
           boolean isCast = false;

           // If the argument is a cast, use the cast type.

           if (argType == lisp.Cast.class) {
               isCast= true;
               argType= ((Cast)args[pindex]).getKlass();
           }

           // If we're not dealing with one of the ambiguous classes
           // (i.e., one that could refer to a primitive type or an
           // object type like int/Integer, boolean/Boolean, etc.),
           // simply count the number of classes in the chain from
           // the argument's class up to the declared parameter's
           // class. If the argument's class is a subclass of the
           // the declared class, the method or constructor is not
```

```
    // applicable and is assigned an infinite distance.

    if (!isPrimAndObject(argType)) {
        if (paramType.isAssignableFrom(argType)) {
            methodDistance +=
                countClassStepsRemoved(paramType, argType);
        } else {
            return INFINITE_DISTANCE;
        }
    } else {
        // It might seem like we would always add zero to the
        // distance if the parameter type is equal to the arg
        // type, but this doesn't work for primitive types. We
        // want to give precedence to the primitive half of
        // a primitive/Object pair like int/Integer, and the
        // actual argument will always be an instance of the
        // object half of the pair. However, if a user explicitly
        // casts to the object half of a pair, we'll honor her
        // wishes.

        if (isCast && paramType == argType) {
            continue;
        }
        // An added wrinkle here is that the isAssignableFrom()
        // method does not succeed for primitive classes.
        // Long.TYPE.isAssignableFrom(Integer.TYPE) returns
        // false! We use our own isPrimAssignableFrom() method
        // in this case.

        final Class primClass = getPrimClass(argType);

        // First, check our primitive conversions to determine
        // if we can assign the arg type across as a primitive
        // type. If that fails, try treating the argument
        // as an instance of the object half of a primitive/object
        // pair.

        if (isPrimAssignableFrom(paramType, primClass)) {
            methodDistance +=
                countClassStepsRemoved(paramType, primClass);

        } else if (paramType.isAssignableFrom(argType)) {
            methodDistance +=
                countClassStepsRemoved(paramType, argType);
        } else {
            return INFINITE_DISTANCE;
        }
    }
```

```
        }
        return methodDistance;
    }


    // Count the distance between two types. For arrays this is the
    // distance between component types; for primitive types it is
    // the separation between entries in our conversion arrays; for
    // other types it is the number of getSuperclass() calls required
    // to reach from one type to another.

    private static int countClassStepsRemoved(
            Class paramType,
            Class argType)
    {
        if (paramType == argType) {
            return 0;
        }
```

In line ❶, the `Class.getComponentType()` methods in the `if` clause return the type of the elements of an array, provided the class represents an array type.

```
        // If we're looking at array types, use their component types.
        // We already know that the types are compatible so we don't
        // need to also check that argType represents an array.

        if (paramType.isArray()) {
            paramType = paramType.getComponentType();
            argType   = argType.getComponentType();
        }

        int distance = 0;
```

`Class.isPrimitive()` in line ❷ indicates whether the class represents a primitive type such as `boolean` or `int`.

```
        // For a primitive type, count the separation between entries
        // in a conversion array.

        if (argType.isPrimitive()) {
            Class[] conversionArray =
                    (Class[])conversions.get(argType);

            for (; distance < conversionArray.length; distance++) {
                if (paramType == conversionArray[distance]) {
                    return distance;
```

```
            }
        }
    }

    // Count the number of classes in the inheritance chain
    // between the two types.

    if (paramType.isInterface()) {
        while (!implementsInterface(argType, paramType)) {
            argType = argType.getSuperclass();
            distance++;
        }

    } else {
        while (argType != paramType) {
            argType = argType.getSuperclass();
            distance++;
        }
    }

    return distance;
}

// Determine if a class directly implements an interface.
private static boolean implementsInterface(Class klass, Class
        interfayce) {
    Class[] interfaces = klass.getInterfaces();

    for (int i = 0; i < interfaces.length; i++) {
        if (interfaces[i] == interfayce) {
            return true;
        }
    }

    return false;
}

// Determine if a class can represent one of the primitive types.

private static boolean isPrimAndObject(Class argType) {
    return getPrimClass(argType) != null;
}

// Look up a class in the hash table defining primitive types.

private static Class getPrimClass(Class argType) {
    return (Class)primAndObjectHash.get(argType);
}
```

```java
// Search a conversion array to determine if one primitive type
// is separated from another by a widening conversion.

private static boolean isPrimAssignableFrom(
   Class paramType,
   Class argType)
{

if (paramType == argType) {
   return true;
}

// Look up the conversions for the argument type.

Class[] assignables = (Class[])conversions.get(argType);

// Search the conversions for the parameter type.

if (assignables != null) {
   for (int i = 0; i < assignables.length; i++) {
      if (assignables[i] == paramType) {
         return true;
      }
   }
}

return false;
}

// Helper methods to initialize type conversion information.

private static void initializeHashEntries(Class c1, Class c2) {
  primAndObjectHash.put(c1, c2);
}

private static void initializeConversions(Class c, Class[]
  carray) {
  conversions.put(c, carray);
}

private static void initializeConverters(Class c1, Class c2,
  Converter conv) {
  converters.put(c1, conv);
  converters.put(c2, conv);
}

private final static Hashtable primAndObjectHash = new
```

```
  Hashtable();

private final static Hashtable conversions     = new Hashtable();
private final static Hashtable converters       = new Hashtable();

static {
  // Initialize the set of classes that must be tried
  // as both primitive and object.

  initializeHashEntries(Boolean.class,    Boolean.TYPE);
  initializeHashEntries(Byte.class,       Byte.TYPE);
  initializeHashEntries(Character.class,  Character.TYPE);
  initializeHashEntries(Short.class,      Short.TYPE);
  initializeHashEntries(Integer.class,    Integer.TYPE);
  initializeHashEntries(Long.class,       Long.TYPE);
  initializeHashEntries(Float.class,      Float.TYPE);
  initializeHashEntries(Double.class,     Double.TYPE);

  // In each case, the first argument to initializeConversions may
  // be implicitly converted to any entry in the second argument.

  initializeConversions(Byte.TYPE,
    new Class[] { Byte.TYPE,
      Short.TYPE,
      Integer.TYPE,
      Long.TYPE,
      Float.TYPE,
      Double.TYPE });
  initializeConversions(Short.TYPE,
    new Class[] { Short.TYPE,
      Integer.TYPE,
      Long.TYPE,
      Float.TYPE,
      Double.TYPE });
  initializeConversions(Integer.TYPE,
    new Class[] { Integer.TYPE,
      Long.TYPE,
      Float.TYPE,
      Double.TYPE });
  initializeConversions(Long.TYPE,
    new Class[] { Long.TYPE, Double.TYPE });
  initializeConversions(Float.TYPE,
    new Class[] { Float.TYPE, Double.TYPE });
  initializeConversions(Double.TYPE,
    new Class[] { Double.TYPE });

  // Create converters that will convert any numeric type into
  // a particular numeric type. These converters may be used
```

```java
        // for both widening and narrowing casts.
        initializeConverters(Byte.class, Byte.TYPE,
           new Converter() {
              Number convert(Number n) {
                 return new Byte(n.byteValue());
              }
           });
        initializeConverters(Short.class, Short.TYPE,
           new Converter() {
              Number convert(Number n) {
                 return new Short(n.shortValue());
              }
           });
        initializeConverters(Integer.class, Integer.TYPE,
           new Converter() {
              Number convert(Number n) {
                 return new Integer(n.intValue());
              }
           });
        initializeConverters(Long.class, Long.TYPE,
           new Converter() {
              Number convert(Number n) {
                return new Long(n.longValue());
              }
           });
        initializeConverters(Float.class, Float.TYPE,
           new Converter() {
              Number convert(Number n) {
                 return new Float(n.floatValue());
              }
           });
        initializeConverters(Double.class, Double.TYPE,
           new Converter() {
              Number convert(Number n) {
                 return new Double(n.doubleValue());
              }
           });
     }

     // A class that converts instances of one numeric class into
     // instances of another.

     abstract static class Converter {
       abstract Number convert(Number n);
     }
}
```

The lisp.prim.LispAFetchFun Class

The `LispAFetchFun` class supports the `afetch` operation, which extracts an item from an array. The `afetch` operation takes the array and an arbitrary number of indices as arguments and returns the specified entry.

In the class definition in Example 14-2, notice use of the `Class.isArray()` method, as previously discussed, to determine if a class represents an array. Also, look for use of `Array.get()` near the end of the class definition. It returns the element at a particular index of an arbitrary array.

Example 14-2 lisp.prim.LispAFetchFun Class

```
package lisp.prim;

import lisp.*;
import java.lang.reflect.*;
import java.util.*;

public class LispAFetchFun extends LispPrimitive {
  public Object apply(Vector args) throws WrongArgCountException,
  NoSuchClassException, LispException {

    if (args.size() < 2) {
     throw new WrongArgCountException(
        "afetch: expected at least 2 args; got " + args.size() + ".");
    }

    Object o = args.elementAt(0);

    if (!o.getClass().isArray()) {
      throw new LispException(
        "afetch may only be applied to arrays; got: " + o);
    }

    // Since Java deals with multidimensional arrays as
    // arrays-of-arrays, we go through a loop for the set of
    // indices, chaining through the nested arrays.

    for (int i = 1; i < args.size(); i++) {
      if (!(args.elementAt(i) instanceof Number)) {
        throw new LispException(
          "Array indices must be numbers; got: " +
          args.elementAt(i));
      }
    }

    // Use the Array.get() reflective operation to fetch
    // an array entry.
```

```
     o = Array.get(o, ((Number)args.elementAt(i)).intValue());
   }
   return o;
 }
}
```

The lisp.prim.LispAStoreFun Class

The `LispAStoreFun` class supports the `astore` operation, which stores an item in an array. The `astore` operation takes the array, an arbitrary number of indices, and a new entry as arguments and stores the entry in the array. Again, notice use of the `Class.isArray()` method. Pay attention also to the `Array.set()` method, which sets the slot at a specified index of an arbitrary array.

Example 14-3 lisp.prim.LispAStoreFun Class

```java
package lisp.prim;

import lisp.*;
import java.lang.reflect.*;
import java.util.*;

public class LispAStoreFun extends LispPrimitive {
  public Object apply(Vector args) throws WrongArgCountException,
  NoSuchClassException, LispException {
    if (args.size() < 3) {
      throw new WrongArgCountException(
          "astore: expected at least 3 args; got " +
          args.size() + ".");
    }

    Object o = args.elementAt(0);

    if (!o.getClass().isArray()) {
      throw new LispException(
          "astore may only be applied to arrays; got: " + o);
    }

    int argCount = args.size();

    // Since Java deals with multidimensional arrays as
    // arrays-of-arrays, we go through a loop for the set of
    // indices, chaining through the nested arrays. The last
    // argument is the new entry, so we stop short of the end.

    for (int i = 1; i < argCount - 2; i++) {
      Object arg = args.elementAt(i);
```

```
    if (!(arg instanceof Number)) {
        throw new LispException(
            "Array indices must be numbers; got: " +
            arg);
        }

    o = Array.get(o, ((Number)arg).intValue());
    }

    // After obtaining the innermost array, we store the
    // new entry.

    Array.set(o, ((Number)args.elementAt(argCount -
        2)).intValue(),args.elementAt(argCount - 1));

    return Boolean.TRUE;
    }
}
```

Sample Session

Following is a sample interactive session with our interpreter. (Note, the complete code for the lisp interpreter is on the *Java by Example* CD-ROM.)

```
(4:49AM) ~jbe> lisp

; Create a string called "exampleString".

==> (define exampleString "this is a test of the emergency broadcast system")
exampleString

; Show its value

==> exampleString
"this is a test of the emergency broadcast system"

; Fetch the third character of the string. Note that characters
; print using the syntax: #\<character>.

==> (exampleString.charAt 2)
#\i

; Oops. No such method.

==> (exampleString.toUpper)
No applicable method found for: toUpper on: java.lang.String

; Invoke the "toUpperCase method of exampleString. Note that method
```

```
; invocation uses '.'.

==> (exampleString.toUpperCase)

"THIS IS A TEST OF THE EMERGENCY BROADCAST SYSTEM"

; Invoke the length method of exampleString.

==> (exampleString.length)
48

; Concatenate exampleString with itself.

==> (exampleString.concat exampleString)
"this is a test of the emergency broadcast systemthis is a test of the
emergency broadcast system"

; Invoke a static method. Note that class names are fully qualified
; and are separated by '/'.

==> (java/lang/String.valueOf 3.14)
"3.14"

; Define "val" to be the static "valueOf" method from java.lang.String.

==> (define val java/lang/String.valueOf)
val

; Invoke the method stored in "val".

==> (val 3.14)
"3.14"

; "val" holds a static method.

==> val
{method: {class: java.lang.String}.valueOf}
; exampleString.toUpperCase refers to an instance method.

==> exampleString.toUpperCase
{method: this is a test of the emergency broadcast system.toUpperCase}

; Define a lisp procedure that will convert a string to upper case.

==> (define (upper str) (str.toUpperCase))
upper

; "upper" holds a procedure.

==> upper
{procedure}

; Invoke the procedure stored in "upper".
```

```
==> (upper "foo")
"FOO"

; A static field in the Character class. Note that field access is
; indicated by ':'.

==> java/lang/Character:MIN_RADIX
2

; Another static field.

==> java/lang/Character:TYPE
char

; Create an instance of java.util.Vector. Note that constructors are
; invoked via <class>.new.

==> (define vec (java/util/Vector.new))
vec

; "vec" holds an empty vector.

==> vec
[]

; Add an element to the vector. Note that void methods return null and
; Java null values print as "#null".

==> (vec.addElement "a string")
#null

; Now "vec" has contents.

==> vec
[a string]

; Change the contents of "vec".

==> (vec.setElementAt "another string" 0)
#null

; Changed.

==> vec
[another string]

; Create an array of 10 strings.

==> (define stringArray (java/lang/String.new[] 10))
stringArray

; The initial value for each string is null.
```

```
==> stringArray
{#null, #null, #null, #null, #null, #null, #null, #null, #null, #null}

; Store a string in slot 2 of the array.

==> (astore stringArray 2 "hello")
#t

; There it is.

==> stringArray
{#null, #null, "hello", #null, #null, #null, #null, #null, #null, #null}

; Fetch it back out.

==> (afetch stringArray 2)
"hello"

; Create a two-dimensional array of strings.

==> (define twoD (java/lang/String.new[] 2 2))
twoD

; The subarrays are also created.

==> twoD
{{#null, #null}, {#null, #null}}

; Store a value into the two-dimensional array.

==> (astore twoD 1 1 "item")
#t

; There it is.

==> twoD
{{#null, #null}, {#null, "item"}}

; Fetch it back out.

==> (afetch twoD 1 1)
"item"

; Store a class in a variable.

==> (define string java/lang/String)
string

; "string" holds the java.lang.String class object.

==> string
{class: java.lang.String}
```

```
; Use "string" anywhere you could use the class.

==> (string.new[] 2 2)
{{#null, #null}, {#null, #null}}

; Create an instance of the "lisp.foo" class -- Here's the definition:
; package lisp;
;
; public class foo {
;     public int bar;
; }
;

==> (define aFoo (lisp/foo.new))
aFoo

; Set the "bar" field of the new instance. Note that Java true values
; print as #t. False values print as #f.

==> (set! aFoo:bar 5)
#t

; Fetch the "bar" field of the instance.

==> aFoo:bar
5

; The following examples show how the '.', '/', and ':' syntax is
; translated on input.  The interpreter never sees the special
; characters. It sees the equivalent expressions below.

; A class name separated by slashes is translated into a call to
; "class".

==> (read)
java/lang/String
(class "java.lang.String")

; A field reference separated by colons is translated into calls to
; "field".

==> (read)
aFoo:bar
(field aFoo "bar")

; A method invocation separated by periods is translated into calls to
; "method".

==> (read)
exampleString.toUpperCase
(method exampleString "toUpperCase")
```

```
; Use the underlying call instead of the special syntax.

==> ((class "java.lang.String").new[] 3)
{#null, #null, #null}

==> (field aFoo "bar")
5

==> ((method exampleString "toUpperCase"))
"THIS IS A TEST OF THE EMERGENCY BROADCAST SYSTEM"

; Throw an exception

==> (throw (java/lang/Exception.new "an exception"))
An exception occurred
java.lang.Exception: an exception
    at java.lang.reflect.Constructor.newInstance(Native Method)
    at lisp.Reflector.invokeConstructor(Reflector.java:164)
    at lisp.Reflector.invokeMethod(Reflector.java:69)
    at lisp.LispEvaluator.eval(LispEvaluator.java:42)
    at lisp.LispEvaluator.evalArgs(LispEvaluator.java:77)
    at lisp.LispEvaluator.eval(LispEvaluator.java:33)
    at lisp.LispInterpreter.readEvalPrint(LispInterpreter.java:86)
    at lisp.Lisp.main(Lisp.java:9)

; Use a "try/finally" construct to make sure "yow!" is printed even
; if an exception is thrown.

==> (try (throw (java/lang/Exception.new)) (finally (print "yow!")))
"yow!"
An exception occurred
java.lang.Exception
    at java.lang.reflect.Constructor.newInstance(Native Method)
    at lisp.Reflector.invokeConstructor(Reflector.java:164)
    at lisp.Reflector.invokeMethod(Reflector.java:69)
    at lisp.LispEvaluator.eval(LispEvaluator.java:42)
    at lisp.LispEvaluator.evalArgs(LispEvaluator.java:77)
    at lisp.LispEvaluator.eval(LispEvaluator.java:33)
    at lisp.TrySpecialForm.eval(TrySpecialForm.java:15)
    at lisp.LispEvaluator.eval(LispEvaluator.java:28)
    at lisp.LispInterpreter.readEvalPrint(LispInterpreter.java:86)
    at lisp.Lisp.main(Lisp.java:9)

; Catch an exception using the "try" construct.  Note that "e" is
; bound to the captured exception.

==> (try (throw (java/lang/Exception.new "got it"))
            ((java/lang/Exception e) (print (e.getMessage))))
"got it"
#t

; Catch another exception using the "try" construct.  Note that the
; "finally" section is executed even if an exception is caught.
```

```
==> (try (throw (java/lang/Exception.new "got it"))
          ((java/lang/Exception e) (print (e.getMessage)))
          (finally (print "done.")))
"got it"
"done."
#t

; Catch an exception, print its message, and rethrow it.

==> (try (throw (java/lang/Exception.new "got it"))
          ((java/lang/Exception e)
           (print (e.getMessage))
           (throw e))
          (finally (print "done.")))
"got it"
"done."
An exception occurred
java.lang.Exception: got it
    at java.lang.reflect.Constructor.newInstance(Native Method)
    at lisp.Reflector.invokeConstructor(Reflector.java:164)
    at lisp.Reflector.invokeMethod(Reflector.java:69)
    at lisp.LispEvaluator.eval(LispEvaluator.java:42)
    at lisp.LispEvaluator.evalArgs(LispEvaluator.java:77)
    at lisp.LispEvaluator.eval(LispEvaluator.java:33)
    at lisp.TrySpecialForm.eval(TrySpecialForm.java:15)
    at lisp.LispEvaluator.eval(LispEvaluator.java:28)
    at lisp.LispInterpreter.readEvalPrint(LispInterpreter.java:86)
    at lisp.Lisp.main(Lisp.java:9)
```

Summary

Reflection is a facility that is derived from the dynamic programming community. In the context of the Java language, reflection refers to the ability to observe and/or manipulate the inner workings of an environment programmatically.

Reflection is often misused. Although you may be tempted to use the reflection operations provided by Java, remember that it is really a special-purpose facility suited to applications such as interpreters and debuggers. Using reflection is appropriate when information about an object's type is not available at compile time, which is a fairly uncommon situation.

Generally speaking, if you're using reflective operations in your programs, you may want to reassess your approach and see if a more general-purpose mechanism will achieve the same end. Use of interfaces is often a more appropriate solution.

CHAPTER
15

- Developing a Java Calculator
- Calculator Classes
- Calculator Interfaces

Putting the Language Pieces Together

Four-Function Calculator

We've now covered enough of Java to work through a larger example. We'll implement a stack-based calculator showing how to use Java features such as interfaces and exception handling to make it elegant and extensible. Commands for the calculator will be single non-numeric characters, and operands will be of type `double`.

The program is used in the following way:

```
java RunCalculator
calc>
```

At the prompt, you can enter functions for the calculator to perform.

The classes that comprise the calculator are grouped together into a `calc` package. This package consists of six classes and three interfaces, as illustrated in Figure 15-1.

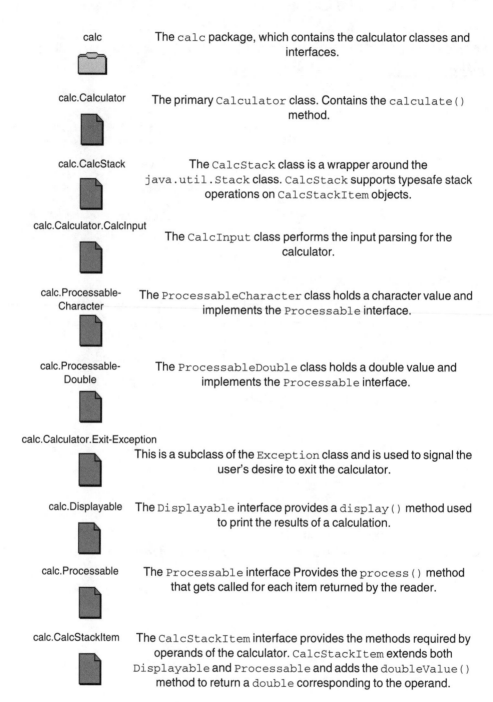

calc	The calc package, which contains the calculator classes and interfaces.
calc.Calculator	The primary Calculator class. Contains the calculate() method.
calc.CalcStack	The CalcStack class is a wrapper around the java.util.Stack class. CalcStack supports typesafe stack operations on CalcStackItem objects.
calc.Calculator.CalcInput	The CalcInput class performs the input parsing for the calculator.
calc.Processable-Character	The ProcessableCharacter class holds a character value and implements the Processable interface.
calc.Processable-Double	The ProcessableDouble class holds a double value and implements the Processable interface.
calc.Calculator.Exit-Exception	This is a subclass of the Exception class and is used to signal the user's desire to exit the calculator.
calc.Displayable	The Displayable interface provides a display() method used to print the results of a calculation.
calc.Processable	The Processable interface Provides the process() method that gets called for each item returned by the reader.
calc.CalcStackItem	The CalcStackItem interface provides the methods required by operands of the calculator. CalcStackItem extends both Displayable and Processable and adds the doubleValue() method to return a double corresponding to the operand.

Figure 15-1 Calculator Class Structure

With this picture in mind, we'll describe each class and interface and how they inter-relate to form a working, four-function calculator program.

The Calculator main() Method

At the top of the calculator is the RunCalculator class that includes a main() method. The RunCalculator class imports the calc package, which has all the classes and interfaces necessary to implement the calculator. The RunCalculator class looks like this:

```
import calc.*;

public class RunCalculator {
    public static void main(String args[]) {
        new Calculator().calculate();
    }
}
```

The Calculator Class

The top-level class in the calc package is the Calculator class. It provides constructors for creating calculators and a calculate() method called in the main() method of RunCalculator. Table 15-1 summarizes the constructors and instance method provided by the Calculator class.

Table 15-1 Calculator Program Class Summary

Package		calc
Imports		java.io
Constructors		public Calculator() public Calculator(Reaader in, Writer out)
Instance Methods	Name:	calculate()
	Returns:	void
	Throws:	None

The Calculator class starts out with package commands. All the classes for the calculator are in package calc. The Calculator class imports a few classes from java.io. Notice that he Calculator class reads a line at a time so it uses a BufferedReader for input. We'll first show the class in its entirety, and then focus on some of the details.

```
package calc;

import java.io.Reader;
import java.io.Writer;
import java.io.InputStreamReader;
import java.io.BufferedReader;
import java.io.PrintWriter;
import java.io.IOException;

public class Calculator {

public Calculator() {
   this(new BufferedReader(
      new InputStreamReader(System.in)),
      new PrintWriter(System.out));
   }
   public Calculator(final Reader in, final Writer out) {
      BufferedReader dataIn;
      PrintWriter    printOut;

      if (!(in instanceof BufferedReader)) {
         dataIn = new BufferedReader(in);
      } else {
         dataIn = (BufferedReader)in;
      }

      if (!(out instanceof PrintWriter)) {
         printOut = new PrintWriter(out);
      } else {
         printOut = (PrintWriter)out;
      }

      input  = new CalcInput(dataIn);   // Handles all input.
      stack  = new CalcStack();         // Operand stack.
      output = printOut;                // Output writer.
   }

   public void calculate() {

      boolean finished = false;

      while (!finished) {
         output.println();
         output.print("calc> ");
         output.flush();
```

```java
        if (!input.readLine()) {
            continue;
        }

         try {
            Processable item;

            while (input.hasInput()) {
                item = input.read(); // Returns a Processable

                if (item != null) {
                    item.process(stack, output);
                }
            }

        } catch (final ExitException e) {
            System.err.println("Exiting.");
            finished = true;

        } catch (final Exception e) {
            System.err.println("An exception occurred:");
            e.printStackTrace();
            stack = new CalcStack();
        }
    }
}

static final class ExitException extends Exception {}

static final class CalcInput {

private static final char SPACE   = ' ';
private static final char TAB     = '\t';
private static final char NEWLINE = '\n';

private static final char DOT     = '.';
private static final char MINUS   = '-';

private static final char EOI     = (char)-1;

public CalcInput(final BufferedReader in) {
    inputReader = in;
}

public boolean readLine() {
    try {
        buffer = inputReader.readLine();
```

```
        } catch (final IOException e) {
            return false;
        }

        bufferLength = buffer.length();

        if (bufferLength == 0) {
            return false;
        }

        index = 0;  // Initialize the offset into the buffer.

        return true;
    }

    public Processable read() {
        if (hasInput()) {
            return readInternal();
        } else {
            return null;
        }
    }

    public boolean hasInput() {
        skipWhite();
        return !bufferExhausted();
    }

    Processable readInternal() {
        final char ch = peekCh();

        if (Character.isDigit(ch) ||
            ch == DOT ||
            (ch == MINUS &&
                (Character.isDigit(peekCh(1)) || peekCh(1) == DOT))) {
            return readNumber();
        } else {
            return new ProcessableCharacter(getCh());
        }
    }

    private Processable readNumber() {
        final StringBuffer buf = new StringBuffer();

        char ch = peekCh();

        if (ch == MINUS) {
            buf.append(getCh());
```

```java
            ch = peekCh();
        }

        while (Character.isDigit(ch) || ch == DOT) {
            buf.append(getCh());
            ch = peekCh();
        }

        final Double doubleObj = Double.valueOf(buf.toString());

        return new ProcessableDouble(doubleObj.doubleValue());
    }

    void skipWhite() {
        while (!bufferExhausted()) {
            final char ch = buffer.charAt(index);

            if (ch != SPACE &&
                ch != TAB &&
                ch != NEWLINE) {
                break;
            }

            index++;
        }
    }

    private char getCh() {
        return buffer.charAt(index++);
    }

    private char peekCh() {
        return peekCh(0);
    }

    private char peekCh(final int numAhead) {
        if (index + numAhead >= bufferLength) {
            return EOI;
        }

        return buffer.charAt(index + numAhead);
    }

    private boolean bufferExhausted() {
        return index == bufferLength;
    }

    private BufferedReader inputReader;
```

```
        private int              index;
        private int              bufferLength;
        private String           buffer;
    }

    private CalcInput    input;
    private CalcStack     stack;
    private PrintWriter  output;
}
```

Now, let's look at this class in a little more detail.

Notice that the `Calculator` class has two constructors. The first one is for creating an interactive calculator that uses `System.in` and `System.out`. The calculator reads a line at a time, so it relies on `BufferedReader` for input.

```
public Calculator() {
   this(new BufferedReader(
       new InputStreamReader(System.in)),
       new PrintWriter(System.out));
```

The second constructor connects the calculator to arbitrary input and output streams. This constructor ensures that the input and output streams are of type `InputStreamReader` and `PrintWriter`, respectively, so that all the operations the calculator needs are available. The `BufferedReader` class provides a `readline()` method that is used to read a line of input at a time. The instance variables introduced here - `input`, `stack`, and `output`, respectively - contain a `Reader` object that parses input, a `CalcStack` that holds operands, and an output stream to display results:

```
public Calculator(final Reader in, final Writer out) {

   BufferedReader dataIn;
   PrintWriter     printOut;

   if (!(in instanceof BufferedReader)) {
      dataIn = new BufferedReader(in);
   } else {
      dataIn = (BufferedReader)in;
   }

   if (!(out instanceof PrintWriter)) {
      printOut = new PrintWriter(out);
   } else {
      printOut = (PrintWriter)out;
   }
```

```
input  = new CalcInput(dataIn);  // Object that handles all input.
stack  = new CalcStack();        // Operand stack.
output = printOut;               // Output writer.
}
```

The `calculate()` method runs a loop, taking user input and printing results until the exit command e is entered. The main loop is then exited. We read a line at a time so extra prompts aren't inserted between the processing of multiple items in a line.

```
public void calculate() {

    boolean finished = false;

    while (!finished) {
        output.println();
        output.print("calc> ");
        output.flush();

        if (!input.readLine()) {
            continue;
        }
```

At this point, the reader has a new line waiting to be parsed. Note that the ensuing `try` block contains the first use of an interface in the program, as item is declared to be of type `Processable`. The `Processable` interface provides one method, `process()`. By using this interface, it would be easy to add new types of items to the calculator without the main class needing to change. Also notice how in the while loop, we process each item in the current input line. The `reader.hasInput()` call returns true as long as there is something other than spaces in its buffer.

```
        try {
            Processable item;

            while (input.hasInput()) {
                item = input.read(); // Returns a Processable
```

Here, we call the `process()` method of item. The `Calculator` class does not need to know anything about the kind of object item is. It only needs to know that item provides a `process()` method.

```
                if (item != null) {
```

```
            item.process(stack, output);
        }
    }
```

We have defined a special exception called `ExitException` that can be thrown by any `Processable`. When it is caught by the calculator, the `calculate()` method exits.

If any exception other than an `ExitException` is thrown (such as an invalid operator), the program displays a stack trace and continues after re-initializing the calculator:

```
    } catch (final ExitException e) {
        System.err.println("Exiting.");
        finished = true;

    } catch (final Exception e) {
```

If any exception other than an `ExitException` occurs, we print a stack trace and reset the calculator state. The `CalcInput` will automatically read a fresh line and needn't be reset.

```
        System.err.println("An exception occurred:");
        e.printStackTrace();
        stack = new CalcStack();
        }
    }
}
```

The CalcInput Class

The calculator encapsulates all input handling in the `CalcInput` class. Each calculator has its own `input` object (created in the constructor for the `Calculator` class). The `CalcInput` class uses several methods, which are summarized in Table 15-2. Take a quick look at these before reviewing the `CalcInput` source code.

Table 15-2 CalcInput Class Summary

Package		`calc`	
Imports		`java.io.InputStreamReader;` `java.io.IOException;`	
Constructors		`public CalcInput(BufferedReader in)`	
`public` **Instance Methods**	**Name:**	`readline()`	
	Returns:	`boolean`	
	Throws:	None	
	Use:	Reads a line from a `BufferedReader` object.	
	Name:	`read()`	
	Returns:	`Processable`	
	Throws:	None	
	Use:	Uses a the `private` method `readInternal()` to read input, if there is any.	
	Name:	`hasInput()`	
	Returns:	`boolean`	
	Throws:	None	
	Use:	Skips whitespace and checks if the buffer is empty.	
`private` **Instance Methods**	**Name:**	`readInternal()`	
	Returns:	`Processable`	
	Throws:	None	
	Use:	Reads the next `Processable` object.	
	Name:	`readNumber()`	
	Returns:	`Processable`	
	Throws:	None	
	Use:	Gathers all the input characters that could be a `double`.	

Table 15-2 CalcInput Class Summary (Continued)

Name:	`peekCh()`
Returns:	`char`
Throws:	None
Use:	Returns the next character in the line buffer without consuming it.
Name:	`peekCh(int n)`
Returns:	`char`
Throws:	None
Use:	Returns the *nth* character remaining in the line buffer without consuming any characters.
Name:	`getCh()`
Returns:	`char`
Throws:	None
Use:	Consumes and returns the next character in the line buffer.
Name:	`bufferExhausted()`
Returns:	`boolean`
Throws:	None
Use:	Returns true if the line buffer is empty.
Name:	`skipWhite()`
Returns:	`void`
Throws:	None
Use:	Consumes spaces, tabs, and newlines in the line buffer.

The `CalcInput` class handles all input for a calculator. It supports reading a line, reading the next entry, and checking if the current line is exhausted. Note that the class definition is followed by use of the `static final` idiom, which is used to define constants for all the special characters that might be entered. You'll also notice that The `CalcInput` class has only one constructor. All it does is save the `BufferedReader` the reader will take input from. The reader holds on to the input stream for the calculator.

When you encounter the the `readLine()` method, notice how it reads a line from the `BufferedReader`. Here, the class must catch `IOException` since `BufferedReader..readLine()` can throw it.

```java
static final class CalcInput {

  private static final char SPACE   = ' ';
  private static final char TAB     = '\t';
  private static final char NEWLINE = '\n';

  // '.' and '-' for numeric input.

  private static final char DOT     = '.';
  private static final char MINUS   = '-';

  private static final char EOI     = (char)-1;

  public CalcInput(final BufferedReader in) {
    inputReader = in;
  }

  public boolean readLine() {
    try {
      buffer = inputReader.readLine();

    } catch (final IOException e) {
      return false;
    }

    bufferLength = buffer.length();

    if (bufferLength == 0) {
      return false;
    }

    index = 0;  // Initialize the offset into the buffer.

    return true;
  }

  // Skip over any whitespace and read the next number or operator.

  public Processable read() {
    if (hasInput()) {
      return readInternal();
    } else {
      return null;
    }
  }

  // Skip whitespace and check if the buffer is empty.
```

```java
public boolean hasInput() {
  skipWhite();
  return !bufferExhausted();
}

// Read either a Double or a Character depending on the first few
// characters of the next item.

private Processable readInternal() {
  final char ch = peekCh();

  if (Character.isDigit(ch) ||
      ch == DOT ||
      (ch == MINUS &&
          (Character.isDigit(peekCh(1)) || peekCh(1) == DOT))) {
    return readNumber();
  } else {
    return new ProcessableCharacter(getCh());
  }
}

// Read and return a Double.

private Processable readNumber() {
  final StringBuffer buf = new StringBuffer();

  char ch = peekCh();

  if (ch == MINUS) {
    buf.append(getCh());
    ch = peekCh();
  }

  while (Character.isDigit(ch) || ch == DOT) {
    buf.append(getCh());
    ch = peekCh();
  }

  final Double doubleObj = Double.valueOf(buf.toString());

  return new ProcessableDouble(doubleObj.doubleValue());
}

// Skip whitespace.

private void skipWhite() {
  while (!bufferExhausted()) {
    final char ch = buffer.charAt(index);
```

```
      if (ch != SPACE &&
          ch != TAB &&
          ch != NEWLINE) {
          break;
    }

    index++;
    }
}

// Return the next character from the buffer and advance the
// buffer offset.

private char getCh() {
   return buffer.charAt(index++);
}

// Look ahead at the next character in the buffer without
// advancing the buffer offset.

private char peekCh() {
   return peekCh(0);
}

// Look ahead "numAhead" characters into the buffer.  Return EOI
// if there are not "numAhead" characters left.

private char peekCh(final int numAhead) {
   if (index + numAhead >= bufferLength) {
       return EOI;
   }

   return buffer.charAt(index + numAhead);
}

// Return whether or not the buffer has been emptied.

private boolean bufferExhausted() {
   return index == bufferLength;
}

private BufferedReader inputReader;
private int            index;
private int            bufferLength;
private String         buffer;
}
```

```
// Instance variables
private CalcInput    input;
private CalcStack    stack;
private PrintWriter output;
}
```

There are a couple details worth reviewing in this class. First of all, notice that the read() method uses a private method, readInternal(), to read input if there is any input available; otherwise the read() method returns null:

```
public Processable read() {
    if (hasInput()) {
        return readInternal();
    } else {
        return null;
    }
}
```

The readInternal() method returns a Processable type. In this simple calculator, a Processable is either a ProcessableCharacter or a ProcessableDouble. Note that here we use the constants previously defined with the static final modifiers:

```
private Processable readInternal() {
    final char ch = peekCh();

    if (Character.isDigit(ch) ||
        ch == DOT ||
        (ch == MINUS &&
            (Character.isDigit(peekCh(1)) || peekCh(1) == DOT))) {
        return readNumber();
    } else {
        return new ProcessableCharacter(getCh());
    }
}
```

The readNumber() method gathers all the characters that could make up a double and uses Double.valueOf() to try to parse the result as a double. If Double.valueOf() fails to parse the characters as a double, it will throw a NumberFormatException:

```
private Processable readNumber() {
    final StringBuffer buf = new StringBuffer();

    char ch = peekCh();

    if (ch == MINUS) {
        buf.append(getCh());
```

```
        ch = peekCh();
    }

    while (Character.isDigit(ch) || ch == DOT) {
        buf.append(getCh());
        ch = peekCh();
    }

    final Double doubleObj = Double.valueOf(buf.toString());

    return new ProcessableDouble(doubleObj.doubleValue());
}
```

Lastly, notice how the peekCh() and peekCh(int numHead) are overloaded methods. Note how peekCh() is simply implemented in terms of peekCh(int n):

```
// Look ahead at the next character in the buffer without
// advancing the buffer offset.

private char peekCh() {
    return peekCh(0);
}

// Look ahead "numAhead" characters into the buffer.  Return EOI
// if there are not "numAhead" characters left.

private char peekCh(final int numAhead) {
    if (index + numAhead >= bufferLength) {
        return EOI;
    }

    return buffer.charAt(index + numAhead);
}
```

The ExitException Class

The ExitException class exists only to have a unique exception class that Calculator.calculate() can check for:

```
package calc;

    // The exception thrown when the user want to exit the program.
    static final class ExitException extends Exception {}
```

Displayable Interface

The Displayable interface is implemented by any object that can be printed on a PrintWriter. For the calculator, this is only CalcStackItem objects:

```java
package calc;

import java.io.PrintWriter;

public interface Displayable {
    void display(PrintWriter output);
}
```

The Processable Interface

All calculator tokens implement the Processable interface. In this calculator, both ProcessableCharacter and ProcessableDouble implement the Processable interface. ProcessableCharacter represents operators, and ProcessableDouble represents operands:

```java
package calc;

import java.io.PrintWriter;

public interface Processable {
    void process(CalcStack stack, PrintWriter output) throws
    Calculator.ExitException;
}
```

The ProcessableCharacter Class

The ProcessableCharacter class represents operators for the calculator. The process() method for ProcessableCharacter determines the operation to perform based on the character input and makes the appropriate changes to the calculator stack. ProcessableCharacter.process pops values off of the calculator stack and performs operations on them, pushing the results. If an invalid operator is found, an error message is printed. If the user enters the exit command e, an instance of ExitException is thrown that will cause the calculator to quit its calculate() method:

```java
package calc;

import java.io.PrintWriter;

public class ProcessableCharacter implements Processable {
    public ProcessableCharacter(char val) {
    characterVal = val;
```

```
    }

    public void process(CalcStack stack, PrintWriter output) throws
    Calculator.ExitException {
        double tempArg;

        switch (characterVal) {
         case '+':
            stack.pushDouble(stack.popDouble() + stack.popDouble());
            break;
         case '-':
            tempArg = stack.popDouble();
            stack.pushDouble(stack.popDouble() - tempArg);
            break;
         case '*':
            stack.pushDouble(stack.popDouble() * stack.popDouble());
            break;
         case '/':
            tempArg = stack.popDouble();
            stack.pushDouble(stack.popDouble() / tempArg);
            break;
         case '=':
            stack.pop().display(output);
            break;
         case 'e':
            throw new Calculator.ExitException();
         default:
            System.err.println("Unknown operator: " + characterVal);
            break;
        }
    }
    private char characterVal;
}
```

The ProcessableDouble Class

The `ProcessableDouble` class holds a `double` value and implements
`CalcStackItem` so it knows how to push it on the stack when `process()` is
called or print it out when `display()` is called:

```
package calc;

import java.io.PrintWriter;

public class ProcessableDouble implements CalcStackItem {
    public ProcessableDouble(double val) {
```

```
      doubleVal = val;
   }
   public void process(CalcStack stack, PrintWriter output) {
      stack.push(this);
   }
   public void display(PrintWriter output) {
      output.println(doubleVal);
   }
   public double doubleValue() {
      return doubleVal;
   }

   private double doubleVal;
}
```

The CalcStack Class

The CalcStack class provides a typesafe Stack that requires no casting. The Stack class in java.util holds instances of Object, so when values are popped they must be cast down to their actual classes. CalcStack uses a java.util.Stack in its implementation. Since CalcStack is not a subclass of Stack, users may not push arbitrary objects onto a CalcStack. The only push() method requires a CalcStackItem argument. Note how popDouble() uses the fact that the CalcStackItem interface provides a doubleValue() method to return a double without casting:

```
package calc;

import java.util.Stack;

public class CalcStack {
    public CalcStack() {
       stack = new Stack();
    }

    public void push(CalcStackItem item) {
       stack.push(item);
    }

    public CalcStackItem pop() {
       return (CalcStackItem)stack.pop();
    }

    public boolean empty() {
       return stack.empty();
    }
```

```
   public CalcStackItem peek() {
      return (CalcStackItem)stack.peek();
   }

   public void pushDouble(double item) {
      stack.push(new ProcessableDouble(item));
   }

   public double popDouble() {
      return pop().doubleValue();
   }

   private Stack stack;
}
```

The CalcStackItem Interface

The CalcStackItem interface represents values on a CalcStack. A class that implements it must support process(), display(), and doubleValue() methods:

```
package calc;

public interface CalcStackItem extends Displayable, Processable {
   double doubleValue();
}
```

Running the Calculator Program

After all the classes in the calc package and the RunCalculator class have been compiled, you can call the java interpreter from the command line to start the calculator:

java RunCalculator

The interpreter will display the calculator prompt on the screen, and you can begin using it:

```
calc> 3 5 * =
15.0
calc> 3 5 + =
8.0
calc> 3 5 - =
-2.0
calc> 3 5 / =
0.6
```

Summary

Many of Java's features come together in this chapter to illustrate a simple, elegant calculator program that can easily be adapted to include new functions. In particular, the calculator program illustrates how Java interfaces, exception handling, I/O, and packages work.

In *Part 2—Writing Java Applets*, we'll expand on some of these topics and also address the specific issues of managing keyboard and mouse events, using animation, images, sound, and other graphical elements you may want to use in Java programs that will run in a web browser.

CHAPTER
16

Remote Method Invocation

What is Remote Method Invocation?

The Java Remote Method Invocation (RMI) mechanism, as its name suggests, provides the means to invoke methods remotely. Practically speaking, this ability enables the development of distributed applications. By using the Java RMI, applications can communicate and execute across multiple systems on a network.

The Java RMI system is Java's mechanism for doing distributed programming. As such, it is extremely flexible and is much easier to use than other distributed programming approaches such as RPC. Using RMI, methods can be invoked on remote objects as easily as they can on local ones. Sending sets of argument objects across the network is handled automatically.

The Java RMI mechanism is supported in the language by the `java.rmi`, `java.rmi.server`, and `java.rmi.registry` packages.

Before getting into the details of these packages, let's take a look at how RMI works.

How RMI Works

An application using RMI makes initial contact with a remote object by looking it up in a registry. The registry returns a stub object that can be used to manipulate its remote counterpart. For example, take a look at Figure 16-1.

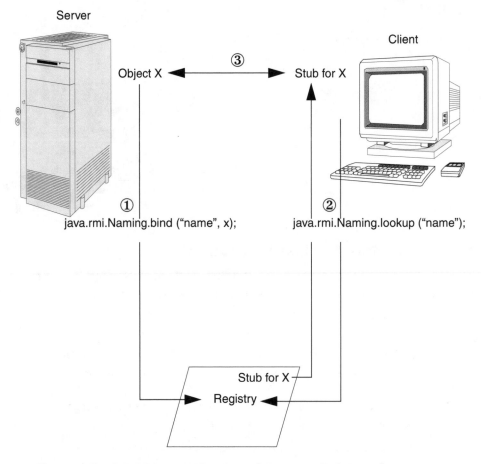

Figure 16-1 RMI Server, Client, and Registry Relationship
① The server process registers the remote object X with the registry using the `Naming.bind()` method.
② The client calls `Naming.lookup()`, which contacts the registry and obtains a stub object for X.
③ The client then uses the stub as if it is a local object, but methods

When a remote method is executed, the `java.rmi` runtime encodes the arguments and sends them over the network to a server that decodes them. The server then invokes the method, encodes the result and sends it back. Finally, the client-side `java.rmi` runtime decodes the result.

To set this picture in motion, let's look at a test program that utilizes RMI.

Calling Remote Methods

Example 12-1 demonstrates the simplest form of an RMI application—a remote object registers itself with a registry and one of its methods is called remotely by another process. The OpTest class looks up a remote object registered as "operator" and invokes the call operation on it. The java.rmi.Naming class is used to perform the lookup. The call operation will be performed in a remote process.

Example 16-1 Calling Remote Methods

```java
package rmi1;

import java.rmi.*;
import java.rmi.server.*;

public class OpTest {

  public static void main(String[] args) {

❶      System.setSecurityManager(new StubSecurityManager());

        try {

❷          RemOp ro = (RemOp)Naming.lookup("operator");

❸          ro.call();

        } catch (Exception x) {
            x.printStackTrace();
            System.exit(-1);
        }
    }
}
```

The purpose of the main() method in this test program is to look up a remote object (operator) and invoke call(). Notice in the call in line ❶ to System.setSecurityManager(). A Java process can have a SecurityManager that specifies security policies related to reading and writing files, making socket connections to other hosts, and so on. By default, no SecurityManager is present; however, Java RMI applications will not run without a SecurityManager. Once a SecurityManager has been set for a Java process, it cannot be changed. A simple, highly restrictive SecurityManager called java.rmi.RMISecurityManager is provided with the RMI distribution.

The object `ro` in line ❷ is an RMI stub that acts as a proxy for a remote object in another process. This is the simplest case for a remote call since no arguments are being passed and no value is returned. The type `RemOp` in the cast is an interface. (*All* remote objects are referenced through interfaces.)

The `Naming.lookup()` method searches for a name in an RMI registry and returns a stub reference to the object stored under that name. (We'll describe registries in more detail shortly.)

Line ❸ invokes the call operation remotely. The remote side of the example consists of two parts: an interface that defines the `call()` operation and a class that implements it. First, let's look at the interface.

The RemOp Interface

The `RemOp` interface in Example 16-2 is a remote interface for an object that supports the call operation.

Example 16-2 Extending the `Remote` Interface

```
package rmi1;

import java.rmi.*;

public interface RemOp extends Remote {
  public void call() throws RemoteException;
}
```

All interfaces for remote operations must extend the `Remote` interface. The `Remote` interface does not define any operations. It merely serves to identify remote objects. Note that all remote operations must declare themselves capable of throwing `RemoteException`.

Now let's look at the class that implements the `RemOp` interface.

The RemImpl Class

The `RemImpl` class in Example 16-3 implements the `RemOp` interface and supports remote invocation of the call operation. The `getName()` method returns a unique string identifying a particular instance of `RemImpl`.

Example 16-3 Implementing the `RemOp` Interface

```
package rmi1;

import java.rmi.*;
import java.rmi.server.*;
```

```
     public class RemImpl extends UnicastRemoteObject
     implements RemOp {

❶   public static void main(String[] args) {
         System.setSecurityManager(new StubSecurityManager());

         try {

             // Register an instance of RemImpl.

             Naming.rebind("operator", new RemImpl());

         } catch (Exception x) {
             x.printStackTrace();
             return;
         }
     }

❷   public RemImpl() throws RemoteException {
     }

❸   public void call() throws RemoteException {
         System.out.println(getName());
         System.out.println("Location: " +
                             System.getProperty("LOCATION"));
     }

     // Return a unique name for a RemImpl object.

     public String getName() {
         return "Remote operation: " + this;
     }

}
```

The main() method in line ❶ registers a new instance of RemImpl with the registry on the local host.

Note that in line ❷, a remote implementation class must have a zero-argument constructor that declares itself capable of throwing RemoteException. (We'll see this in a number of our examples in this chapter.)

The call() method in line ❸ prints the name of the RemImpl instance and the value of the LOCATION property. We set the LOCATION property when running the examples to distinguish between server and client processes. The property will be set to "server" in the server process and "client" in the client process.

Running the rmi1 Example

All of the examples in this chapter assume that each process is running on a separate system. You can, however, run these processes in the background on one system to emulate the behavior of the test application in a distributed, networked environment. (This is true of all the examples in this chapter.) Specifically, to run this example:

1. Set your CLASSPATH to include the applications/RMI directory and the java.rmi directory from the CD.

2. Start a registry using the rmiregistry executable in the JDK bin directory:

On Solaris: rmiregistry&

On Windows: start rmiregistry or javaw rmiregistry

3. Start the server for the application with this command:

java -DLOCATION=server -Djava.security.policy="*<path to cd>***\code\applications\RMI\policy" rmi1.RemImpl**

A security policy must be specified when running a server. The policy contained in the policy file on the CD is WIDE OPEN. Do not use it in a real system! For a full discussion of the current Java security policy model, see:

http://java.sun.com/products/jdk/1.2/docs/guide/security/PolicyFiles.html

http://java.sun.com/products/jdk/1.2/docs/guide/security/permissions.html

4. Use the following command to run the example:

java -DLOCATION=client -Djava.security.policy="*<path to cd>***\code\applications\RMI\policy" rmi1.OpTest**

Note that the operation is performed on the server. The interpreter will display output similar to the following:

```
Remote operation: rmi1.RemImpl[RemoteStub [ref: [endpoint:
[206.133.172.142:1079]
(local),objID:[0]]]]
Location: server
```

Building RMI Applications

Now that we've seen an introductory example, let's take a closer look at how to build an RMI application. Constructing an RMI application consists of three steps:

- Defining remote interfaces
- Creating classes that implement the interfaces
- Creating stub and skeleton classes for the implementation classes

Let's look at what is involved at each step.

Defining Interfaces

All methods that can be run remotely must be declared as part of an interface that extends Remote. In our first example, the RemOp interface extends Remote and declares the method call(). As we mentioned in the introduction, the Remote interface does not declare any methods of its own. It is only used to identify remote objects:

```
public interface RemOp extends Remote {
  public void call() throws RemoteException;
}
```

A class may implement any number of remote interfaces. It may also define methods that are not included in a remote interface, but these other methods will not be available remotely.

Creating Classes That Implement the Interfaces

Classes that implement remote interfaces must be defined. They must be subclasses of the RemoteObject class. RemoteObject provides support for the hashCode(), equals(), and toString() methods as applied to remote instances. hashCode() and equals() are redefined so that remote references to an object may be used as keys in hash tables. In practice, implementation classes extend a subclass of RemoteObject.

Example 16-4 shows the class structure.

Example 16-4 Object **and** RemoteObject **Class Structure**

```
java.lang.Object
   java.rmi.server.RemoteObject
      java.rmi.server.RemoteServer
         java.rmi.server.UnicastRemoteObject
```

Subclasses of RemoteServer, such as UnicastRemoteObject, define the semantics of remote requests. It is possible to define different subclasses of RemoteServer to create replicated remote objects, persistent remote objects, and

so on. The `UnicastRemoteObject` provides a non-replicated point-to-point remote object model. Individual instances reside in processes and can be contacted in order to run methods. All the remote object classes we will look at extend `UnicastRemoteObject`.

Every method defined in an implementation class that will be made available remotely must declare itself capable of throwing `RemoteException`. In addition, a zero-argument constructor must be defined that can throw `RemoteException`, as in this example:

```
public RemImpl() throws RemoteException {
}
```

The important things to remember when writing a remote implementation class are:

- Extend `UnicastRemoteObject`

- Implement one or more remote interfaces

- Declare all remote methods capable of throwing `RemoteException`

- Define a zero-argument constructor that throws `RemoteException`

Creating Stub and Skeleton Classes

RMI uses classes called *stub* and *skeleton* to provide the interface to application programs. Stub classes are the client-side images of remote object classes. They implement the same interfaces as the remote classes and forward methods invoked on their instances to the corresponding remote instances.

Conversely, skeleton classes reside on the server. When a remote method request arrives, a skeleton instance calls the actual method on an implementation instance and then returns the results to the client.

Stubs and skeletons are generated from an implementation class using the `rmic` (RMI compiler) program. For our `RemImpl` class, the following command will generate a stub and skeleton class in the current directory:

```
rmic rmi1.RemImpl
```

The two files produced are:

```
RemImpl_Stub.class
RemImpl_Skel.class
```

Passing Arguments to Remote Methods

To invoke methods on remote objects, the arguments to the methods and the return values must be sent across the network. The Java RMI handles this in one of two ways, depending on whether an argument or return value is an instance of

`RemoteObject` or not. For arguments and return values that *are* remote objects, a reference is passed over the network and a stub that refers to the remote object is created on the other side.

Arguments and return values that are *not* remote objects are copied over the network. Other objects referred to by an argument object are copied as well. In fact, all the non-remote objects that can be reached by a chain of references from an argument are copied. (The remote ones are passed by reference).

Let's assume that we have two classes, NR and R, which stand for non-remote and remote. R is a subclass of `RemoteObject`. In Figure 16-2 and Figure 16-2, arg, nr1, nr2, and nr3 are instances of NR; r1 is an instance of R.

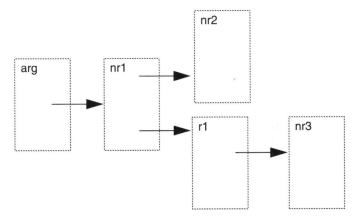

Figure 16-2 Passing Arguments to Remote Methods on Client Side

If a remote method was invoked with arg as an argument, the following would happen:

1. arg would be copied.

2. The reference from arg to nr1 would be followed, and nr1 would be copied.

3. The reference from nr1 to nr2 would be followed, and nr2 would be copied.

4. The reference from nr1 to r1 would be followed, but since r1 is a remote object, a reference would be passed. On the server side, the copy of nr1 would contain a reference to a stub for r1.

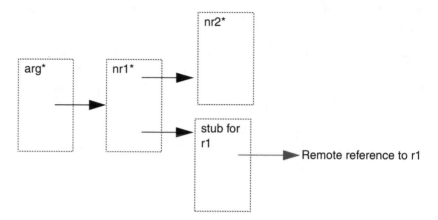

Figure 16-3 Passing Arguments to Remote Methods on Server Side

The process of encoding arguments for network transmission is known as *marshaling*. The inverse process is *unmarshaling*. Marshaling and unmarshaling of objects for RMI is handled by the Java Object Serialization system. Object serialization in Java is automatic and in most cases need not be a concern of RMI application writers, even though support is available for special-purpose serialization routines if necessary.

The notions of client and server for an RMI application are only meaningful in the context of a single remote method call. For instance, after the call that caused `arg` in our diagram to be copied to the server, a method on the server side could be invoked on the stub for `r1`. This would cause a remote call back to the originating process, reversing the roles of client and server.

The next example demonstrates RMI arguments passed both by copying and by reference. It also demonstrates client/server role reversal. The first call made by the test program passes a remote object. When its `execute()` method is called, the method runs in the same process as the test program. The second call passes a non-remote object. When its `execute()` method is called, it runs in the server process.

Figure 16-4 shows the package overview for the next test application that uses the Java RMI.

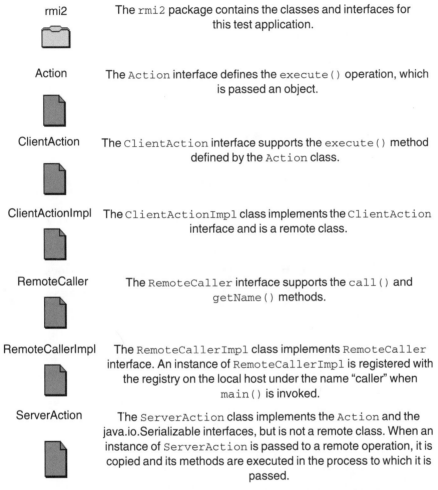

rmi2	The `rmi2` package contains the classes and interfaces for this test application.
Action	The `Action` interface defines the `execute()` operation, which is passed an object.
ClientAction	The `ClientAction` interface supports the `execute()` method defined by the `Action` class.
ClientActionImpl	The `ClientActionImpl` class implements the `ClientAction` interface and is a remote class.
RemoteCaller	The `RemoteCaller` interface supports the `call()` and `getName()` methods.
RemoteCallerImpl	The `RemoteCallerImpl` class implements `RemoteCaller` interface. An instance of `RemoteCallerImpl` is registered with the registry on the local host under the name "caller" when `main()` is invoked.
ServerAction	The `ServerAction` class implements the `Action` and the java.io.Serializable interfaces, but is not a remote class. When an instance of `ServerAction` is passed to a remote operation, it is copied and its methods are executed in the process to which it is passed.

Figure 16-4 Classes for Passing Arguments to Remote Arguments

`ActionTest` in Example 16-5 creates two objects that implement the `Action` interface (see page 355). One is a remote object of type `ClientActionImpl`. The other is a non-remote object of type `ServerAction`. When the `ClientActionImpl` instance is passed to a `RemoteCaller`, its `execute()` method will run in the same process as the `ActionTest main()` method. When the `ServerAction` instance is passed, its `execute()` method will run in the same process as the `RemoteCaller` call method.

Example 16-5 `rmi2.ActionTest` **Class**

```java
package rmi2;

import java.rmi.*;
import java.rmi.server.*;

public class ActionTest {
  public static void main(String[] args) {
      System.setSecurityManager(new StubSecurityManager());

      try {

          // Create a new remote action object.

          ClientActionImpl cai = new ClientActionImpl();

          // Create a new non-remote action object.

          ServerAction    sa = new ServerAction();

          // Find an instance of RemoteCaller in the local
          // registry.

          RemoteCaller    rc =
            (RemoteCaller)Naming.lookup("caller");

          // Pass the remote action object to the remote caller.

          rc.call(cai);

          // Pass the non-remote action object to the remote
          // caller.

          rc.call(sa);

      } catch (Exception x) {
          x.printStackTrace();
          System.exit(-1);
      }
  }
}
```

The Action Interface

The `Action` interface in Example 16-6 defines the `execute()` operation that is passed an object. The argument is typically the object that invoked `execute()`.

Example 16-6 `rmi2.Action` **Interface**

```
package rmi2;

import java.rmi.*;

public interface Action {
  public void execute(Object o) throws RemoteException;
}
```

The ServerAction Class

The `ServerAction` class in Example 16-7 implements the `Action` interface but is not a remote class. When an instance of `ServerAction` is passed to a remote operation, it is copied and its methods are executed in the process it is passed to.

Example 16-7 `rmi2.ServerAction` **Class**

```
package rmi2;

import java.rmi.*;
import java.rmi.server.*;

public class ServerAction implements Action,java.io.Serializable{

❶    public void execute(Object o) throws RemoteException {
        if (o instanceof RemoteCaller) {
            System.out.println(((RemoteCaller)o).getName());
        } else {
            System.out.println(o);
        }

        System.out.println("Location: " +
                        System.getProperty("LOCATION"));
    }
}
```

The `execute()` method in line ❶ displays the name and location of the object `o`. The location will be either "server" or "client" depending on whether `execute()` runs in the server or client process. (You'll notice that we use this convention in examples throughout this chapter.)

The ClientAction Interface

The ClientAction interface in Example 16-8 supports the execute() method defined by Action and is implemented by remote objects. When an instance of a class that implements ClientAction is passed to a remote operation, a stub is passed as a proxy. Methods invoked on the stub are executed in the process that passed the stub, not the process that received it.

Example 16-8 rmi2.ClientAction Interface

```
package rmi2;

import java.rmi.*;

public interface ClientAction extends Remote, Action {
  public void execute(Object o) throws RemoteException;
}
```

The RemoteCaller Interface

The RemoteCaller interface in Example 16-9 supports two methods: call() and getName(). The call() method takes an Action as an argument and is intended to call execute() on the action. The getName() method returns the unique name of a particular RemoteCaller.

Example 16-9 rmi2.RemoteCaller Interface

```
package rmi2;

import java.rmi.*;

public interface RemoteCaller extends Remote {

  // Execute the Action "a".

  public void call(Action a) throws RemoteException;

  // Return a unique name for a RemoteCaller.

  public String getName() throws RemoteException;
}
```

The RemoteCallerImpl Class

The `RemoteCallerImpl` class in Example 16-10 implements the
`RemoteCaller` interface. An instance of `RemoteCallerImpl` is registered with
the registry on the local host under the name "caller" when `main()` is invoked.

Example 16-10 `rmi2.RemoteCallerImpl` **Class**

```
package rmi2;

import java.rmi.*;
import java.rmi.server.*;

public class RemoteCallerImpl extends UnicastRemoteObject
implements RemoteCaller {

  public static void main(String[] args) {
      System.setSecurityManager(new StubSecurityManager());

      try {
❶       Naming.rebind("caller", new RemoteCallerImpl());
      } catch (Exception x) {
         x.printStackTrace();
         return;
      }
  }

❷ public RemoteCallerImpl() throws RemoteException {
  }

❸ public String getName() throws RemoteException {
      return "Remote operation: " + this;
  }

❹ public void call(Action a) throws RemoteException {
      a.execute(this);
  }
}
```

Line ❶ registers an instance of `RemoteCallerImpl` with the local registry under
the name "caller."

As we've already seen in our first RMI example, all remote implementation
classes must have a zero-argument constructor that declares itself capable of
throwing `RemoteException`, which we do in line ❷.

The getName() method in line ❸ returns the unique name of a RemoteCallerImpl. The call() method in line ❹ invokes the Action object passed as an argument.

The ClientActionImpl Class

The ClientActionImpl class in Example 16-11 implements the ClientAction interface and is a remote class. When an instance of ClientActionImpl is passed to a remote operation, a stub is passed as a proxy. Methods invoked on the stub are executed in the process that passed the stub.

Example 16-11 rmi2.ClientActionImpl **Class**

```
package rmi2;

import java.rmi.*;
import java.rmi.server.*;

public class ClientActionImpl extends UnicastRemoteObject
implements ClientAction {

  // All remote implementation classes must have a
  // zero-argument constructor that declares itself
  // capable of throwing RemoteException.

  public ClientActionImpl() throws RemoteException {
  }

  // Display the name and location of the object "o". The
  // location will be either "server" or "client" depending
  // on whether execute() runs in the server or client
  // process.

  public void execute(Object o) throws RemoteException {
      if (o instanceof RemoteCaller) {
          System.out.println(((RemoteCaller)o).getName());
      } else {
          System.out.println(o);
      }

      System.out.println("Location: " +
                          System.getProperty("LOCATION"));
  }
}
```

Running the rmi2 Example

This example assumes that each process is running on a separate system. To run this example follow these four steps.

1. Set your CLASSPATH to include the applications/RMI directory and the java.rmi directory from the CD.

2. Start a registry using the rmiregistry executable in the JDK bin directory:

    On Solaris: rmiregistry&

    On Windows: start rmiregistry or javaw rmiregistry

3. Start the server for the application with this command:

    java -DLOCATION=server -Djava.security.policy="*<path to cd>*\code\applications\RMI\policy" rmi2.RemoteCallerImpl**

4. Use the following command to run the example:

    java -DLOCATION=client -Djava.security.policy="*<path to cd>*\code\applications\RMI\policy" rmi2.ActionTest**

The first call runs on the client, and the second on the server. The interpreter will display output similar to the following:

```
Remote operation: rmi2.RemoteCallerImpl[RemoteStub [ref: [endpoint:
[206.133.172.
142:1086](local),objID:[0]]]]
Location: client

Remote operation: rmi2.RemoteCallerImpl[RemoteStub [ref: [endpoint:
[206.133.172.
142:1086](local),objID:[0]]]]
Location: server
```

Managing Multiple RMI Client Processes

The next example demonstrates cooperation between multiple RMI client processes. References to remote objects can be freely passed between any number of processes and methods can be invoked that will run in the process containing the actual implementation object. In the next example, one process sends a remote reference to another process, which then becomes the target of a method invocation from a third process. To make things a little more interesting, the initial method invocation by the third process changes the action that will be executed on the second invocation.

The next test application has the same set of classes as the one in Figure 16-4, only some of the implementations are different. The two test classes in this example are ActionTestSet and the ActionTestCall. The ActionTestSet class sends a remote object to the server process that is then invoked by the ActionTestCall class.

The ActionTestCall class in Example 16-12 looks up a RemoteCaller in line ❶ and invokes its call() method twice. If the RemoteCaller was initialized with a ClientActionImpl object, the second time call() is invoked, and it will execute an instance of ServerAction that the ClientActionImpl object associated with the RemoteCaller.

Example 16-12 rmi3.ActionTestCall **Class**

```
package rmi3;

import java.rmi.*;
import java.rmi.server.*;

public class ActionTestCall {
  public static void main(String[] args) {
      System.setSecurityManager(new StubSecurityManager());

      try {

          // Look up a RemoteCaller and invoke its call() method
          // twice.

          RemoteCaller rc = (RemoteCaller)Naming.lookup("caller");
          rc.call();
          rc.call();

      } catch (Exception x) {
          x.printStackTrace();
          return;
      }
  }
}
```

❶

The ActionTestSet Class

The ActionTestSet class in Example 16-13 initializes the action associated with a RemoteCaller object (line ❷). The initial value is an instance of clientActionImpl that will reset the action when its execute() method is invoked. Notice in line ❶ that the ClientActionImpl instance cai will set the action for a RemoteCaller to a copy of the ServerAction instance sa when its execute() method is invoked.

Example 16-13 rmi3.ActionTestSet **Class**

```
package rmi3;

import java.rmi.*;
import java.rmi.server.*;

public class ActionTestSet {

  public static void main(String[] args) {
      System.setSecurityManager(new StubSecurityManager());

      try {

          ServerAction      sa  = new ServerAction();
          ClientActionImpl cai = new ClientActionImpl();

          cai.setServerAction(sa);

          RemoteCaller     rc  =
          (RemoteCaller)Naming.lookup("caller");

          // Initialize the action for "rc" to an instance
          // of ClientActionImpl.

          rc.setAction(cai);

      } catch (Exception x) {
          x.printStackTrace();
          return;
      }
  }
}
```

Line markers: ❶ at `cai.setServerAction(sa);`, ❷ at `(RemoteCaller)Naming.lookup("caller");`

The ClientActionImpl Class

The ClientActionImpl class in Example 16-14 implements the ClientAction interface and is a remote class. When an instance of ClientActionImpl is passed to a remote operation, a stub is passed as a proxy.

Methods invoked on the stub are executed in the process that passed the stub. An instance of ClientActionImpl will change the saved action object associated with a RemoteCaller when the RemoteCaller invokes its execute() method.

Example 16-14 rmi3.ClientActionImpl **Class**

```
package rmi3;

import java.rmi.*;
import java.rmi.server.*;

public class ClientActionImpl extends UnicastRemoteObject
implements ClientAction {

  public ClientActionImpl() throws RemoteException {
  }

  public void setServerAction(ServerAction sa) {
      serverAction = sa;
  }

  public void execute(Object o) throws RemoteException {
      if (o instanceof RemoteCaller) {
          RemoteCaller rc = (RemoteCaller)o;
          System.out.println(rc.getName());
          rc.setAction(serverAction);

      } else {
          System.out.println(o);
      }

      System.out.println("Location: " +
                          System.getProperty("LOCATION"));
  }

  ServerAction serverAction;
}
```

❶ — `public void execute(Object o) throws RemoteException {`

❷ — `rc.setAction(serverAction);`

Notice that the execute() method in line ❶ displays the name and location of the object o, and the location will be either "server" or "client" depending on whether execute() runs in the server or client process. This is the same as in the previous examples. However, this implementation of the execute() method also replaces the action associated with the argument with an instance of ServerAction (line ❷).

The RemoteCaller Interface

The `RemoteCaller` interface in Example 16-15 supports three methods:

- `setAction()` — Stores a reference to an action object in the RemoteCaller
- `call()` — Is intended to call `execute()` on the action
- `getName()` — Returns the unique name of a particular RemoteCaller

Example 16-15 `rmi3.RemoteCaller` **Interface**

```
package rmi3;

import java.rmi.*;

public interface RemoteCaller extends Remote {

    // Store an instance of Action in the RemoteCaller.

    public  void setAction(Action a) throws RemoteException;

    // Execute the action stored in the RemoteCaller.

    public void call() throws RemoteException;

    // Return a unique name for a RemoteCaller.

    public String getName() throws RemoteException;
}
```

The RemoteCallerImpl Class

The `RemoteCallerImpl` class in Example 16-16 implements the `RemoteCaller` interface. An instance of `RemoteCallerImpl` is registered with the registry on the local host under the name "caller" when `main()` is invoked.

Example 16-16 `rmi3.RemoteCallerImpl` **Class**

```java
package rmi3;

import java.rmi.*;
import java.rmi.server.*;

public class RemoteCallerImpl extends UnicastRemoteObject
implements RemoteCaller {

  // Register an instance of RemoteCallerImpl with the
  // local registry under the name "caller".

  public static void main(String[] args) {
      System.setSecurityManager(new StubSecurityManager());

      try {
         Naming.rebind("caller", new RemoteCallerImpl());
      } catch (Exception x) {
         x.printStackTrace();
         return;
      }
  }

  public RemoteCallerImpl() throws RemoteException {
  }

  // Return the unique name of a RemoteCallerImpl.

  public String getName() throws RemoteException {
      return "Remote operation: " + this;
  }

  // Set the local action object for a RemoteCallerImpl.

  public void setAction(Action a) throws RemoteException {
      action = a;
  }

  // Invoke execute() on a stored Action object.

  public void call() throws RemoteException {
      action.execute(this);
  }

  private Action action;
}
```

Running the rmi3 Example

To run this example:

1. Set your CLASSPATH to include the applications/RMI directory and the java.rmi directory from the CD.

2. Start a registry using the rmiregistry executable in the JDK bin directory:

    On Solaris: rmiregistry&

    On Windows: start rmiregistry or javaw rmiregistry

3. Start the server for the application with this command:

    java -DLOCATION=server -Djava.security.policy="*<path to cd>***\code\applications\RMI\policy" rmi3.RemoteCallerImpl**

4. Initialize a remote action with the following command:

    java -DLOCATION=client -Djava.security.policy="*<path to cd>***\code\applications\RMI\policy" rmi3.ActionTestSet**

5. Use the following command to run the example:

    java -DLOCATION=client2 -Djava.security.policy="*<path to cd>***\code\applications\RMI\policy" rmi3.ActionTestCall**

The two operations run in the client and server process, but not in the client2 process. The interpreter will display output similar to the following:

```
Remote operation: rmi3.RemoteCallerImpl[RemoteStub [ref: [endpoint:
[206.133.172.
142:1230](local),objID:[0]]]]
Location: server

Remote operation: rmi3.RemoteCallerImpl[RemoteStub [ref: [endpoint:
[206.133.172.
142:1230](local),objID:[0]]]]
Location: client
```

RMI and Threads

When an RMI application makes a remote method call, a thread is spawned on the remote server to process the request. Since Java threads are not guaranteed to be preemptive, it's possible for a remote call to hang waiting for an opportunity to execute in the remote process. In the next example, the remote call back to the `ActionTestSet` process cannot complete until the computation thread calls `Thread.yield()`. Without the call to `Thread.yield()`, the remote call could hang indefinitely.

This test application relies on the classes in interfaces shown in Figure 16-5.

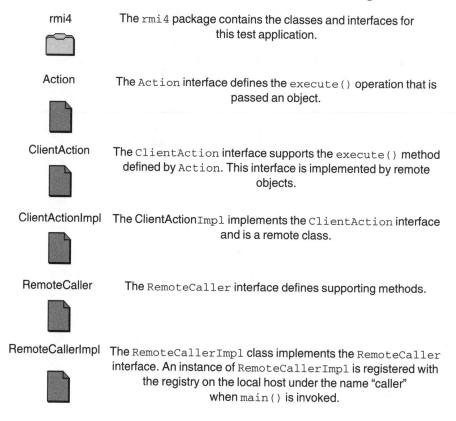

rmi4	The `rmi4` package contains the classes and interfaces for this test application.
Action	The `Action` interface defines the `execute()` operation that is passed an object.
ClientAction	The `ClientAction` interface supports the `execute()` method defined by `Action`. This interface is implemented by remote objects.
ClientActionImpl	The ClientAction`Impl` implements the `ClientAction` interface and is a remote class.
RemoteCaller	The `RemoteCaller` interface defines supporting methods.
RemoteCallerImpl	The `RemoteCallerImpl` class implements the `RemoteCaller` interface. An instance of `RemoteCallerImpl` is registered with the registry on the local host under the name "caller" when `main()` is invoked.

Figure 16-5 Classes for the RMI Threads Example

The next example shows the interaction between threads and RMI. Like the previous `rmi3` example, one process sends a remote object to a server, which is invoked by another process. In this case, the original process goes into a busy loop after sending the object. The remote call initiated by the second process cannot be completed until the thread containing the busy loop in the first process yields.

The `ActionTestCall` class in Example 16-17 looks up a `RemoteCaller` and invokes its `call()` method.

Example 16-17 `rmi4.ActionTestCall` **Class**

```
package rmi4;

import java.rmi.*;
import java.rmi.server.*;

public class ActionTestCall {
  public static void main(String[] args) {
      System.setSecurityManager(new StubSecurityManager());

      try {
         RemoteCaller rc = (RemoteCaller)Naming.lookup("caller");
         rc.call();

      } catch (Exception x) {
         x.printStackTrace();
         return;
      }
   }
}
```

The ActionTestSet Class

The `ActionTestSet` class in Example 16-18 initializes the action associated with a `RemoteCaller` object. The initial value is an instance of `ClientActionImpl`. `ActionTestSet` then enters a loop that `yields()` periodically. Remote operation requests may only be serviced when the main thread yields.

Example 16-18 `rmi4.ActionTestSet` **Class**

```
package rmi4;

import java.rmi.*;
import java.rmi.server.*;

public class ActionTestSet {
  public static void main(String[] args) {
      System.setSecurityManager(new StubSecurityManager());
```

```
try {

    // Initialize the action object for a RemoteCaller.

    ClientActionImpl cai = new ClientActionImpl();
    RemoteCaller    rc  =
                 (RemoteCaller)Naming.lookup("caller");
    rc.setAction(cai);

    // Go into a loop waiting for a remote request.

    int bigNumber = (int)(Math.random() * 10) + 1000000;

    for (int i = 0; i < bigNumber; i++) {
        for (int j = 0; j < bigNumber; j++) {
            k = k + 1;
        }

        System.out.println(i);

        // Yield so other threads can run. A remote request
        // can only be handled here.

        Thread.yield();
    }

    System.out.println(k);

} catch (Exception x) {
    x.printStackTrace();
    return;
}
}

    private static long k;
}
```

The ClientActionImpl Class

The ClientActionImpl class in Example 16-19 implements the
ClientAction interface and is a remote class. When an instance of
ClientActionImpl is passed to a remote operation, a stub is passed as a proxy.
Methods invoked on the stub are executed in the process that passed the stub.

Example 16-19 `rmi4.ClientActionImpl` **Class**

```java
package rmi4;

import java.rmi.*;
import java.rmi.server.*;

public class ClientActionImpl extends UnicastRemoteObject
implements ClientAction {

  public ClientActionImpl() throws RemoteException {
  }

  public void execute(Object o) throws RemoteException {
      if (o instanceof RemoteCaller) {
          RemoteCaller rc = (RemoteCaller)o;
          System.out.println(rc.getName());

      } else {
          System.out.println(o);
      }

      System.out.println("Location: " +
                         System.getProperty("LOCATION"));
  }
}
```

Running the rmi4 Example

As we've mentioned in the previous examples, in a true RMI application, each Java process would be running on a separate system. You can, however, run these processes in the background on one system to emulate the behavior of the test application in a distributed, networked environment. Specifically, to run this example follow these steps:

1. Set your `CLASSPATH` to include the `applications/RMI` directory and the `java.rmi` directory from the CD.

2. Start a registry using the `rmiregistry` executable in the JDK `bin` directory:

On Solaris: `rmiregistry&`

On Windows: `start rmiregistry` or `javaw rmiregistry`

3. Start the server for the application with this command:

java -DLOCATION=server -Djava.security.policy="*<path to cd>***\code\applications\RMI\policy" rmi4.RemoteCallerImpl**

4. Initialize a remote action with the following command:

```
java -DLOCATION=client -Djava.security.policy="<path to
cd>\code\applications\RMI\policy" rmi4.ActionTestSet
```

5. Use the following command to run the example:

```
java -DLOCATION=client2 -Djava.security.policy="<path to
cd>\code\applications\RMI\policy" rmi4.ActionTestCall
```

The message from the remote operation is not printed until immediately after a number is printed (i.e., when the client process calls `Thread.yield()`). The interpreter will display output similar to the following:

```
1
2
3
4
5
6
Remote operation: rmi4.RemoteCallerImpl[RemoteStub [ref:
[endpoint:[206.133.172.
142:1143](local),objID:[0]]]]
2304
Location: client
7
8
9
```

Registries

To begin a remote interaction via RMI, an initial connection to a remote object must be obtained. This is done via a *registry*. Registries are objects associated with a particular host and port that provide dictionaries of remote objects referenced by name.

Finding Objects in a Registry

A typical RMI session begins with a client contacting a registry and obtaining a reference to a remote object. A registry may be contacted directly or by using the URL based `java.rmi.Naming` interface.

Example 16-20 shows sample code that uses the `Registry` interface directly.

Example 16-20 Using the `Registry` Interface Directly

```
Registry registry = LocateRegistry.getRegistry();
Builder builder1 = (Builder)registry.lookup(args[1]);
Builder builder2 = (Builder)registry.lookup(args[2]);
```

Example 16-21 shows a sample call using the `Naming` class to look up a registry.

Example 16-21 Contacting a Registry Using the `Naming` **Class**

```
RemoteCaller rc = (RemoteCaller)Naming.lookup("caller");
```

In both these examples, the host and port for the registry have been set by default to the local host and the standard default registry port.

To specify a different host and/or port, the `getRegistry()` call may take any of the following forms (where *host* is a string and *port* is an `int`), as in Example 16-22.

Example 16-22 Specifying a Host or Port With `getRegistry()` **Method**

```
Registry registry = LocateRegistry.getRegistry(host);
Registry registry = LocateRegistry.getRegistry(port);
Registry registry = LocateRegistry.getRegistry(host, port);
```

To specify host and port information to the `Naming` interface, URLs are used as in Example 16-23.

Example 16-23 Specifying a Host or Port With the `Naming` **Interface**

```
Remote o = Naming.lookup("rmi://host/object_name");
Remote o = Naming.lookup("rmi://host:port/object_name");
```

Both the `Registry` interface and the `Naming` interface also support listing the entries in the registry, as in Example 16-24.

Example 16-24 Listing Registry Entries

```
String[] entries = registry.list();
String[] entries = Naming.list(URL);
```

Changing the Contents of a Registry

Objects can be added to a registry using the `bind()` and `rebind()` methods (Example 16-25). `rebind()` is just like `bind()`, except that `bind()` throws an `AlreadyBoundException` if an object is already stored in the registry under the specified name.

Example 16-25 Adding Contents to a Registry

```
Registry registry = LocateRegistry.getRegistry();
registry.rebind("a name", new BuildImp()); // or registry.bind()
Naming.bind("another name", new RemImpl()); // or Naming.rebind()
```

Objects are removed from a registry either via an `unbind()` call or by having a different object attached to the same name with `rebind()`, as in Example 16-26.

Example 16-26 Removing Contents From a Registry

```
registry.unbind("a name");
Naming.unbind("another name");
```

Not all remote objects need to be stored in a registry. It's only necessary that an object be there to make initial contact. After that, remote references to other objects may be created and passed back and forth as arguments and return values.

Garbage Collection of Remote References

The RMI runtime keeps track of every remote reference to a remote object. When all remote references have been dropped, the object behaves like a normal object and may be garbage collected when there are no more references to it. The RMI runtime maintains *weak* references to remote objects. A weak reference is one that is ignored by the garbage collector. If an object has only weak references referring to it, the garbage collector is free to collect it.

If a remote object needs to be notified when it is no longer referred to remotely, it can implement the `java.rmi.server.Unreferenced` interface. When the last remote reference is dropped, `unreferenced()` will be called on the object. It is possible for `unreferenced()` to be called multiple times. If other remote references to the object are generated before it is garbage collected, `unreferenced()` will be called when those references are dropped.

Maintaining Object References Across Multiple Processes

Our final example shows just how easy it is to deal with remote objects using RMI. The program will construct a remote linked list in which every other node is in a different process and none of them are in the main process. The list will then be traversed just as if it were local.

This test application relies on the classes and interfaces shown in Figure 16-6.

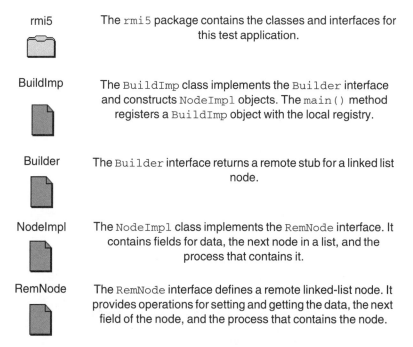

rmi5 — The rmi5 package contains the classes and interfaces for this test application.

BuildImp — The BuildImp class implements the Builder interface and constructs NodeImpl objects. The main() method registers a BuildImp object with the local registry.

Builder — The Builder interface returns a remote stub for a linked list node.

NodeImpl — The NodeImpl class implements the RemNode interface. It contains fields for data, the next node in a list, and the process that contains it.

RemNode — The RemNode interface defines a remote linked-list node. It provides operations for setting and getting the data, the next field of the node, and the process that contains the node.

Figure 16-6 Classes for the RMI Linked List Example

This test application relies on the Builder interface, which constructs new remote nodes. Two processes containing BuildImp objects will construct nodes and hand them back to the top-level ListTest program. The ListTest program will alternately create list nodes in either of two BuildImp processes. It will then traverse the list twice, first printing the list contents and then printing the locations of each list node.

The ListTest class in Example 16-27 creates a linked list that is spread across two remote processes. The nodes in the list alternate between the two processes. First the data elements, and then the process locations of the list cells are printed.

As you look through the code, notice how we create node builders in two different processes in lines ❶ and ❷.

Example 16-27 rmi5.ListTest **Class**

```
package rmi5;

import java.rmi.*;
import java.rmi.server.*;
import java.rmi.registry.*;

public class ListTest {
  public static void main(String[] args) {
      if (args.length != 3) {
        System.err.println(
          "Usage: java rmi5.ListTest <count> <server1> <server2>");
        System.exit(-1);
      }

      System.setSecurityManager(new StubSecurityManager());

      try {

          // Find the local registry.

          Registry registry = LocateRegistry.getRegistry();

          // Read in the length of the list.

          int      count    = Integer.parseInt(args[0]);

          // Create node builders in two different processes.
          // The processes should be registered under the
          // names found in arguments 1 and 2.
```

❶
❷
```
          Builder  builder1 = (Builder)registry.lookup(args[1]);
          Builder  builder2 = (Builder)registry.lookup(args[2]);

          // The head of the list.

          RemNode  list     = null;

          // Create "count" list nodes, alternating between
          // processes and attach them to the list.
```

```java
        for (int i = 0; i < count; i++) {
            RemNode node = builder1.newNode();
            node.setNext(list);
            node.setData(i);
            list          = node;

            // Swap the two node builders so that the
            // next time around the other one will be used.

            Builder temp = builder2;
            builder2     = builder1;
            builder1     = temp;
        }

        // Print the data elements in the list.

        RemNode listptr = list;
        System.out.print("[ ");

        while (listptr != null) {
            System.out.print(listptr.getData() + " ");
            listptr = listptr.getNext();
        }

        System.out.println("]");

        // Print the process locations of each node
        // in the list.

        listptr = list;
        System.out.print("[ ");

        while (listptr != null) {
            System.out.print(listptr.getLocation() + " ");
            listptr = listptr.getNext();
        }

        System.out.println("]");

    } catch (Exception x) {
        x.printStackTrace();
        System.exit(-1);
    }
  }
}
```

The Builder Interface

The `Builder` interface in Example 16-28 defines the `newNode()` method that returns a remote stub for a linked list node.

Example 16-28 `rmi5.Builder` **Interface**

```
package rmi5;

import java.rmi.*;

public interface Builder extends Remote {
  public RemNode newNode() throws RemoteException;
}
```

The BuildImp Class

The `BuildImp` class in Example 16-29 implements the `Builder` interface and constructs `NodeImpl` objects. The `main()` method registers a `BuildImp` object with the local registry.

Example 16-29 `rmi5.BuildImp` **Class**

```
package rmi5;

import java.rmi.*;
import java.rmi.server.*;
import java.rmi.registry.*;

public class BuildImp extends UnicastRemoteObject
implements Builder {
  public static void main(String[] args) {
      if (args.length != 1) {
          System.err.println(
            "Usage: java rmi5.BuildImp <binding name>");
          System.exit(-1);
      }

      System.setSecurityManager(new StubSecurityManager());

      try {

          // Register a BuildImp object in the local registry
          // under the name in argument zero.

          location        = args[0];
          Registry registry = LocateRegistry.getRegistry();
          registry.rebind(location, new BuildImp());
```

```
        } catch (Exception x) {
            x.printStackTrace();
            System.exit(-1);
        }
    }

    public BuildImp() throws RemoteException {
    }

❶  public RemNode newNode() throws RemoteException {
        NodeImpl node = new NodeImpl();
        node.setLocation(location);
        return node;
    }

    private static String location;
}
```

Notice that the newNode() method (line ❶) returns an instance of the remote class NodeImpl. Its location field will contain the same value as the BuildImp object's location field.

The RemNode Interface

The RemNode interface in Example 16-30 defines a remote linked-list node. Operations are provided to set and get the data and the next and location fields of the node. The location field refers to the process that contains the node.

Example 16-30 rmi5.RemNode **Interface**

```
package rmi5;

import java.rmi.*;

public interface RemNode extends Remote {
  public RemNode getNext() throws RemoteException;
  public void    setNext(RemNode next) throws RemoteException;

  public int     getData() throws RemoteException;
  public void    setData(int data) throws RemoteException;
```

```
    public String getLocation() throws RemoteException;
    public void setLocation(String location) throws RemoteException;

}
```

The NodeImpl Class

The NodeImpl class implements the RemNode interface. It contains instance variables for data, the next node in a list, and the process that contains it. Notice while looking through the code that the getLocation() method in line ❶ obtains the name under which this node's builder is registered. Each process containing a node builder should have it registered under a distinct name. Also, note that line ❷ sets the process location for this node. This is used by the node builder that creates a node. The name under which the builder is registered is stored in the node's location instance variable.

Example 16-31 rmi5.NodeImpl **Class**

```
package rmi5;

import java.rmi.*;
import java.rmi.server.*;
import java.rmi.registry.*;

public class NodeImpl extends UnicastRemoteObject
implements RemNode {

  public NodeImpl() throws RemoteException {
  }

  // Return the next node in a list.

  public RemNode getNext() throws RemoteException {
      return next;
  }

  // Set the next node in a list.

  public void setNext(RemNode next) throws RemoteException {
      this.next = next;
  }
```

```
// Return the data value for this node.

public int getData() throws RemoteException {
    return data;
}

// Set the data value for this node.

public void setData(int data) throws RemoteException {
    this.data = data;
}
```

❶
```
public String getLocation() throws RemoteException {
    return location;
}
```

❷
```
public void setLocation(String location) throws RemoteException {
    this.location = location;
}

    private RemNode next;
    private int      data;
    private String   location;
}
```

Running the rmi5 Example

To run this example:

1. Set your CLASSPATH to include the applications/RMI directory and the java.rmi directory from the CD.

2. Start a registry using the rmiregistry executable in the JDK bin directory:

    On Solaris: rmiregistry&

    On Windows: start rmiregistry or javaw rmiregistry

3. Start two servers with the following commands:

    java -Djava.security.policy="<*path to*
    *cd>***\code\applications\RMI\policy" rmi5.BuildImp** *name1*

    java -Djava.security.policy="<*path to*
    *cd>***\code\applications\RMI\policy" rmi5.BuildImp** *name2*

4. Use the following command to run the example:

```
java -Djava.security.policy="<path to
cd>\code\applications\RMI\policy" rmi5.ListTest length_of_list name1
name2
```

The two outputs are:

- The contents of the list

- The process locations of each node

Assuming the length of the list were 8 and the two servers were named name1 and name2, the Java interpreter would display output similar to the following:

```
[ 5 4 3 2 1 0 ]
[ -nine seven-of -nine seven-of -nine seven-of ]
```

Summary

The java.rmi package supports the creation of distributed, networked applications. In the Java RMI implementation, a server process registers a remote object with a registry. A client, in turn, contacts the registry and obtains a stub for the named remote object. The client then uses that stub as if it were a local object, but methods are actually executed on the remote object.

Building an RMI application involves three primary steps: defining remote interfaces, creating classes that implement those interfaces, and creating stub and skeleton classes for the implementation classes. Stub and skeleton classes are generated by the rmic compiler, and they are the client-side images of remote object classes.

CHAPTER
17

- Learning About JDBC

- Basics of Developing JDBC Applications

- Implementing an Employee Lookup in JDBC

Java
Database
Connectivity

What is Java Database Connectivity?

It was clear very early in the development of Java that access to databases would become important. Many business applications depend on databases but, more importantly for Java, a very large number of Internet applications include some form of data retrieval.

Most of the programming languages (Perl, for example) that compete with Java in the world of web applications already provide support for database access in one form or another. Any Java solution, however, must be generic and platform-independent. As it turns out, there already exists a relational database API that meets these criteria: the X/Open SQL Call Level Interface (CLI). The X/Open SQL CLI is the basis for the Microsoft Open Database Connectivity (ODBC) interface. Unfortunately, since ODBC is a C-based interface, using it directly from Java would introduce a variety of problems associated with native method interfaces. Instead of a direct connection to ODBC, JavaSoft is specifying a similar interface called Java Database Connectivity (JDBC), which is a Java-based counterpart to ODBC. Database vendors will supply JDBC *drivers* for their databases so that Java programs may access them transparently. (The need for a driver and a database to use JDBC means that most of you reading this book will not be able to run the examples in this chapter.)

In this chapter, we will show how to use JDBC by implementing the back end of an example we used in our chapter on *Exception Handling*—a hypothetical `lookup()` method to retrieve employee information.

Structure of a JDBC Application

A JDBC application consists of at least these four parts:

- The application code
- The JDBC runtime
- A JDBC driver
- A relational database

Figure 17-1 shows how the four parts communicate.

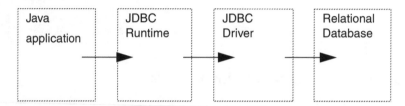

Figure 17-1 JDBC Structure

A fifth part may be added if a JDBC driver is not available for a particular database. A component called the JDBC-ODBC bridge can be used to implement JDBC on top of an ODBC driver for a database, as illustrated in Figure 17-2.

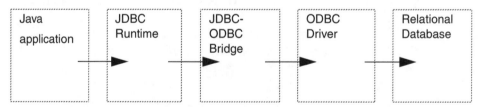

Figure 17-2 JDBC-ODBC Bridge in JDBC Structure

In either case, the application uses the standard JDBC interface to communicate with the database.

Any number of JDBC drivers may be loaded into a Java runtime. The actual driver selected for a particular interaction is determined at database connection time.

Database Connections

A JDBC application begins by requesting a database connection. It does this by calling one of the `java.sql.DriverManager.getConnection()` methods, as in Example 17-1. The most general version takes a URL and a set of properties as arguments. The URL specifies the protocol used to connect to the database and the particular database to connect to. The set of properties is encoded as an instance of `java.util.Properties` which is a subclass of `java.util.Hashtable`. The properties usually include at least a user and a password.

Example 17-1 Connecting to a Database

```
import java.sql.*;
import java.util.*;
  .
  .
  .
Properties props = new Properties();
props.put("user", "Judy");
props.put("password", "Argyle");

Connection conn =
  DriverManager.getConnection("jdbc:myprotocol:employee", props);
```

The JDBC runtime searches its list of drivers until it finds one that understands the `myprotocol` protocol. It then asks that driver for a connection. The syntax of the URL argument is:

jdbc : *subprotocol* : *subname*

It is recommended that a *subname* that includes a network address be in the following form:

/ / *hostname* : *port* / *subsubname*

where *subsubname* can have any desired syntax. Here's an example of a network JDBC URL:

```
jdbc:myprotocol://empserver:9876/employee
```

The set of drivers included in a JDBC runtime is derived from two sources:

- The `jdbc.drivers` property specified on the Java command line

- Calls to `Class.forName`(*driver class name*)

In the first case, the `jdbc.drivers` property contains a colon-separated list of driver class names:

```
java -Djdbc.drivers=empdb.Driver:custdb.Driver
localclasses.jdbcServer
```

In the second case, an application class can explicitly load a driver via:

```
Class.forName("empdb.Driver");
```

The static initializer for a driver class creates an instance of itself and registers it with the `DriverManager`.

Interacting With a Database

Once a connection has been established to a database, an application can use the methods defined by `java.sql.Connection` to construct SQL statements that can be applied to the database.

This is done by creating instances of `java.sql.Statement` and executing them. For instance, we can create an employee table, as in Example 17-3.

Example 17-2 Interacting With a Database

```
Statement s = conn.createStatement();
s.executeUpdate("create table employee " +
                "(name char(30), age integer, salary integer)");
```

`Statement.executeUpdate()` is used to execute statements without results such as updates, insertions, deletes, creates, or drop calls for tables and indexes. Queries that return results are executed with `Statement.executeQuery()`.

Now, Example 17-3 shows how to return all employees with last name *Grindstaff*.

Example 17-3 Returning Entries From a Table

```
ResultSet rs =
  s.executeQuery("select * from employee where name like '%
            Grindstaff'");
```

`Statement.executeQuery()` returns an instance of `java.sql.ResultSet`, which can be iterated through to obtain individual rows.

Enquiring minds may want to print information about the Grindstaffs, which can be accomplished as in Example 17-4.

Example 17-4 Printing a Query Result

```
while (rs.next()) {// ResultSet.next() returns false when there
                   // are no more results.

  String name   = rs.getString(1);  // "name" will be padded
                                     // to 30 chars
  int    age    = rs.getInt(2);
  int    salary = rs.getInt(3);

  System.out.println(name + " " + age + " " + salary);
}
```

As you can see, fetching individual fields from a row is done using type specific get* methods.

SQL/Java Type Correspondence

Table 17-1 shows the type correspondence between SQL and Java.

Table 17-1 SQL/Java Type Correspondence

SQL Type	Java Type
BIGINT	long
BINARY	byte[]
BIT	boolean
CHAR	String
DATE	Date (java.sql.Date)
DECIMAL	Numeric (java.sql.Numeric)
DOUBLE	double
FLOAT	double
INTEGER	int
LONGVARBINARY	byte[]
LONGVARCHAR	String
NUMERIC	Numeric (java.sql.Numeric)
REAL	float
SMALLINT	short
TIME	Time (java.sql.Time)
TIMESTAMP	Timestamp (java.sql.Timestamp)

Table 17-1 SQL/Java Type Correspondence (Continued)

SQL Type	Java Type
TINYINT	byte
VARBINARY	byte[]
VARCHAR	String

Each Java type that corresponds to an SQL type has a `get` method for `ResultSet`, as shown in Table 17-2.

Table 17-2 `ResultSet.get` Methods

Java Type	Corresponding get Methods
boolean	getBoolean()
byte	getByte()
byte[]	getBytes()
double	getDouble()
float	getFloat()
int	getInt()
Date (java.sql.Date)	getDate()
Numeric (java.sql.Numeric)	getNumeric()
String	getString()
Time (java.sql.Time)	getTime()
Timestamp (java.sql.Timestamp)	getTimestamp()

All of these `get` methods may be passed either the integer index of the column (starting at 1) or the name of the column. So, for Example 17-4 on page 387, `rs.getInt(2)` and `rs.getInt("age")` would be equivalent.

To determine if the value of a column is SQL null, it is necessary to first fetch it and then call `ResultSet.wasNull()`. The `wasNull()` method returns true if the last column fetched was null.

Executing Precompiled SQL

It is often useful when writing database applications to *precompile* an SQL statement and then execute it multiple times with different parameters. This is accomplished in JDBC using the `java.sql.PreparedStatement` class, as in Example 17-5.

Example 17-5 Executing Precompiled SQL

```
PreparedStatement ps =
  conn.prepareStatement("update employee set salary = ?
                        where name = ?");
```

Each "?" must be replaced by a parameter value before executing the statement. For instance:

```
ps.setInt(1, 150000);
ps.setString(2, "Myrnie");
ps.executeUpdate();
```

Table 17-3 shows the type correspondence between Java and SQL.

Table 17-3 Java/SQL Type Correspondence

Java Type	SQL Type
boolean	BIT
byte	TINYINT
byte[]	VARBINARY
double	DOUBLE
float	FLOAT
int	INTEGER
Date (java.sql.Date)	DATE
Numeric (java.sql.Numeric)	NUMERIC
String	VARCHAR
Time (java.sql.Time)	TIME
Timestamp (java.sql.Timestamp)	TIMESTAMP

In the cases of byte[] and String, if the values are too large for VARBINARY and VARCHAR, they are mapped onto LONGVARBINARY and LONGVARCHAR.

The `PreparedStatement` class includes `set*` methods that correspond to Java types, as shown in Table 17-4.

Table 17-4 `PreparedStatement.set` Methods

Java Type	Corresponding set Methods
boolean	setBoolean()
byte	setByte()
byte[]	setBytes()
double	setDouble()
float	setFloat()
int	setInt()
Date (java.sql.Date)	setDate()
Numeric (java.sql.Numeric)	setNumeric()
String	setString()
Time (java.sql.Time)	setTime()
Timestamp (java.sql.Timestamp)	setTimestamp()

There is also a `PreparedStatement.setNull()` call to set a parameter to SQL null.

Generic get and set Methods

Both `ResultSet.get` methods and `PreparedStatement.set` methods have generic counterparts. `ResultSet.getObject()` will return an instance of the Java class that matches the SQL type of a column. If the SQL type were INTEGER, an instance of `java.lang.Integer` would be returned. `PreparedStatement.setObject()` sets a database column to the SQL type that corresponds to its Java instance argument.

Resources

Both the `ResultSet` and `Statement` classes provide `close()` methods that will free any resources associated with them. It is a good idea to call `close()` explicitly when instances of `ResultSet` and `Statement` are no longer needed because their resources will not be freed automatically until they are garbage collected. (This means that potentially, they may *never* be freed because Java objects are not guaranteed to be collected.)

Metadata

JDBC allows users to determine what facilities are provided by a database or a driver using methods defined in the `java.sql.DatabaseMetaData` class. Many specifics including whether or not a database or driver supports outer joins, stored procedures, unions, or a particular transaction isolation level can be queried by using these methods.

Transactions

A JDBC user can choose between two styles of transaction support. A connection can be in *auto-commit* mode, in which case every statement is committed immediately, or an ongoing transaction can be maintained that is ended with a call to `Connection.commit()` or `Connection.abort()`. Instances of `PreparedStatement` and `ResultSet` are closed on either call. Switching between the two styles is done via a call to `Connection.setAutoCommit(boolean)`.

The actual semantics of transactions are based on the underlying database support. `DatabaseMetaData` methods are available to determine support.

Cursors

Limited cursor support is provided by JDBC. The cursor associated with a result set can be obtained and used in positioned update and delete statements. The cursor is returned by the `ResultSet.getCursorName()` method. It remains valid until the `ResultSet` resources are freed either by the closing of the `ResultSet` or its parent `Statement`.

Exercising the JDBC

Now let's revisit our employee lookup example we introduced in our chapter on *Exception Handling*. To implement this type of lookup with JDBC, we need to support the call:

```
TableEntry entry = lookup("Marianna", "employee");
```

Example 17-6 on page 392 shows how we would go about doing this. First, however, look at Figure 17-3, which shows the classes supporting our JDBC lookup implementation.

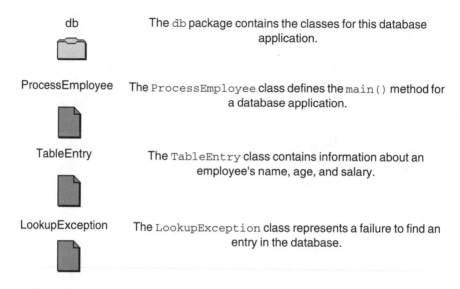

db	The db package contains the classes for this database application.
ProcessEmployee	The ProcessEmployee class defines the main() method for a database application.
TableEntry	The TableEntry class contains information about an employee's name, age, and salary.
LookupException	The LookupException class represents a failure to find an entry in the database.

Figure 17-3 Classes Supporting JDBC Employee Lookup

As you look through the example, notice that the ProcessEmployee class provides a main() method that takes an employee's first name, looks up the employee, and prints his or her information. If there are multiple entries with the same first name, only the first one is processed. Note that the lookup() method itself (line ❶) executes an SQL select statement and retrieves its results. The results are returned in a TableEntry instance. You might also pay attention to the initDatabase() method in line ❷. It establishes a connection to a database using the java.sql.DriverManager.getConnection() method.

Example 17-6 Employee Lookup Example

```
package db;

import java.sql.*;
import java.util.*;

public class ProcessEmployee {

  // The main() method initializes the database, looks up an
  // employee, and processes the results.

  public static void main(String[] args) {
      if (args.length != 1) {
```

```
            System.err.println("Usage: java db.ProcessEmployee
                            <name>");
            System.exit(-1);
        }

        try {
            // Set up a connection to the database.

            initDatabase();

           // look up the command line argument in "employee" table.

            TableEntry entry = lookup(args[0], "employee");

          // Process the result from the lookup. If the lookup failed
          // an exception would have been thrown and we would not
          // have arrived at this point.

            process(entry);

        } catch (LookupException e) {
            e.printStackTrace();
            System.exit(-1);
        }
    }

    // The lookup() method executes an SQL select statement and
    // retrieves its results. The results are returned in a
    // TableEntry instance.

    private static TableEntry lookup(String name, String table)
    throws LookupException {
        try {
            // Create an instance of java.sql.Statement associated
            // with a particular database connection.

            Statement s = getConnection().createStatement();

            // Execute the query statement and capture the results.

            ResultSet rs = s.executeQuery("select * from " + table +
                                    " where name like '" +
                                    name + " %'");

            // Check to make sure there is at least one row.

            if (!rs.next()) {
                throw new LookupException();
```

```
            }

                // Fetch the columns out of the returned row.

                String fullName = rs.getString(1);
                int     age      = rs.getInt(2);
                int     salary   = rs.getInt(3);

              // Free up any resources associated with the statement and
              // result set.

                s.close();

                // Return the entry.

                return new TableEntry(fullName, age, salary);

          } catch (SQLException e) {
              e.printStackTrace();
              System.exit(-1);
          }

          return null;
      }

      // initDatabase() establishes a connection to a database using
      // the java.sql.DriverManager.getConnection() method.

❷     private static void initDatabase() {
          try {
              Properties props = new Properties();
              props.put("user", "hr");
              props.put("password", "eyesonly");

          connection =
            DriverManager.getConnection("jdbc:myprotocol:db",
                                                    props);

          } catch (SQLException e) {
              e.printStackTrace();
              System.exit(-1);
          }
      }

      // Print the results of a query.

      private static void process(TableEntry entry) {
          System.out.println(entry);
```

```
  }

  private static Connection getConnection() {
      return connection;
  }

 private static Connection connection; // the database connection.
}

// The TableEntry class contains information about employees. An
// employee's name, age, and salary are stored.

class TableEntry {

  // Construct a new TableEntry instance.
  TableEntry(String entryName, int entryAge, int entrySalary) {
      name   = entryName;
      age    = entryAge;
      salary = entrySalary;
  }

  // Return an employee's name.

  String getName() {
      return name;
  }

  // Return an employee's age.

  int getAge() {
      return age;
  }

  // Return an employee's salary.

  int getSalary() {
      return salary;
  }
```

```
    // Display the information about an employee in a nice format.

    public String toString() {
        return "EMPLOYEE:\n" + "  NAME:    " + name   + "\n" +
                                "  AGE:     " + age    + "\n" +
                                "  SALARY: " + salary + "\n";
    }

    private String name;
    private int    age;
    private int    salary;
}


    // The LookupException class represents a failure to find an entry
    // in the database.

    class LookupException extends Exception {
    }
```

The Java interpreter will display output similar to the following:

```
> java db.ProcessEmployee Marianna
EMPLOYEE:
  NAME:   Marianna Gaudaur
  AGE:    39
  SALARY: 200000
>
```

Summary

The Java JDBC interface provides an easy-to-use platform independent means of working with relational databases. JDBC is largely derived from ODBC, but is completely Java based. An application may talk to multiple databases using different JDBC drivers. Drivers are installed either via the `jdbc.drivers` property or via explicit loading by an application. JDBC operations are invoked through `Connection`, `Statement`, and `ResultSet` classes. There are `get` and `set` methods provided that correspond between Java types and SQL types.

Part 2—Writing Java Applets

CHAPTER
18

Introduction to Applets

Introduction

Applets are simple Java programs that run in web browsers. The ways applets differ from standalone Java programs are largely a result of the environment in which they run. Applets are invoked through a different interface than a `main()` method. Applets are also different in that they are not allowed to make changes to the machine on which they are running. This security is enforced by the Java runtime system.

In this part of the book, we'll describe several applets, highlighting different programming techniques along the way. Note that all the applets we discuss are available on the CD accompanying this book. We encourage you to try them out to see how they work before reading about how they are constructed.

Java's Applet Tools and Class Support

Applets are almost always graphical applications. As such, they use the Java Abstract Window Toolkit, otherwise known as the *awt*. The awt (actually, it's the `java.awt` class library) allows you to write graphics code that is independent of the target platform. The awt avoids potential inconsistencies with the behavior of native windowing systems by actually using components from the native system. These components are called *peers*. You don't generally need to deal directly with peers when writing Java applets, but their presence is evident when writing event handling routines.

In Java parlance, graphics objects such as panels, scrollbars, containers, labels, buttons, and so on are generically referred to as *components*. That is because most graphic objects are derived from the Component class in the awt. The awt.Component class includes some of the most commonly used methods in applets. These include the paint(), repaint(), and update() methods. Table 18-1 summarizes their use.

Table 18-1 Commonly Used awt.Component **Methods**

Common awt.Component Methods	Description
paint()	The paint() method paints the component.
repaint()	The repaint() method schedules a call to the component's update() method as soon as possible.
update()	The update() method is responsible for redrawing the applet. The default version redraws the background and calls the paint() method.

The Java Applet class (in the applet package) provides another set of methods particularly important when writing applets. Chief among these are the init(), start(), stop(), and destroy() methods. Table 18-2 summarizes their use.

Table 18-2 Commonly Used applet.Applet **Methods**

Common applet.Applet Methods	Description
init()	When a document with an applet is opened, the init() method is automatically called to initialize the applet. You do not need to explicitly call this method in an applet, although you can override it if an applet needs to initialize state. The init() method is called only once for an applet.
start()	When a document with an applet is opened, the start() method is automatically called to start the applet. You do not need to explicitly call this method in the applet, although you can override it if necessary. The start() method is called every time the document is opened.
stop()	When a document with an applet is no longer displayed, the stop() method is automatically called. This method is always called before the destroy() method is called.
destroy()	After the stop() method has been called, the destroy() method may be called to clean up any resources that are being held.

Displaying Applet Output

For consistency and ease of illustration, all of the applets in this part of the book are used in the following way:

```
appletviewer applet_name.html
```

In this syntax, *applet_name*.html is a minimal HTML file that can be used as an argument to the appletviewer. The HTML file looks like this:

```
<title>
<hr>
<applet code="applet_name.class" width=200 height=80>
</applet>
<hr>
```

Each applet on the CD included with this book has a corresponding HTML file that can be used as an argument to the appletviewer. Of course, these applets could also be displayed within a Java-enabled web browser, as long as the web page includes the appropriate HTML applet tag to call the applet.

A Simple Applet

To begin with applets, recall from the first chapter the HelloWorldApplet. This is one of the simplest possible applets:

```
import java.applet.Applet;
import java.awt.Graphics;

public class HelloWorldApplet extends Applet {
  public void paint(Graphics g) {
    g.drawString("Hello Brave New World!", 50, 25);
  }
}
```

The only thing an applet really *has* to do is define a paint() method. The paint() method will be called automatically when the applet is displayed or resized. The argument to paint() is a Graphics object. Graphics objects store the current color, font, and other information used when performing graphics operations. They also provide methods for drawing objects such as lines, images, and strings.

Figure 18-1 shows this applet in the appletviewer:

Figure 18-1 Hello World Applet

A simple applet like this one is pretty easy to put together. However, applets that can be configured with HTML tags and applets that perform dynamic actions on the screen need to do more than simply define a paint() method. We'll examine what it takes to develop more sophisticated applets in the following sections.

Configurable Applets

Applets can be written so that they can be configured with HTML code. In effect, the applet makes a set of parameters *configurable*, and if those parameters are specified in the HTML code, they override the default settings specified in the applet. In this section, we'll show exactly how to do this.

Displaying a Static Label

In the next applet, we create a StaticLabel class. It displays a text string. It also includes parameters for the label and for the font, which the user can specify in the HTML file to override the default values. This applet will also center the label, which will show some other useful features.

The most important things to note in the example are the init() method and the use of getParameter(). If an applet needs to initialize state, it can override the default init() method that is normally called when a document with an applet is opened. The init() method is called automatically before the applet is started.

This example uses the init() method to read the user-defined parameters specified in the HTML code and set the label and font. The getParameter() method takes a String argument and returns the value of the user-specified parameter with that name in the source HTML file. If no value has been specified for the parameter, getParameter() returns null. The applet supplies default values for `label`, `fontname`, `fontsize`, `fontslant`, and `fontweight`. These default values will be used if the user doesn't specify these parameters in the HTML file.

Other points to note are the use of the `size()` method to return the width and height of the applet and the use of the `FontMetrics` class to examine features of a font. Here's the code for the `StaticLabel` class:

Example 18-1 StaticLabel Applet

```
import java.awt.*;

// The StaticLabel class takes a text string and displays it centered
// in an applet. The font and label can be passed as parameters from
// html.

public class StaticLabel extends java.applet.Applet {
    public void init() {

        // Read in parameters and set values for textValue,
        // and textFont.

        // The "label" parameter holds the text to be displayed.

        String param = getParameter("label");

        if (param != null) {
            textValue = param;
        }

        // The four parameters: "fontname", "fontslant",
        // "fontweight", and "fontsize" are used to select a font for
        // the label. In the Java font model, "fontslant" and
        // "fontweight" are combined into font "style".

        String fontName  = FONTNAME;
        int    fontStyle = FONTSTYLE;
        int    fontSize  = FONTSIZE;

        param = getParameter("fontname");

        if (param != null) {
            fontName = param;
        }

        param = getParameter("fontslant");
```

```
    if (param != null &&
        (param.equals("italic") || param.equals("ITALIC"))) {
        fontStyle |= Font.ITALIC;
    }

    param = getParameter("fontweight");

    if (param != null &&
        (param.equals("bold") || param.equals("BOLD"))) {
        fontStyle |= Font.BOLD;
    }

    param = getParameter("fontsize");

    if (param != null) {
        fontSize = Integer.parseInt(param);
    }

    // Create a font object from the font parameters.

    textFont = new java.awt.Font(fontName, fontStyle, fontSize);
}

public void paint(Graphics g) {

// Paint the label.

// We recompute dimensions every time in case the applet is
// resized.
//
// "dim"       is the applet width and height.
// "metrics"   is the set of font parameters for the font we have
//             chosen.
// "textWidth" is the width of the label in the chosen font.
// "x"         is the horizontal position of the beginning of
//             the label.
// "y"         is the vertical position of the baseline of
//             the label. The "baseline" is the position
//             of bottom of a line of text not counting
//             the tails of lower case "g", "y", etc. The
//             extra space taken up by the tails is called
//             the _descent_ of the font.

Dimension   dim       = getSize();
FontMetrics metrics   = getFontMetrics(textFont);
int         textWidth = metrics.stringWidth(textValue);
```

```
// The label will be clipped if "x" and "y" are outside
// the applet.

int        x       = (dim.width  - textWidth) / 2;
int        y       = (dim.height - metrics.getHeight()) / 2 +
                     metrics.getHeight() - metrics.getDescent();

// Draw the label.

g.setFont(textFont);
g.setColor(textColor);
g.drawString(textValue, x, y);
}

// Default values for applet parameters. These values will be
// used if the user leaves "label", "fontname", "fontsize",
// "fontslant", or "fontweight" unspecified.

private static final String LABEL     = "Hello, world.";
private static final String FONTNAME  = "TimesRoman";
private static final int    FONTSIZE  = 24;
private static final int    FONTSTYLE = Font.PLAIN;

// Private state variables.

private String  textValue   = LABEL;
private Font    textFont    = null;
private Color   textColor   = Color.black;
}
```

Output From the Static Label Applet

Using the appletviewer on a simple HTML file that just specifies the
`StaticLabel.class` will display it with its default values:

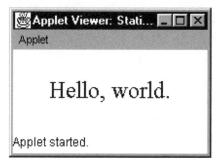

Now, assume an HTML file with the following parameters set in it:

```
<title>Static Label</title>
<hr>
<applet code="StaticLabel.class" width=200 height=80>
<param name=label value="Java By Example">
<param name=fontname value="Courier">
<param name=fontslant value="italic">
<param name=fontweight value="bold">
<param name=fontsize value="24">
</applet>
<hr>
```

Figure 18-2 shows the `StaticLabel` applet with the parameters specified in this HTML file.

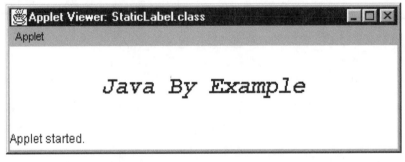

Figure 18-2 A Configurable Applet
The Hello World display is defined in the HTML file, which overrides the default values defined in the applet code.

The HTML applet parameters take precedence over the default font characteristics defined in the `StaticLabel` applet. (See *The HTML applet and param Tags* on page 544 for more information.)

Incorporating Images and Sound

Including images, sound, or both in an applet is easy. However, doing interesting things with them can be tricky. We'll look at animation and active images a little later, but first let's see how to read in and display images and sounds. The next example adds a definition for the `start()` method that will override the default `start()` method. The `start()` method is called when the applet's document is visited.

The `ImageWithSound` class reads in a `.gif` image and a `.au` audio file. (These files reside in the `Image` and the `Audio` directory on the CD included with this book.) The applet displays the image and plays the sound. The `MediaTracker` class is used to wait for an image to be completely loaded before displaying it or playing the sound. The `IMAGE` and `AUDIO static final` variables hold default values for the image and sound file names. Following is the code for the `ImageWithSound` class.

Example 18-2 ImageWithSound Applet

```
import java.awt.*;
import java.applet.*;

public class ImageWithSound extends Applet {

  public void init() {

    // Read in an Image and an AudioClip.

    String imageName = IMAGE;
    String audioName = AUDIO;
    String param = getParameter("image");

    if (param != null) {
       imageName = param;
    }

    param = getParameter("audio");

    if (param != null) {
       audioName = param;
    }

    // Create a MediaTracker to inform us when the image has
    // been completely loaded.

    tracker = new MediaTracker(this);

    // getCodeBase() returns the URL of the applet's directory.
    // These calls will read in image and sound files relative to
    // the applet's directory.

    sound = getAudioClip(getCodeBase(), audioName);

    // getImage() returns immediately. The image is not
    // actually loaded until it is first used. We use a
    // MediaTracker to make sure the image is loaded
```

```
    // before we try to display it.

    image = getImage(getCodeBase(), imageName);

    // Add the image to the MediaTracker so that we can wait
    // for it.

    tracker.addImage(image, 0);
  }

  // Display the image. The "this" argument to drawImage() is there
  // because drawImage() expects an "ImageObserver". An image may
  // not be complete when drawImage() returns. If so, the
  // ImageObserver argument is notified later. The ImageObserver
  // is notified via its "imageUpdate" method. Applets that do
  // elaborate image processing can override imageUpdate() to
  // get information about the state of images.

  public void paint(Graphics g) {
    g.drawImage(image, 0, 0, this);
  }

  // Play the audio clip.

  public void start() {

    // Load the image and wait until it's done.

    try {
      tracker.waitForID(0);
    } catch (InterruptedException e) {
    }

    repaint();
    sound.play();
  }

  // Default values for the image and sound file names.

  private static final String IMAGE = "Images/kidsintree.gif";
  private static final String AUDIO = "Audio/gong.au";

  // Private state variables.

  private Image        image;
  private AudioClip     sound;
  private MediaTracker tracker;
}
```

Output From the ImageWithSound Applet

Figure 18-3 shows sample output from the ImageWithSound applet. (You'll have to imagine the gong.)

Figure 18-3 An Applet With Image and Sound
A gong rings when the image of these coconuts is displayed in the applet.

Active Applets

An applet that runs continuously introduces a new requirement. It needs to provide a separate thread of control so that it doesn't interfere with the operation of the rest of the system. In most cases, the applet's start() method starts the thread and its stop() method stops the thread. We haven't seen a stop() method yet, but it gets called when the applet's document is no longer displayed.

The next applet relies heavily on the repaint() method, so before looking at the applet, let's look at how repaint(), update() and paint() work together to redraw an applet. The repaint() method is called when an applet is resized or exposed, and can be called directly by an applet. Despite its name, repaint() does not immediately redraw the applet; instead, it schedules a redraw as soon as possible. When the redraw occurs, the applet's update() method is called. There is a default update() method defined in awt.Component that redraws the background of the applet and then calls paint(). Although this is generally sufficient, it is sometimes necessary to override update() to avoid redrawing the background. (We'll show this in some of our later applet examples.)

The repaint() method has four different signatures, as shown in Table 18-3.

Table 18-3 Forms of the repaint() Method

Signature	Description
repaint()	Repaint the entire applet as soon as possible.
repaint(long maxTime)	Repaints the entire applet within maxTime milliseconds.
repaint(int x, int y, int width, int height)	Repaint just the area of the applet specified by the arguments.
repaint(long maxTime, int x, int y, int width, int height))	Repaint the specified area within the specified maximum time.

We'll use the first and third forms of repaint() in our applet examples.

Now, with that as background, let's look at an applet that displays a label that blinks on and off at a user-specifiable rate.

Displaying a Flashing Label

The FlashingLabel class is based on the StaticLabel class previously described. The FlashingLabel class takes a text string and displays it in the center of an applet. When displayed, the text will blink on and off at a rate determined by the sleepTime parameter. The font, label, and sleepTime (in milliseconds) parameters can be passed from the HTML file. The applet supplies default values that will be used if the user fails to specify them in the HTML file. Example 18-3 shows the code for the `FlashingLabel` class.

Example 18-3 FlashingLabel Applet

```java
import java.applet.Applet;

// The FlashingLabel class takes a text string and displays it
// centered in an applet. The text will blink on and off at a rate
// determined by the "sleepTime" parameter. The font, label, and
// sleepTime (in milliseconds) can be passed as parameters from html.

public class FlashingLabel extends Applet implements Runnable {
    public void init() {

        // Read in parameters and set values for sleepValue, textValue,
        // and textFont.
        // The "sleeptime" parameter tells how long to pause between
        // flashes (in milliseconds).

        String param = getParameter("sleeptime");

        if (param != null) {
            sleepValue = Integer.parseInt(param);
        }

        // The "label" parameter holds the text to be displayed.

        param = getParameter("label");

        if (param != null) {
            textValue = param;
        }

        // The four parameters: "fontname", "fontslant", "fontweight",
        // and "fontsize" are used to select a font for the label.
        // In the Java font model, "fontslant" and "fontweight" are
        // combined into font "style".

        String fontName  = FONTNAME;
        int    fontStyle = FONTSTYLE;
        int    fontSize  = FONTSIZE;

        param = getParameter("fontname");

        if (param != null) {
            fontName = param;
```

```
    }

    param = getParameter("fontslant");

    if (param != null &&
        (param.equals("italic") || param.equals("ITALIC"))) {
        fontStyle |= Font.ITALIC;
    }

    param = getParameter("fontweight");

    if (param != null &&
        (param.equals("bold") || param.equals("BOLD"))) {
        fontStyle |= Font.BOLD;
    }

    param = getParameter("fontsize");

    if (param != null) {
        fontSize = Integer.parseInt(param);
    }

    // Create a font object from the font parameters.

    textFont = new Font(fontName, fontStyle, fontSize);
}

public void paint(Graphics g) {
    // Paint the label every other time "paint" is called.

    paintThisTime = !paintThisTime;

    if (paintThisTime == false) {
        return;
    }

    // We recompute dimensions every time in case the applet is
    // resized.
    //
    // "dim"       is the applet width and height.
    // "metrics"   is the set of font parameters for the font we
    //             have chosen.
    // "textWidth" is the width of the label in the chosen font.
    // "x"         is the horizontal position of the beginning of
    //             the label.
    // "y"         is the vertical position of the baseline of
    //             the label. The "baseline" is the position
    //             of bottom of a line of text not counting
```

```
    //                 the tails of lower case "g", "y", etc.  The
    //                 extra space taken up by the tails is called
    //                 the _descent_ of the font.

    Dimension   dim       = getSize();
    FontMetrics metrics   = getFontMetrics(textFont);
    int         textWidth = metrics.stringWidth(textValue);

    // The label will be clipped if "x" and "y" are outside
    // the applet.

    int         x         = (dim.width  - textWidth) / 2;
    int         y         = (dim.height - metrics.getHeight()) / 2 +
        metrics.getHeight() - metrics.getDescent();

    // Draw the label.

    // We set the font first so that the FontMetrics will return
    // a correct value for the width of the label.

    g.setFont(textFont);
    g.setColor(textColor);
    g.drawString(textValue, x, y);
}

public void start() {

    // Create a thread for this applet and start it.

    flashThread = new Thread(this);
    flashThread.start();
}

public void stop() {

    // Stop the applet's thread.

    timeToGo = true;
}

public void run() {

    // Run the applet sleeping "sleepValue" milliseconds between
    // each repaint.

    while (!timeToGo) {
        try {
            flashThread.sleep(sleepValue);
```

```
                } catch (InterruptedException e) {
                }
                repaint();
        }
    }

    // Default values for applet parameters. These values will be used
    // if the user leaves "label", "fontname", "fontsize",
    // "fontslant", "fontweight", or "sleeptime" unspecified.

    private static final String LABEL     = "Hello, world.";
    private static final String FONTNAME  = "TimesRoman";
    private static final int    FONTSIZE  = 24;
    private static final int    FONTSTYLE = Font.PLAIN;
    private static final int    SLEEPTIME = 650;

    // Private state variables.

    private String  textValue     = LABEL;
    private int     sleepValue    = SLEEPTIME;
    private Font    textFont      = null;
    private Thread  flashThread   = null;
    private boolean paintThisTime = false;
    private Color   textColor     = Color.black;
}
```

Output From the Flashing Label Applet

Figure 18-4 shows sample output from the `FlashingLabel` applet, with some HTML parameters overriding the default text values.

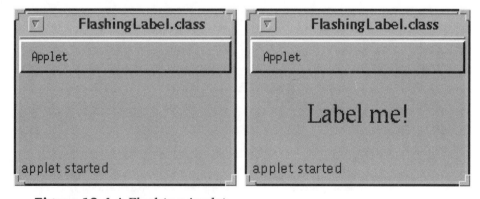

Figure 18-4 A Flashing Applet
The first display shows the text flashing off, and the second shows the text flashing on.

Summary

This chapter provides a brief introduction to applets. It highlights the use of the basic methods from the `Applet` class and the awt, and illustrates circumstances when you would override those methods. The applets themselves show how to read applet parameters specified in HTML code and how to create multiple threads.

We haven't yet shown any graphics programming, form creation, or event handling. These will be discussed in the following chapters. Understanding how Java deals with these areas is necessary for writing interesting applets, but at this point you at least understand the basics of the applet model.

CHAPTER
19

- Using Containers

- Standard Layout Managers

- Using GridBagLayout

- Custom Layout Managers

Forms in Applets

Introduction

Many applications that interact with users display forms of one kind or another. The applets we've seen so far have been composed of single components. However, Java supports developing applets composed of multiple components. There are some special classes in the awt package that support this. In particular, the Container class and LayoutManager interface are useful for developing applets with multiple components. In this chapter, we'll describe these classes and illustrate their use to create a forms-based, multicomponent applet.

Containers

Instances of the Container class group other components. Applets themselves are containers since the Applet class extends the Panel class which extends the Container class. All containers provide operations to add, remove, and paint their components. Containers also provide methods to determine which component is under the mouse and to deliver an event to a particular component.

Using containers, you can group related components together and treat them as a unit. In general, this simplifies the program, and it is particularly useful in arranging components on the display.

Layout Managers

Containers do not do the whole job of grouping components. You need some way to arrange components on the screen. This is accomplished by instances of the `LayoutManager` interface. Each container has an associated layout manager that arranges its components within the container. (Java provides several types of layout managers.) Components are arranged according to a plan that is specific to each particular type of layout manager.

The `Panel` class uses an instance of `FlowLayout` for its default `LayoutManager`. That means that `FlowLayout` is the default layout manager for applets, since the `Applet` class extends the `Panel` class. (All the applets discussed up to this point have implicitly used `FlowLayout`.) The `FlowLayout` manager adds components to a row until the row is full, and then it moves to the next row. This is much like the way an HTML page is formatted by default.

The Java environment provides the following set of layout managers:

- `BorderLayout` — Lays out the components around the sides and in the center of the container in north, east, west, south, and center positions. The gaps between components can be specified.

- `CardLayout` — Only one component is visible at a time. The user can switch between different components. The components can themselves be containers, which allows switching between multiple layouts.

- `FlowLayout` — Places components left to right until there is no more room, then moves to the next line. The lines can be aligned to the left, center, or right.

- `GridBagLayout` — Arranges components both vertically and horizontally using an elaborate set of constraints to determine how much space is allocated to each component and how it should be placed relative to previous components. (We use `GridBagLayout` in the next example.)

- `GridLayout` — Lays out grids of identically sized components. The horizontal and vertical gaps between components may be specified.

A Forms-based Applet

Using most of these layouts is straightforward. The next applet example, however, uses the most complicated layout manager provided in the Java environment—the `GridBagLayout`.

This applet attempts to determine a person's occupation (within an engineering organization) based on certain traits such as coffee consumption, fashion sense, and a few others. The values are entered using a simple form, as illustrated in Figure 19-1.

![Applet Viewer screenshot showing the OccupationOracle form with fields for Name, Age, Binary World View checkbox, Coffee consumption, Fashion sense radio buttons (Low, Medium selected, High), and Occupation showing "Unknown".]

Figure 19-1 A Sample Form

Following is the code for the multiple component applet. While looking through the class definition, notice the use of `GridBagLayout` and the accompanying `GridBagConstraints` (used to specify details about the layout) to structure the form. This layout manager is the most complex and powerful in Java, so consider this example a simple introduction. If you want to dive into the details of using `GridBagLayout`, you'll want to find a more comprehensive awt reference[1].

---

1. See Geary, David (1998). *Graphic Java*. Prentice Hall.

Example 19-1 OccupationOracle Applet

```java
import java.applet.Applet;
import java.awt.*;
import java.awt.event.*;

// The OccupationOracle class makes a guess at a person's occupation
// within an engineering organization based on a few "key" traits.
// Invalid entries in numeric fields result in an "Unknown"
// occupation. This applet uses the awt.GridBagLayout class to
// structure the occupation form. The awt.GridBagLayout class allows
// fields to be placed in rows and columns within a form. Each
// component is given a "display area" based on the constraints in
// effect when it is added to the layout. For this applet, we do a
// full recalculation when any component changes state so we share
// our event handling routines among all the controls.

public class OccupationOracle extends Applet implements
    ActionListener, ItemListener {

    // Construct the form. Create each component of the form and
    // add it to the layout. Initialize the occupation to "Unknown".

    public void init() {

        // Use the GridBagLayout layout to construct rows and
        // columns.

        GridBagLayout gridbag = new GridBagLayout();

        // Create a new set of constraints to use when adding
        // a component to the layout. The constraint values
        // in effect when a component is added to the layout
        // are cloned and stored in conjunction with the component
        // by the layout.

        GridBagConstraints constraints = new GridBagConstraints();

        // Set the font for the form.

        setFont(new Font("TimesRoman", Font.BOLD, 18));

        // Associate the GridBagLayout object with the applet.

        setLayout(gridbag);

        // The "anchor" constraint determines how a component
        // is justified within its display area.
```

```
constraints.anchor = GridBagConstraints.WEST;

// Determines how much space should be given to this component.
// if left at 0.0, all components clump up in the middle as the
// padding is applied to the outside.

constraints.weighty = 1.0;

// Create a name label and text field.

makeNameField();

// Setting the "gridwidth" constraint to 1 will
// cause the component to take up the minimum
// horizontal space in its row.

constraints.gridwidth = 1;

// "addFormComponent" will associate the current constraints
// with a component and add the component to the form.

addFormComponent(gridbag, nameLabel, constraints);

// Setting the "gridwidth" constraint to REMAINDER will
// cause the component to fill up the remainder of its row.
// i.e. it will be the last entry in the row.

constraints.gridwidth = GridBagConstraints.REMAINDER;

// The "fill" constraint tells what to do if the item is in
// a area larger than it is. In this case we want to fill
// any extra horizontal space.

constraints.fill = GridBagConstraints.HORIZONTAL;
addFormComponent(gridbag, nameField, constraints);
nameField.addActionListener(this);

// Create and add an age label and text field.

makeAgeField();
constraints.gridwidth = 1;
constraints.fill      = GridBagConstraints.NONE;
constraints.weightx   = 0.0;
addFormComponent(gridbag, ageLabel, constraints);
constraints.gridwidth = GridBagConstraints.REMAINDER;
constraints.weightx   = 1.0;
addFormComponent(gridbag, ageField, constraints);
```

```
ageField.addActionListener(this);      // Listen for text events

// Create and add a world view label and a single checkbox
// for a true/false value.

makeWorldViewField();
constraints.gridwidth = 1;
constraints.weightx   = 0.0;
addFormComponent(gridbag, worldViewLabel, constraints);
constraints.gridwidth = GridBagConstraints.REMAINDER;
constraints.weightx   = 1.0;
addFormComponent(gridbag, worldViewField, constraints);
worldViewField.addItemListener(this);

// Create and add a coffee consumption label and text field.

makeCoffeeField();
constraints.gridwidth = 1;
constraints.weightx   = 0.0;
addFormComponent(gridbag, coffeeLabel, constraints);
constraints.gridwidth = GridBagConstraints.REMAINDER;
constraints.weightx   = 1.0;
addFormComponent(gridbag, coffeeField, constraints);
coffeeField.addActionListener(this);  // Listen for text events

// Create and add a fashion sense label and a checkbox
// group that has three mutually exclusive values.

makeFashionField();
constraints.gridwidth = GridBagConstraints.REMAINDER;
constraints.weightx   = 0.0;
constraints.weighty   = 0.0;
addFormComponent(gridbag, fashionLabel, constraints);

// The three checkboxes that represent fashion sense.

addFormComponent(gridbag, low, constraints);
addFormComponent(gridbag, medium, constraints);
addFormComponent(gridbag, high, constraints);
low.addItemListener(this);
medium.addItemListener(this);
high.addItemListener(this);

// The Occupation field is output only.

makeOccupationField();
constraints.gridwidth = 1;
constraints.weightx   = 0.0;
```

```
   constraints.weighty    = 1.0;
   constraints.fill        = GridBagConstraints.NONE;
   addFormComponent(gridbag, occupationLabel, constraints);
   constraints.fill        = GridBagConstraints.HORIZONTAL;
   constraints.gridwidth = GridBagConstraints.REMAINDER;
   constraints.weightx    = 1.0;
   addFormComponent(gridbag, occupationField, constraints);

   // Display the initial "Unknown" occupation.
   recalculateOccupation();
   resize(500, 350);
}

   // The paint() method for this applet just calls the
   // paintComponents() method which is defined by the Container
   // class. It causes all the components visible within the
   // Container to get painted.

   public void paint(Graphics g) {
       paintComponents(g);
   }

   // This method is invoked when activity occurs in the text fields
   // where we added a listener. While we could use the passed in
   // event information to make a decision as to what we want to do,
   // we are defaulting to call the recalculateOccupation() method
   // regardless of the invoking event.
   //

   public void actionPerformed(ActionEvent event) {
       recalculateOccupation();
   }

   // This method is similar to the actionPerformed() method. We
   // added listeners for the checkbox and buttons on our form.
   // When a change in state is sensed the itemStateChanged() method
   // is invoked. Again, we could query the event information to
   // make further decisions as to what to do. As previously in
   // all cases we are calling the recalculateOccupation() method.
   //

   public void itemStateChanged(ItemEvent event) {
       recalculateOccupation();
   }

   // A helper function that associates constraints with a component
   // and adds it to the form.
```

```java
private void addFormComponent(GridBagLayout grid, Component comp,
                              GridBagConstraints c) {
    grid.setConstraints(comp, c);
    add(comp);
}


// recalculateOccupation() fetches the values of each component
// and computes an occupation based on some truly stupid
// heuristics.
private void recalculateOccupation() {

// If we don't have a name yet we might incorrectly categorize
// the CEO!

    if (nameField.getText() == "") {
        occupationField.setText("Unknown");
    }

    // Fetch other important values that we'll use in our
    // calculations.

    int     age;
    int     coffeeConsumption;
    boolean binaryView = worldViewField.getState();

    // Try to fetch integer values for age and coffeeConsumption.
    // If the values in the fields can't be parsed as integers,
    // set the occupation to "Unknown".

    try {
        age                = Integer.parseInt(ageField.getText());
        coffeeConsumption =
                        Integer.parseInt(coffeeField.getText());
    } catch (Exception e) {
        occupationField.setText("Unknown");
        return;
    }

    // Check for the CEO.

    String name = nameField.getText();

    if (name.endsWith("II")  ||
        name.endsWith("III") ||
        name.endsWith("IV")) {

        if (age < 35 || coffeeConsumption < 4) {
            occupationField.setText("Junior Executive");
```

```
        } else {
            occupationField.setText("CEO");
        }

        return;
    }

    // Fashion sense is a critical piece of information.
    // The getCurrent() method of CheckboxGroup returns whichever
    // Checkbox in the group is currently selected. Only one
    // can be selected at a time.

    Checkbox fashionValue = fashionGroup.getSelectedCheckbox();

    if (fashionValue == low || fashionValue == medium) {

        // There are two kinds of people in the world: those who
        // divide people into two kinds and those who don't.

        if (binaryView && coffeeConsumption >= 4) {
            occupationField.setText("Engineer");

        } else if ((age > 40 && binaryView) ||
                   (age < 40 && coffeeConsumption >= 4)) {
            occupationField.setText("Engineering Manager");

        } else {
            occupationField.setText("Product Manager");
        }

    } else {

        // High fashion sense. Not an engineer!

        if (binaryView || coffeeConsumption >= 4) {
            occupationField.setText("Vice President");
        } else {
            occupationField.setText("Product Marketing");
        }
    }
}

// Helper functions to create form components.

private void makeNameField() {
    nameLabel = new Label("Name: ");
    nameField = new TextField(40);
}
```

```java
private void makeAgeField() {
    ageLabel = new Label("Age: ");
    ageField = new TextField(3);
}

private void makeOccupationField() {
    occupationLabel = new Label("Occupation: ");
    occupationField = new TextField(40);
}

private void makeWorldViewField() {
    worldViewLabel = new Label("Binary World View: ");
    worldViewField = new Checkbox();
}

private void makeCoffeeField() {
    coffeeLabel = new Label("Coffee consumption: ");
    coffeeField = new TextField(3);
}

private void makeFashionField() {
    fashionLabel = new Label("Fashion sense:");

    fashionGroup = new CheckboxGroup();
    low        = new Checkbox("Low   ", fashionGroup, false);
    medium     = new Checkbox("Medium", fashionGroup, true);
    high       = new Checkbox("High  ", fashionGroup, false);
}

// Text fields.

private TextField    nameField;
private TextField    ageField;
private TextField    coffeeField;
private TextField    occupationField;

// Labels.

private Label        nameLabel;
private Label        ageLabel;
private Label        coffeeLabel;
private Label        fashionLabel;
private Label        worldViewLabel;
private Label        occupationLabel;

// Checkboxes.
```

```
    private Checkbox        worldViewField;
    private Checkbox        low;
    private Checkbox        medium;
    private Checkbox        high;

    // The fashion sense checkbox group.
    private CheckboxGroup fashionGroup;
}
```

Output from the Occupational Oracle Applet

Figure 19-2 shows sample output from the OccupationOracle applet.

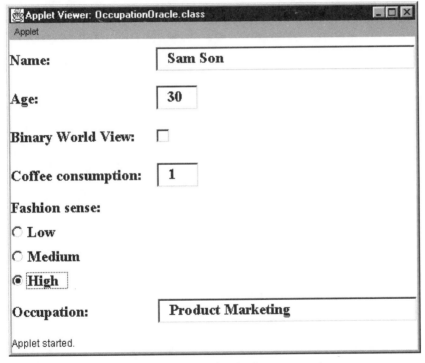

Figure 19-2 An Applet With Multiple Components
In this case, the Occupation Oracle predicts a 30 year old fellow who consumes 1 cup of coffee a day and who has a high sense of fashion is destined to fill a role

Summary

Working with forms involves incorporating multiple components into an applet. The sample applet in this chapter shows use of radio buttons, text fields, and check boxes. This applet shows use of one of Java's default LayoutManagers—`GridBagLayout`. The applet uses `GridBagLayout` to arrange components vertically and horizontally in the display. In later applets, we'll show alternatives to using `GridBagLayout`.

CHAPTER 20

- The Wonderful World of Animation
- The Ticker-Tape Example
- Supporting Animated Display Sequences

Animation in Applets

Incorporating Animation

One of the things that excites a lot of people about Java is the potential for lively pages on the world-wide web—not just pictures and sound, but movement as well. Java provides ample support for such animated applets. We'll focus our discussion of animation in applets on one of the most popular applets in use: the ticker-tape.

A Ticker-tape Applet

This `Ticker` applet will scroll a message across the screen like the news tickers in airports or at sports arenas. This is a configurable applet, so you can specify parameters in the HTML file to override the default values for the text, the font, and the foreground and background colors of the ticker-tape.

The key point of this applet is the use of *double buffering* to produce flicker-free animation. Double buffering refers to the technique of first drawing an image offscreen and then displaying it. In the example, the scrolling text is first written to an instance of `Image`, which is then displayed on the screen.

Other interesting characteristics of this applet to note are the use of the `Graphics.draw3DRect` call to draw an indented rectangle for a border and the use of the `java.util.StringTokenizer` class to divide a string at specified delimiters.

Example 20-1 lists the code for the `Ticker` class.

Example 20-1 Ticker Applet

```java
import java.awt.*;
import java.util.StringTokenizer;
import java.applet.Applet;

// The Ticker class displays a ticker tape of text that scrolls
// across the screen in a loop. When the text scrolls completely
// off one end it reappears on the other end. The text, font,
// foreground and background can be set via parameters. The font is
// specified by fontname, fontsize, fontweight and fontslant. The
// colors may be entered by name or by rgb values. To avoid
// flickering, the text is first drawn into an
// offscreen image and the image is then displayed all at once.

public class Ticker extends Applet implements Runnable {

    // The init() method initializes the Ticker. It sets the text,
    // font, foreground and background. The background is defaulted
    // to pink, the foreground to black, and the font to Helvetica.

    public void init() {
      tape        = "Java by Example: The Java Book for Programmers";
        String param = getParameter("text");
        if (param != null) {
            tape     = param;
        }

        // Get the user's font parameters, with 12 point Helvetica
        // font as the default.

        textFont = getFont("Helvetica", Font.PLAIN, 12);

        // We use the font height and font descent to draw the text
        // centered in the scrolling area. The width is used to
        // determine how far to scroll before starting over.

        FontMetrics metrics = getFontMetrics(textFont);
        textHeight        = metrics.getHeight();
        textDescent       = metrics.getDescent();
        textWidth         = metrics.stringWidth(tape);

        // Get the colors specified by the user with black as the
        // default foreground and pink as the default background.

        getColors(Color.black, Color.pink);
```

```
        // Initialize the size, number of scrolling steps and the
        // offscreen image used to draw the text.

        setupTape();
    }

// The start() method create a new thread to scroll the text and
// starts it.

public void start() {
    scrollThread = new Thread(this);
    scrollThread.start();
}

// The stop() method stops the scrolling thread.

public void stop() {
    scrollThread = null;
}

// The Ticker update() method just calls paint() since we are
// covering the background with our offscreen image.

public void update(Graphics g) {
    paint(g);
}

// The paint() method first checks if the Ticker has grown wider
// or taller. If it has grown taller, it is resized back to the
// right height for the font. If it has grown wider, setupTape()
// will create a new wider offscreen image and reset the number
// of steps required to scroll all the way across.
//
// After checking for resize, paint() draws the string into the
// offscreen image at the current scroll position then draws the
// image on the display.

public void paint(Graphics g) {

    // Adjust for resize if necessary.

    setupTape();

    // Draw the string into the offscreen image.

    Graphics offg = offscreenImage.getGraphics();
    offg.setColor(getBackground());
```

```
        offg.fillRect(0, 0, getSize().width - (RECTMARGIN * 2),
                textHeight);
        offg.setColor(getForeground());
        offg.setFont(textFont);

    // previousWidth is the width of the displayed area in pixels.
    // The text starts at the right edge of the Ticker at a position
    // previousWidth pixels from the left. Each time it is
    // repainted it is drawn one pixel farther to the left.

        offg.drawString(tape, previousWidth - tapeIndex,
                textHeight - textDescent);

    // totalTapeSteps is set to the width of the display area +
    // the width of the text. After the text has scrolled the
    // width of the display area it is at the left end of the
    // display and it must scroll its own width to complete
    // one traversal.

        tapeIndex = (tapeIndex + 1) % totalTapeSteps;

    // Draw a 3D rectangle just within the display area for a
    // border.

        g.draw3DRect(RECTMARGIN, RECTMARGIN,
                getSize().width - RECTMARGIN,
                getSize().height - RECTMARGIN,
                false);

    // Draw the offscreen image within the rectangle.

        g.drawImage(offscreenImage, RECTMARGIN + 1,
                RECTMARGIN + TEXTMARGIN + 1,
                this);
    }

// The run() method just pauses briefly between repaints.

public void run() {
    Thread currentThread = Thread.currentThread();
    while (scrollThread == currentThread) {
        try {
            scrollThread.sleep(SCROLLPAUSE);
        } catch (InterruptedException e) {
        }
        repaint();
    }
}
```

```
// The getColors() method retrieves color parameters from the
// user for foreground and background colors. If either is
// unspecified, the arguments are used as defaults.

private void getColors(Color foreground, Color background) {

    // Get either a named foreground color or an rgb value.

    String param = getParameter("foreground");

    if (param != null) {
        setForeground(lookupColor(param, foreground));

    } else {
        param = getParameter("foreground-rgb");

        if (param != null) {
            setForeground(lookupRGBColor(param, foreground));
        } else {

            // no parameter, use the default.

            setForeground(foreground);
        }
    }

    // Get either a named background color or an rgb value.

    param = getParameter("background");
    if (param != null) {
        setBackground(lookupColor(param, background));

    } else {
        param = getParameter("background-rgb");
        if (param != null) {
            setBackground(lookupRGBColor(param, background));
        } else {

            // no parameter, use the default.

            setBackground(background);
        }
    }
}

// The lookupColor() method looks up a color by name. All the
// predefined colors in the Color class are available except
```

```
// the shades of gray. The "colors" array holds {"colorname",
// color} pairs. If the name argument does not match any color
// in the array, the defaultColor argument is used.

private Color lookupColor(String name, Color defaultColor) {
    for (int i = 0; i < colors.length; i++) {
        if (name.equals(colors[i][0])) {
            return (Color)colors[i][1];
        }
    }
    return defaultColor;
}


// The lookupRGBColor() method takes a string that is expected to
// have the form: "rval,gval,bval" where rval, gval and bval are
// integers between 0 and 255. If the string matches this format,
// a color is returned with the specified rgb values; otherwise,
// defaultColor is returned.
//
// The Java StringTokenizer class is used to split the
// "description" argument into separate red, green, and blue
// values.

private Color lookupRGBColor(String description, Color
                            defaultColor) {
    try {

        // If any error occurs trying to parse the string, return
        // the default color. Possible errors are that there are
        // not enough tokens or and malformed integers.

        StringTokenizer tokens = new StringTokenizer(description,
                                                    ",");
        int red   = Integer.parseInt(tokens.nextToken());
        int green = Integer.parseInt(tokens.nextToken());
        int blue  = Integer.parseInt(tokens.nextToken());

        // ignore any extra stuff

        return new Color(red, green, blue);
    } catch (Exception e) {
        return defaultColor;
    }
}

// The getFont() method retrieves user specified font parameters.
// Any parameter not set by the user is replaced by the
// corresponding default argument. The "style" argument subsumes
```

```java
// the "fontweight" and "fontslant" parameters.

private Font getFont(String name, int style, int pointSize) {
    String param = getParameter("fontname");
    if (param != null) {
        name = param;
    }

    // Since the Java font model conflates slant and weight into
    // style we need to keep track of whether or not any style
    // parameters have been specified. If "fontweight" was
    // specified, then "fontslant" should be "or'd" with it;
    // otherwise, the "fontslant"
    // should completely replace the default.

    boolean styleSpecified = false;
    param                   = getParameter("fontweight");

    if (param != null) {
        styleSpecified = true;

        if (param.equals("bold") || param.equals("BOLD")) {
            style = Font.BOLD;

        } else {

            // Since the only two weights are "bold" and "plain",
            // we'll set the style to "plain" if it isn't bold.

            style = Font.PLAIN;
        }
    }
    param = getParameter("fontslant");

    if (param != null) {
        if (param.equals("italic") || param.equals("ITALIC")) {
            if (styleSpecified) {
                style |= Font.ITALIC;
            } else {
                style = Font.ITALIC;
            }

        } else if (!styleSpecified) {

            // Since the only two slants are "italic" and "plain",
            // we'll set the style to "plain" if it isn't italic.

            style = Font.PLAIN;
```

```
            }
        }
        param = getParameter("fontsize");

        if (param != null) {
            pointSize = Integer.parseInt(param);
        }

        return new Font(name, style, pointSize);
    }

    // The setupTape() method adjusts the state of the Ticker after a
    // resize. If the height has changed, it is reset to the
    // appropriate height for the selected font. If the width has
    // changed, the number of steps required for a complete scroll
    // traversal is reset and a new offscreen
    // image is created to draw into.

    private void setupTape() {
        Dimension dim = getSize();

        // resize() does nothing if the size hasn't changed.

        resize(dim.width, textHeight + (TEXTMARGIN * 2) + (RECTMARGIN
            * 2));

        // If the width hasn't changed, we're done.
        if (dim.width == previousWidth) {
            return;
        }

        // Save the width to compare against next time.

        previousWidth  = dim.width;

        // Reset the tape to the beginning.

        tapeIndex      = 0;

    // The total steps required for a scroll traversal is the width
        // of the display area + the width of the text.

        totalTapeSteps = dim.width + textWidth;

    // If there is already an existing offscreen image, destroy it.

        if (offscreenImage != null) {
            offscreenImage.flush();
```

```
    }

    // Create a new image to fit the current display area.

    offscreenImage = createImage(dim.width - (RECTMARGIN * 2),
                          textHeight);
}

// Constants.

private static final int TEXTMARGIN  = 3;
private static final int RECTMARGIN  = 1;
private static final int SCROLLPAUSE = 15;
private Thread scrollThread;        // Thread that scrolls text.
private String tape;                // The text being displayed.
private Image  offscreenImage = null; // Offscreen image we write
                                    // text into before displaying
                                    // it.
private Font   textFont;            // The displayed font.
private int    tapeIndex;           // Current index into the
                                    // text.
private int    totalTapeSteps;      // Number of steps required to
                                    // to traverse a complete
                                    // scroll.
private int    textWidth;           // Width of text in pixels.
private int    textHeight;          // Height of text in pixels.
private int    textDescent;         // How far the text goes
                                    // below the font's baseline
                                    // in pixels.
private int   previousWidth = -1;   // How wide the Ticker was the
                                    // last time we drew it.

// Colors indexed by name. Used by lookupColor to select a color
// value.

private Object[][]  colors = { { "white",  Color.white  },
                               { "WHITE",  Color.white  },
                               { "gray",   Color.gray   },
                               { "GRAY",   Color.gray   },
                               { "black",  Color.black  },
                               { "BLACK",  Color.black  },
                               { "red",    Color.red    },
                               { "RED",    Color.red    },
                               { "pink",   Color.pink   },
                               { "PINK",   Color.pink   },
                               { "orange", Color.orange },
                               { "ORANGE", Color.orange },
                               { "yellow", Color.yellow },
```

```
                                    {  "YELLOW",   Color.yellow  },
                                    {  "green",    Color.green   },
                                    {  "GREEN",    Color.green   },
                                    {  "magenta",  Color.magenta },
                                    {  "MAGENTA",  Color.magenta },
                                    {  "cyan",     Color.cyan    },
                                    {  "CYAN",     Color.cyan    },
                                    {  "blue",     Color.blue    },
                                    {  "BLUE",     Color.blue    } };
}
```

Output From the Ticker-tape Applet

Figure 20-1 shows output from the Ticker applet.

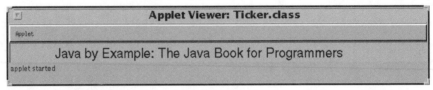

Figure 20-1 Ticker Applet Display

Summary

The ticker-tape applet is a common and useful one. The key point illustrated in this example is the use of double buffering to prevent the screen display from flickering. The ticker-tape applet also shows how to draw an indented rectangle for a border and the use of the `java.util.StringTokenizer` class to divide a string at specified delimiters.

CHAPTER 21

- Demonstrating Simple Event Handling

- Events and Threads

- Sample Event Handling Applets

Events and Threads in Applets

Introduction

Graphical user interfaces in Java are based on the processing of events, such as mouse clicks or keyboard key sequences. A programmer defines the actions to be taken when various events occur. In this chapter we'll describe two applets, the first of which simply responds to user events, and the second of which introduces an independent thread of control that interacts with the event processing.

In all the examples, the event handling methods return `boolean` values. When a method returns a `true` value, it means that the method has handled the event and no further processing is required. If an event handling method returns a `false` value, the event is forwarded to the current component's peer. This mechanism allows programmers to override the default behavior of native windowing components when necessary and rely on the built-in behaviors otherwise.

Simple Event Handling

The first event handling applet is a simple puzzle that demonstrates how to respond to events generated by the user. We'll define how the puzzle operates by creating a `Puzzle` class.

Puzzle Applet

This applet is a simple puzzle in which the goal is to change all the squares on the board to black. Figure 21-1 shows the puzzle applet display.

Figure 21-1 Puzzle Applet Display

Each time the mouse changes squares, the new square is advanced one step through the color sequence. To make the game a little bit harder, moving the mouse directly back to the previous square doesn't change anything. The only events monitored in the example are the `mouseMove` and `mouseDrag` events.

Example 21-1 shows the code for the `Puzzle` class:

Example 21-1 Puzzle Applet

```
import java.applet.*;
import java.awt.*;
import java.awt.event.*;

// The Puzzle class implements a simple puzzle in which the goal is to
// change all the squares on the board to black. Each mouse move is
// checked to see if the mouse has changed squares. If the mouse has
// moved to a square other than the one it was in one move earlier,
// the new square is advanced one step through the color sequence.

public class Puzzle extends Applet implements MouseMotionListener {
    // To initialize the puzzle we create a board which has the
    // dimensions: appletWidth/50, appletHeight/50. We read the
    // to determine the length of the color sequence for the applet. A
    // "numcolors" parameter longer color sequence makes the puzzle
    // harder.
```

```java
public void init() {
   scale = 50;   // Each square is 50 pixels on a side.

   // Make sure the height and width are multiples of "scale".

   appletWidth   = Math.max(getSize().width,  scale) / scale  *
                   scale;
   appletHeight  = Math.max(getSize().height, scale) / scale *
                   scale;

   // lastX, lastY, nextToLastX, nextToLastY record the previous
   // square and the previous square once removed.

   lastX         = -1;
   lastY         = -1;
   nextToLastX   = -1;
   nextToLastY   = -1;

   // The dimensions of the board.

   cellWidth     = appletWidth  / scale;
   cellHeight    = appletHeight / scale;
   board = new char[cellWidth][cellHeight];

   // Determine the length of the puzzle's color sequence. A
   // longer sequence is harder. If the parameter value is
   // greater than the number of colors, use the total number
   // of colors. If the value is less than 2, use 2. If the
   // number of colors is unspecified, use DEFAULT_NUM_COLORS.

   String param = getParameter("numcolors");

   if (param != null) {
      numColors = Integer.parseInt(param);

      if (numColors > colors.length) {
         numColors = colors.length;

      } else if (numColors < 2) {
         numColors = 2;
      }
   } else {
      numColors = DEFAULT_NUM_COLORS;
   }

   // Resize to a multiple of the scale value.

   resize(appletWidth, appletHeight);
```

```
        // Initialize the colors of the board to random values and
        // draw it.

        reset();
        addMouseMotionListener(this);
    }
// The reset method is called at the start of the applet and every
// time the puzzle is successfully completed. It sets the colors
// of the board to random values. The board is an array of chars
// to save space. Each cell of the board holds an index into the
// array of colors.

private void reset() {
    for (int i = 0; i < cellWidth; i++) {
        for (int j = 0; j < cellHeight; j++) {

            // Initialize the cell to a random value between 0 and
                // the number of colors - 1.

            board[i][j] = (char)((Math.random() * 10) % numColors);
            }
        }
        repaint();
    }

// Test for the solution of the puzzle. If all the cells contain
// the index of the first color, the puzzle is solved. When
// the puzzle is solved, play the "winning" sound and reset the
// board.

private void testWin() {
    for (int i = 0; i < cellWidth; i++) {
        for (int j = 0; j < cellHeight; j++) {
            if (board[i][j] != 0) {
                return;
                }
            }
        }
        getAudioClip(getCodeBase(), "Audio/gong.au").play();
        reset();
    }

// Repaint the board. This method could be made more efficient by
// only repainting the changed square. We'll make this
// optimization in later examples.

public void paint(Graphics g) {
    for (int i = 0; i < cellWidth; i++) {
```

```
        for (int j = 0; j < cellHeight; j++) {
            g.setColor(colors[board[i][j]]);
            g.fillRect(i * scale, j * scale, scale, scale);
        }
    }
}
```

```
// This is the method that handles the "mouseMoved" event.
// Anytime the mouse moves without a button pressed, "mouseMoved"
// is called. If a button is being held down, "mouseDragged" is
// called. We want to do the same thing in either case so
// "mouseMoved" and "mouseDragged" can both call the same routine.

public void mouseMoved(MouseEvent mEvent) {
    processMovement(mEvent);
}
```

```
// Here is "mouseDragged".

public void mouseDragged(MouseEvent mEvent) {
    processMovement(mEvent);
}
```

```
// This is the routine that does all event handling for the
// applet. The event location is scaled into cell coordinates
// and the scaled x and y values are compared to the last two
// cells. If the new cell is distinct
// from either of the previous two cells, the color of
// the new cell is updated. A special version of repaint()
// is called, which tells Java to clip changes that fall outside
// the current square.

private boolean processMovement(MouseEvent evt) {

    // Scale the pixel coordinates to cell coordinates.

    int cellX = evt.getX() / scale;
    int cellY = evt.getY() / scale;

    // If the new cell is the same as the last one or the next to
    // last one, do nothing.

    if ((cellX == lastX && cellY == lastY) ||
        cellX == nextToLastX && cellY == nextToLastY) {
        return true;
    }

    // If the new cell coordinates fall outside the board, do
```

```java
    // nothing.

    if (cellX >= cellWidth || cellY >= cellHeight) {
        return true;
    }

    // Update the color index of the current cell.

    board[cellX][cellY] = (char)((board[cellX][cellY] + 1) %
        numColors);

    // Save the previous two cells.

    nextToLastX = lastX;
    nextToLastY = lastY;
    lastX       = cellX;
    lastY       = cellY;

    // Repaint the applet, clipping the painted region to the
    // the changed square.

    repaint(0, cellX * scale, cellY * scale, scale, scale);

    // Check if the puzzle is solved.

    testWin();

    // Return true so the event is not forwarded to this
    // component's peer.

    return true;
}

// If the number of colors is not specified, default to 4.

private static final int DEFAULT_NUM_COLORS = 4;
private int      appletHeight;  // Height of the applet.
private int      appletWidth;   // Width of the applet.
private int    numColors;      // Number of colors in the puzzle.
private int    scale;          // One side of a square in pixels.
private char    board[][];      // Game board.
private int      lastX;          // X index of previous cell.
private int      lastY;          // Y index of previous cell.
private int      nextToLastX;    // X index of next to last cell.
private int      nextToLastY;    // Y index of next to last cell.
private int      cellWidth;      // Width of game board in cells.
private int      cellHeight;     // Height of game board in cells.
```

```
// The maximum number of colors in the puzzle is 6.

private Color    colors[]    = { Color.black,
                                 Color.white,
                                 Color.red,
                                 Color.green,
                                 Color.blue,
                                 Color.yellow };
```

Output From the Puzzle Applet

It's hard to show a graphical puzzle game being played in a book, but Figure 21-2 shows the Puzzle applet, as displayed by the `appletviewer`.

Figure 21-2 An Applet That Manages Mouse Movements
The first frame shows the Puzzle applet after being started, and the second frame shows the game nearly completed. One more move and the remaining square changes to black and the gong sounds.

Managing Events and Threads

Now that we've seen simple handling of mouse events, let's look at a little more complicated example. In the next example, we'll introduce a separate thread of control.

Memory Game Applet

This next applet is a memory game in which a pattern is displayed that the user must try to remember and duplicate. The display thread uses calls to the `Thread.sleep()` method to pause between squares. Selected squares are highlighted by changing their colors using the `Color.brighter()` method.

The `Memory` class implements a game in which the user uses the mouse to duplicate a sequence of squares that have been highlighted. Each time the user successfully duplicates the pattern, the pattern display speeds up. Eventually, the pattern slows back down, increases in number by one square, and starts speeding up again. If the user fails in reproducing the sequence, the game starts over. Here's the code for the `Memory` class:

Example 21-2 Memory Applet

```java
import java.applet.*;
import java.awt.*;
import java.awt.event.*;

// This class implements a memory game. A sequence of squares is
// highlighted which the user must remember and reproduce. If she is
// successful, the sequence display gets faster and then longer. If
// the user fails in reproducing the sequence, the game starts over.

public class Memory extends Applet implements Runnable {
    // To initialize the applet, scale the height and width by the
    // number of colors.  Set the display time and pattern length
    // to easy values. (Long for the display time and short for the
    // pattern length).

    public void init() {
        // The first time we get updated we want to paint everything.

        fullPaint = true;

        // Each row and column has one cell of each color.

        numCellsOnSide = colors.length;

        // Scale width and height to multiples of the number of cells
        // on a side.

        int appletHeight = Math.max(getSize().width, numCellsOnSide) /
            numCellsOnSide * numCellsOnSide;
        int appletWidth  = Math.max(getSize().height, numCellsOnSide) /
            numCellsOnSide * numCellsOnSide;

        // Set the width and height of the cells for painting.

        cellWidth  = appletWidth  / numCellsOnSide;
        cellHeight = appletHeight / numCellsOnSide;

        // Listen for mouse activity
```

```java
    addMouseListener(new MemoryMouseListener());
    addMouseMotionListener(new MemoryMouseMotionListener());

    // Initialize the display time and the pattern length to
    // easy values.

    getReallyEasy();

    // Resize to our new width and height.

    resize(appletWidth, appletHeight);
}

// Create a thread for the pattern display.  We start the game by
// immediately displaying a pattern so call Thread.start() right
// away.

public void start() {
  displayThread = new Thread(this);
  displayThread.start();
}

// Stop the display thread.  This is only called when the applet
// is exited.

public synchronized void stop() {
  displayThread = null;
}

// This applet implements the Runnable interface so it must define
// a "run" method.  This method will be called when the Thread's
// start method is called.  The call to reset() creates a new
// pattern and displays it.  The display thread is then suspended
// until a new pattern is needed.

public void run() {
      Thread currentThread = Thread.currentThread();
      while (displayThread == currentThread) {
          try {
              synchronized (this) {
               reset();
               wait();
               }
          } catch (InterruptedException e) {
           // Here we consider being interrupted as equivalent
           // to being notified.
          }
```

```
        }
    }

    // We redefine the update method derived from java.awt.Component.
    // The default version redraws the background each time
    // and our applet completely covers the background, so drawing it
    // is unnecessary.

    public void update(Graphics g) {
        paint(g);
    }

    // In this paint method we optimize for the painting of single
    // cells. When a method makes a change to a single cell, it sets
    // "fullPaint" to false and sets paintColor, paintX, and paintY
    // before calling repaint.  If fullPaint is false, we just redraw
    // the cell at (paintX, paintY); otherwise we redraw the entire
    // grid.

    public void paint(Graphics g) {
        if (fullPaint) {
            for (int i = 0; i < numCellsOnSide; i++) {
                for (int j = 0; j < numCellsOnSide; j++) {
                    g.setColor(colors[i][j]);
                g.fillRect(i * cellWidth, j * cellHeight, cellWidth,
                                cellHeight);
                }
            }
        } else {

            // paintColor, paintX, and paintY must be set before this
            // method is called with fullPaint == false.

            g.setColor(paintColor);
            g.fillRect(paintX, paintY, cellWidth, cellHeight);
            fullPaint = true;
        }
    }

    private class MemoryMouseListener extends MouseAdapter {
        // All the following event handling routines check the value
        // of the "resetting" flag and do nothing if it is set. The
        // "resetting" is set while the current pattern is being
        // displayed.

        // When the user presses a button down in a square
        // we highlight the square and begin watch mouse movement. If
        // she then releases the button in the same square we consider
```

```
// the square selected and process her move. If the mouse
// leaves the square we just unhighlight the square and
// proceed as if nothing had happened.

public void mousePressed(MouseEvent mEvent) {
    int x = mEvent.getX();
    int y = mEvent.getY();

    // If the pattern is being displayed, do nothing.

    if (resetting) {
        return;
    }

    // Scale the pixel coordinates to cell coordinates.

    int cellX = x / cellWidth;
    int cellY = y / cellHeight;

    // Set "paintX", "paintY" and "paintColor" so the paint
    // method will know which square to redraw and what color
    // to paint it.

    paintX     = cellX * cellWidth;
    paintY     = cellY * cellHeight;
    paintColor = colors[cellX][cellY].brighter();

    // Tell the paint method to only paint a single square.

    fullPaint = false;

    // Schedule an update.

    repaint();

    // Set the current cell X and Y coordinates so we can
    // determine if the user releases the mouse in the same
    // cell.

    currentX = cellX;
    currentY = cellY;

    // Set the checkMove flag so that we pay attention to drag
    // and mouseUp events.

    checkMove = true;
    return;
}
```

```
// If the mouse button is released and the button had been
// pressed within the applet, unhighlight the square and add
// the square to the user's pattern. Check if the user has
// completed the pattern or selected the wrong square.

public void mouseReleased(MouseEvent mEvent) {
    synchronized (Memory.this) {
        int x = mEvent.getX();
        int y = mEvent.getY();

        // If we're currently displaying the pattern or no
        // mouse down occurred within the applet, do nothing.

        if (resetting || !checkMove) {

        return;
    }

        // Scale the pixel coordinates to cell coordinates.

        int cellX = x / cellWidth;
        int cellY = y / cellHeight;

        // Set "paintX", "paintY" and "paintColor" so the paint
        // method will know which square to redraw and what color
        // to paint it.

        paintX     = cellX * cellWidth;
        paintY     = cellY * cellHeight;
        paintColor = colors[cellX][cellY];

        // Tell the paint method to only paint a single square.

        fullPaint = false;

        // Schedule an update.

        repaint();

        // testPattern() will try to match the user's
        // selection with the next cell in the pattern.  If it
        // matches, the pattern index is advanced and a check
        // is made to see if the user has completed the
        // pattern.  If the selection doesn't match, the
        // current game ends and a new game starts.

        testPattern(cellX, cellY);
```

```
            checkMove = false;
            return;
        }
    }
}

private class MemoryMouseMotionListener extends
    MouseMotionAdapter {
// The following event handling routine check the value of the
// "resetting" flag and does nothing if it is set.  The
// "resetting" is set while the current pattern is being
// displayed.

public void mouseDragged(MouseEvent mEvent) {
    int x = mEvent.getX();
    int y = mEvent.getY();

    // If we're currently displaying the pattern or no mouse down
    // occurred within the applet, do nothing.

    if (resetting || !checkMove) {
        return;
    }

    // Scale the pixel coordinates to cell coordinates.

    int cellX = x / cellWidth;
    int cellY = y / cellHeight;

    // If the mouse has not left the mouse down square, do nothing.

    if (cellX == currentX && cellY == currentY) {
        return;
    }

    // Set "paintX", "paintY" and "paintColor" so the paint method
    // will know which square to redraw and what color to paint it.
    // Note that we don't repaint the square the mouse is now in
    // but, instead, the square the mouse just left.

    paintX = currentX * cellWidth;
    paintY = currentY * cellHeight;
    paintColor = colors[currentX][currentY];

    // Tell the paint method to only paint a single square.

    fullPaint = false;
```

```
    // Schedule an update.

    repaint();

    // Return to the default state.

    checkMove = false;
    return;
  }
}


// This routine compares a cell with the next cell in the stored
// pattern.  If it matches, a check is made for the pattern being
// complete.  If it fails, the game ends and a new game is started.
// Each time a pattern is completed, the pattern display is speeded
// up or the pattern is lengthened.

private synchronized void testPattern(int x, int y) {
    int[] nextMatch = pattern[next++];

    if (nextMatch[0] == x && nextMatch[1] == y) {

        // If the current cell matched, check if we're at the
        // end of the pattern.

        if (next == patternLength) {

            // If the pattern is complete, play a winning sound and
            // make the next pattern harder.  Resume the pattern
            // display thread to display a new pattern.

            win();
            getHarder();
            notify();
        }
    } else {

        // If the user failed to match the current cell, play a
        // losing sound and make the next pattern really easy.
        // Resume the pattern display thread to display a new
        // pattern.

        lose();
        getReallyEasy();
        notify();
    }
}
```

```
// Play a "winning" sound.

private void win() {
    getAudioClip(getCodeBase(), "Audio/gong.au").play();
}

// Play a "losing" sound.

private void lose() {
    getAudioClip(getCodeBase(), "Audio/beep.au").play();
}
// Make the pattern harder. Decrement the display time until it
// gets too fast then slow it down and make the pattern longer.

private void getHarder() {
    if (sleepTime > minimumSleepTime) {
        sleepTime -= sleepTimeDecrement;
    } else {
        patternLength++;
        sleepTime = resetSleepTime / 2;
    }
}

// Make the pattern really easy.  Make the display time very long
// and the pattern very short.  This is used to start a new game.

private void getReallyEasy() {
    sleepTime = resetSleepTime / 2;
    patternLength = initialPatternLength;
}

// reset() starts a new pattern.  It generates the pattern, and
// displays it to the user.  The pattern sequence is generated
// using the Math.random() method and each square in the pattern
// is displayed as it is generated.

private synchronized void reset() {

    // Set "resetting" to true so events will be ignored while the
    // pattern is displayed.

    resetting = true;
    checkMove = false;
    fullPaint = true;

    // Display a flashy color rolling effect to signal the start
    // of a new pattern.
```

```
        loopColors();

    // Initialize the current index into the pattern to 0.  This
    // is used to keep track of where the user is in duplicating
    // the pattern.

    next = 0;

    // Create a new pattern array.  Each element is a pair of
    // X and Y coordinates.  We could save space using chars or
    // shorts but this is always a small array so it doesn't
    // really matter.

    pattern = new int[patternLength][2];

    for (int i = 0; i < patternLength; i++) {

        // Select random X and Y coordinates.

      int randomX = (int)((Math.random() * 10) % numCellsOnSide);
      int randomY = (int)((Math.random() * 10) % numCellsOnSide);

        // Set the next pattern entry to the new coordinates.

        pattern[i][0] = randomX;
        pattern[i][1] = randomY;

      // Display the pattern square by redrawing it briefly in a
        // brighter version of its current color.

        paintColor = colors[randomX][randomY].brighter();
        paintX     = randomX * cellWidth;
        paintY     = randomY * cellHeight;
        fullPaint = false;
        repaint();

        // Sleep so the user can see the bright color before we
      // darken it again.  The sleep time decreases as patterns
        // are successfully duplicated.

        goToSleep(sleepTime);

      // Redraw the square in its original color before going to
        // the next square.

        paintColor = colors[randomX][randomY];
        fullPaint = false;
        repaint();
```

```
        // Sleep between squares.

        goToSleep(repaintSleepTime);
    }

    // Allow mouse events to be processed.

    resetting = false;
}

// Rotate the colors of the grid to signal a new pattern.  Sleep
// between each rotation so the user can see it.

private void loopColors() {

    // Rotate as many times as there are colors so we return to
    // our initial color pattern.

    for (int i = 0; i < colors.length; i++) {
        rotateColors();
        repaint();
        goToSleep(rotateSleepTime);
    }
}

// Rotate the entries in the color array.

private void rotateColors() {
    Color[] temp = colors[0];

    for (int i = 0; i < colors.length - 1; i++) {
        colors[i] = colors[i + 1];
    }

    colors[colors.length - 1] = temp;
}

// In this applet we don't care if a sleep is interrupted so we
// do nothing with an InterruptedException.

private void goToSleep(int n) {
    try {
        Thread.currentThread().sleep(n);
    } catch (InterruptedException e) {
    }
}
```

```java
// Constants.

private static final int resetSleepTime      = 1500;
private static final int repaintSleepTime    = 30;
private static final int rotateSleepTime     = 300;
private static final int minimumSleepTime    = 150;
private static final int sleepTimeDecrement   = 100;
private static final int initialPatternLength = 4;
private Thread  displayThread;    // Thread that resets display.
private int     cellWidth;        // The pixel width of a cell.
private int     cellHeight;       // The pixel height of a cell.
private int     numCellsOnSide;   // Number of cells on one side
                                  // of the grid.
private int     sleepTime;        // How long to sleep while
                                  // displaying a pattern square.
private int     next;             // Current index into the pattern.
private int     currentX;         // X coordinate of the square in
                                  // which a mouse down occurred.
private int     currentY;         // Y coordinate of the square in
                                  // which a mouse down occurred.
private int     paintX;           // X coordinate of the square to
                                  // paint.
private int     paintY;           // Y coordinate of the square to
                                  // paint.
private int[][] pattern;          // The current pattern.
private int     patternLength;    // Length of current pattern.
private boolean fullPaint;        // Whether or not to paint a
                                  // single cell.
private boolean checkMove;        // Whether or not a mouse down
                                  // has occurred.
private boolean resetting;        // Whether or not the pattern is
                                  // currently being displayed.
private Color   paintColor;       // Color of single cell to paint.
private Color   colors[][] =      // The colors in the grid.
  {
      { Color.blue.darker(),
        Color.yellow.darker(),
        Color.red.darker(),
        Color.green.darker() },
      { Color.yellow.darker(),
        Color.red.darker(),
        Color.green.darker(),
        Color.blue.darker() },

      { Color.red.darker(),
        Color.green.darker(),
        Color.blue.darker(),
        Color.yellow.darker() },
```

```
        { Color.green.darker(),
          Color.blue.darker(),
          Color.yellow.darker(),
          Color.red.darker() }
    };
}
```

Output From the Memory Game Applet

Figure 21-3 shows the output from the Memory game applet.

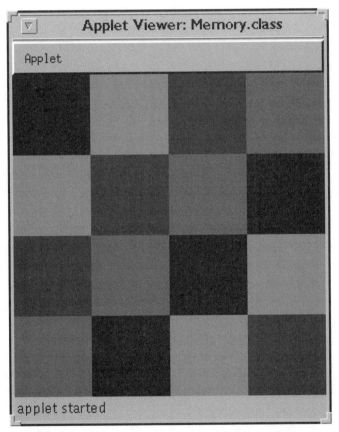

Figure 21-3 Applet Managing Events and Threads
The applet flashes a color pattern. The user must duplicate the

Summary

Developing interesting applets most likely requires managing events such as mouse and keyboard actions. Also, many applets are manipulated by the user, so the applet needs to perform ongoing operations at the same time it is interacting with the user. This requires multiple threads of execution in the applet. In this chapter, we've illustrated event handling and threads in applets. Next, we'll develop these concepts and illustrate applets that combine these with forms to see how to create a Java graphical user interface.

CHAPTER
22

- Using a Custom Layout Manager

- Developing a Complex Applet

- Using synchronized in an Applet

Putting the Applet Pieces Together

Introduction

To complete discussion of applets, we'll describe a complex applet that will use techniques applied in previous examples. This applet will use interfaces, event handling, multiple threads of execution, and add some interesting new features.

This example will be the longest program we discuss and should help understand how to construct large Java applications or applets. The applet is a *cellular automaton construction kit*. That sounds like a mouthful, but don't be put off by the name. You may already be familiar with a particular cellular automaton—the computer game of Life. In the game of Life, the cells of a grid structure are filled, as if under their own power. In this chapter, we'll build an applet (the cellular automaton construction kit) that lets you define new automata and watch them evolve.

Constructing the Cellular Applet

This applet uses a two-dimensional grid of cells, a set of possible cell values, and a rule that tells how cell values change over time. The rule determines the next value contained in a cell. The next value is based on the cell's current value and the current values of the eight cells that surround it, as illustrated in Figure 22-1.

Figure 22-1 Cellular Applet Grid
In the grid, C is the current cell and N is a neighbor cell. The next value of a cell is based on the cell's current value and the current values of the eight cells that surround it.

The game of Life has two possible cell values—off and on—and a simple rule that says:

```
IF the current cell is off
  IF exactly 3 of the current cell's neighbors are on
    Turn the current cell on.
  ELSE
    Leave the current cell off.

ELSE (the current cell is on)
  IF 2 or 3 of the current cell's neighbors are on
    Leave the current cell on.
  ELSE
    Turn the current cell off.
```

By changing the rule and changing the set of values we can define different automata that have completely different—and sometimes surprising—behavior.

Applet Overview

The Cellular applet consists of four different parts:

- A user interaction piece that displays the automata and takes user input
- A layout manager that arranges the display canvas and controls for the applet
- An *arena* in which the evolution of the automata takes place
- A rule module that provides support for defining rules and sets of cell values

These parts correspond to the program structure, which we'll show later in the chapter in our discussion of applet class structure. Before doing that, let's look at how it works.

Operation of the Applet

The applet can run in two modes:

1. An interactive mode in which the user can select a set of rules and define the starting configuration of cells before launching the automaton.

2. A scripted mode in which the applet runs automatically according to a pre-defined set of rules and configurations.

When the applet is run in its interactive mode, four controls are provided to start and stop the evolution, clear the canvas, and switch to a different rule set, as illustrated in Figure 22-2.

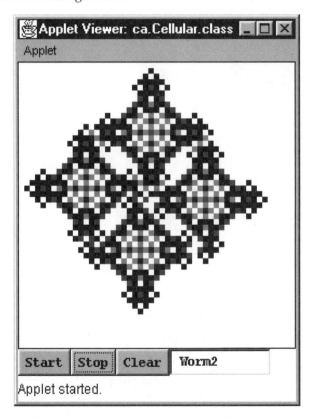

Figure 22-2 Cellular Applet in Interactive Mode
In interactive mode, the user can start, stop, or clear the board.
The user can also enter a new set of rules in the text field.

When the applet is running in scripted mode, it looks something like this:

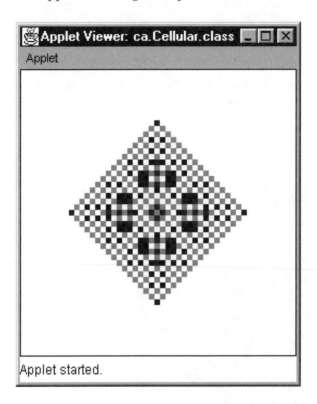

Figure 22-3 Cellular Applet in Scripted Mode
In scripted mode, the applet plays according to a predefined
script. There are no controls for user interaction.

A user can zoom in on the activity by making the applet bigger. This makes each
individual cell larger, so it's easier to see the pattern of changing cells.

The Cellular applet also employs some special techniques and features worth
noting before looking in detail at the code. These include use of the
`synchronized` keyword, a custom layout manager, an easy-to-modify rule set,
and the scripting capability we already alluded to. It is helpful to look at each of
these to better understand how the entire applet works.

Use of synchronized in the Applet

The Cellular applet is the first example in which we've used the Java synchronized keyword. We use it to synchronize changes to the cells of an automaton. The user can change the values of cells by using the mouse, but the ongoing thread that handles the evolution of the automaton may be about to change that cell as well, or the cell might be about to repainted. So we use the synchronized keyword to avoid conflicts.

A Custom Layout Manager

This applet is unable to make use of any of the default layout managers discussed in *Layout Managers* on page 418. The problem is that, when resizing the applet canvas, the width and height must always be integral multiples of the number of cells on a side. Otherwise, there would be leftover bits of cells around the edges. The default layout managers don't provide any way to handle this particular resizing problem. As a result, we have written our own layout manager called BoardLayout.

The BoardLayout layout manager arranges a board and a set of controls, and it handles the resizing problem. It's called BoardLayout because it could easily be used to manage a board for a game like chess or checkers. This layout manager tries to make a square board as large as possible within the space provided by its parent and arranges the controls in the remaining space. If the controls won't fit when the board is reduced to its minimum size, they are not shown.

Defining Rules

The Cellular applet is designed to make it easy to define new rules. Each rule set is a class that must define three methods, as described in Table 22-1.

Table 22-1 Cellular Applet Rule Methods

Rule Methods	Description
getColors()	Returns an array of colors representing cell values.
getInitialValue()	Returns the index into the color array of the starting value for cells.
apply()	Returns the new value for a cell.

Several helper methods are provided to obtain the values of the current cell and its neighbors. Here is the rule set for the game of Life:

```java
// All rule sets should be in the ca.rules package.

package ca.rules;

// All rule sets must extend the ca.Rules class. The process() method
// of the ca.Rules class initializes the set of neighbors and the
// value of the current cell before calling a rule set's apply()
// method. The ca.Rules class also provides support methods for
// selecting particular neighbors and determining how many
// neighboring cells have a particular value.

import ca.Rules;
import java.awt.Color;

public class Life extends Rules {
  public Life() {
    colors     = new Color[2];
    colors[0] = Color.white;
    colors[1] = Color.black;
  }

  // Return the set of colors this rule set wants to display for
  // its cell values.

  public Color[] getColors() {
    return colors;
  }

  // Cells should be initialized to the zero'th color in this rule
  // set's color array (i.e. white).

  public int getInitialValue() {
    return 0;
  }

  // The apply() method determines the new value for a cell given
  // its current value and the values of its neighbors.

  public int apply() {

    // The numCells() method returns the number of neighbors that
    // currently have the value passed as its argument. In this
    // case, it returns the number of cells that have the value "1"
    // (the cells which are on).
```

```
    int num = numCells(1);

    // The self() method returns the current value of the current
    // cell.

    if (self() == 0) {

        // If the current cell is off, there must be exactly three
        // neighbors that are on before it gets turned on.

        if (num == 3) {
            return 1;

        } else {
            return 0;
        }

    } else {

        // If the current cell is on, there must be two or three
        // neighbors that are on or it gets turned off.

        if (num == 2 || num == 3) {
            return 1;

        } else {
            return 0;
        }
    }
  }
  private Color colors[];
}
```

In this rule set, note the use of the numCells() method to determine how many neighbors have a particular value. numLinear() and numDiag() methods are also provided. These methods determine how many cells have specified values in the *rook move* and *bishop move* directions on the board.

Different rule sets can be dynamically loaded into the applet by typing their names into the text field at the bottom of the applet (see Figure 22-2 on page 467).

Scripting the Applet

Automata are entertaining to watch. For those wishing to be mesmerized, it's possible to use HTML code to script the applet so that it executes a predefined set of rules and patterns. The two HTML parameters for the applet are script and numcells. The script parameter allows you to specify rules and configurations. The numcells parameter determines the *grain size* of the applet (that is, the number of cells across one side of the applet). The width of the applet divided by the number of cells specified determines the minimum size of a cell on the screen. The cells can be made larger by increasing the size of the applet, but they cannot be made smaller than their initial size. More cells allows for more generations and more of a birds-eye view of the automaton, but it also makes each generation take longer to calculate.

Example 22-1 shows a sample HTML script for the Cellular applet.

Example 22-1 Sample Cellular Script

```
<applet code="ca.Cellular.class" width=300 height=300>
<param  name="script"
value="Worm2:edge:25,25,1;Life:10:25,23,1:25,24,1:25,25,1:25,26,1
:25,27,1">
<param  name="numcells" value="51">
</applet>
```

For each entry in the script, you can define three parameters: the rule set to use, when to stop running the rule set, and the initial configuration of cells. Here's the syntax of a script entry:

<Rule set name> : *<bound behavior>* : *<initial configuration>*

So, in the following single script entry:

```
Worm2:edge:25,25,1;
```

the script says to start the applet with the Worm2 rule and execute it until it reaches the edge or until its pattern stops changing. This entry also says to start the applet with a single cell set to color number 1 at location 25,25.

The *<initial configuration>* parameter (and the colon preceding it) are optional. An *<initial configuration>* consists of triples separated by colons. Each triple is of the form: *x*, *y*, *color*.

After executing the first script entry, the applet then switches to the Life rule set, as specified in Example 22-1. The Life rule set initializes cells to color number 1 at 5 locations. The color and locations are specified in a series of triples separated by colons. The Life rule set runs for 10 generations or until its pattern stops changing. Then the applet repeats executing from the beginning.

The execution pattern display can terminate two ways:

• When the pattern reaches the edge of the canvas

• After a certain number of steps

Also, the pattern can run continuously, unless it stops changing. (The evolution of an automaton always stops if it does not change between two generations.)

Applet Class Structure

As previously mentioned, the Cellular applet has four functional parts: a user interaction part, a layout part, an arena part, and a rule part. Figure 22-4 on the next page shows the high-level organization of the classes that provide these four parts.

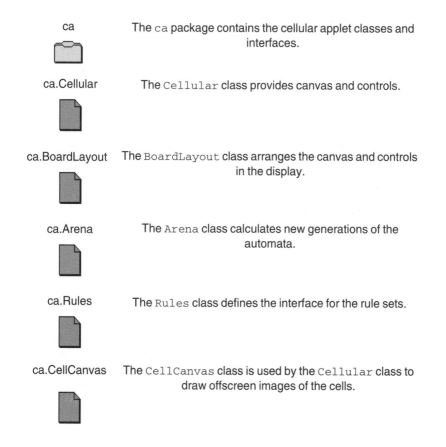

ca   The `ca` package contains the cellular applet classes and interfaces.

ca.Cellular   The `Cellular` class provides canvas and controls.

ca.BoardLayout   The `BoardLayout` class arranges the canvas and controls in the display.

ca.Arena   The `Arena` class calculates new generations of the automata.

ca.Rules   The `Rules` class defines the interface for the rule sets.

ca.CellCanvas   The `CellCanvas` class is used by the `Cellular` class to draw offscreen images of the cells.

Figure 22-4 The Cellular Applet's Class Structure
All of these classes are in the `ca` package.

Table 22-2 describes these classes in more detail.

Table 22-2 Cellular Applet Class Summary

`Cellular` **Class**	
Package	`ca`

Imports	`java.applet.Applet`
	`java.awt.*`
	`java.util.*`

Interfaces	`Runnable`
Subclass of	`Applet`
Description	The `Cellular` class is the top-level class for the applet. It reads parameters and provides a canvas and controls for manipulating components of the applet.

`BoardLayout` **Class**	
Package	`ca`
Imports	`java.util.*` `java.awt.*`
Interfaces	`LayoutManager`
Subclass of	`Object`
Description	The `BoardLayout` class implements the `LayoutManager` interface. It arranges the display canvas and controls for the applet, reshaping them if necessary when the display is resized.

`Arena` **Class**	
Package	`ca`
Imports	None
Interfaces	None
Subclass of	`Object`
Description	The `Arena` class takes care of actually calculating new generations for the automata. It loops through the current array of cells, saves new values for each cell in a separate array, and then swaps the arrays.

`Rules` **Class**	
Package	`ca`
Imports	`java.awt.Color`
Interfaces	None
Subclass of	`Object`

Table 22-2 Cellular Applet Class Summary (Continued)

Description	The Rules class is an *Abstract* class that defines the interface for rule sets and provides support methods for defining rules. (For a review of abstract classes, see *Native Methods* on page 35.)

CellCanvas **Class**	
Package	ca
Imports	None
Interfaces	None
Subclass of	Canvas
Description	The CellCanvas is *not* public as it is only useful within the context of the Cellular class. CellCanvas does the actual display of automata. It calls the arena's apply() method repeatedly and redraws the cells that have changed. All drawing is done to an offscreen image, which is then displayed on the screen. When the display is resized, the offscreen image is recreated and the cellSize and cellSide are recomputed.

The Cellular Applet

We've gone into a fairly lengthy discussion of the Cellular applet—what's going on in it and how it works. Now let's take a look at the code.

The Cellular class provides the canvas for displaying and controls for manipulating cellular automata. It can be used in two modes:

- A running display mode that automatically steps through predefined patterns

- A manual mode with controls for starting, stopping, and clearing the display and changing the automaton rules and initial cell configuration

This applet uses the BoardLayout layout manager to place the canvas and controls. Example 22-2 shows the code for the Cellular class, as well as the definition of the CellCanvas class.

Example 22-2 Cellular Applet

```
package ca;

import java.applet.Applet;
import java.awt.*;
import java.util.*;
import java.awt.event.*;

// The Cellular applet provides a canvas and controls for
// manipulating and displaying cellular automata. It can be used in
// two modes: a running display mode that automatically steps through
// predefined patterns and a manual mode with controls for starting,
// stopping, and clearing the display and changing the automaton
// rules and initial cell configuration. This applet uses the
// BoardLayout layout manager to place the canvas
// and controls.

public class Cellular extends Applet implements Runnable {

    // The init() method retrieves parameter values from the user and
    // creates the components of the applet. If the applet is running
    // in automatic mode, no controls are added to the layout. The
    // components of the applet are:
    //
    // 1) a canvas for displaying automata.
    // 2) a start button to initiate the evolution of an automaton.
    // 3) a stop button to suspend the evolution.
    // 4) a clear button that clears the display and suspends
    // evolution.
    // 5) a text field holding the name of the current rule set. This
    //    value can be changed to load a new rule set.

    public void init() {

        // The initial size of the canvas defaults to the size of the
        // applet.
        // It may change later to become an integral multiple of the
        // number of cells on a side.

        canvasWidth = getSize().width;

        // Retrieve the number of cells on a side of the display. This
        // value combined with the canvasWidth is used to determine the
        // size of a single cell on the display in pixels.

        String param = getParameter("numcells");
        int numSideCells;
```

```
if (param != null) {
        numSideCells = Integer.parseInt(param);
} else {

   // If the number of cells is not specified, compute it
   // from the width of the canvas and the default cell size.

   numSideCells = canvasWidth / DEFAULT_CELL_SIZE;
}

cellSize = canvasWidth / numSideCells;

if (cellSize == 0) {
   cellSize = 1;
}

// We recompute the canvasWidth so that it is an integral
// multiple of the number of cells.

canvasWidth = numSideCells * cellSize;

// Get the patterns defined by the user. If none are defined,
// a default pattern is used. A pattern consists of:
//
// 1) The name of a rule set
// 2) The bounds of the pattern. This is either a number of
//    steps to run, the string "edge", indicating the pattern
//    should stop upon reaching the edge of the canvas, or
//    the string "none", indicating the pattern should
//    continue running until no more changes occur.
// 3) (optional) An initial configuration of cells.
//
// The syntax of these patterns is described in the getPatterns()
// method.

Vector patterns = getPatterns();

// If the first pattern has an initial configuration, start
// automatically; otherwise, create the canvas and add a set
// of controls so that the user can specify a configuration.

Pattern firstPattern = (Pattern)patterns.firstElement();

startAutomatically = (firstPattern.getConfiguration().size() >
                   0);

// Set the font for the buttons and rule set name field.
```

```
setFont(new Font("Courier", Font.BOLD, 12));

// Create the layout manager for the applet. The BoardLayout
// will guarantee that the canvas is always resized to an
// integral multiple of the number of cells on a side.

BoardLayout boardLayout = new BoardLayout();
setLayout(boardLayout);

// Create the canvas and add it to the applet.

cellCanvas  = new CellCanvas(canvasWidth, cellSize, cellThread,
                            patterns);
add(cellCanvas);

// Add the canvas to the layout as the "board".

boardLayout.addBoard("Canvas", cellCanvas, numSideCells,
                    canvasWidth, BORDER_WIDTH);

if (!startAutomatically) {

    // If we're not running through predetermined patterns,
    // add a set of controls to the applet and layout.

    startButton       = new Button("Start");
    stopButton        = new Button("Stop");
    clearButton       = new Button("Clear");
    String ruleName = firstPattern.getRuleName();
    ruleField         = new RuleTextField(ruleName, RULENAME_SIZE,
                        cellCanvas);
    add(startButton);
    add(stopButton);
    add(clearButton);
    add(ruleField);

    startButton.addActionListener(
        new ActionListener() {
            public void actionPerformed(ActionEvent event) {
                            cellCanvas.resume();
            }
        });

    stopButton.addActionListener(
        new ActionListener() {
            public void actionPerformed(ActionEvent event) {
                            cellCanvas.suspend();
            }
```

```
        });

        ActionListener defaultListener =
            new ActionListener() {
                public void actionPerformed(ActionEvent event) {
                                       cellCanvas.clear();
                }
            };

        clearButton.addActionListener(defaultListener);
        ruleField.addActionListener(defaultListener);

        boardLayout.addControl("start", startButton);
        boardLayout.addControl("stop", stopButton);
        boardLayout.addControl("clear", clearButton);
        boardLayout.addControl("rules", ruleField);
    }

    // Resize to the preferred size for the applet. This will be
    // determined by the preferredLayoutSize() method of the
    // layout manager.

    resize(getPreferredSize());
}

// The start() method creates a thread for recalculating cell
// values.

public synchronized void start() {
    cellThread = new Thread(this);
    cellThread.setPriority(Thread.MIN_PRIORITY);
    cellThread.start();
}

// The stop() and destroy methods allow the recalculation thread
// to finish that the applet won't consume resources while
// offscreen.

public synchronized void stop() {
    cellThread = null;
}

public void destroy() {
    cellThread = null;
}

// The run() method checks if the applet is starting
// automatically and, if not, causes the thread to wait.
```

```
public void run() {
   if (!startAutomatically) {
      cellCanvas.suspend();
   }

   cellCanvas.execute();
}

// The update() method paints the border around the board then
// paints the board and controls using the paintComponents()
// method defined in awt.Container.

public void update(Graphics g) {
   paint(g);
   paintComponents(g);
}

// Paint the border around the board.

public void paint(Graphics g) {
   Rectangle r = cellCanvas.getBounds();
   g.setColor(Color.black);
   g.draw3DRect(r.x - 1, r.y - 1,
            r.width + 1, r.width + 1, false);
}

// The CellCanvas class does the actual display of automata. It
// calls the arena's apply() method repeatedly and redraws the
// cells that have changed. All drawing is done to an offscreen
// image which is then displayed on the screen. When a resize
// occurs, the offscreen image is recreated and the cellSize and
// cellSide are recomputed.

private static class CellCanvas extends Canvas {
   // Create a new CellCanvas. The instance variables are
   // initialized and the current pattern is set to be the first
   // pattern in the pattern vector.

   CellCanvas(int width, int newCellSize, Thread thread, Vector
            patterns) {

      // mySide is compared to the current width at repaint time.
      // If it is different, the offscreen image is rebuilt and
      // dimensions are recomputed. Set its value to -1 the
      // first time to force a rebuild.

      mySide = -1;
      cellSide    = width / newCellSize;
```

```
    cellSize     = newCellSize;
    cellThread   = thread;
    cellPatterns = patterns;
    Pattern firstPattern = (Pattern)patterns.firstElement();
    setPattern(firstPattern);

    // Listen for activity

    addMouseListener(new CellCanvasListener());
  }

// The update() method for a CellCanvas just calls paint()
// since there is no background showing.

public void update(Graphics g) {
    paint(g);
  }

// The paint() method first adjusts dimensions if the applet
// has been resized. Then it draws changed cells into an
// offscreen image and displays it.

public void paint(Graphics g) {
    // If the current width of the canvas is different then the
    // remembered width, rebuild the offscreen image and
    // recompute the cellSize. Save the new width for next
    // time.

    if (getSize().width != mySide) {

        // Save the new width.

        mySide = getSize().width;

        // recompute the cell size.

        cellSize = mySide / cellSide;

        // If there is an existing offscreen image, free its
        // resources.

        if (offscreen != null) {
            offscreen.flush();
        }

        // Create a new image with the current dimensions.

        offscreen = createImage(mySide, mySide);
```

```
    }

// Use the graphics object for the offscreen image for
// drawing cells.

Graphics og = offscreen.getGraphics();

synchronized (arena) {

    // When the user puts a cell on the display with the
    // mouse,"singleCell" is set so that only that cell is
    // redrawn. The mouseUp method sets "paintColor",
    // "cellX", and "cellY".

    if (singleCell) {
        og.setColor(paintColor);
        og.fillRect(cellX, cellY, cellSize, cellSize);
        g.drawImage(offscreen, 0, 0, this);
        singleCell = false;
    } else if (specific) {

        // After a generation is computed, we only draw the
        // cells that have changed. Flags telling which
        // cells have changed are stored in the "changed"
        // array. If nothing changes for a generation we
        // move on to the next pattern if there is one or
        // pause the cell computation thread if there isn't.

        boolean somethingChanged = false;

        for (int i = 0; i < cellSide; i++) {
            for (int j = 0; j < cellSide; j++) {

                // If cell(i,j) has changed, draw it.
                // Note the change if this is the first one.

                if (arena.getChanged(i, j)) {
                    if (!somethingChanged) {
                        somethingChanged = true;
                    }

                    // If the stopAtEdge flag is set and
                    // we're at one of the edges, stop.

                    if (stopAtEdge &&
                        (i == 0 || j == 0  ||
                            i == cellSide - 1 ||
                            j == cellSide - 1)) {
```

```
                        atEdge = true;
                        return;
                    }

                    // Draw the changed cell.

                og.setColor(getColors()[arena.getCell(i,
                                                 j)]);
                og.fillRect(i * cellSize, j * cellSize,
                        cellSize, cellSize);
                }
            }
        }

        // Display the updated image on the screen.

        g.drawImage(offscreen, 0, 0, this);
        specific = false;

        // Check for a change. If nothing changed,
        // nothing ever
        // will so stop the current pattern and go to the next
        // one if there is one.

        if (!somethingChanged) {
            if (cellPatterns.size() > 1) {
                noChange = true;
            } else {
                suspend();
            }
        }

    } else {

    // Redraw all the cells. This is used after a resize
    // and at startup.

    for (int i = 0; i < cellSide; i++) {
        for (int j = 0; j < cellSide; j++) {
          og.setColor(getColors()[arena.getCell(i, j)]);
          og.fillRect(i * cellSize, j * cellSize,
                  cellSize, cellSize);
        }
    }

    g.drawImage(offscreen, 0, 0, this);
    }
}
```

```
    }

    // The resume() method notifies the calculation thread if it
    // is waiting.

    void resume() {
        if (threadWait) {
            threadWait = false;

            synchronized (arena) {
                arena.notify();
            }
        }
    }

    // The suspend() method just sets a flag so that when the
    // execute method has completed the calculation of the current
    // generation the calculation thread will wait.

    void suspend() {
        if (!threadWait) {
            threadWait = true;
        }
    }

    // The clear() method first checks to see if the calculation
    // thread is running. If it is, it just sets a flag telling
    // execute to clear the display and calls suspend so that
    // calculation will stop after the display is cleared. If the
    // calculation thread is not running, the arena is cleared and
    // the applet is repainted.

    void clear() {
        synchronized(arena) {
            if (threadWait) {
                arena.clear();
                specific = false;
                repaint();
            } else {
                clearArena = true;
                suspend();
            }
        }
    }
    // The setRules methods are used to change the current rule
    // set. They change the rule set of the current arena (which
    // also clears it). Like clear(), if the calculation thread
    // is not running, the rule set change is done immediately;
```

```
// otherwise, a flag is set that execute can act on. When
// setRules() is called from nextPattern(), it sets the
// waitFlag to false since there won't be any pending
// calculation or repaint waiting.

void setRules(Rules newRules) {
    setRules(newRules, true);
}

void setRules(Rules newRules, boolean waitFlag) {
    if (arena != null) {
        synchronized(arena) {
            if (!waitFlag || threadWait) {
                arena.setRules(newRules);
                setColors(newRules.getColors());
                specific = false;
                repaint();

            } else {
                rules = newRules;
                suspend();
            }
        }
    } else {

        // If this is the first time, create a new arena.

        arena = new Arena(cellSide, cellSide, newRules);
        setColors(newRules.getColors());
    setBackground(getColors()[newRules.getInitialValue()]);
    }
}

// The execute() method is the master method for the canvas.
// It recalculates new generations and performs various
// actions based on flags set by other methods. If the
// clearArena flag is set, the arena is cleared. If the rules
// variable is not null, the rule set is changed to its value.
// If threadWait is set, the calculation thread is paused.
// Finally, if the number of steps for the current pattern has
// run out, the pattern reached the edge of the display with
// stopAtEdge set, or the pattern remained unchanged through a
// generation, execute advances to the next pattern.

void execute() {
    while (cellThread != null) {

        // Clear the arena.
```

```java
        if (clearArena) {
          arena.clear();
          clearArena = false;
          repaint();
         } else if (rules != null) {

           // Switch to a new rule set.

           arena.setRules(rules);
           setColors(rules.getColors());
          rules = null;
           repaint();
          }

      // If a method has requested that the thread wait,
      // make it wait.

      if (threadWait) {
         try {
            synchronized (arena) {
            arena.wait();
            }
            } catch (InterruptedException e) {
        }
      }

      // Check if it's time to end the current pattern. If so,
         // reset the flags and step count.

        if (steps++ == maxSteps || atEdge || noChange) {
           steps    = 0;
           atEdge   = false;
           noChange = false;
           nextPattern();
           repaint();
        }

        // Calculate the next generation.

        synchronized(arena) {
           arena.apply();
        }

        // Paint the cells that have changed.

        specific = true;
        repaint();
```

```
        // Be a good citizen and sleep briefly.

        try {
            Thread.currentThread().sleep(SLEEP_TIME);

        } catch (InterruptedException e) {
        }
    }
}

private class CellCanvasListener extends MouseAdapter {
    // The mouseReleased() method increments the color value
    // in the cell pointed to by the mouse. If the color value
    // exceeds the maximum, it wraps around to 0. This method
    // is synchronized on the arena so that a new value added
    // by the user won't be lost.

    public void mouseReleased (MouseEvent mEvent) {
        int x = mEvent.getX();
        int y = mEvent.getY();
        synchronized (arena) {

            // Find the current cell.

            int xoffset = x / cellSize;
            int yoffset = y / cellSize;

            // If we're outside the board, do nothing. This can
            // occur if someone presses the mouse within the
            // canvas then drags it out before releasing.

            if (xoffset < 0 || xoffset >= cellSide ||
                yoffset < 0 || yoffset >= cellSide) {
                return;
            }

            // Get the current value out of the cell.

            int val = arena.getCell(xoffset, yoffset);
            val = (val + 1) % colors.length;

            // Write the updated value.

            arena.setCell(xoffset, yoffset, val);

            // Set the new parameters so that repaint can
            // redraw the right cell in the right color.
```

```
                    paintColor = getColors()[val];
                    cellX      = xoffset * cellSize;
                    cellY      = yoffset * cellSize;

                    // Set "singleCell" to true so that repaint()
                    // will only draw one cell.

                    singleCell = true;

                    repaint();
                    return;
                }
            }
        }
```

```
// The nextPattern() method advances the current pattern to the
// next pattern in the set. If it reaches the end, it goes back
// to the first pattern.

private void nextPattern() {
    pattern = (pattern + 1) % cellPatterns.size();

  Pattern current =(Pattern)cellPatterns.elementAt(pattern);
    setPattern(current);
}
```

```
// setPattern() sets the boundary flags, the rule set and the
// initial cell configuration based on a new pattern.

private void setPattern(Pattern current) {

  // We stop at the edge of the display if there are multiple
  // patterns or the single pattern says to.

    stopAtEdge = cellPatterns.size() > 1 || current.stop();
    maxSteps   = current.steps();

    setRules(current.getRules(), false);
    setInitialConfiguration(current.getConfiguration());
}
```

```
// setInitialConfiguration() sets an initial set of cells in
// the arena to prespecified values. This is used for
// the automatic display mode.

private void setInitialConfiguration(Vector cells) {
    Enumeration e = cells.elements();
```

```
        while (e.hasMoreElements()) {
            CellValue c = (CellValue)e.nextElement();

            arena.setCell(c.x, c.y, c.color);
        }
    }

// Return array of colors obtained from the current rule set.

    private Color[] getColors() {
        return colors;
    }

    // Set the current array of colors.

    private void setColors(Color colorArray[]) {
        colors = colorArray;
    }

    // The amount of time to sleep between calculations.

    private static final int SLEEP_TIME = 10;

    // The offscreen image where cells are drawn.

    private Image    offscreen      = null;

    // The thread used to recalculate cell values.

    private Thread  cellThread;

    // The rule set that will become current at the next time
    // through execute().

    private Rules    rules          = null;

    // The array of colors obtained from the current rule set.

    private Color    colors[];

    // Flags passed to repaint().

    private boolean singleCell     = false;
    private boolean specific       = false;

    // The color and location of a particular cell to repaint().

    private Color   paintColor;
```

```java
    private int     cellX;
    private int     cellY;

    // The number of cells on a side of the canvas.

    private int     cellSide;

    // The width of a single cell in pixels.

    private int     cellSize;

    // The width of the canvas in pixels.

    private int     mySide;

    // The number of generations that have been computed for the
    // current pattern.

    private int     steps           = 0;

    // Maximum number of generations before stopping the current
    // pattern. It's initialized to -1 by default so that "steps"
    // will likely never reach it.

    private int     maxSteps        = -1;

    // The current index into the vector of patterns.

    private int     pattern         = 0;

    // Flags passed to execute.

    private boolean threadWait = false;
    private boolean clearArena = false;
    private boolean stopAtEdge = false;
    private boolean atEdge     = false;
    private boolean noChange   = false;

    // The current set of patterns.

    private Vector cellPatterns;

    // The arena which calculates cell values.

    private Arena arena = null;
}

// The Pattern class holds a rule set, a rule name, boundary
```

```java
// behavior information and a set of CellValue objects
// representing an initial automaton configuration.

private static class Pattern {

    // Set and get the rule set.

    void setRules(Rules newRules) {
        rules = newRules;
    }
    Rules getRules() {
        return rules;
    }

    // Set and get the rule name.

    void setRuleName(String name) {
        ruleName = name;
    }
    String getRuleName() {
        return ruleName;
    }

    // Add another cell value to the initial configuration.

    void addCellValue(CellValue cval) {
        cellValues.addElement(cval);
    }

    // Get the initial configuration.

    Vector getConfiguration() {
        return cellValues;
    }

    // Set and get the flag indicating whether or not to stop at the
    // edge of the canvas.

    void setStop(boolean flag) {
        stopFlag = flag;
    }
    boolean stop() {
        return stopFlag;
    }

    // Set and get the maximum number generations for the pattern.

    void setSteps(int steps) {
```

```
            numSteps = steps;
        }
        int steps() {
            return numSteps;
        }


        Rules    rules;
        String   ruleName;
        Vector   cellValues = new Vector();
        boolean  stopFlag   = false;
        int      numSteps    = -1;
}


// The RuleTextField class holds the name of the current rule
// set for a Cellular applet. It overrides keyDown to load a
// new rule set when a newline or carriage return is pressed.
// If no rule set can be found with the new name, the field will
// revert to its previous value.

private static class RuleTextField extends TextField {

    // Create a new RuleTextField. The canvas it's associated
    // with is saved so that its setRules() method can be called.

    RuleTextField(String text, int size, CellCanvas canvas) {
        super(text, size);
        previousText = text;
        myCanvas     = canvas;

        addKeyListener(new RuleTextKeyListener());
    }

    private class RuleTextKeyListener extends KeyAdapter {
        // Check the key that was just pressed. If it was a
        // newline or carriage return, try to load the rule class
        // named in the text field. If the load fails, restore
        // the previous rule class name.

        public void keyPressed(KeyEvent kEvent) {
            int key = kEvent.getKeyChar();
            if (key == '\n' || key == '\r') {
                Rules rules = Rules.loadRules(getText());

                if (rules != null) {
                    myCanvas.setRules(rules);
                    previousText = getText();
                } else {
                    setText(previousText);
```

```
                    }
                }
            }
        }

        // The rule name from the last successful load.

        private String previousText;

        // The canvas whose rules we set.

        private CellCanvas myCanvas;
    }

    // The CellValue class encapsulates x and y positions and a color
    // index for a cell so that they may be manipulated as a unit.

    private static class CellValue {

        // Create a new CellValue.

        CellValue(int cellX, int cellY, int cellColor) {
            x     = cellX;
            y     = cellY;
            color = cellColor;
        }
        int x;
        int y;
        int color;
    }

    // The getPatterns() method retrieves the "script" parameter from
    // the user and builds a Vector of Pattern structures based on
    // its value. If there is no script specified, a default pattern
    // is used.
    //
    // The syntax of a script entry is:
    //
    // <Rule set name>:<bound behavior>:<initial configuration>
    //
    // where <initial configuration> (and the colon preceding it) are
    // optional. An <initial configuration> consists of
    // triples separated by colons. Each triple is of the form:
    // x,y,color.
    //
    // Here is a sample script:
    //
//"Worm2:edge:25,25,1;Life:10:25,23,1:25,24,1:25,25,1:25,26,1:25,2
```

```
    // 7,1"
    //
    // This says to start with the Worm2 rule set and a single cell
    // containing color number 1 at (25,25). Run until it reaches the
    // edge or stops changing, then switch to the Life rule set, with
    // cells initialized to color number 1 at 5 locations and run for
    // 10 generations or until it stops changing. Then repeat from
    // the beginning.

    private Vector getPatterns() {

        // Create a vector to hold the patterns read from the user. The
        // vector will be returned as the value of this method.

        Vector patterns = new Vector();
        String param    = getParameter("script");

        // If no script specified, load the rules for Life by default.

        if (param == null) {
            Pattern pat = new Pattern();
            pat.setRuleName("Life");
            pat.setRules(Rules.loadRules("Life"));
            patterns.addElement(pat);

        } else {

            // Use StringTokenizers to break up the pattern strings
            // from the script. Patterns are separated by semicolons.

            StringTokenizer pats = new StringTokenizer(param, ";");

            // For each pattern, break it up into name, boundary
            // behavior and configuration.

            while (pats.hasMoreTokens()) {

                // The parts of a pattern are separated by colons.

                StringTokenizer patValues =
                  new StringTokenizer(pats.nextToken(), ":");
                try {

                    // Get the name of the rule set and try to load it.
                    // If the load fails, skip to the next pattern.

                    String ruleName = patValues.nextToken();
                    Rules patRules  = Rules.loadRules(ruleName);
```

```
    if (patRules == null) {
        continue;
    }

    // Create a new pattern.

    Pattern pat = new Pattern();

// Set the rule name and rules for the new pattern.

    pat.setRuleName(ruleName);
    pat.setRules(patRules);

    // Set up the boundary behavior for the pattern,
    // setStop() means the pattern should stop upon
    // hitting the edge of the display. setSteps()
    // sets the maximum number of generations to
    // run before stopping.

    String steps = patValues.nextToken();

    if (steps.equals("edge")) {
        pat.setStop(true);
    } else if (steps.equals("none")) {
        pat.setStop(false);
    } else {
        pat.setSteps(Integer.parseInt(steps));
    }

    // Collect all the cell values for the initial
    // configuration. The x position, y position,
    // and color index are separated by commas.

    while (patValues.hasMoreTokens()) {
        StringTokenizer patCells =
        new StringTokenizer(patValues.nextToken(),
                        ",");
        int cellX =
        Integer.parseInt(patCells.nextToken());
        int cellY =
        Integer.parseInt(patCells.nextToken());
        int color =
        Integer.parseInt(patCells.nextToken());

        pat.addCellValue(new CellValue(cellX, cellY,
                            color));
    }
```

```
                    // Add the new pattern to the set of patterns.

                    patterns.addElement(pat);

                } catch (Exception e) {
                    e.printStackTrace();
                }
            }

        // If all the patterns in the script failed to load, use
        // the default pattern.

        if (patterns.size() == 0) {
            Pattern pat = new Pattern();
            pat.setRuleName("Life");
            pat.setRules(Rules.loadRules("Life"));
            patterns.addElement(pat);
        }
    }

    return patterns;
}

// Constants.

private static final int DEFAULT_CELL_SIZE = 4;
private static final int BORDER_WIDTH      = 1;
private static final int RULENAME_SIZE     = 10;

// The thread used to recalculate cell values.

private Thread cellThread = new Thread(this);

// The canvas on which the automata are displayed.

private CellCanvas cellCanvas;

// The start, stop, and clear controls.

private Button startButton;
private Button stopButton;
private Button clearButton;

// The text field with which to enter a rule name.

private RuleTextField ruleField;

// The width of the cell canvas in pixels.
```

```
    private int canvasWidth;

    // The width of a cell in pixels.

    private int cellSize;

    // Whether or not to start running the display immediately.

    private boolean startAutomatically;
}
```

The BoardLayout Class

The applet has sizing requirements that are not adequately handled by Java's default layout managers, so we create a custom layout manager for the Cellular applet. The BoardLayout class implements the LayoutManager interface. It arranges the display canvas and controls for the applet, reshaping them if necessary when the display is resized.

The layout is divided into two areas: the board and the controls. The board is guaranteed to be sized into a square whose side is an integral multiple of the side of a single square on the board. A border can be specified for the board that will be taken into account when it is laid out. The user controls flow into the space below the board. If the controls cannot be made to fit in the space below the board, they are not displayed. If the board cannot fit even when shrunk to its minimum size, it will be clipped at the right and bottom:

Example 22-3 BoardLayout Class

```
package ca;

import java.util.*;
import java.awt.*;

// The BoardLayout class provides layout support for grids of cells
// as might be used in a board game. The layout is divided into two
// areas: the board and the controls. The board is guaranteed to be
// sized into a square whose side is an integral multiple of the side
// of a single square on the board. A border can be specified for the
// board that will be taken into account when it is laid out. The
// controls "flow" into the space below the board. If the controls
// can not be made to fit in the space below the board they are not
// displayed. If the board cannot fit even when shrunk to its minimum
// size it will be clipped at the right and bottom.

public class BoardLayout implements LayoutManager {
```

```
// The two addBoard() methods add the board component to the
// layout. The long form: addBoard(String, Component, int, int,
// int) allows the three board parameters to be set at the same
// time.

public void addBoard(String name, Component newBoard, int
            numCellsOnSide,int boardSide, int borderWidth) {

   board = newBoard;
   setCellParameters(numCellsOnSide, boardSide, borderWidth);
}

public void addBoard(String name, Component newBoard) {
   board = newBoard;
}
```

```
// setCellParameters() sets the three defining values for a board:
// The number of cells on a side, the minimum allowed length of a
// side in pixels, and the width of the border around the board.

public void setCellParameters(int numCellsOnSide, int
                 minBoardSide,int borderWidth) {
   cells   = numCellsOnSide;
   minSide = minBoardSide;
   border  = borderWidth;
}
```

```
// addControl() is a more descriptive name for the generic
// "addLayoutComponent" that all LayoutManagers must implement.
// It adds a "control" to the layout (usually a button, textItem,
// etc.).

public void addControl(String name, Component comp) {
   addLayoutComponent(name, comp);
}
```

```
// addLayoutComponent() just adds a component to the Vector of
// controls.

public void addLayoutComponent(String name, Component comp) {
                        controls.addElement(comp);
}
```

```
// removeLayoutComponent() will remove a control from the
// Vector of controls and hide it.

public void removeLayoutComponent(Component comp) {
   controls.removeElement(comp);
```

```
    comp.setVisible(false);
  }


  // The layoutContainer() method formats the board and controls.
  // It is called automatically when an applet is resized. The
  // approach for this layout is to make the board as large as
  // possible while leaving room for the controls. If the controls
  // will not fit, either horizontally or vertically, they are
  // not displayed. The vertical space taken up by the controls
  // depends on the width of the applet. As many controls as
  // possible are placed in each control row.

  public void layoutContainer(Container parent) {

// The area available for board and controls is the size of the
// parent minus the parent's "insets" and the border width
// specified in the layout parameters. Insets are padding
// around the edges of some Containers.

Insets insets= parent.getInsets();

// The width available for the board is the parent's width
// minus the left and right insets and a border on two sides of
// the board.

int    innerWidth= parent.getSize().width -
  (insets.left + insets.right + border * 2);

// The height available for the board and controls is the
// parent's height minus the top and bottom insets and a
// border on two sides of the board.

int    innerHeight= parent.getSize().height -
  (insets.top + insets.bottom + border * 2);

// The maximum height available for controls is the innerHeight
// minus the minimum height of the board.

int    maxControlHeight= innerHeight - minSide;

// The maximum width available for controls is the maximum board
// width plus the borders since the controls are not constrained
// by the borders around the board.

int    maxControlWidth = innerWidth + (border * 2);

// Fetch the width, height, rowHeights, and rowLengths for
// the controls given the maximum width.
```

```
ControlParameters cParams = controlParameters(maxControlWidth);

// If the controls will not fit, remove them and just show the
// board.

if (cParams.width  > maxControlWidth ||
    cParams.height > maxControlHeight) {
    layoutBoardOnly(insets, innerWidth, innerHeight);
    return;
}

// Now we determine how big the board will be. We know the board
// at its minimum size will fit vertically from our previous
// calculations for controls. If the minimum board width is
// greater than the available width, draw the board at its
// minimum size and let it be clipped at the right.

int side;

if (innerWidth < minSide) {

    // If the available space is smaller than the minimum board
    // size, use the minimum board size (the board will be clipped).

    side = minSide;
} else {

    // If there is room for the board horizontally, round the
    // smaller of the width and height dimensions down to
    // a multiple of the number of cells.

    side = Math.min(innerWidth, (innerHeight - cParams.height))
      / cells * cells;
}

// Reshape the board. If the board is too wide for its area,
// position it at 0 and let it be clipped; otherwise, center
// it in the available space.

board.setBounds(
    Math.max(innerWidth  - side, 0) / 2 + insets.left + border,
    (innerHeight - cParams.height - side) / 2 + insets.top + border,
    side,
    side);

// Make the board visible.
```

```
board.setVisible(true);

// Place the controls. The ControlParameters object cParams
// contains all the information necessary: the lengths of the rows
// and their heights, and the total height of the controls.

Enumeration e    = controls.elements();
int          cols = 0;
int          row  = 0;

// Horizontally, the controls start at the very left of the area
// inside the container's padding.

int          xoffset = insets.left;

// Vertically, the controls start just below the board and its
// border. i.e. after the top inset, the top border, the board,
// and the bottom border.

int          yoffset = (innerHeight - cParams.height) + insets.top +
                 (border * 2);

// Step through the controls and place them. Use the row lengths
// from the ControlParameters to determine when to move to the
// next row. Use the row heights from the ControlParameters to
// determine how tall to make each control. Use the minimum
// width for each control.

while (e.hasMoreElements()) {
    Component c    = (Component)e.nextElement();
    Dimension d    = c.getMinimumSize();

    // The height of the current row.

    int        rHeight =
      ((Integer)cParams.heights.elementAt(row)).intValue();

    // The length of the current row.

    int        rLength =
      ((Integer)cParams.lengths.elementAt(row)).intValue();

    // Reshape the current component. Place it at the current
    // x and y offsets and make it minimum width and the height
    // of the current row.

    c.setBounds(xoffset, yoffset, d.width, rHeight);
```

```
        // Make the component visible.

        c.setVisible(true);

        // Advance to the next column. If we're at the end of the
        // current row, reset the column to 0 and the x offset to
        // the left inset then add the height of the current row
        // to the y offset.

        if (++cols >= rLength) {
            cols = 0;
            xoffset = insets.left;
            yoffset+= rHeight;
            row++;
        } else {

            // If we haven't reached the end of the row, just add
            // the width of the current component to the x offset.

            xoffset += c.getSize().width;
        }
    }
}
// The preferredLayoutSize() method is used by enclosing
// Containers to determine how much space to allocate to a
// Component. For the board layout, we'll treat preferred and
// minimum the same since there isn't any well-defined "preferred"
// size for a board.

    public Dimension preferredLayoutSize(Container parent) {
        return minimumLayoutSize(parent);
    }

    // The minimumLayoutSize() method returns the smallest area the
    // layout can occupy without violating its structure in some way.
    // For the board layout, this is an area that is as wide as the
    // greater of the board's minimum width and the maximum width
    // of any control and as tall as the minimum board height plus
    // the controls. It's possible that a smaller area could be
    // generated by making the layout wider rather than taller but
    // we're not pursuing that approach. The minimum width will
    // always be as small as possible.

    public Dimension minimumLayoutSize(Container parent) {

        // Find the widest control. We can't make the board layout
        // any narrower than that.
```

```
    int       minControlWidth = maxWidthOfControls();

    Insets    insets  = parent.getInsets();
    Dimension d  = new Dimension();

    // Set the minimum width to the greater of the minimum size
    // of the board and the width of the widest control.

    int innerWidth = Math.max(minSide, minControlWidth);

    // The actual minimum size of the layout has to take into
    // account the insets and the borders of the board.

    d.width  = insets.left + innerWidth + insets.right +
            border * 2;

    // The minimum height of the layout is the top and bottom
    // insets plus the minimum height of the board plus the
    // borders plus the calculated height of the controls given
    // the width.

    d.height = insets.top + minSide +
        controlParameters(innerWidth).height + insets.bottom +
        border * 2;

    return d;
}

// The layoutBoardOnly() method displays the board when there is
// no room for the controls. It makes the controls invisible
// and devotes all the available space to the board.

private void layoutBoardOnly(Insets insets, int innerWidth,
        int innerHeight) {

    // Set the size of the board to the maximum that will fit or
    // to the boards minimum size if it won't fit.

    int side = Math.max(Math.min(innerWidth, innerHeight),
            minSide) / cells * cells;

    // Reshape the board. If the board is too large for the
    // available space, clip it on the right and bottom.

    board.setBounds(
        Math.max(innerWidth - side, 0) / 2 + insets.left + border,
        Math.max(innerHeight - side, 0) / 2 + insets.top + border,
            side, side);
```

```
    // Make the board visible.

    board.setVisible(true);

    // Make the components invisible.

    Enumeration e = controls.elements();

    while (e.hasMoreElements()) {
        Component c= (Component)e.nextElement();

        c.setVisible(false);
    }
}
```

```
// The maxWidthOfControls() method simply steps through the set of
// controls and returns the minimum width of the widest control.

private int maxWidthOfControls() {
    Enumeration e   = controls.elements();
    int         max = 0;

    while (e.hasMoreElements()) {
        Component c= (Component)e.nextElement();
        max     = Math.max(max, c.getMinimumSize().width);
    }

    return max;
}
```

```
// The controlParameters() method determines the width, height,
// row lengths and row heights for a set of controls. It adds
// controls to a row until the maximum width is reached then
// adds another row. The row height for a row is set to the
// maximum height of any element in the row.

private ControlParameters controlParameters(int maxWidth) {
    int rowWidth    = 0;  // The width of the current row.
    int totalHeight = 0;  // The total height of all controls.
    int rowHeight   = 0;  // the height of the current row.
    int totalWidth  = 0;  // the total width of all controls.
    int numColumns  = 0;  // the number of columns in a row.

    // We keep track of the heights and lengths of each row.

    Vector rowHeights = new Vector();
    Vector rowLengths = new Vector();
```

```
Enumeration e = controls.elements();
while (e.hasMoreElements()) {
   Component c = (Component)e.nextElement();
   Dimension d = c.getMinimumSize();
   rowWidth+= d.width;

   // For each component, if its width does not overflow the
   // maximum width for a row, increment the number of
   // columns for the row and adjust the row height to the
   // height of the new component if it is taller than any
   // of the previous components in the row.

   if (rowWidth <= maxWidth) {
      numColumns++;
      rowHeight = Math.max(rowHeight, d.height);

   } else {

      // If the current component makes the row too wide,
      // end the row. Add the current height and number
      // of columns for the row to the vectors of row
      // parameters, adjust the maximum width of controls
      // if necessary, and reset the row width, row height,
      // and number of columns to start a new row.

      rowHeights.addElement(new Integer(rowHeight));
      rowLengths.addElement(new Integer(numColumns));
      totalWidth   = Math.max(totalWidth, rowWidth -
                     d.width);
      totalHeight += rowHeight;
      rowWidth     = d.width;
      rowHeight    = d.height;
      numColumns   = 1;
   }
}

// End the final row.

rowHeights.addElement(new Integer(rowHeight));
rowLengths.addElement(new Integer(numColumns));
totalWidth   = Math.max(totalWidth, rowWidth);
totalHeight += rowHeight;

// Return an instance of ControlParameters that contains all
// the information about the controls.

return new ControlParameters(totalWidth, totalHeight,
                   rowHeights, rowLengths);
```

```java
        // The instance variables used by the layout. The layout keeps
        // track of the board, the set of controls, the number of cells
        // on one side of the board, the minimum length of a side of the
        // board and the width of the border around the board.

        private Component board;
        private Vector    controls = new Vector();
        private int       cells;
        private int       minSide;
        private int       border;
}

// The ControlParameters class is a helper class that wraps up
// several values associated with the layout of a set of controls so
// that they can be returned from a function as a single value. This
// is similar to the use of Dimension, Point, Rectangle, etc. in the
// awt package.

class ControlParameters {

    // Create a new instance of ControlParameters.

    ControlParameters(int cWidth, int rHeight, Vector rowHeights,
                    Vector rowLengths) {
      width= cWidth;
      height= rHeight;
      heights = rowHeights;
      lengths = rowLengths;
    }

    // The parameters of interest.

    int    width;
    int    height;
    Vector heights;
    Vector lengths;
}
```

The Arena Class

The Arena class takes care of actually calculating new generations for the automata. It loops through the current array of cells, saves new values for each cell in a separate array, and then swaps the arrays. Two copies of the cell array are maintained so that the current state of each cell may be used in computing the next states of its neighbors:

Example 22-4 Arena Class

```
package ca;

// The Arena class creates an array of cells and applies a set of
// rules to each cell. Two copies of the cell array are maintained
// so that the current state of each cell may be used in computing
// the next states of its neighbors.

public class Arena {

    // Create a new Arena with dimensions x and y and a new rule set.
    // Each cell is initialized with the result of the rule set's
    // getInitialValue() method.

    public Arena(int x, int y, Rules newRules) {
        cellWidth  = x;
        cellHeight = y;

        // The "cells" array holds the current cell values.

        cells   = new int[x][y];

        // The "newCells" array is where newly computed values
        // are placed.

        newCells = new int[x][y];

        // The "changed" array keeps track of which cells have changed
        // and will need to be redrawn.

        changed    = new boolean[x][y];

        setRules(newRules);
    }

    // The setRules() method associates a new set of rules with the
    // arena and calls the clear() method to initialize the cells to
    // the rule set's initial value.
```

```java
public void setRules(Rules newRules) {
  rules = newRules;
  clear();
}

// The clear() method steps through each cell and initializes its
// value to the initial value for the current rule set.

public void clear() {
  int initialValue = getInitialValue();
  for (int i = 0; i < cellWidth; i++) {
    for (int j = 0; j < cellHeight; j++) {
      cells[i][j] = initialValue;
    }
  }
}

// Return the initial value obtained from the arena's current rule
// set.

public int getInitialValue() {
  return rules.getInitialValue();
}

// Return the value of a cell.

public int getCell(int x, int y) {
  return cells[x][y];
}

// Set the value of a cell.

public void setCell(int x, int y, int val) {
  cells[x][y] = val;
}

// Return the "changed" flag associated with a particular cell.
// The entry in the changed array for a cell is set to true if
// the value calculated for it during an apply is different from
// its current value.

public boolean getChanged(int x, int y) {
  return changed[x][y];
}

// The apply() method steps through the cells and calls the current
// rule set's process method on each cell. The result is placed in
// the newCells array. If the result is different than the current
```

```
// value of the cell, an entry is made for the cell in the changed
// array. After all the cells have been processed, the roles of
// the cells and newCells arrays are reversed so that the newCells
// array becomes the cells array for the next apply().

  public void apply() {
     for (int i = 0; i < cellWidth; i++) {
        for (int j = 0; j < cellHeight; j++) {
           int result     = rules.process(cells, i, j);
           newCells[i][j] = result;
           changed[i][j]  = (cells[i][j] != result);
        }
     }

     // Reverse the roles of the cells and newCells arrays.
     swap();
  }

  // The swap() method exchanges the cells and newCells arrays.

  private void swap() {
    int tempcells[][] = cells;
    cells     = newCells;
    newCells  = tempcells;
  }

     private int      cellWidth;      // Width of the cells array.
     private int      cellHeight;     // Height of the cells array.
    private int     cells[][];     // The array of current cell values.
     private int      newCells[][];  // The array of new cell values.
     private boolean changed[][];   // Flags to indicate which cells
                                    // have changed.
     private Rules    rules;         // The current rule set.
}
```

The Rules Class

The Rules class is an abstract class that defines the interface for rule sets and provides support methods for defining rules. (For a review of abstract classes, see *Abstract Methods* on page 34.) Several helper methods are defined in the Rules class that make it easier to write rules. An apply() method can use the methods in formulating rules. All the helper methods are declared protected since they only make sense when called by the apply() method of a subclass:

Example 22-5 Rules Class

```java
package ca;

import java.awt.Color;

// The Rules class supports the definition of different "rule sets"
// for a cellular automaton. Each new rule set extends the Rules
// class and defines three methods:
//
// getColors()        -- Return an array containing the colors used
//                        by a rule set.
//
// getInitialValue()  -- Return the index of the initial color value
//                        for the cells.
//
// apply()            -- Return a new color index for a cell based
//                        on the values of its neighbors. This is called
//                        for each cell in the grid.
//
// Several helper methods are defined in the Rules class that make it
// easier to write rules. An apply() method can use the methods in
// formulating rules. All the helper methods are declared
// "protected" since they only make sense when called by the
// apply method of a subclass.

public abstract class Rules {

    // The three methods that all subclasses of Rules must define.

    public abstract Color[] getColors();
    public abstract int     getInitialValue();
    public abstract int     apply();

    // The loadRules() method looks up the name of subclass of Rules
    // in the "ca.rules" package and returns an instance of the class
    // if it's found; otherwise it returns null.

    public static Rules loadRules(String name) {
      try {
        Class ruleClass = Class.forName("ca.rules." + name);
        return (Rules)ruleClass.newInstance();

      } catch (Exception e) {
        return null;
      }
    }
```

```
// The process() method is called by an instance of Arena for each
// cell. It initializes the set of neighbors for the cell then
// calls the apply method.  "cellVal" will wrap around to the other
// side of the board if it is called at an edge.

public int process(int cells[][], int i, int j) {
  neighbors[0] = cellVal(cells, i - 1, j - 1);
  neighbors[1] = cellVal(cells, i, j - 1);
  neighbors[2] = cellVal(cells, i + 1, j - 1);
  neighbors[3] = cellVal(cells, i - 1, j);
  neighbors[4] = cellVal(cells, i + 1, j);
  neighbors[5] = cellVal(cells, i - 1, j + 1);
  neighbors[6] = cellVal(cells, i, j + 1);
  neighbors[7] = cellVal(cells, i + 1, j + 1);
  selfValue    = cellVal(cells, i, j);

  return apply();
}


// Helper functions that return the values of particular
// neighboring cells.

// Upper left.

protected int ul() {
  return neighbors[0];
}

// Upper center.

protected int uc() {
  return neighbors[1];
}

// Upper right.
protected int ur() {
  return neighbors[2];
}

// Left.
protected int l() {
  return neighbors[3];
}

// Right.
protected int r() {
  return neighbors[4];
}
```

```java
// Lower left.
protected int ll() {
  return neighbors[5];
}

// Lower center.
protected int lc() {
  return neighbors[6];
}

// Lower right.
protected int lr() {
  return neighbors[7];
}

// The current cell.
protected int self() {
  return selfValue;
}

// The getNeighbors() method returns the entire array of neighbor
// values in case a rule set wants to perform some operation that
// iterates over the set of neighbors.

protected int[] getNeighbors() {
  return neighbors;
}

// The anyCell() method returns true if any of the neighbors have
// the value "val".

protected boolean anyCell(int val) {
  for (int i = 0; i < numNeighbors; i++) {
    if (neighbors[i] == val) {
      return true;
    }
  }

  return false;
}

// The numCells() method returns the number of neighbors that have
// the value "val".

protected int numCells(int val) {
  int result = 0;
```

```
   for (int i = 0; i < numNeighbors; i++) {
      if (neighbors[i] == val) {
         result++;
      }
   }

   return result;
}

// The numLinear() method returns the number of "rook move"
// neighbors that have the value "val".

protected int numLinear(int val) {
   int result = 0;

   if (uc() == val) {
      result++;
   }

   if (l() == val) {
      result++;
   }

   if (r() == val) {
      result++;
   }

   if (lc() == val) {
      result++;
   }

   return result;
}

// The numDiag() method returns the number of "bishop move"
// neighbors that have the value "val".

protected int numDiag(int val) {
   int result = 0;

   if (ul() == val) {
      result++;
   }

   if (ur() == val) {
      result++;
   }
```

```java
    if (ll() == val) {
      result++;
    }

    if (lr() == val) {
      result++;
    }

    return result;
  }

  // The cellVal() method encapsulates the behavior of the automaton
  // at the edge of the board. Negative x and y positions and
  // position values that are too large wrap around to the opposite
  // side of the board.

  private int cellVal(int cells[][], int x, int y) {

    if (x < 0) {
      x = cells.length + x;
    } else if (x >= cells.length) {
      x = x - cells.length;
    }

    if (y < 0) {
      y = cells[0].length + y;
    } else if (y >= cells[0].length) {
      y = y - cells[0].length;
    }

  return cells[x][y];
  }

  // The number of neighbors for a cell. This can be used in
  // apply methods that iterate through the set of neighbors.

  protected static final int numNeighbors = 8;

  // The array of neighbors. This array is filled by the process
  // method before an apply method is called.

  private int[] neighbors = new int[numNeighbors];

  // The value of the current cell. It is set by the process method
  // before an apply method is called.

  private int   selfValue;
}
```

Summary

This chapter and final example applet bring together many features of the Java language discussed throughout this book—arrays, interfaces, event handling, type comparisons, threaded execution, and so on. The Cellular applet emphasizes use of packages to organize Java programs into functional groups. Also, since the Cellular applet places demands on sizing that the default Java layout managers can't support, we develop a custom `BoardLayout` class. Not only does this class support the Cellular applet, but it could also be used for other board-oriented games such as chess or checkers.

This completes our discussion and examples of Java applets. In *Part 3— Appendixes*, we provide a high-level introduction to object-oriented programming and a quick reference to the Java language.

Part 3—Appendixes

PART THREE

APPENDIX

A

- Classes

- Instances

- Inheritance

- Encapsulation

- Overloading

- Polymorphism

Object-Oriented Programming

Overview

Although Java's syntax will be familiar to C programmers, its object-oriented features may not. In this appendix, we'll cover some basic characteristics of object-oriented (OO) programming as it pertains to Java. For C++ programmers and others already familiar with OO programming, you may want to skip this appendix. It is just a summary of Java's basic OO language features, and they are quite similar to those in C++. For C programmers who are new to object-oriented programming, successfully working with Java means you'll have to grasp a few OO concepts:

- **Classes** — The fundamental structure in Java. Classes are similar to structured types in C.

- **Instances** — Similar to a value of a structured type

- **Inheritance** — Language construct that allows for classes to be related to one another so that a subclass can *inherit* features of its superclass

- **Encapsulation** — Language construct that enables programmers to limit access to parts of a program

- **Overloading** — The ability to use the same name for multiple methods (Java methods are similar to C functions)

- **Polymorphism** – Ability to deal with multiple types based on a common feature

We'll talk briefly about each of these in this appendix.

Note that we only intend to provide a simple introduction to object-oriented programming.

Classes

The fundamental structure in Java is a *class*, and a Java program consists of a set of class definitions. A class is a data structure, similar to a `record` in Pascal or a `struct` in C, with some extra features. A Java program is a set of class definitions, with at least one of those class definitions containing a function (called a *method*) named `main`.

In traditional programming languages, functions and statements are the primary elements. Data structures serve a secondary purpose. FORTRAN and the original version of Basic are extreme examples of this, providing only simple arrays as data structures. This primary emphasis on functions and secondary emphasis on data structures is reversed in an object-oriented language like Java. In Java, the class is primary.

Unlike C and other traditional programming languages, Java does not support free-standing functions. All functions in Java are associated with classes. Instead of building a program around a set of interrelated functions, you build a Java program out of a set of data structures and their affiliated operations.

Let's look at an example. Suppose we want to write a word processing program. Using a traditional approach, we would probably begin by thinking about the operations the program needs to perform. Our list of operations might look something like this:

- Read files
- Write files
- Accept user input
- Support cursor movement
- Insert and delete text
- Format paragraphs

We would then write a program with functions to carry out these operations.

Object-oriented programming languages such as Java encourage a different approach. Instead of thinking about the operations the word processor needs to perform, we would start by determining the sorts of objects the word processor needs to manipulate. If we were working with an object-oriented language, our list would look something like this:

- Files

- Characters

- Lines of text

- Paragraphs

The advantage of the object-oriented approach is that the code we write will tend to be more generic and reusable than code written in the traditional way. Instead of writing code that is narrowly focussed on completing the current task, we'll develop a set of general-purpose operations that make sense for an object such as a file or a line of text.

Instances

Classes in Java correspond to structured types in a language such as C or Pascal. A member of a class, like a member of a structured type, is called an *instance* of the class. (Note that the use of the term member here should not be confused with the use of member in C++, which refers to the attributes of an object.) Creating an instance is referred to as *instantiating* the class. At the time a class is instantiated, memory is allocated for the new instance and that memory is initialized with appropriate values.

Inheritance

Classes can be related to one another. One class may be a *subclass* of another class. For example, say we had a class describing wagons, and we called it the Wagon class. Then, if we want a class describing red wagons—the RedWagon class—we could make it a subclass of Wagon. (Wagon—or any parent class—is referred to as a *superclass*.) This means that all the attributes and operations defined for the Wagon class would also be applicable to the RedWagon class. (This is generally referred to as *single inheritance*.)

Using inheritance can eliminate a lot of code redundancy since many operations need only be defined once and can be used for free within subclasses. Membership in a subclass implies membership in the superclass. That is, a RedWagon is a Wagon. Some object-oriented languages allow a class to be a direct subclass of more than one other class. (This is generally referred to as *multiple inheritance*.) This is *not* allowed in Java. However, Java does provide a facility that approximates the behavior of multiple inheritance. We discuss this facility in detail in *Interfaces as Types* on page 75.

Encapsulation

Java provides the ability to limit access to parts of a program. A programmer can provide an abstraction such as a stack or a tree without letting the user of the abstraction see inside it. Not only does this prevent the user from accidentally breaking a program by changing its internal state in an incorrect way, but it also prevents them from writing code that depends on the implementation details of such an abstraction. This makes code much easier to maintain and modify since a programmer knows exactly which code will be affected if the implementation of an abstraction is changed.

As a result of encapsulation, the code you write tends to be modular. As a general rule, programs should be organized into discrete groups so that information is shared on a need-to-know basis. That way, when a feature changes, you only need to update the parts of the program that really depend on that feature. An object-oriented approach makes this kind of programming straightforward by grouping all the operations that need to know about the internals of a data structure within that data structure. For example, with our word processing example in mind, only the operations defined for a line of text are given access to the internals of that structure. Example A-1 shows how such a structure might look in Java.

Example A-1 Encapsulation in a Class

```java
public class LineOfText {
  // Return the length of the line.
  public int getLength() {
    return length;
  }

  // Return the current index.
  public int getCurrentIndex() {
    return index;
  }

  // Advance the current index by one if it's not already
  // at the end.
  public void forwardCharacter() {
    if (index < length - 1) {
      index++;
    }
  }

  private int length;
  private int index;
  private String buffer;
```

The important point to make about this example is that the LineOfText object has length, index, and buffer fields that are *not* exposed to any piece of code outside of this particular class. These fields are private, and are specified so by use of the private keyword. Only the getLength(), getCurrentIndex(), and forwardCharacter() methods in the LineOfText class are visible to other parts of the program that use this class.

Overloading

Overloading refers to using the same name for multiple methods (Java methods are similar to C functions) within a class. In Java, we can do this. The only stipulation is that the argument list and return type for each method must be unique. The selection of the correct method to call is based on the types of the arguments in a call expression. For example, in Example A-2, the class Example has two methods called doubleIt.

Example A-2 Method Overloading

```
   class Example {
❶     public static int doubleIt(int x) {
           return x * 2;
       }

❷     public static String doubleIt(String x) {
           return x + x;
       }
   }
```

In Example A-2, lines ❶ and ❷ both define methods named doubleIt. However, as long as the argument lists in each have different types, each method is distinct, and there is no confusion. A program can call both methods without a problem, as illustrated in Example A-3.

Example A-3 Calling an Overloaded Method

```
❶ int intResult    = Example.doubleIt(3);
❷ String stringResult= Example.doubleIt("wow");
```

In this example, the method doubleIt is *overloaded*. Specifically:

❶ Is a call to the doubleIt() method (in the Example class) that returns an integer. intResult would hold the integer 6.

❷ Is a call to the `doubleIt()` method (in the `Example` class) that returns a string. `stringResult` would hold the string wowwow.

Polymorphism

In C, functions can only operate on a specific set of argument types. This is inconvenient and can lead to code redundancy. For example, the following code shows a C function that checks to see if its argument's color is blue:

```c
/* take an automobile and return true if it's blue */

int
is_blue(struct car *c)
{
    return c->color == BLUE;
}
```

Unfortunately, this function only works for cars. It would be nice if we could have a generic test for the quality of "blueness," but C has no way of expressing this. In Java, we could write a method like this one:

```java
class Example {
  static boolean isBlue(ColoredObject o) {
    return o.getColor() == Colors.blue;
  }
}
```

This is polymorphism at work. Any class could declare itself to be a `ColoredObject` and its instances could then be passed to the `isBlue()` method. A method that can operate on arguments of multiple types is referred to as polymorphic. This ability to deal with multiple types based on a common feature is very powerful, as illustrated in the chapter on *Interfaces as Types* on page 75.

APPENDIX

B

- Java for C Programmers

- Java for C++ Programmers

- Data Types

- Operators

- Control Flow and Iteration

- Comments

- Keywords

- Deprecated Methods

- HTML applet and param Tags

Quick
Reference

Java for C Programmers

Table B-1 compares some typical C syntax and the Java equivalents.

Table B-1 Java Syntax Equivalents for C Programmers

C Syntax	Java Equivalent
`char *foo;`	`String foo;`
`char **foo;`	`String[] foo;`
`int *foo = (int *) malloc(` `    5 * sizeof(int));`	`int[] foo = new int[5];`
`int foo[3][4];`	`int[][] foo = new int[3][4];`
`#define foo 5`	`static final int foo = 5;`
`printf(` `    " Value equals: %d\n",val);`	`System.out.println(` `    " Value equals: " + val);`
`char c = getc(stdin);`	`char c = (char)System.in.read();`
`free(ptr);`	`N/A`
`int x = foo.bar;` `int x = foo->bar;`	`int x = foo.bar;` `int x = foo.bar;`
`int main (int argc, char **argv);`	`public static void main (String[] args);`

Java for C++ Programmers

Table B-2 compares some typical C++ syntax and the Java equivalents.

Table B-2 Java Syntax Equivalents for C++ Programmers

C++ Syntax	Java Equivalent
`char* foo;`	`String foo;`
`char** foo;`	`String[] foo;`
`int* foo = new int[5];`	`int[] foo = new int[5];`
`int** foo = new int[3][4];`	`int[][] foo = new int[3][4];`
`const int foo = 5`	`static final int foo = 5;`
`cout    << "The answer is: "` `<< answer;`	`System.out.println(` `"The answer is: " + answer);`
`char c; cin >> c;`	`char c = (char)System.in.read();`
`delete ptr;`	`N/A`
`int x = foo.bar;` `int x = foo->bar;`	`int x = foo.bar;` `int x = foo.bar;`
`int main (int argc, char **argv);`	`public static void main (String[] args);`

Data Types

Table B-3 describes the Java data types and their default values.

Table B-3 Simple Data Types

Data Type	Sizes	Description	Default Value
byte	1 byte	Machine independent and signed integers	0
short	2 bytes	Signed, twos complement	0
int	4 bytes	Signed, twos complement	0
long	8 bytes	Signed, twos complement	`0L`
float	4 bytes	Single precision float	`0.0f`
double	8 bytes	Double precision float	`0.0d`
char	2 bytes	Unsigned integer that uses the Unicode character set	`'\u0000'`
boolean	1 bit	Contains a `true` or `false` value; not a number	`false`

Operators

Table B-4 describes the Java operators.

Table B-4 Java Operators

Type	Operator	Data Type	Description
Additive Operators	x + y	x,y: Arithmetic types	Sum of x and y.
	x - y	x,y: Arithmetic types	Difference of x and y.
Multiplicative Operators	x * y	x,y: Arithmetic types	Product of x and y.
	x / y	x,y: Arithmetic types y != 0	Quotient of x and y.
	x % y	x,y: Arithmetic types y != 0	Remainder of x and y.
Equality Operators	==	x,y: Arithmetic types	x equals y.
		x,y: Boolean	x and y both true or false.
		x,y: Object	x and y refer to the *same* object.
Increment/ Decrement Operators	x++	x: Arithmetic types	Add one to x, returning the previous value.
	++x	x: Arithmetic types	Add one to x, returning the new value.
	x--	x: Arithmetic types	Subtract one from x, returning the previous value.
	--x	x: Arithmetic types	Subtract one from x, returning the new value.
Other Unary Operators	~x	x: Integral	Bitwise complement of x.
	!x	x: Boolean	Logical complement of x.
	+x	x: Arithmetic types	Unary plus.
	-x	x: Arithmetic types	0 - x.

Table B-4 Java Operators (Continued)

Type	Operator	Data Type	Description
String Concatenation Operator	x + y	x or y: String	If either x or y is a String, the other is converted to a String and then they are concatenated. null converts to "null". booleans convert to "true" and "false". An object reference is converted using its toString() method.
Bitwise & Logical Operators	x & y	x: Integral or boolean.	x AND y.
	x ^ y	x: Integral or boolean.	x XOR y.
	x | y	x: Integral or boolean.	x OR y.
Relational Operators	x < y	x,y: Arithmetic	x less than y.
	x > y	x,y: Arithmetic	x greater than y.
	x <= y	x,y: Arithmetic	x less than or equal to y
	x >= y	x,y: Arithmetic	x greater than or equal to y.

Table B-4 Java Operators (Continued)

Type	Operator	Data Type	Description
Shift Operators	x << y	x,y: Integral	x * (2 ** y).
	x >> y	x,y: Integral	x / (2 ** y).
	x >>> y	x,y: Integral	The bits of x are shifted right y places with zero extension.
Assignment Operators	x = y	x,y: Arithmetic	The value of y is placed in x.
	x += y	x,y: Arithmetic	x = x + y.
	x -= y	x,y: Arithmetic	x = x - y.
	x *= y	x,y: Arithmetic	x = x * y.
	x /= y	x,y: Arithmetic	x = x / y.
	x %= y	x,y: Arithmetic	x = x % y.
	x <<= y	x,y: Integral	x = x << y.
	x >>= y	x,y: Integral	x = x >> y.
	x >>>= y	x,y: Integral	x = x >>> y.
	x &= y	x,y: Integral or boolean	x = x & y.
	x ^= y	x,y: Integral or boolean	x = x ^ y.
	x |= y	x,y: Integral or boolean	x = x | y.
Conditional Operators	x && y	x,y: Boolean	True if x and y both true.
	x || y	x,y: Boolean	True if x or y true.
	x ? y : z	x: Boolean	If x is true, then y, otherwise, z.
		y,z: Arithmetic, boolean, or object references.	

Control Flow and Iteration

The control structures in Java are largely the same as C or C++ with a few exceptions. For one, there is no goto statement. Another difference is that break and continue can take a single argument, indicating which of a set of nested loops they refer to. The loop must have a label which is used as the argument. For example, consider the following program:

```java
import java.io.*;

public class LoopTest {
   public static void main(String[] args) {

     outer:
      for (int i = 0; i < 3; i++) {
         for (int j = 0; j < 3; j++) {
            if (i + j == 3) {
               continue outer;
            }

            System.out.println("i = " + i + "; j = " + j);
         }
      }
   }
}
```

This program would print the following:

```
i = 0; j = 0
i = 0; j = 1
i = 0; j = 2
i = 1; j = 0
i = 1; j = 1
i = 2; j = 0
```

Comments

Table B-5 shows the comment forms you can use in Java code.

Table B-5 Java Comments

Comment Form	Notes
`/* A comment */`	C-style comment. All text between /* and */ is ignored.
`// A comment`	C++ style comment. All text from // to the end of the line is ignored.
`/** A comment */`	Comment used before a declaration. Running the `javadoc` program on the file will automatically generate HTML documentation for any comment in this form.

Keywords

Table B-6 shows Java keywords and summarizes their use.

Table B-6 Java Keywords

Keyword	Description
`abstract`	A class or method modifier. An `abstract` class is used for classes that include `abstract` methods. An `abstract` method is used for methods that are generic and that will have their operations fully defined in subclasses of the class. An interface is implicitly abstract, since the methods in it have their operations defined in the classes that implement the interface.
`boolean`	One of Java's primitive types. By default, initialized to `false`.
`break`	Standard control transfer statement. Passes control to the end of an enclosing iteration.
`byte`	One of Java's primitive types. By default, initialized to `0`.
`case`	Standard control flow in a `switch` statement.
`cast`	Not currently used.
`catch`	Keyword used in exception handling. (See *try and catch* on page 108.)
`char`	One of Java's primitive types. By default, initialized to `'\u0000'`.
`class`	Keyword used to introduce a new type. (See *Classes and Methods* on page 25.)
`const`	Not currently used.
`continue`	Standard control transfer statement. Passes control to the loop-continuation point of an iteration statement.
`default`	Standard default action of a `switch/case` block.

Table B-6 Java Keywords (Continued)

Keyword	Description
do	Standard loop. Executes until value of its expression is `boolean` false.
double	One of Java's primitive types. By default, initialized to `0.0`.
else	Standard conditional control flow.
extends	Keyword that specifies the superclass or superclasses of the class or interface being declared.
final	A class, method, or variable modifier. A `final` class cannot be subclassed. A `final` method cannot be overridden. A `final` variable cannot have its initialized value changed.
finally	Keyword used in exception handling. (See *The finally Statement* on page 109.)
float	One of Java's primitive types. By default, initialized to `0.0f`.
for	Standard loop. Executes until value of its test expression is false. You can omit the test expression, in which case the implied test expression is `true`.
future	Not currently used.
generic	Not currently used.
goto	Not currently used.
if	Standard conditional control flow.
implements	Keyword that specifies the interface(s) that will be provided by the class being declared.
import	Keyword that specifies packages or classes that can be used within a program.
inner	Not currently used.
instanceof	A type comparison operator.
int	One of Java's primitive types. By default, initialized to `0`.
interface	Keyword used to introduce a new interface. (See *Interfaces as Types* on page 75.)
long	One of Java's primitive types. By default, initialized to `0L`.
native	A method modifier. A native method indicates the method body will be written in C and linked into the interpreter.
new	Keyword used to create an instance of a class.
null	Keyword indicating the absence of a reference.
operator	Not currently used.
outer	Not currently used.

Table B-6 Java Keywords (Continued)

Keyword	Description
package	Keyword used to name a group of related classes.
private	A constructor, method, or variable modifier. A private constructor, method, or variable can be accessed only within the same class.
protected	A constructor, method, or variable modifier. A protected constructor, method, or variable can be accessed by other methods in the class, methods in subclasses of the class, or methods in classes in the same package as the class.
public	A class, constructor, method, or variable modifier. A public class, constructor, method, or variable can be directly accessed or imported from other packages.
rest	Not currently used.
return	Standard control transfer statement. Passes control to the caller of the current method.
short	One of Java's primitive types. By default, initialized to 0.
static	A method or variable modifier. A static method is used to declare a class method. (See *Class Methods* on page 30.) A static variable is used to declare a class variable, which will be shared among all instances of a class.
super	Keyword used to reference a class's immediate superclass or a constructor defined in the superclass.
switch	Standard conditional control flow.
synchronized	A method or block modifier. A synchronized method or block acquires a lock on a resource, executes the specified code, and releases the lock. Used for multithreading.
this	Keyword used to reference the current class or a constructor defined in the current class.
throw	Standard control transfer statement. Indicates a runtime exception. By convention, the argument to throw is a subclass of the Exception class.
throws	A method keyword that lists all the exceptions the method can throw.
transient	A variable modifier indicating the variable is not part of the persistent state of an object.
try	Keyword used in exception handling. (See *try and catch* on page 108.)
var	Not currently used.

Table B-6 Java Keywords (Continued)

Keyword	Description
void	Standard null return type.
volatile	A variable modifier indicating the variable may be asynchronously modified.
while	Standard loop. Executes until value of its test expression is `boolean false`.

Deprecated APIs

The JDK 1.2 introduces a number of classes and specific class members that are intended to replace functionality in previous versions of the JDK. These new APIs are improvement upon their predecessors. represent improved

Table B-5 shows the deprecated classes in the JDK1.2.

Table B-7 Deprecated Classes

Deprecated Class	JDK 1.2 Replacement
LineNumberInputStream	java.io.LineNumberInputStream
StringBufferInputStream	java.io.StringBufferInputStream
Certificate	java.security.Certificate

Table B-5 shows the deprecated class members in the JDK1.2.

Table B-8 Deprecated Class Members

Class	Deprecated Class Member
java.awt.BorderLayout	addLayoutComponent()
java.awt.CardLayout	addLayoutComponent()
java.awt.CheckboxGroup	getCurrent() setCurrent()
java.awt.Choice	countItems()
java.awt.Component	getPeer() enable() disable() show() hide()

Table B-8 Deprecated Class Members (Continued)

Class	Deprecated Class Member
	`location()`
	`move()`
	`size()`
	`resize()`
	`bounds()`
	`reshape()`
	`preferredSize()`
	`minimumSize()`
	`layout()`
	`inside()`
	`locate()`
	`deliverEvent()`
	`postEvent()`
	`handleEvent()`
	`mouseDown()`
	`mouseDrag()`
	`mouseUp()`
	`mouseMove()`
	`mouseEnter()`
	`mouseExit()`
	`keyDown()`
	`keyUp()`
	`action()`
	`gotFocus()`
	`lostFocut()`
	`nextFocus()`
`java.awt.Container`	`countComponents()`
	`insets()`
	`layout()`
	`preferredSize()`
	`minimumSize()`
	`deliverEvent()`
	`locate()`
`java.awt.FontMetrics`	`getMaxDecent()`

Table B-8 Deprecated Class Members (Continued)

Class	Deprecated Class Member
java.awt.Frame	DEFAULT_CURSOR CROSSHAIR_CURSOR TEXT_CURSOR WAIT_CURSOR SW_RESIZE_CURSOR SE_RESIZE_CURSOR NW_RESIZE_CURSOR NE_RESIZE_CURSOR N_RESIZE_CURSOR S_RESIZE_CURSOR W_RESIZE_CURSOR E_RESIZE_CURSOR HAND_CURSOR MOVE_CURSOR setCursor() getCursorType()
java.awt.Graphics	getClipRect()
java.awt.List	countItems() addItem() clear() delItem() isSelected() allowsMultipleSelections() setMultipleSelections() preferredSize() minimumSize() delItems() countItems()
java.awt.MenuBar	countMenus()
java.awt.MenuComponent	getPeer() postEvent()
java.awt.MenuContainer	postEvent()
java.awt.MenuItem	enable() disable()
java.awt.Polygon	getBoundingBox() inside()
java.awt.Rectangle	reshape() move() resize() inside()
java.awt.ScrollPane	layout()

Table B-8 Deprecated Class Members (Continued)

Class	Deprecated Class Member
java.awt.ScrollBar	getVisible() setLineIncrement() getLineIncrement() setPageIncrement() getPageIncrement()
java.awt.TextArea	insertTextArea() appendText() replaceText() preferredSize() minimumSize()
java.awt.TextField	setEchoCharacter() preferredSize() minimumSize()
java.awt.Window	postEvent()
java.awt.geom.AffineTransform	prepend() append()
java.awt.image.BufferedImage	getGraphics()
java.awt.swing.AbstractButton	getLabel() setLabel()
java.io.ByteArrayOutputStream	toString()
java.io.DataInputStream	readLine()
java.io.ObjectInputStream	readLine()
java.io.PrintStream	PrintStream()
java.io.StreamTokenizer	StreamTokenizer()
java.Lang.Character	isJavaLetter() isJavaCharacter() isJavaLetterOrDigit() isSpace()
java.lang.ClassLoader	defineClass()
java.Lang.Runtime()	getLocalizedInputStream() getLocalizedOutputStream()
java.lang.SecurityManager	inCheck() getInCheck() classDepth() classLoaderDepth() inClass() inClassLoader()
java.lang.String	String() getBytes()
java.lang.System	getenv()

Table B-8 Deprecated Class Members (Continued)

Class	Deprecated Class Member
java.lang.Thread	stop() suspend()a resume()
java.lang.ThreadGroup	suspend() resume()
java.net.Socket	Socket()
java.rmi.registry.RegistryHandler	registryStub() registryImpl()
java.security.Identity	addCertificate() removeCertificate() certificates()
java.security.Signature	setParameter() getParameter()
java.security.Signature.Spi	engineSetParameter() engineGetParameter()
java.sql.Date	Date() getHours() getMinutes() getSeconds() setHours() setMinutes() setSeconds()

Table B-8 Deprecated Class Members (Continued)

Class	Deprecated Class Member
java.sql.Time	getYear()
	getMonth()
	getDay()
	getDate()
	setYear()
	setMonth()
	setDate()
java.sql.Timestamp	Timestamp()
java.util.Date	Date()
	UTC()
	parse()
	getYear()
	setYear()
	getMonth()
	setMonth()
	getDate()
	setDate()
	getDay()
	getHours()
	setHours()
	getMinutes()
	setMinutes()
	getSeconds()
	setSeconds()
	toLocaleString()
	toGMTString()
	getTimezoneOffset()

The Java Classes and Interfaces

The following list provides a simple overview of the JDK packages:

- java.applet — Provides support for Java programs that will execute within a web browser.

- java.awt — Provides support for graphics in Java programs.

- java.awt.color — Provides classes for color spaces.

- java.awt.datatransfer — Provides interfaces and classes for transferring data between applications and within applications.

- java.awt.dnd — Provides interfaces and classes to support drag-and-drop operations.

- java.awt.event — Provides interfaces and classes for dealing with different types of events used in AWT components.

- `java.awt.font` — Provides classes and interface relating to fonts.
- `java.awt.geom` — Provides Java 2D classes for operations that have to do with two-dimensional geometry.
- `java.awt.im` — Provides classes and an interface for the input method framework.
- `java.awt.image` — Provides classes for creating and modifying images.
- `java.image.renderable` — Provides classes and interfaces for producing rendering independent images.
- `java.awt.print` — Provides classes and interfaces that define a general printing API.
- `java.awt.swing` — Provides a set of lightweight Java components that the same on all platforms.
- `java.awt.swing.border` — Provides classes and interface for drawing specialized borders around a `Swing` component.
- `java.awt.swing.event` — Provides classes and interface for events dealing with different kinds of events used in Swing components.
- `java.awt.swing.plaf` — Provides an interface and abstract classes that Swing components use to provide common look-and-feel capabilities.
- `java.awt.swing.table` — Provides classes and interfaces for control over table construction, updates, and rendering.
- `java.awt.swing.text` — Provides classes and interfaces that deal with text components.
- `java.awt.swing.text.html` — Provides the `RTFEditorKit` class and other classes for creating rich-text format text editors.
- `java.awt.swing.text.rtf` — Provides the `HTMLEditorKit` class and other classes for creating HTML text editors.
- `java.awt.swing.tree` — Provides classes and interfaces for control over tree construction, updates, and rendering.
- `java.awt.swing.undo` — Provides support for undo and redo operations in a text editor application.
- `java.beans` — Provides support for developting Java beans.
- `java.beans.beancontext` — Provides classes and interfaces relating to bean context.

- `java.io` — Provides support for input/output in Java programs.

- `java.lang` — Provides the base classes of the Java language. This package is always available without being imported.

- `java.lang.ref` — Provides reference object classes, allowing a program to interact with the Java garbage collector.

- `java.lang.reflect` — Provides classes and interfaces for obtaining information internal to classes and objects.

- `java.math` — Provides classes for performing arbitrary-precision integer arithmetic and arbitrary-precision decimal arithmetic.

- `java.net` — Provides support for network applications.

- `java.rmi` — Provides the Remote Method Invocation (RMI) package.

- `java.rmi.activiation` — Provides support for RMI object activation.

- `java.rmi.dgc` — Provides classes and interface for RMI distributed garbage collection.

- `java.rmi.registry` — Provides a class and two interfaces for the RMI registry.

- `java.rmi.server` — Provides classes and interfaces for supporting RMI on the server side.

- `java.security` — Provides the classes and interfaces for the security framework.

- `java.security.acl` — The classes and interfaces in this package have been replaced by classes in the `java.security` package.

- `java.security.cert` — Provides classes and interfaces for parsing and managing certificates.

- `java.security.interfaces` — Provides interfaces for generating Rivest, Shamir and Adleman AsymmetricCipher algorithm (RSA) keys as defined in the RSA Laboratory Technical Note PKCS#1, and DSA (Digital Signature Algorithm) keys as defined in NIST's FIPS-186.

- `java.security.spec` — Provides classes and interfaces for key specifications and algorithm parameter specifications.

- `java.sql` — Provides the Java Database Connectivity (JDBC) package.

- `java.text` — Provides classes and interfaces for handling text, dates, numbers, and messages.

- `java.util` — Provides useful classes such as hashtables, stacks, and so on.

- `java.util.jar` — Provides classes for creating and reading Java Archive (JAR) files.

- `java.util.mime` — Provides classes for dealing with Multipurpose Internet Mail Extension (MIME) types.

- `java.util.zip` — Provides classes for computing checksums of data and for compressing and decompressing data using ZIP and GZIP formats.

The HTML applet and param Tags

To call an applet from within a web page, you use the HTML `applet` tag. Minimally, you can use a single-line call, as in Example B-1. (Assume that we're calling the `StaticLabel` applet on page 403.)

Example B-1 The Basic HTML `applet` Tag

```
<applet code="StaticLabel.class" width=200 height=80> </applet>
```

You can also include a set of parameters to specify exactly how you want the applet displayed, as in Example B-2. Applet parameters are specified using the `param` tag. The syntax for the `param` tag is:

```
<param name="name" value="value">
```

All parameters are passed to an applet as strings.

If specified within the web page, these HTML parameters override the default parameters specified in an applet. For instance, the StaticLabel applet described on page 403 has default parameters for label, fontname, fontslant, fontweight, and fontsize. However, the param tags in Example B-2 would override those default values.

Example B-2 The HTML param Tag

```
<applet code="StaticLabel.class" width=200 height=80> <param
name=label value="I'm a static label.">
<param name=fontname value="Courier">
<param name=fontslant value="italic">
<param name=fontweight value="bold">
<param name=fontsize value="24">
</applet>
```

Index

Sun Microsystems, Inc.

Binary Code License Agreement

READ THE TERMS OF THIS AGREEMENT AND ANY PROVIDED SUPPLEMENTAL LICENSE TERMS (COLLECTIVELY "AGREEMENT") CAREFULLY BEFORE OPENING THE SOFTWARE MEDIA PACKAGE. BY OPENING THE SOFTWARE MEDIA PACKAGE, YOU AGREE TO THE TERMS OF THIS AGREEMENT. IF YOU ARE ACCESSING THE SOFTWARE ELECTRONICALLY INDICATE YOUR ACCEPTANCE OF THESE TERMS BY SELECTING THE "ACCEPT" BUTTON AT THE END OF THIS AGREEMENT. IF YOU DO NOT AGREE TO ALL OF THESE TERMS, PROMPTLY RETURN THE UNUSED SOFTWARE TO YOUR PLACE OF PURCHASE FOR A REFUND OR, IF THE SOFTWARE IS ACCESSED ELECTRONICALLY, SELECT THE "DECLINE" BUTTON AT THE END OF THIS AGREEMENT.

1. **License to Use.** Sun grants to you a non-exclusive and non-transferable license for the internal use only of the accompanying software and documentation and any error corrections provided by Sun (collectively "Software"), by the number of users and the class of computer hardware for which the corresponding fee has been paid.

2. **Restrictions**. Software is confidential and copyrighted. Title to Software and all associated intellectual property rights is retained by Sun and/or its licensors. Except as specifically authorized in any Supplemental License Terms, you may not make copies of Software, other than a single copy of Software for archival purposes. Unless enforcement is prohibited by applicable law, you may not modify, decompile, disassemble, or otherwise reverse engineer Software. Software is not designed or licensed for use in on-line control of aircraft, air traffic, aircraft or navigation or aircraft communications; or in the design, construction, operation or maintenance of any nuclear facility. You warrant that you will not use Software for these purposes. You may not publish or provide the results of any benchmark or comparison tests run on Software to any third party without the prior written consent of Sun. No right, title or interest in or to any trademark, service mark, logo, or trade name of Sun or its licensors is granted under this Agreement.

3. **Limited Warranty.** Sun warrants to you that for a period of ninety (90) days from the date of purchase, as evidenced by a copy of the receipt, the media on which Software is furnished (if any) will be free of defects in materials and workmanship under normal use. Except for the foregoing, Software is provided "AS IS". Your exclusive remedy and Sun's entire liability under this limited warranty will be at Sun's option to replace Software media or refund the fee paid for Software.

4. **Disclaimer of Warranty.** UNLESS SPECIFIED IN THIS AGREEMENT, ALL EXPRESS OR IMPLIED CONDITIONS, REPRESENTATIONS AND WARRANTIES, INCLUDING ANY IMPLIED WARRANTY OF MERCHANTABILITY, FITNESS FOR A PARTICULAR PURPOSE, OR NON-INFRINGEMENT, ARE DISCLAIMED, EXCEPT TO THE EXTENT THAT THESE DISCLAIMERS ARE HELD TO BE LEGALLY INVALID.

5. **Limitation of Liability.** TO THE EXTENT NOT PROHIBITED BY APPLICABLE LAW, IN NO EVENT WILL SUN OR ITS LICENSORS BE LIABLE FOR ANY LOST REVENUE, PROFIT OR DATA, OR FOR SPECIAL, INDIRECT, CONSEQUENTIAL, INCIDENTAL OR PUNITIVE DAMAGES, HOWEVER CAUSED AND REGARDLESS OF THE THEORY OF LIABILITY, ARISING OUT OF OR RELATED TO THE USE OF OR INABILITY TO USE SOFTWARE, EVEN IF SUN HAS BEEN ADVISED OF THE POSSIBILITY OF SUCH DAMAGES. In no event will Sun's liability to you, whether in contract, tort (including negligence), or otherwise, exceed the amount paid by you for Software under this Agreement. The foregoing limitations will apply even if the above stated warranty fails of its essential purpose.

6. **Termination.** This Agreement is effective until terminated. You may terminate this Agreement at any time by destroying all copies of Software. This Agreement will terminate immediately without notice from Sun if you fail to comply with any provision of this Agreement. Upon termination, you must destroy all copies of Software.

7. **Export Regulations.** All Software and technical data delivered under this Agreement are subject to U.S. export control laws and may be subject to export or import regulations in other countries. You agree to comply strictly with all such laws and regulations and acknowledge that you have the responsibility to obtain such licenses to export, re-export, or import as may be required after delivery to you.

8. **U.S. Government Restricted Rights.** Use, duplication, or disclosure by the U.S. Government is subject to restrictions set forth in this Agreement and as provided in DFARS 227.7202-1(a) and 227.7202-3(a) (1995), DFARS 252.227-7013(c)(1)(ii) (Oct 1988), FAR 12.212(a)(1995), FAR 52.227-19 (June 1987), or FAR 52.227-14 (ALT III) (June 1987), as applicable.

9. **Governing Law.** Any action related to this Agreement will be governed by California law and controlling U.S. federal law. No choice of law rules of any jurisdiction will apply.

10. **Severability.** If any provision of this Agreement is held to be unenforceable, this Agreement will remain in effect with the provision omitted, unless omission of the provision would frustrate the intent of the parties, in which case this Agreement will immediately terminate.

11. **Integration.** This Agreement is the entire agreement between you and Sun relating to its subject matter. It supersedes all prior or contemporaneous oral or written communications, proposals, representations and warranties and prevails over any conflicting or additional terms of any quote, order, acknowledgment, or other communication between the parties relating to its subject matter during the term of this Agreement. No modification of this Agreement will be binding, unless in writing and signed by an authorized representative of each party.

For inquiries please contact: Sun Microsystems, Inc., 901 San Antonio Road, Palo Alto, California 94303

JAVA™ DEVELOPMENT KIT VERSION 1.2
SUPPLEMENTAL LICENSE TERMS

These supplemental terms ("Supplement") add to the terms of the Binary Code License Agreement ("Agreement"). Capitalized terms not defined herein shall have the same meanings ascribed to them in the Agreement. The Supplement terms shall supersede any inconsistent or conflicting terms in the Agreement.

1. Limited License Grant. Sun grants to you a non-exclusive, non-transferable limited license to use the Software without fee for evaluation of the Software and for development of Java™ applets and applications provided that you: (i) may not re-distribute the Software in whole or in part, either separately or included with a product. (ii) may not create, or authorize your licensees to create additional classes, interfaces, or subpackages that are contained in the "java" or "sun" packages or similar as specified by Sun in any class file naming convention; and (iii) agree to the extent Programs are developed which utilize the Windows 95/98 style graphical user interface or components contained therein, such applets or applications may only be developed to run on a Windows 95/98 or Windows NT platform. Refer to the Java Runtime Environment Version 1.2 binary code license (http://java.sun.com/products/JDK/1.2/index.html) for the availability of runtime code which may be distributed with Java applets and applications.

2. Java Platform Interface. In the event that Licensee creates an additional API(s) which: (i) extends the functionality of a Java Environment; and, (ii) is exposed to third party software developers for the purpose of developing additional software which invokes such additional API, Licensee must promptly publish broadly an accurate specification for such API for free use by all developers.

3. Trademarks and Logos. This Agreement does not authorize Licensee to use any Sun name, trademark or logo. Licensee acknowledges as between it and Sun that Sun owns the Java trademark and all Java-related trademarks, logos and icons including the Coffee Cup and Duke ("Java Marks") and agrees to comply with the Java Trademark Guidelines at http://java.sun.com/trademarks.html.

4. High Risk Activities. Notwithstanding Section 2, with respect to high risk activities, the following language shall apply: the Software is not designed or intended for use in on-line control of aircraft, air traffic, aircraft navigation or aircraft communications; or in the design, construction, operation or maintenance of any nuclear facility. Sun disclaims any express or implied warranty of fitness for such uses.

5. Source Code. Software may contain source code that is provided solely for reference purposes pursuant to the terms of this Agreement.

About the CD

Welcome to the *Java by Example 1.2* CD. This CD contains source code for the Java applications and applets referred to in the book. The files are organized as follows:

Classes	This directory contains the applet and application class files referred to in the book.
Classes.zip	This file contains the applet and application class files referred to in the book in zip format.
Code	This directory contains the applets and applications directories described below.
applets	This directory contains sample applets, audio and image files and HTML files that you can use to view the applets with the Java appletviewer.
applications	This directory contains sample applications that you can use, modify or study to help you learn the language.
Code.zip	This directory contains the applets and applications directories described above in zip format.

Please note: Because the final version of the JDK 1.2 was not available at press time, this CD does NOT include a copy of the JDK. To obtain the most current version of the JDK, go to http://java.sun.com and follow the instructions provided for downloading and installing the JDK. Use of the JDK is subject to the Binary Code License terms and conditions on page 559.

The *Java by Example 1.2* CD is a standard ISO-9660 disc formatted with RockRidge and Joliet extensions. The software on this CD requires Solaris 2.x, Windows 95, or Windows NT. Windows 3.1 is not supported.

Technical Support

Prentice Hall does not offer technical support for this software. If there is a problem with the media, however, you may obtain a replacement CD by emailing a description of the problem. Send your email to:

disc_exchange@prenhall.com